Contents

Managing multimedia

Project management for interactive media

2nd edition

Elaine England

Andy Finney

ADDISON-WESLEY

Harlow, England ■ Reading, Massachusetts ■ Menlo Park, California
New York ■ Don Mills, Ontario ■ Amsterdam ■ Bonn ■ Sydney ■ Singapore
Tokyo ■ Madrid ■ San Juan ■ Milan ■ Mexico City ■ Seoul ■ Taipei

Pearson Education Limited
Edinburgh Gate
Harlow
Essex CM20 2JE
England

and Associated Companies throughout the World.

Visit us on the World Wide Web at:
http://www.pearsoneduc.com

Text design by Claire Brodmann
Illustrations by Gary Weston
Typeset in Stone sans and Palatino by 30
Printed in Great Britain by Henry Ling Ltd., at the Dorset Press, Dorchester, Dorset

First printed 1999.

ISBN 0-201-36058-6

British Library Cataloguing-in-Publication Data
A catalogue record for this book is available from the British Library

10 9 8 7 6 5
04 03 02 01 00

Introduction

How to use the book and CD-ROM

Who is it for?

This book is useful for anyone studying or practicing multimedia, whether online through the World Wide Web or offline using CD-ROMs or any other appropriate medium. It addresses the multimedia management role of head of a project. There are a variety of titles that are used to denote this – producer, managing editor, analyst, or senior software engineer, for example. The term **project manager** is used here because it is a neutral term, which does not betray any media origins, since new media is produced from a fusion of talents across several media.

Project management theory and practice offer insights to help you keep control of projects. Multimedia projects are notoriously difficult to keep within time and budget because there are so many variables. This book analyzes all the variables within projects from clients to techniques; from team members to applying project management principles.

Because the book follows the life cycle of a project, it broadens the understanding of the multimedia context for those with a single specialism such as programming or graphics, while giving a practical business and management slant for others.

It will prove useful for those commissioning new media, as the client's roles and responsibilities are defined in parallel with the project manager's. It clearly identifies the phases of a project, and acts as an introduction to the process. It can act as a reference for those new to multimedia.

The structure of the book

The chapters are organized around the development of a project from initiation to completion. Administration, management and production processes are interweaved, reflecting the way they happen during a project. Because some phases occur simultaneously, the linear nature of the chapters misrepresents the overall process to an extent. However, we have tried to cover all the phases for developing a team-based, client-driven, commercial project that uses the equivalent of some original video footage, a range of audio assets, commercially sourced and in-house-produced graphics, and text content.

We used this type of project as the default because it has the greatest number of tasks and resources. Other multimedia projects – non-commercial and non-team-based – would need many but not all of the aspects covered here. Web site projects can use just a selection or all of the media, depending on the specific project. Multimedia games and entertainment titles sometimes have a different development cycle if they are truly market driven. This market-driven model is mentioned as a point of comparison with client-centred projects but is not explained in detail. Research and international projects have more phases, and are referred to when appropriate.

The main differences between non-commercial and commercial projects are the amount and type of rights clearances that are needed, as well as the smaller production scale, where fewer staff are used in audio, video and graphics production. If you are working on these types of project you may not have as many administrative and legal aspects to cover, but many will be the same, albeit on a smaller scale.

The glossary will serve as a ready reference for any terms that need further explanation. We have tried to make it as comprehensive as possible, and it is also included on the CD.

The structure of the chapters

Chapters 1 and 2 give the background knowledge for the topics of multimedia, projects, and new media project management, both on- and offline. These will provide a common base of understanding.

Icon of Project manager's responsibilities

From Chapter 3, we follow the development of a project. Each chapter begins with a resumé of the project manager's responsibilities. This will prepare you for the concepts that will be covered, and will help focus your interpretation of them on the role outlined. During the book, the complete range of responsibilities builds up into the equivalent of a job description. If you are reading the book for a general purpose, then you can skip the resumés and read the chapters for salient information.

Icon of Theory into practice

During the chapters you will find suggested tasks. These are to help you transfer the principles into practical activities of relevance to your own situation. Because there are so many types of multimedia project we have tried to stick to principles that can be applied across the greatest variety of projects.

Icon of Refer
to CD-ROM

Icon of
Summary

Icon of
Recommended
reading

But the principles will serve you for your own situation only if you take the time and effort to apply them. The 'theory into practice' tasks can help you build up project-specific sets of reference materials that suit the range and type of projects you develop.

Where appropriate during the chapters you will be referred to the CD and Web site for information that is represented better in an electronic form, and for practical exercises on visual and audio examples.

Each chapter has a summary. This reinforces the main points covered in the chapter, but can also be used as a quick reference when you are developing a project and reach the phase being discussed. Some people prefer to read the summary prior to reading a chapter to decide if it has direct relevance for them. Others read the summary first to preview the chapter, to prepare them for it.

Where possible we have included recommended reading at the ends of chapters, but a few of the aspects covered here have relied on practical experience and represent the authors' interpretation of that experience rather than insights from defined theory.

The structure of the CD-ROM

The CD with this book aims to be both a companion to and an extension of the book itself, and is a mixed-mode disc combining digital audio and data.

The structure of the CD-ROM corresponds to the chapters in the book, and you can find the examples and exercises that are referenced during the text in the book. With these, we have tried to overcome the static and monochrome limitations of the printed page by means of colour illustrations, some audio, video and animation, and hyperlinks. There is also an electronic, searchable copy of the glossary. Along with this there are a variety of demonstration software packages. These include examples of the kind of software that is commonly used in multimedia production, and will give a good introduction to some of the tools that you will use as you produce your applications. They will help you to extend your understanding of the principles covered in the chapters dealing with audio, video, and graphics.

As well as CD-ROM data this disc contains a few CD audio tracks, which can be played on any compact disc player as well as on most CD-ROM drives. These are examples for Chapters 8 and 13, and they start with Track 2 of the disc. Please do not try to play Track 1 of the disc since this contains CD-ROM data and, if you hear it at all, it may damage your equipment.

The CD-ROM is based around an HTML document, which can be read with the same software you would use to surf the World Wide Web on the Internet. We have done this to allow the greatest access to the disc. This disc is in a standard format, called ISO 9660, which can be read on a wide range of computers including PC and Macintosh. Most of the material can be used with other platforms, as can the HTML document, since the files are stored, where possible, in standard formats.

The most up-to-date information on the CD can be found in the ReadMe file on the CD-ROM itself. This is a text file, which can be read with any word processor, and is the best point for you to start. To start to explore the CD itself you use your browser to open the document called START.HTM and then follow the links.

The CD will point you to our Web site, where there are extra resources, such as links to resource information and information on courses available for multimedia professionals. http://www.atsf.co.uk/manmult

Acknowledgements

Many thanks to all those who gave their time and expertise to comment on the drafts and helped shape the book:

Judith Aston, Lecturer in Multimedia Production, Faculty of Art, Media and Design, University of the West of England, Bristol, UK.
Chris Barlas, Chairman, Authors Licensing & Collecting Society, UK.
Jardine Barrington Cook, Logica, UK.
Birte Christensen-Dalsgaard, UNI.C, Danish Computing Centre for Research and Education, Aärhus, Denmark.
Mark Dillon, Director, On-Line Services, GTE Entertainment, USA.
Mike Philips, MediaLab Arts Course, School of Computing, University of Plymouth, UK.
Malcolm Roberts, Senior Manager, Bank of Montreal Institute for Learning, Scarborough, Ontario, Canada.
Gisella Rosano, Designer/Developer, Bank of Montreal Institute for Learning, Scarborough, Ontario, Canada.
Henry Steele, Head of International Business and Marketing, Lingnan College, Hong Kong.
William S. Strong, Partner, Kotin Crabtree & Strong Attorneys at Law, Boston, USA.
Charles Walker, Partner, Walker Tomaszewski Solicitors, London, UK.

We both recognize that many of our past and present colleagues have contributed to the span of experience covered here, and we thank you all – too numerous to name individually.

Finally we also recognize the debt to all the pioneers who persevered against the odds and kept the faith that multimedia would be mainstream. You were right.

Elaine England
Andy Finney
March 1998

1

The background: multimedia and projects

What is multimedia?

Multimedia is the seamless integration of text, sound, images of all kinds and control software within a single digital information environment.

Tony Feldman, multimedia consultant

This definition applies to interactive media productions for distribution both online, such as Web pages, and offline, such as kiosks and CD-ROM. Throughout this book the term **multimedia** is used to encompass both online and offline projects, and has relevance for other interactive media such as interactive TV and on-demand services. The use of the word 'seamless' in this context is important from an artistic as well as a technical perspective. The viewer (or user if you like) of a computer should be cushioned from the technology as much as possible, and the designer should be able to choose the best medium to get the particular message across.

An **offline** project is self-contained, does not interact with anything outside its immediate environment, and usually communicates with nothing outside the computer it runs on except for the user. An **online** project needs to communicate with distant resources and sometimes distant users. Sometimes the application will actually be running on a distant computer, but more often your local application will be gathering information and assets from distant resources over a network. Some projects have elements of both on- and offline

Online, offline and hybrid projects.

projects, and we will refer to these as **hybrid Web/CD** projects. Online projects, having originally been predominantly text and graphics biased, are now taking advantage of increasing bandwidth to integrate animation, sound and video, as and where appropriate. Offline projects are rarely constricted in their choice of media components nowadays.

Multimedia has a chameleon-like ability to pretend to be many things. In designing an application you have the freedom to use so many disparate media types and techniques that it can be a challenge to understand which ones are relevant for a particular type of project. Animation, sound and pictures can help to attract your viewer to the screen on the one hand and make the most tedious of help screens interesting on the other.

The disciplines of multimedia are as diverse as the media types. Familiarity and expertise are required in all the facets of media production as well as a facility with computer software and even journalistic skills. The skills you need when working in multimedia production include project management and cost control, computer system architecture and logic, video and audio editing, text and image manipulation … plus the need to be able to integrate the disparate elements in a meaningful and appropriate way.

Of course there is a downside to this integration. Computer-related projects are notoriously difficult to scope and to budget, and this is often a problem for people coming into multimedia from other media backgrounds. Multimedia is more complex, because you first have to decide on your delivery format from components that are constantly changing and shifting, and then once you have made a choice, this has an impact on how you can treat the content. This is analogous to building a videotape recorder at the same time as editing the tape. Coupled with this there is often a lack of knowledge of what can be achieved with the technology (and this applies to developers as well as the clients), as ever more is offered by developments in computers and other equipment. Software techniques change too, as do fashions in the tools that are used to build the final application. The pace of change in the use of tools and interface design can be easily seen if we compare Internet sites over several years.

For people with a computing background there is the difficulty of scoping and specifying the way in which the application is to work, in the knowledge that the content is usually more important than the computer program that controls and displays it. The software team leader will often be reporting to someone who does not share his or her intricate knowledge of computing. This person may find it hard to believe that superficially simple things can need difficult programming, and yet seemingly complicated changes in structure can be achieved by quick changes in the code.

For end users, whether they are in a classroom, in the home or at work, multimedia improves the flow of ideas and information. It is a rich canvas on which to communicate, but this richness brings with it complexities and challenges, and quite often the only way to see what can be done is to try it.

What is a multimedia project?

Varieties of project

A project in multimedia comprises a series of tasks that deliver a combination of media and have a computer component to integrate them. There are hardware-oriented multimedia projects where the aim might be to specify, introduce, and integrate a delivery platform, such as video conferencing with a tailored user front-end, into an organization. There are software development projects that combine media components into an application to run on a delivery platform. The delivery platform will be one that can support an interactive combination of video, graphics, animation, sound and text. This could include anything from the Internet to interactive TV.

This book will concentrate on client-centred software development projects that need a team to work together to achieve the project. This type of project covers the majority of circumstances that will be met in both on- and offline project management and production. There are some multimedia professionals who carry out all aspects of a project alone, so they will not need the staff management aspects covered here. However, the principal stages of a multimedia project are the same. Managing the project cycle and handling clients need the same skills whether you are working alone or as part of a team, and whether you are producing on- or offline products.

Projects can be initiated in many different ways. Often the client makes the first approach. Sometimes the sales force drives the initial stages; sometimes analysis of market needs prompts projects. This book will not look at these aspects in detail since the premises underlying project management need to be applied by the end of the first major stage however the project is initiated. If the sales force is involved in winning business, they have to be aware of the process that the company will employ via the project leader or equivalent.

They also need to liaise with them to ensure they do not make false promises that the team will not be able to deliver within the time and cost.

Varieties of client

It will help if you consider that a client is anyone who has the authority to control time and budget, and has the right to sanction design decisions. This definition covers both internal and external clients. Internal clients are those who commission a project from within your own company, for example. External clients are people outside your company who commission projects.

The process of developing a project is in principle the same for all clients except that the contractual agreements will probably, but not always, be more straightforward for internal clients – if such agreements exist at all. The company's internal procedures will determine whether formal agreements are needed between departments where budget transfer is concerned. You will still need to establish ways of working together, and the project will need to run to time and resource constraints. Beware the internal client who does not agree the way of working, and expects you to do everything they ask in impossible times, regardless of your resources. Putting a nominal costing on your resource time is a good discipline even if you do not have to exchange money. It gives you a common ground for understanding if you tell the internal client that your section has spent the equivalent of a small fortune for them. It makes them think things through more carefully, and begins to educate them about the potential cost of changes.

So, there are diverse projects and ways of classifying projects, but they all share some of the characteristics that are explored in the main chapters.

The client-centred multimedia project cycle: overview

During the definition stage you are trying to get an understanding of what the client wants so that you can match their needs to a multimedia solution. This often needs to be carried out quickly, so you work from assumptions rather than facts. We refer to this as **scoping the project**.

Once you have scoped the needs of the project and have a time-scale, you can begin to work out the costs so that you can formulate a proposal for the client. The proposal indicates the range and scope of the work you will produce according to the time and cost you define.

When the client accepts the proposal the project explodes into activity, with several layers of operations happening simultaneously. In the book we shall cover one strand or one major part of a strand at a time, but the project cycle diagram demonstrates the true nature of the process.

You need to establish how you will work with the client because you will depend on them at certain points to give you assets or decisions to allow you to continue the work according to schedule. While you are establishing the ways of working and the legal aspects of the contracts, work starts on the project development. The details of the content, platform, media and techniques to be used, interface and interactive design are firmed up and production gets under way.

The production could not happen without personnel, so the team is also being assembled by recruitment or by use of internal staff at this time. While the production team are working together, the management aspects of teamwork come into play.

Of course, the actual asset production work – text, graphics, audio, video – that leads to integration of the assets gets under way. Coupled with asset production is the administration of the rights in the materials used. This is not a trivial task because of the lack of consensus on how to treat multimedia by those who hold or administer copyright. Offline projects have become easier to work with because more companies now recognize and have policies for them, but online has moved so quickly that they have been caught out again. For online projects expect this job to be problematic until standard agreements are reached.

Meanwhile, as asset production evolves, so does the testing to ensure that all the pieces will meet the specifications so that integration can take place as smoothly as possible. As the media components are integrated, the code underlying integration needs to be tested thoroughly in a variety of circumstances on the equivalent of the final delivery platform. The development platform may well have been different, and there are often adjustments that have to be made for the delivery platform to ensure that the software operates according to specification, or behaves properly on different computers or different browsers.

The client will be uneasy about giving final sign-off because they recognize that they lose any bargaining position they have at this point. You have to have an end point that is clear, or the budget quickly turns into overspend. The precise terms for final sign-off need to be negotiated before the end of the project to help the process run smoothly.

Finally, it is tempting to consider final sign-off and delivery as the end of the project. For most projects it is, but many people forget the importance of archiving the project in a systematic, well-documented way. If there is return business for upgrading the application or Web site, or if reuse of assets is needed for the same client in another project, you'll save time, confusion and money if it is easy to locate any asset, piece of code, or documentation that might be needed.

This then is the main model of multimedia project definition and production that will be expanded in the following chapters. There are many more stages that occur within each of the major stages identified here. These represent the tip of the iceberg, so to speak. The simultaneous nature of levels 1 to 6 in the project cycle diagram should indicate the complexity of the interaction between the team members and the processes of production. This should also serve to demonstrate why project management principles need to be applied to help control this complex interaction.

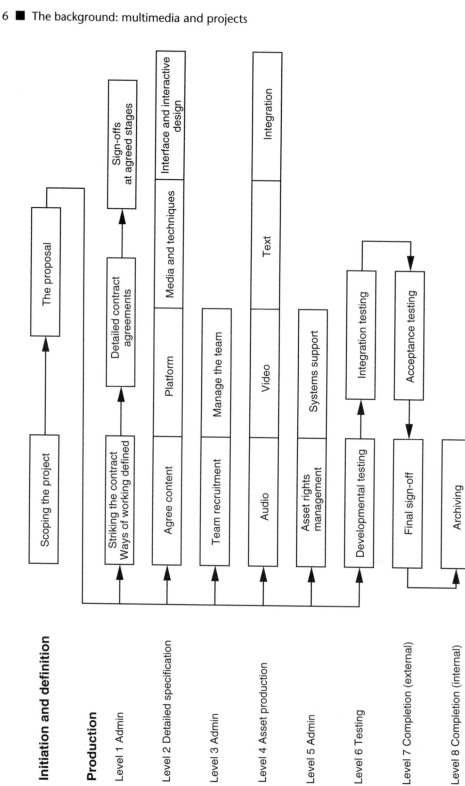

The client-centred multimedia project cycle.

Initiation and definition

Production

Level 1 Admin

Level 2 Detailed specification

Level 3 Admin

Level 4 Asset production

Level 5 Admin

Level 6 Testing

Level 7 Completion (external)

Level 8 Completion (internal)

The proposal

Scoping the project

Sign-offs at agreed stages

Detailed contract agreements

Interface and interactive design

Striking the contract
Ways of working defined

Media and techniques

Platform

Agree content

Team recruitment

Manage the team

Audio

Video

Text

Integration

Asset rights management

Systems support

Developmental testing

Integration testing

Final sign-off

Acceptance testing

Archiving

Summary

- Multimedia is the seamless integration of text, sound, images of all kinds, and control software within a single digital information environment.

- The skills needed to produce multimedia are diverse.

- Apart from competence in software and media design and production, cost control and staff management skills are needed.

- A client is anyone that has the authority to control the time and budget, or to sanction the design.

- A client-centred project follows stages of initiation and definition, followed by production. The production phase has several levels, which are interrelated. It is not a linear process.

Recommended reading

There is no specific support material recommended for this chapter. The definitions are based on experience.

2

The background: multimedia project management

Multimedia: industry fusion or confusion?

Because multimedia uses many skills, and because its people come from a variety of backgrounds, the multimedia environment does not have a single, defined way of working. New media companies tend to have a bias according to their origin and the background of their management. The bias will usually reflect journalism, advertising, video production, computing, publishing, or interactive training/education. Functional specifications have to blend with storyboards, and source code coexists with time code.

Each of these disciplines has different role names, phases of production, methods for documenting production, ways of working, organizational structures, and cultures. The individuals who work in the companies have their own specialisms. Some will recognize the environment they find themselves in, but many will not. They will have to adapt to the new terminology and structure.

Communication across the disciplines is problematic. Imagine a person with a Web design background being asked to produce a Web site extension product on DVD, or someone with a video producer's background being asked to produce a functional and technical specification, or a programmer being asked to produce a storyboard and assimilate time code data from an edit shot list. This happens.

Table 2.1 Comparison of multimedia origins.

	Web site production	Video production	Computing	Publishing	Interactive training/ Education
Roles	Web manager	Executive producer	Project manager	Commissioning editor	Training analyst
		Producer	Analyst	Senior editor	
		Director		Editor	
		Production assistant			
	Web editor	Scriptwriter	Programmer	Author	Interactive designer
	Web programmer				
	Web designer	Video graphics artist	Computer graphics artist	Print graphics artist Illustrator Cartoonist	
Production phases		Commission		Commission	
	Analyze	Research script	Analyze	Research/write,	Analyze
	Design		Prototype	Review	Design
	Produce	Shoot		Rewrite	Prototype
	Redesign	Offline edit	Program	Proof	Redesign
		Online edit	Test		
	Publish			Produce	Produce
	Update	Distribute	Release	Distribute	Test
					Release
					Evaluate
Documentation (client/ commissioner receives)	Proposal	Storyboard	Functional specification	Proposal	Proposal
	Script	Script	Technical specification	Drafts	Outline design
	Rewrites	Rewrites	Change management procedures	Redrafts	Detailed design
				Proofs	Sign-off agreements

Table 2.1 shows how each industry has developed its own way of producing a media product. As soon as an interactive application uses a mix of media components, aspects from all of these can prove invaluable for successful production.

Where does project management fit into this?

Although there are obvious differences, the industries share the production of media products. Their ways of working have evolved to suit the production methods for a particular medium, market and distribution cycle, in some cases over many decades. We often imagine television to be a new medium, but it has been around since the mid-1930s, and drew on practices from radio and the movie industry.

They are all team-based, complex activities with one role acting as the team leader/coordinator. They are all producing a particular end-product as the result of the team effort. Each product has unique properties. These aspects are characteristics of project management, and they apply to both on- and offline multimedia management too.

A project manager is expected to produce a product by organizing and controlling resources according to planned expenditure, in a certain time frame, and to a defined quality level. This fits the description of a person in charge of a new media project. For the purposes of this book the term 'project manager' will be used to denote a person with this role irrespective of the specialist origins, where the role might be called producer or designer.

Is multimedia project management the same as project management?

Although project management methods offer a good basis for multimedia project management, there are limitations and confusions that need to be recognized and considered. Some of these are inherent in project management methods, and some occur because of the particular nature of multimedia.

Limitations of project management methods

Traditional project management principles were derived from engineering projects, where the link between time for production, the cost of the product, and the quality of the end-product was established. The principles state that if any one of these factors is changed, the others are affected. Once a project has started, the project manager needs to monitor changes and assess the impact on the planned time, cost and quality of the product.

Some of these principles were used as the basis for the computer-based project management software packages that exist today. They provide a method to help define the breakdown of the project into tasks and the sequence of tasks that need to be performed according to a time line. This is called a **Gantt chart**. Some tools link the use of resources to the costs incurred, and some attempt to link the dependence between tasks, time and resources.

Check out the following tools to get a feel of what is available. Project management tools have proliferated in the last few years. Some are better for certain tasks and organizations than others. It is important for you to monitor developments in this field, as the tool that finally meets the real needs of multimedia projects will be invaluable.

The tools have derived from the analysis of different sets of needs within the profession. Some have emerged from the administration of the management of the volume of electronic multimedia assets. They formulate tasks and times around the changes needed to convert the raw assets into the delivery of integrated assets. Take note of the reference to Bulldog's Web site at the end of the chapter to see an example of this approach to a project management tool.

Microsoft Project is derived from more conventional project management wisdom of deciding milestones, tasks and resources. Different tools will suit different companies and ways of working.

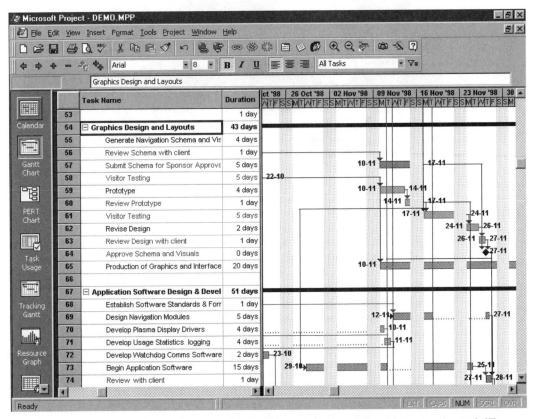

Gantt chart example. (Screen shot reproduced with permission from Microsoft Corporation and IST)

The tasks, sequence of production, resources needed, and cost breakdown need to be defined in some way as part of the multimedia project manager's role, and this is not straightforward.

Traditional project management methods tried to address the interrelation of the dependencies between tasks to the sequence of production and time. This was done using a technique called **network analysis**, which was also known as **critical path analysis**.

Network analysis encouraged project managers to use a diagram to show the logical links between tasks, illustrating which ones would be in simultaneous development and which ones were dependent on others' reaching a certain stage before work could begin. The critical path is derived from this analysis. It is the sequence of development of tasks that allows the optimum progress through the project.

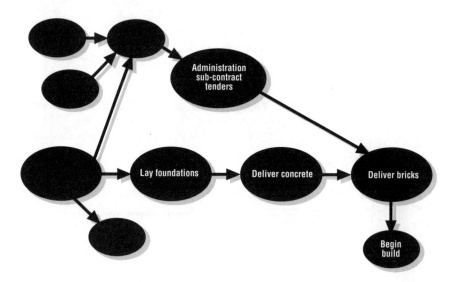

Multimedia network analysis: Example 1.

For example, in a building project (Example 1) the delivery of ready-mixed, quick-setting concrete is dependent upon the foundations' being ready to receive it. If there is a delay with the foundations, the delivery of the concrete has to be delayed. The one is critically dependent on the other. But in this case the opposite is not true because the digging doesn't have to stop if the concrete is going to be late. The subcontract tender process for the bricks doesn't have to stop if the foundations are delayed.

Sometimes, however, the dependence *does* work both ways. Sometimes dependence states change. Sometimes something that was not dependent can become dependent. Sometimes something that wasn't critical becomes critical. It begins to sound mysterious – it is, and there are no set rules for when or why things change their nature!

To give a multimedia example, your project may be going well, and you have worked out the sequence of production with a good understanding of which parts can be under production simultaneously without affecting each other and which major parts need to wait for several processes all to be complete.

Example 2 is for the purposes of demonstration, and represents only a small part of the project. It addresses major parts of the project, not detailed processes.

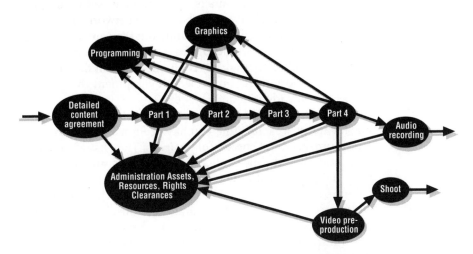

Multimedia network analysis: Example 2.

It shows that while computing and graphics tasks begin as soon as one part of the content/script is agreed, audio and video production wait until all the relevant content is agreed. This is usual, because audio and video production is often better done in one phase than in pieces. You want to hire a video crew or a sound studio for a voice-over only once for a defined time, for example, whereas your graphics and programming resources have a longer commitment to the project.

But consider this problem while looking at the diagram. You are likely to know how many voice-over artistes are needed from the initial agreement of the structure of the application, but not exactly how much or what they will say until the whole content has been agreed. The client has specified that they want to use a particular artiste in this project because his voice has become identified with their products through advertising. He is an actor as well as a voice-over artiste but is known best for minor character roles.

The project is almost halfway through the content stage. You have had to adjust the time-scale of developments because of hold-ups on sign-off of Part 1, but you are getting more confident that the next stages will run pretty smoothly. You decide to check out the availability of the artiste with an indication of which month you'll need him and most likely which week. You find he'll be filming on location for two and a half months around then for a TV series. He can manage to give you only one or two days, and these are a full month before your content should be finished if nothing else affects its planned progress. You can't afford to wait until he finishes his location shooting because the project release date is linked to a fixed conference day in your clients' organization, and you've already lost a lot of contingency time. Although you try to influence the client to change, they insist on using this artiste.

Completing the audio script now becomes more critical than completing the rest of the content. This is an example of something becoming critical when it wasn't previously a problem. The network analysis would have to be reworked in a radical way to separate out the way of working to achieve this. The voice-over date would be fixed, and would influence all the phases of production linked to it whatever else occurred in the project. Fixed dates and times have more effect on project development than anything else, so the sooner they are identified, the better.

In a similar way, the critical path of a Web site project could be affected by outside influences. Imagine you have begun a project to create a Web site for a medium-sized but successful business. They have agreed the general structure, budget and time-scale. The Web site is due to be rolled out stage by stage, beginning with the corporate profile, then products and services, distributors, and finally a 'what's new' section. The content underlying all the sections is large, and needs separate sign-offs. You haven't yet completed the profile or obtained agreement on the general interface design. Suddenly, news of a new product is leaked, and the company decides to meet the demand for information on the Web, since their switchboard is being swamped with queries.

The information has to be accessible by the following Monday morning, three days away with only one day to source materials from others – they will disappear for the weekend even though you won't – write up the material and have it signed-off before constructing some temporary pages. This leak of information and the reaction would obviously have a radical impact on any critical path that had been defined. During the day it emerges that this new product is dependent on two previous complementary products and services. This triggers debate in the company that these should be featured too, or the new product information would not be clear enough. This means that you have to liaise with more people than originally expected during the day, and of course they are 'out on business'; you'll also have to produce some pages on existing products and link between them and the new one. You weren't due to begin that section for another two weeks!

Some of the problems in using network analysis are evident in this example. Although it was popular during the 1980s, its popularity has waned. The first difficulty is met when the level of detail needs to be decided. It is possible to clutter the diagram with connections between tasks very easily. A large amount of space is needed to outline a complex project, and relatively small changes can mean a complete reworking of the level of detail, as in the case shown above. Sometimes network analysis makes the process appear so complicated that there seems to be no clear development path. It is also difficult for others to grasp its meaning and relevance. It is very time consuming to maintain if the project environment is prone to as many changes as online and offline multimedia.

However, the impact of the consequent changes in use of resources, different priorities for completing tasks, and the dangers of not meeting the date, need to be recorded in some way that all understand. At the moment this is usually done by word of mouth, backed up by a written account if the project manager is experienced. Project management software tools can show fixed deadlines in the Gantt chart, but the reasons behind the line-up of tasks is not clear, and with so much going on all the time it is sometimes easy to forget why you made a seemingly odd decision. This is why other documentation becomes important.

If we return to looking at project management methods and tools, the computer tools can prove useful in the planning stage of the project, particularly if the clients help to construct the schedule and agree to their time involvement on tasks. It also helps if they get an understanding of the process so that they can appreciate why you suggest certain solutions to problems that arise.

What is quality in interactive media?

The first limitation of conventional project management tools lies in the definition of quality. In engineering projects it is easier to specify quality in measurable terms: for example, the dimensions of the product, its durability, the physical mechanisms and how they operate, the components, and so on. But in any media project how is quality defined in measurable terms?

How do you measure multimedia quality?

It is easy to define technical levels of quality, such as whether the audio is mono or stereo, and whether it is encoded at a specific digital level, but the quality of design is more problematic. Without such a definition, it is very difficult to measure the impact of changes in time and cost on quality.

Time, cost, quality triangle.

Project management tools do not help in defining the quality level that is agreed between client and producer. The link between time, cost and quality of product is not shown in any breakdown of tasks, or in the resource/cost schedule, and this is a problem. The three are interrelated, so that a change to any one will affect the others, but there is no direct correlation. There is a tendency for project managers to overlook the impact of time and cost on quality because of this. Because the quality level is not specified as exactly in multimedia projects as it is in manufacturing projects, for example, it is harder for project managers to define the impact because it is so intangible.

Hanspeter Bürgin, coordinator for the interactive media awards at the 5th World Conference for Banking and Finance, Basle 1995, came face to face with the dilemma posed by people having different perspectives on the meaning of quality in multimedia. His set of judges came from different backgrounds in interactive development, and so were looking for different features. These features were perfectly valid for each perspective, but meant that it was difficult to get a consensus. So the judges then reached agreement on a set of criteria before making their decisions.

This difference of perspective on the nature of quality is similar to what happens within multimedia teams because the members come from different media backgrounds. It occurs between developers and clients for the same reason. There can also be a gap between the team's understanding of quality and that of their management. So the definition of quality in interactive media is a major problem.

If we look back at Table 2.1, quality has been defined in different ways in the different disciplines. Video production produces a storyboard and script for the client to agree content and visual treatment. Computing uses a functional specification to define how the application will operate and a prototype to show how it will look and feel. Publishing uses editors and peer review processes to control the quality of work submitted. Interactive training and education uses the outline and detailed design documents to agree the quality level of content and a prototype for the look and feel. Web site design documentation and agreement procedures have not yet been standardized. They are open to interpretation and multiple practices. In market-driven projects quality is assessed by whether the product is successful in the market. The production quality relies on the creativity of the development team.

This highlights some of the problems in defining quality in multimedia. There are objective parameters for some of the technical aspects, but many subjective aspects for design quality. Each project will define its own 'quality' priorities according to the subject and the target audience.

How then can the time–cost–quality equation work for multimedia? It can only work with a guiding principle defined as quality – one so general that it will operate for all multimedia projects. The principle needs to be viewed with the understanding that it is only acting as a control mechanism for time and cost.

For budgetary purposes then, the following definition of quality will be useful. Underlying all the processes are the definition and agreement of content and its treatment. The content means the information that is going to be presented, and the treatment means which media and which techniques will be used, and what it will look like.

Design quality for media projects = Content and treatment agreement

This definition is intentionally broad, and can therefore be linked to whatever project is being considered. Some people will not accept this as a definition; they find that it omits aspects they would like to see covered. However, most problems during development relate to changes in the content and treatment. The overall aspects of robustness of the product and fitness for purpose for the audience are important, of course. But we have moved those to be part of the testing cycle, which moves in parallel with the development of content and treatment. These aspects are covered in Chapter 18, *Testing*, where we discuss how to devise a testing strategy to suit the client and yourselves.

The definition of quality in interactive media can be split into each media component, and can be debated by each professional group. The concept of quality that is achievable in professional terms, and which is considered 'leading edge', may not be compatible with the quality that relates to that achieved by a particular team for the budget and time they have. It may not even be a quality level that is wanted or needed by the client. The approach that needs to be adopted here is to set levels of quality that are appropriate and achievable for a given purpose to achieve defined results. It is a business-driven rather than a specialism-driven approach.

It is hard for professionals to accept the idea of producing less than what they consider 'top quality', as they tend to be judged by their projects in the eyes of their peers. Within each level of quality that is dictated by the constraints of the project, however, there is still room to be creative and professional, as well as aspiring for the best that can be achieved for that level. This dilemma of specialism versus business needs is one that underlies many a project conflict. It should be brought into the open, and the peer pressure relieved. It would help if this debate was addressed in all spheres and all courses as a priority, and remains one of the fundamental gaps between an academic and business perspective.

How are time, cost and quality linked in multimedia?

The relationship between time, cost and quality is far from linear. If we consider a classic request from a client in a less complicated process than multimedia and study the effects, it will give a clear indication of the relationship between time, cost and quality, and demonstrate the principles that should be applied in multimedia.

'Oh! and there's just a small change ...'

You are a specialist furniture craftsman. A client has ordered an armchair in a particular style using particular materials, with a particular fabric and a particular fitting. You have worked out the cost and delivery time accordingly, to a formula that takes into account the type and availability of the materials and the complexity of production.

However, after a week, the client changes his mind about the fabric. What are the implications for cost and time? The knock-on cost will depend on how far along production the original request has got.

■ *Project management note 1. Change may have cost implications for administration and production.*
The original fabric could be at any of the following stages at different times of the process: it could have been cut out, or sewn, or fitted. So the customer may well have to accept some charges and a changed delivery date. In this case the fabric has been cut and sewn, so there is redundant work and materials, and rework. You will have to start the production again.

■ *Project management note 2. Change may have time implications because of rework.*
When you explain the time and cost knock-ons, the client insists that he really needs the chair in the original time. There may be no way that this can happen. You may not be able to achieve it, as the time limit may now be too short. The new fabric choice is from a special supplier, and is much more expensive than the original choice. When you contact them, they are out of stock. It will take time to order.

■ *Project management note 3. Change may make the project impossible to achieve if it results in factors beyond your control. Also, there are some processes that cannot be speeded up.*

If you make it into a special order where the workers will need to work overtime, more costs need to be passed to the customer.

■ *Project management note 4. If time-scales are immovable but you have to absorb changes, the workload increases and causes extra cost.*

You might offer a standard fitted cover rather than a loose one, as this takes less time but is of a different quality. Alternatively, you might suggest a different style and shape for the chair that is easier and faster to produce.

■ *Project management note 5. The quality of the product can be changed to meet the time constraint.*

It has taken a few hours for you to assess the situation, time and cost implications and relay three alternatives to the client. You need a quick decision because your new time-scales and costs are based on starting immediately. Your client doesn't reply to your fax immediately. You phone his company the next day to be told he's out of the country on business for two days and isn't contactable! Your work's supervisor is reworking the production schedule and is on hold waiting for the decisions! The fabric supplier keeps phoning to ask if you're placing the order or not!

■ *Project management note 6. Never be fooled by 'it's just a small change'.*

Theory into practice 1

Look back at the example and substitute the following. It should give you an insight into the repercussions of change in an online or offline multimedia project.

The style of the chair	= Content agreed
(type of wood, springs and stuffing)	
The shape of the chair	= Structure agreed
The fabric	= Treatment of content agreed
	(usually known as 'look and feel')

Even though there were only three quality variables here – style, shape and fabric – it is easy to understand how a relatively small change can have significant repercussions according to when the change was requested, how far into production the product was, and how quickly new decisions are agreed.

Multimedia has many levels of quality and variables within each of the production processes – video, audio, graphics, text, animation, content treatment. Each of these has several stages to production, so any changes at any point can have upward, downward, backward, forward and diagonal effects.

The schedule and plan become difficult to change and update. You have to predict the time and cost implications of slippage, and this means consulting members of the team who will be affected by the proposed change. You also have to balance what can be absorbed with the effect this has on any contingency you had allowed in time and cost.

You have to agree the change and the knock-ons with the clients. Then you have to communicate the changes and the impact to the whole team because they are making decisions based on the time they're allowed. A change a day is not uncommon, so imagine the impact on your time from the administration of these changes.

The main difficulties inherent in the use of the project management methods and tools are as follows.

■ The quality level isn't specified within the existing methods in such a way that the impact of changes on it is measurable. If there are changes, the project manager has to predict all the consequences and update the plan of time and costs accordingly. The tools are not dynamic enough in prediction of the impact on time, resource and cost in relation to quality level. The value of the network analysis technique from traditional methods is difficult to define. Its value even for traditional projects is questioned. The importance of defining the dependences and their changing states is right in principle but difficult in practice.

■ In the armchair example, the quality was agreed in detail before the project started. In multimedia applications, the quality levels are often not well defined because the client and producer have little common ground in communication. When the multimedia specialists try to explain, their language is incomprehensible to clients. The clients can't specify what they want because they are not sure what they can have to begin to match it to what they want. The producer cannot specify cost and time accurately until there is a clear specification, so a lot of time needs to be spent to understand the scope of the project. It is because of this initial effort that many companies ask for staged payments to make sure that their costs are covered even if the project never goes ahead.

■ If you start from a poor definition, the clients will make so many changes that the project will get out of control quickly. We will deal with how to get a good definition later. Even if you are market driven and not client driven, if you don't have a good definition at the beginning the product will evolve and take more time and effort to complete than might be necessary. Sometimes the time of release of a product to market is vital – in time for Christmas presents, for example – or the market's characteristics have changed and it is no longer receptive to the style of product.

How the nature of multimedia affects the project management process

The time, cost and quality principles are important but do not translate directly to multimedia. They can be applied when a process is well defined and the clients understand their role in the development process. In the building project example the client and architect would have taken a long time to define the shape, structure and cost of the building before work commenced. The client recognizes that once the foundations have begun they cannot change the shape of the end-product. They may try to change the construction materials or some features of the building, but the points at which they can no longer affect the process are clear. The structure of a multimedia project is not as readily recognizable but the consequences of changes to it past a certain point in production are as bad as changing the shape of a building under construction.

In part, this problem is due to the seemingly fluid nature of computer software. There is no definite relationship between the elements of a program that comes near to the definite way a building sits on its foundations. This does not mean that such dependencies do not exist. In the development of offline projects, good programming practice can minimize problems due to change – object-oriented programming being one element of this practice – but it cannot remove it. For example, adding a section into a program where this requires another item to be added to a menu can be very problematic if the menu has been built up in a sophisticated visual style with many layers of video and stills. In Web site design there is more flexibility, and changes can be made efficiently without major disruption if component parts of the site structure need changes. But many small changes quite quickly add up to days of extra work.

On- and offline multimedia management is much more like managing innovation. The process and end-product are constructed according to unique circumstances. Each multimedia application is hand-crafted because the content is unique, even if standard tools are used. The personal qualities of the project manager – leadership style, team management, client management, credibility – come to the fore. Aspects related to general management, such as level of authority, level of control over resources, and level of control over budget, are connected to the structure of the organization where the project manager works. These can have a significant effect on projects, and can either help or hinder the project manager in developing a project.

Planning, monitoring, and control of time, cost and quality are still prime factors in a project management role, but because the whole environment is unstable and intangible, the complexity increases and the risks of failure are higher. The total organizational structure contributes to success or failure, but often the project manager has to accept the blame unfairly for setbacks.

Successful managers of innovation try to control the project earlier in the process than traditional project managers because the earlier control is taken the sooner the risks from disrupted project progress decrease. The link between planning and control is stronger. Rather than just plan time, cost and quality, you need to anticipate risk areas and take measures to decrease the risks. This includes controlling the expectations of the client, the development team and the company management. In market-driven projects, you try to minimize risks through market analysis, by having strong distribution channels and through marketing and advertising the product to give it the maximum chance for success. So to manage innovation, knowledge of likely risks and how to cover them is crucial.

These personal and managerial qualities, like the concept of quality level, are not as definable as time and cost. They have to be put in context, in the environment where the project manager needs to operate. It is easy to recognize that multimedia does not have one environment but is a hybrid because of the range of skills of the people involved and the different approaches taken, depending on the bias of the company (see Table 2.1).

Because of this, only a few of the basic principles will be put into context here to demonstrate the extent to which a project's success can be affected by organizational structure, team leadership, and risk analysis. Each individual environment and mix of people needs assessment to reach a more detailed understanding.

Organizational structure effects

If you are a project manager working in an organization with a traditional hierarchical structure, certain characteristics may have a tendency to interfere with your ability to get on with the job. You will have been assigned a project team, but some key members may continue to receive instructions and take their lead from their functional superiors. This is sometimes referred to as **dotted line** responsibility because of the way it is shown on an organizational chart, and is quite common in the technical side of media companies.

In multimedia the programmer may have a senior programmer and the graphics artist may have a senior graphics artist who set their standards of work and, in addition, will generally control their workload as well. They may be working for other project managers on other projects during the timescale of your project. In this case, their seniors will control their time and effort on your project. You may find that your programmer cannot complete the task you need on time because another project has been given priority.

You end up fighting for resources without the authority to influence the situation. This shows a definite role conflict. You cannot be held responsible for your project slippage if you don't have control of people's time. Control of time should be one of your biggest responsibilities. You might be able to allow your team member to work on some other tasks for their functional manager, but the manner and exact amount of time should be within your control and governed by *your* project demands. This type of conflict, which interferes with project progress, also applies to non-human resources. If your team members don't have access to the right equipment at the right time because others have been given priority, there are further hold-ups.

There is a need for shared resources in a business, and the management will only be seen to be doing their job if they try to get the most from the least, to increase margins. But there's a fine balance between downtime costs when sharing resources and savings from labour and equipment charges.

It doesn't take long for a hierarchical allocation of resources to get abused by those best placed to do so in the organization. This is mainly because everyone's projects fall prey to shifts in expected workloads and all is fair in a hierarchical war depending on your rank!

If you are working in an organization where functional and project managers coexist, both roles need to be tightly defined. The functional manager's role needs to change to a more generalist role because the project manager's role is specifically tied to the project and is therefore specialist. The authority over people and equipment for the term of the project has to be established, and it needs to rest with the project manager. If not, there is no real role for a manager of this type.

Any request for resource time or equipment that has been allocated to the project should go through the project manager. Otherwise, the programmer and graphics artist tend to agree to the extra work for the functional manager without being fully aware of the present status of the project. For example, they wouldn't know that you are trying to block a major change resulting from a phone call from the client at the moment they agree to extra work. You finish the phone call but have failed to block the change and need them to absorb the extra work on your project.

As the project manager's role is also to monitor the time and cost of the project, a functional structure may cause problems. Many multimedia organizations operate control over time and costs via time sheets. There needs to be some mechanism for monitoring time and translating it into real costs rather than projected costs, and time sheets are a well-accepted practice. However, there are many debates about how much time can be allocated to projects against time used for organizational administration, general meetings and the like.

If the internal and external resources for your project fill in time sheets, which go to the finance/accounts function, then it is their responsibility to have up-to-date records of costs for you to keep track of how much you have left to spend. The project manager has to make many decisions on reallocation of budget and spending. If the accounts section is behind with inputting the hours from your project, you may not be able to get an accurate picture of how much you have left.

You will find there are occasions when you need to know daily exactly how much you have left, especially as you get near the end of the project, when spending becomes more critical. Confusion can arise if items of equipment or software form part of the budget costs, depending on how the invoices are dealt with. These invoices may go to the respective functional heads and then to accounts, and the first you know of them is a sudden drop in your actual budget. You may have been expecting them, but sometimes the actual point when they are paid is important. You need to take the figure off your expected outlay of money so that you then have a better understanding of exactly what you have left against the remainder of the expected outlay.

Accounts departments rarely keep project information at this detailed level. They don't need the information, but you do. They have to reconcile the overall project payments to overall spending, and reconcile it with the information from other expenses. They have different interests to serve in reporting the overall position to management.

The whole question of how the financial data for each project is kept, and who needs what information when, is a real problem. But as project manager you need to have detailed breakdowns of projected cost and actual costs to use in negotiations with the client. You need to make decisions on how much might be absorbed for small changes for the client as gestures of goodwill and when to charge for other changes because there is a real danger of the projects going over budget.

The structure of the organization will dictate who has what type of financial information, who can have access to which financial data, and under what circumstances. If there is the equivalent of a project manager role in the organization, the financial structure should facilitate this role and its needs as well as the executive management information. Many multimedia organizations that have the equivalent of a project manager role do not organize their financial data to help the role. Without accurate records of cost, a project management role cannot be fulfilled.

It used to be the traditional project manager's responsibility to keep track of the budget and report on it, but the need for better, up-to-date, executive management information on the overall position of the company tends to centralize the financial data. Only a fully automatic system, in which time-sheet data is input regularly and collated with freelance and external project costs, will fully serve the needs of a project-led company.

This is an area that needs to be worked out according to the needs of the company and its employees, and will become more important as companies grow larger.

A hierarchical organization will tend to have strict control over who can spend money. If the project manager or equivalent does not have a good level of authority over spending, projects may get held up waiting for the correct authorization. It is right that there is control over spending, but authority levels need to be allocated according to criteria worked out by the management according to the company's needs.

There are two points to note here. First, project managers will only spend wisely within a defined level if they have good information on current spending, otherwise they will be spending blind. So authority to spend should be linked to the responsibility for monitoring the overall budget of the project to avoid this. Second, if project managers buy a piece of software they have a responsibility to ensure that it is really necessary, that the company doesn't already have a copy, that the licence agreement is recorded and filed according to company policy, and that the correct people are fully informed of what they have done. This will avoid others' replicating the same spending later through lack of knowledge of the existence of the software.

Theory into practice 2

Your designer has met a problem that one piece of software will solve. The company doesn't own it. The technical director who must sanction software purchases is on leave, and the systems manager who acts as his unofficial deputy is on a stand at a conference for three days. You have a deadline in two days and don't have the authority to spend company money.

What should you do?

There are no wrong answers. Some might be better than others. Here are some replies from project managers. They might match yours and give you some new insights.

■ Buy it myself and claim it back later on expenses.

■ Never start a project unless you've agreed some authority to spend money unsanctioned.

■ I used to buy things myself but it took so long and so much hassle to get repaid, I ended up out of pocket because I went overdrawn. They didn't care. Then they just expect you to do it all the time. It's in their interest, really. Now I just explain to the clients why I can't make the deadline – they have a go at the management, who have a go at me, but I'd get the software. One day they'll listen, I suppose.

■ I'd find someone with some authority and get them to buy it. But it takes so much time to justify why you need it. They're always busy, and blame you for not sorting something out sooner.

In an alternative organizational structure, a team is constructed for a particular project under the project manager's control. The core of the organization is organized to support and facilitate projects, general administration and general management. The project team may exist for only one project and then be disbanded or moved into other teams.

This is more like the model of video production. The producer recruits people and facilities according to budget and needs. He or she has authority to spend within budget but has to report back within the company on progress and spending.

Within this type of structure there is more flexibility, which seems to be needed in creative projects, but the organization has to work hard to facilitate, coordinate, record and communicate. There are central needs that have to be controlled – allocation of team space, meeting space, access to phones, network and so on. The larger the organization the harder this becomes, and the informal ways need to become more formalized without becoming restrictive. This is the challenge for management.

There is a third structure emerging as a model for project-run companies; it is based on a retail model, in which people are tasked to find business for the company. Their salaries tend to be linked to commission based on the amount of business they bring in. Their skills of persuasion and influence are important, but there are dangers for the project manager and also the company under this structure. Because they need to win the business, they tend to offer too much on too little information and raise clients' expectations of what they will receive. One of the features of managing innovation that we mentioned earlier was the need to control expectations as early as possible. There is an inherent conflict between these roles.

Again, the management needs to recognize this, and then make decisions on how best to resolve it.

A project manager may move between several types of organizational structure if freelance. The strengths and limitations of the working environment affect the risks to projects so it is as well to become aware of them. You need to build in more contingency time for achieving tasks if the organization is chaotic!

The project manager as team leader

A multimedia team can vary in size and skills. Different projects need different teams to achieve them. The team may grow and shrink during the course of the project. Parts may be subcontracted out if necessary. Sometimes a team member may take on two roles – graphics and authoring, for example. The team definition will begin from the definition of the major components of the project. Then those with skills that match the requirements will be allocated or recruited.

The project manager as team leader.

In terms of roles, a typical team may have:

- a leader, who might also use his or her specialism from a media background to contribute to part of the project development;
- someone who will agree the content and treatment with the client and the relevant members of the team;
- someone to produce the computer graphics;
- someone to program or, for Web pages, write HTML or CGI;
- someone to arrange and manage the audio and video production, if these are necessary.

There are support roles that you'd expect to find as part of the organization structure, such as technical support and secretarial/admin. There are often important support roles that the organization may need to employ if they don't have the skills in house and the project needs them: project/personal assistants, picture researchers, cartoonists, animators, rights clearer, video graphics artists, translators, specialist programmers, computing consultants and technical consultants, for example.

All the usual problems of personality conflict and professional conflict can occur in a team. But a leader of a multidisciplined, professional project team made up of individual specialists also faces people used to making and taking decisions for themselves within their own specialisms.

The control of a creative, skilled group is not easy. In multimedia, the members of the group all have a relevant perspective on the way the content should be structured and treated. All the key people will have some training in their professional background to analyze and treat information within their discipline. This is a potential strength but also a potential weakness of the group. The project manager will have a bias from a background specialism which will be evident in the perspective of the treatment.

The first management decision – of whether you will impose a general design solution on your team or involve them fully in the creative decisions – is often made for you, and is outside your control. An initial specification might have defined the media mix in general terms because of the budget agreed up front. For example, colleagues might have worked up the proposal for the clients because they had the time available. The budget for a CD-ROM might have been based on the cost of ten minutes of video for Windows, computer graphics (approximately 100 screens), a few five-second low-level animations, 30 minutes of audio, and so on. It is possible that neither you nor your team members had any involvement in the initial specification. Or a company Web site might have been specified as a maximum of 18 pages of text and graphics, no audio, no video, and no animation.

This type of specification acts as a constraint under which you have to try to work irrespective of whether the detailed examination of the content indicates a different media selection mix. Most projects can't get off the ground without such a high-level specification. If the detailed understanding of the content suggests a better media mix, and you feel it is in everyone's interest to point out the improved benefits to the client, the same conditions apply to your suggestions for changes to the programme structure as to suggestions coming from the client. You need to convince them to pay more or sacrifice some other aspects of the programme.

This directive management approach to your team sounds harsh. However, if the time allowed for decisions at the beginning of a project is severely limited then this will be a set of circumstances where an initial directive stance may be appropriate. It does not mean that you continue to dictate solutions to the team. Wherever possible their input is needed to give a rounded product, so your management style has to adapt to the changing circumstances of the project as explained in Chapter 12, *Team management principles.*

The main difficulty is in deciding what treatments to use for the various parts of the content. The decisions are often made quite early in relation to the agreed budget. Your team will have plenty of ideas on what will work more effectively. They have freedom of thought in relation to the top quality that they could attain in their specialist areas, and are often frustrated by the decisions that have been made.

They are not subject to the constraints of time and cost in their thinking, and if they haven't experienced the difficult dynamics that occur between the company and the clients to reach enough of an agreement to proceed, they find it hard to compromise their enthusiasm and professional opinions. You need to make clear the reasons behind the decisions, and focus your team on tailoring their suggestions to improvements, consistent with the time and costs, that will serve the user best.

Some of the most difficult problems arise if your team members suggest ideas in front of clients. Once clients have been motivated by an idea that sounds good, you are in a vulnerable position. It is essential that you brief the team to make suggestions openly at any time *except* when they are in meetings with clients. In market-driven applications the working atmosphere is different. Creative brainstorming between the team members is common both before and during the production. Because all the decisions can be taken quickly and internally, more time is created for fine tuning and experimentation. This can still get out of control, so someone has to focus the team on the deadlines and call the tune of how much the changes are costing in terms of effort.

It also causes problems if your team members respond to clients' suggestions in meetings by agreeing that they can do what is wanted. They will be concerned to demonstrate their technical and professional competence. But it is not what is possible that is the issue, it is what is possible within the constraints. The team members feel free of the constraints and will not make the wisest decisions. This is a common cause of tension between creative decision makers and business decision makers. The project manager has a foot in both camps!

You need to make the reasons clear, and set ground rules for how team members communicate with clients. They should not make any agreements for changes unless they directly affect only the material they are working on and they can contain the changes within the next working deadline. You have to be kept informed of the changes if these are agreed independently with the client – on the phone, for example. If they receive requests from the client that fall outside these parameters then these have to be referred to you. Some clients may play you and a team member off against each other in order to achieve a change in the design. In this case it is important that your team tell you of anything of this nature that they discuss with the client.

When ideas are suggested by team members, your problem is to determine how much they can affect the quality without incurring time and cost penalties. If you do not allow them to shape the programme in some ways you run the risk of missing out on genuine improvements, and of losing the team's motivation, trust and respect. If you allow them to influence the structure but don't control them, then there is a big risk of overrun on time and costs. You face a dilemma. Should you tap into the team's appropriate strengths only up to a level that can be contained within cost or budget, or should you fight on their behalf to convince your management and the client that the cost of the increase in quality is justified?

If the project manager shares a discipline perspective with a team member the balance of power in decisions can easily be unbalanced. It is difficult to listen to suggestions objectively when your own discipline is driving your thinking in a different direction. So the split role of project manager and specialist complicates the job.

Sometimes the time-scale of the project is so tight that decisions have to be taken quickly and imposed on the team. Allow changes only for technical efficiency. The team will try to affect the structure and look and feel, but in this case you should focus them on the shortness of time and make sure that what is specified is technically possible in the time.

On other occasions you need to offer a defined time to the team to talk through the agreed outline structure and ask for any suggestions for improvements. This team effort is valuable at the early stages of the project. It is important that you influence their decisions on which suggestions to implement according to time, cost, and benefit to the user. The time for suggestions has to have a limit because the later into a project changes occur, the more impact they have on the remaining time.

You need to consider whether there may be hidden agendas. This is problematic if the suggestions are outside your own specialism. There may be personal motives driving the suggestions, as the members of the team may want to create an opportunity to try out some of the latest techniques purely to obtain the experience that will keep them abreast of the latest advances in their area. These might not be in the project's scope or interest. This is a balancing act, but you need to understand your team's motives and accommodate them within your constraints.

It is true that you cannot time creative ideas. Many good ones will occur during the project that will have to be rejected. As the detail of the content emerges, the conception of the best treatment will be affected. You do not want to discourage ideas. They are part of professional development, and there's value in the team's recognizing their worth. They will serve other projects because the factors that led up to the ideas will be recognized earlier in subsequent projects where it is easier to implement them.

Throughout the project, as team leader you have to represent the views of the users. They are the most important group but they have no representatives on the project. The project's success depends on the users' reaction. Your decisions on which changes have priority over others should try to serve the users above all others. There are many interests that drive the project in one direction or another. Often the client will prevail even when they make decisions that are counter to professional advice because they are in a position to call the tune.

If user interface and cognition are not your strengths, then identify the people in the team who have these skills. If necessary, bounce the suggestions off other colleagues who have strengths in these areas to test them out. You need to ask all those who make suggestions for change, including yourself, to define the benefit to the user. It is surprising how often this will help the decision making.

This has been a rapid overview of some circumstances and how they can affect the management role of the project manager. The full chapter on team management (Chapter 12) examines some of the principles behind management styles. Consequently, the pressure, time and cost constraints on decision making are less evident there. However, a project manager is expected to employ the appropriate style for a given set of circumstances.

Project Manager's role

The role of the multimedia project manager

It should now be clear that the project manager's role is to control the progress of the project against any detrimental influences to the time, cost and quality that can occur from the client, the place of work, the market forces, and the team. The needs of the user should drive priorities and decisions during the course of design and production, and that is true for both client-centred and market-driven projects, and for both on- and offline projects.

This is not a recognized definition within multimedia as it operates today. Project managers, or their equivalent, have usually evolved from specialist roles of computing, graphics, video production, or interactive education and training. Most have received little or no exposure to general business and management principles. Any training is usually confined to professional development within their specialism. This is driven by the constant changes within the professional areas and the need to keep abreast of them. As the tools and standards become more stable, there may be more time to broaden the scope of their training.

Summary

- Project management principles unite the disparate ways of working in interactive media development.

- Not all project management methods transfer well to multimedia development.

- Time, cost and quality principles are important but the overall concept of quality in multimedia is embryonic.

- The project's multimedia design quality = the content and treatment agreement reached for that project.

- The impact of changes on time, cost and quality can put the project at risk.

- Multimedia management shares similarities with the management of innovation.

- Anticipation of risk and measures of control are important.

- Organizational structure affects the project manager's role, responsibility, authority and control.

- The multimedia project manager has a difficult role as team leader because of the diverse, creative team.

Recommended reading

Block R. (1983). *The Politics of Projects*. New York: Yourdon Press Computing Series

Brooks F.P. Jr (1982). *The Mythical Man-Month. Essays on Software Engineering*. Reading, MA: Addison-Wesley

Chicken J. (1994). *Managing Risks and Decisions in Major Projects*. London: Chapman & Hall

Reiss G. (1992). *Project Management Demystified*. London: E. & F.N. Spon

Webb A. (1994). *Managing Innovative Projects*. London: Chapman & Hall

Young T.L. (1993). *Planning Projects*. London: The Industrial Society

Bulldog Web site: http://www.bulldog.ca

3

Scoping a project

Project manager's responsibilities

- To ascertain the client's brief
- To attune yourself to the client and their culture
- To clarify unclear information
- To gather sufficient information to write a clear proposal
- To explain any queries the client has

Your objectives

At the first meeting with the client you are trying to decide whether their brief is realistic in terms of the time for development, the expected use of media, and the results needed from the project. You need to understand these in order to define the cost and quality level that can be produced in the available time, and to define the number and type of resources you'll need for the project.

The way in which initial meetings are conducted varies from company to company, and will to some extent depend on the way the initial approach by the client was handled (if the client is new) or the past history (if the client is an established customer). That will affect the number and type of people who attend a meeting, which could vary from a single person hosting an initial briefing to a full-scale meeting attended by representatives of the main disciplines involved: production and management, graphics and software.

Many companies rely on the experience of the person conducting the interview to ensure that relevant information is obtained. There is no standard approach, and this means that projects tend to evolve differently, displaying a variety of problems. This can often be traced back to early meetings where some vital facts were missed, so it is important for more than one person to take notes and for any unclear points to be revisited. It might be useful to finish the meeting by confirming the action points for both sides, especially if the clients have to undertake some contributory work.

The fundamental requirement of such a meeting is for you as a developer to understand what the client wants. Unfortunately this is not necessarily as simple as it might seem, because you and your client will probably have different backgrounds, and your client may be unfamiliar with the strengths and weaknesses of interactive media. At its worst this results in the client's seeming not to know what they want. (This is a different problem from the situation where the client genuinely does not know what they want. In this case you would hope that the client would ask your advice.)

The training field has recognized this problem and has come up with an answer called **needs analysis**. Some trainers specialize in this, and are called **training analysts**. Multimedia could learn a lot from the techniques to define and refine clients' wishes because it saves time later in the project. Trainers have had to invest in needs analysis because they are accountable not just for the transfer of information but also for proving that the learners have absorbed it. If there is no clear, agreed definition from clients of which knowledge and skills are important to transfer, trainers cannot devise tests to prove that the correct transfer has taken place. Similarly, if you do not define what your clients are trying to achieve with new media, you will not be able to agree that you have provided what they wanted.

A clear, agreed definition of what the client says they want at the beginning of a project is useful if they try to change the scope of the project as new information arrives or if new people are brought into the project and influence its direction. Without the definition the project can meander around, and you won't have any grounds for asking for extra time or costs for the changes.

It would be good practice for companies to spend time collating the experience of their project managers/producers to produce clear, flexible guidelines and check-lists for stages of the project, which could serve as the company's defined way of working. There are drawbacks to using such guidelines rigidly, and these will be pointed out. The following specimen questionnaires will provide you with a check-list and ensure a sound basis for obtaining the first level of information for an online and an offline interactive project. Each category will be explained so that it is clear why the information is important. A copy of the questionnaires is included at the end of the chapter, and can be found on the CD.

Whatever type of interactive project you are responsible for, the initial set of questions you ask will define the scope of the project. The delivery platform of the project will have an influence on the overall look and feel and the type of interactivity; the budget and production time will affect your design decisions. The questions have to be tailored to the type of project. We include generic samples of online and offline questionnaires here. So if you are responsible for interactive TV programmes, you will need to use the following as examples to formulate a set of scoping questions. If you have a definite market bias – Web sites for large advertising companies, for example – then you will be able to refine the questions to suit the market. Hybrid projects – a CD-ROM with volatile content kept on a Web site for pulling into the package as appropriate, for example – will need to combine elements of both of the questionnaires outlined below.

Online interactive media scoping questionnaire

Client's previous multimedia experience

Project name/no:

Contact details

Client/Organization name:

Address:

Tel: Fax: Email:

Web site:

Project contacts:

Name(s):   Position(s):

Direct line   Email:

Previous interactive media experience

Online

None ☐   A little ☐   Fair ☐   Good ☐   Experienced ☐

Offline

None ☐   A little ☐   Fair ☐   Good ☐   Experienced ☐

Experience description

Online

Products: Producer:

Offline

Products: Producer:

Prior experience affects everyone, and clients are no exception. It sets up expectations, which you need to understand. They may have had good and bad experiences. You can learn what they like and don't like in terms of ways of working as well as in interactivity. If they are return customers you need to find out as much as you can from the people who worked with them before. In fact you should have done this prior to the first meeting if it was recognized that they had been clients previously. Even if they are previous clients it is still good practice to find out what they particularly liked and disliked the last time.

You need to cover both on- and offline experience, whatever sort of project you are working on, as experience in one has both positive and negative impact when moving to the other, and colours expectations. For example, a client may have a large text-based Web site, which the user navigates by using a search facility, because the company deals primarily in information. Marketing consultancies would fall into this category, where they offer summaries of their respective reports to tempt people to buy the whole report. The text-driven nature of the Web site may well be the most appropriate way to convey the information. But if the company decides to develop a marketing CD, the interactivity of the Web site will not be the best model for the new purpose and delivery medium, even if they believe it will be. Some of the content may be useful, but it needs a new treatment to achieve the impact they want.

Statement of what the client wants

> **Client's initial statement of what they want**

It helps to formulate what the client says they want at the beginning of the interview. They may be very focused and know their needs precisely. In this case the rest of the questions confirm their needs and develop the detail. Or, they can be very vague. They may have a notion but not be able to define it precisely. The more precise they are the easier your job will be, unless they have misjudged what can be achieved or how to make best use of the medium. The more vague they are the harder you will have to work to get a good specification. An example of what you might enter here would be:

> *This is a specialist small firm producing garden furniture and ornaments. They want to set up a Web site to evaluate the potential for sales of their products over the Net.*

Notice that they have not said that they want to sell their products on the Net. At the moment a database of products and payment structure for selling online would not be a confirmed need.

Alternatively, you might have put:

> *This is a specialist small firm producing garden furniture and ornaments. They think they want a Web site but first they want advice as to what information to place there, some costings based on different types of site, and the type of bene-fits they could expect from their investment.*

This should trigger you to shelve the questionnaire, show them examples of your work, and demonstrate the features of some equivalent small specialist retail sites to help define the component parts of a site that would suit them. Once they have an understanding of what is possible they should be allowed to discuss the possibilities and probably return for a more productive meeting. It might help them to take the questionnaire away in this case so that they can prepare the answers to the queries.

Type of project

The delivery medium affects the specific type of project that will be produced. Online projects serve a much wider range of needs than offline projects, and new uses are continually emerging as the Internet develops as a mass communication delivery platform. Classification of project types in this fast-moving marketplace has not yet become as codified as in offline, which has developed well-defined areas such as point of sale and edutainment publishing. So the following is offered as the starting point, and should be tailored accordingly.

Online project type

Internet ☐   Hybrid Web/CD ☐   Intranet ☐   Extranet ☐

Set up new facility ☐

(If yes, domain name suggestions?)

_____

_____

_____

Add/change existing facility ☐

Internet/intranet/extranet

It is important to clarify the differences between these three categories. The Internet offers general public access to electronic information. An intranet

provides closed access to electronic information, and is usually company specific. An extranet allows nominated companies or individuals access to all or
part of an intranet. If the site will be new then the company needs to put forward suggestions for its domain name. This is not always straightforward, as
others may have already taken the most obvious choice. The sooner this is
confirmed the better, and if they cannot come up with suggestions ask them
to give you three approved alternatives as soon as possible.

The general scope of the project will be linked to the type of delivery and the
access to the online facilities. Setting up a secure international corporate intranet
and providing the design templates for each division to insert their own content
while retaining the common 'corporate' approach is very different from designing a small company profile Web site to be published on the Internet.

In the intranet example the technical specification aspects can be complex,
with several servers spread around the world and the security implications of
linking them through the Internet. Such data links may already be in place but
it is not uncommon for a large organization's IT structure to have organically
grown, and it may be difficult to find out exactly what is in place and who is in
charge of the various parts. On the content side the number and type of templates will take a long time to establish, with the potential for cultural or
linguistic differences and even office politics conspiring to confuse the issue. It
may well emerge that a database might be the most efficient way of dealing
with varying amounts of the data, and this might have to be built from scratch.
Training people to input the data is likely to be necessary as well.

The small company profile, on the other hand, may mean no more than
several sets of pages linked by a straightforward structure with the option for
the client to come back with material to update the pages as and when they
wish. The technical and design aspects are much more straightforward in this
case. The company will either have its own server or will be renting space
from an Internet service provider (ISP), but in either case setting the Web site
up on the server will be relatively straightforward. Hopefully the only awkward issue will be getting the right domain name.

Hybrid Web/CD

The term 'hybrid' can have many meanings. A hybrid CD-ROM, for example,
is a CD that mixes different CD formats, usually CD audio and CD-ROM
data. As it is possible to make an application that mixes both on- and offline,
we can now also refer to an Internet/CD hybrid, or a Web/CD hybrid. This
could be a CD that can take updates from the Internet, or it could be a Web
site that picks its larger assets, such as movies, from a local CD.

It is more common than many realize that clients begin by wanting an
Internet site but end up wanting a CD-ROM as well, and expect it for no extra
cost! The CD often takes data from the site to feed into certain calculations, or
refers out to extended resources found on the Net. Many clients imagine that
once the data has been structured for the Web site it can be put on a CD and
distributed as well. This is rarely straightforward, and the general expecta-

tions of the media to be found on a CD, and how they operate are different from the Web. A hybrid Internet/CD project needs the information to be structured differently to optimize transfer between the different delivery mechanisms, and often needs a lot of extra data of different types. A shift in the audience for the CD is common, and this means that the new market sector or specialized sector needs new information.

A hybrid project needs to combine elements of this questionnaire and the offline questionnaire. In your negotiations they should be treated like two separate projects and costed as such, taking into account any overlap of assets and data. Often the client does not understand the term 'hybrid', and it raises the idea for them to consider. In this case, you should take the opportunity to explain the issues and indicate that if they want a CD-ROM it needs separate specification and costing.

In this way there are no hidden expectations, and they will expect separate costs to be associated with a CD-ROM from the beginning of the relationship. If they originally reject the notion but suddenly change their mind in the middle of the project and want a CD, you will be able to remind them of the discussion and indicate that they originally wanted a Web site only. Accordingly, the assets and information have been oriented to that delivery platform only, and a CD will mean more work for you and therefore cost more now than if they had decided on a hybrid in the first place. As long as you have covered this earlier, it makes it more palatable to the client even though they are usually annoyed – more with themselves, it should be said.

Market sector

Market sector			
Commercial ☐	Corporate ☐	Government ☐	Education ☐

The major categories of commercial, corporate, government and education are included as an indicator of your potential administrative overhead. Small commercial sites allow you more freedom and versatility as a rule when compared with the others. Decisions can be given to you faster, and your work can progress more smoothly. With the other three sectors, and with large commercial clients, it is often much harder to get clear statements and directions. You may be held up for long periods waiting for confirmation of how to proceed even if you follow the advice given in other chapters about establishing authority and sign-off. The internal cultural and political nuances associated with large commercial sites or the other three sectors cannot be ignored in your attempt to size up the scope of the project.

Project bias

Project bias	Importance ranking	Size of section (large, medium, small)
Company profile		
Information gathering		
Information dissemination		
Retail (products or services)		
Marketing/advertising		
Redesign site		
Others (specify)		

The projects will often span several of the components under this heading, and it helps to understand this as soon as possible. The bias on the type of data will help to determine the type of interactivity needed, which will in turn have an effect on the programming and design. A recruitment agency, for example, may need part company profile, part information gathering (prospective job candidates), and part information dissemination (database of current jobs on offer). These begin to give a good indication for the scope of the project, as you may then try to refine exactly what is needed under each component. You should be beginning to recognize the need for coordinating and agreeing the essential aspects of content for the company profile, form design for form filling, several layers of search facility, and so on.

If the site is to have a retail bias then an online catalogue of products and services with payment options may be necessary. Bear in mind that taking credit card numbers over the Internet is still regarded as risky, and many people (and some companies) leave the transaction to more 'conventional' methods such as fax or telephone. Others make use of encryption and secure servers, and in areas such as computer software, where the purchased item can be instantly downloaded, online payment has many attractions.

Any marketing and advertising bias indicates that there needs to be a clear understanding of the image the company wants to convey and who they are trying to reach. These components have a particular bearing on the look and feel of the site, and need careful treatment. The same is true if you are asked to redesign a site. In this case your client will be wanting to improve their image and may have identified the need for new components. Because the medium is so volatile, the breakthroughs in programming suddenly allow new features of interactivity or design. Redesigning sites is often connected with introducing these new features. As they occur frequently, it is not uncommon for high-profile sites to be redesigned every six months or so. This creates a drive for others to keep up with fashion, and causes a ripple effect across other sites. However, while new Web browsers bring new technologies and techniques to the Web designer, not all Web users keep up with the trends, and so any use of new Web features has to be made knowing that not all potential viewers will see them.

Importance ranking

If the clients have identified more than one component, use the ranking column. Because the amount and type of information can be infinite, you need to get the client to recognize their priorities. This is to encourage them to be realistic, and to help you to apportion your effort. If, later, the client does not like your quote, it will help you make edit decisions to prune the material that is least important to them. They may well say that each component has the same importance, so you might enter equal ranking numbers for them. The important point here is that you need to understand if and where there might be leeway.

Size of section

The amount of information you are given to structure for the site affects the time needed to complete the project and therefore the cost. Although it is all relative, you have to try and understand the amount of material within each section to get a feel of how to apportion time and resources as well as cost. One company's expectations of a company profile might be succinct and neatly contained in a few pages; another might see the profile as a major component, with several subsections and lots of media. They might both have ranked the profile as the most important to them, but their expectations of how you will deliver it can be very different. These queries might tease out several aspects that are important for you to note, so have some blank sheets ready. They often prompt healthy discussion between the client's representatives themselves, and they may want to consider their options before they answer. That's fine. Get them to note down the queries they want to discuss but continue with the questionnaire, as other questions might prompt similar responses and they will need to go away to consider their answers to all of them.

Site maintenance

It is important to raise site maintenance early in the discussion. If the client is going to maintain it, you have to know the competence level of those who will

Site maintenance

Client to maintain

You to maintain

be involved so that you can design templates accordingly. You may have to provide training as part of the deal, and this has to be costed. If you are going to maintain the site, a whole set of agreements on how often, how much, and what to do about introducing new elements will be needed. Maintenance is often forgotten, but is crucial for all companies to consider. Many still underestimate the ongoing involvement in updating a site after its launch – and the ongoing costs. The responsibilities should be sorted out early on to avoid difficulties later. Remember that a Web site is more like a magazine than a book – it needs to be updated regularly to stay alive. In fact, some Web sites are more like newspapers, and update very regularly – even continuously.

Benefits/achievements wanted

Benefits/achievements wanted

Not applicable   (Reason)

The organization will benefit by/objectives/wants:

1.
2.
3.
4.
5.
6.

The users will benefit by/objectives/needs:

1.
2.
3.
4.
5.
6.

If the client has been able to define their initial statement earlier, this set of questions will probe their understanding to clarify their thinking. It is not easy to define objectives for the company or for the users, but if the client does not attempt this, the specification will lack direction, and will tend to meander. You will be given mountains of information to structure for no real reason unless you get the client to focus on these core issues. It is their responsibility to provide the answers to these questions rather than for you to surmise why they want the site and what they expect from it in terms of their company and their own clients.

Access and use

Access and use

The audience/users		Access to what information	
Internet	▭		
General public	▭	▭▭▭	
Specific market sector(s)	▭	▭▭▭	
(specify)	▭▭▭	▭▭▭	
	▭▭▭		
Intranet	▭		
Corporate/government/	▭	▭▭▭	
education/other:			
In-house (all)	▭	▭▭▭	
Exec	▭	▭▭▭	
Managers	▭	▭▭▭	
Sales force	▭	▭▭▭	
Other	▭	▭▭▭	
Extranet	▭		
No. of sites to connect	▭		
Who will need access	▭▭▭		
(specify)	▭▭▭		

This section will encourage the client to clarify their thinking even more. The benefits and achievements section will have given you high-level company and user needs, while this section will give you more detail about the content in relation to the user. The connection between the users and the reason they want access to certain types of information is the most important one to establish, whatever the medium. The type of user influences the structure and the level of interactivity. Consider designing information for 5 to 7 year olds to access as a resource from the Web, compared with teenagers accessing information on their favourite pop group, or investors checking their portfolio shares on an investment company's Web site.

The same information may need to be accessed by several different types of user, and this will determine the range, depth and structure of the information. The analysis for this section can be complex, and stimulates most discussion. But it is wise to raise the issues quickly so that the client realizes that, with so much on offer, it is no mean feat to prioritize the categories and match them to the reasons why the user will want to access them. This section will need to be refined and reworked at subsequent meetings.

If the client has not considered this in enough detail, ask them to make it an action point, and request written replies within a specified period. They need to prioritize the range of information types and the sorts of user they expect or want to attract. You will not be able to do a good cost analysis until you are confident about these features, and about the amount of information that needs to be gathered and structured. Don't worry if your client thinks you are asking for them to do too much. Very often clients do not understand the process, and have not been able to raise the right issues for themselves. This is why they may appear vague. You have to raise the right issues and then they can respond to them. Alternatively, the client has not thought the project through in enough detail, and has not planned resource from their side accordingly. By raising the issues, you help them to clarify their involvement. Remember, the common goal for both of you is to start the project from a clear definition of what is expected from both parties in order to progress through the stages smoothly and purposefully towards a known finishing point.

You need to gather enough information to make decisions such as the number and type of browsers the project must adapt and work with, whether it will have frames or not, whether it will need higher-end programming components, and so on. These decisions have to be balanced against the client's needs, the time for development, and the costs.

Media mix

Media mix					
Client's media expectations	None, wants suggestions		Animation		%
	Text	%	Audio		%
	Graphics	%	Video		%

The client may have a vague conception of their site in terms of the media they expect to see as part of it. It is good to get these expectations out in the open, as you may well already have an indication of which media to use based on the emerging understanding of the audience and content. Allow them to state what they would like or expect, and use this to explain why you would not recommend video or audio, for example, in their case. Alternatively, according to what they say you might find yourself arguing for the inclusion of some video and audio for a particular section where you feel that higher-end users would respond well to the added cachet of those media, even though the client has seen the site in terms of text and graphics only.

Content (existing assets)

Content (existing assets)			
Written			Contact:
Relevant databases		Spec:	Contact:
Graphics/stills		Spec:	Contact:
Audio		Spec:	Contact:
Video footage		Spec:	Contact:
Content experts			Contact:

The cost of development in any interactive medium is affected by the number and type of suitable assets that the client already has, as long as their specification will retain enough quality for reuse in a new way. Perceptions of quality in intergrated media are different for online and offline delivery. Lower quality is tolerated in online delivery because of the limitations of the delivery system. This is constrained by the bandwidth of the connections and the power of the computer receiving the data. Sites have to be optimized for a spectrum of uses, and for users who will have varying computer power. If a complete mix of media is needed, then compromises have to be made to optimize across this range. Many sites remain heavily text driven with some graphics because of these considerations. The client may not be fully aware of the possibilities or of the compromises needed. The sooner you can contact the relevant people and understand what assets are available the better. You should be able to work out the gaps, check the rights position, and cost the reworking of existing assets and the generation of new ones.

Time for development

Time for development

Client expectation	_____	(months)	Start date _____
			End date _____
Any fixed dates	_____		
(demos etc.)	_____		_____
	_____		_____
To be specified in	_____		
proposal			

There is often a mismatch between clients' and developers' expectations of the development time that is needed for a project. Clients do not usually appreciate the complexity of some of the processes involved. Their expectations may be impossible to achieve, and the scope of a project may have to be reduced to meet a definite time-scale.

You need to understand any factors that are driving clients in their decisions on the time-scale to see if they might be negotiable. This is why any fixed dates become important. This is the right place to establish as much as you can about the client's needs for completion, because this will help to determine how much content and what media might be achievable. You might suggest scheduling completion of one component before another to meet their needs, or you might be able to suggest publishing components as soon as they are ready, with placeholders in the other sections, or developing skeleton pages in each component just to give a feel for the overall structure. Online delivery is more flexible in this regard than offline, where prototyping tends to be more complex.

Budget

Budget

	_____	£/$ approx
Budget holder:	_____	Position _____
Tel:	_____	
Email:	_____	
Project cost to be prepared and negotiated ____		
Separate costs to be put forward for maintaining and updating ____		

In an ideal world (for the developer), projects would be scoped and specified and clients would then pay for work done on a time and materials basis. Unfortunately, clients will usually want a fixed price up front, and will not want to change that even if circumstances change. Doubly unfortunate is the difficulty of accurately costing any software project, let alone one with as many constituent parts as multimedia. For the sake of this discussion we shall assume a fixed-quote budget.

This can turn into a see-saw battle. It is common for the client to withhold their actual budget figure because they know you will scope to the top of that budget. Many clients prefer you to draft a few alternatives with a range of costs so that they have an indication of the quality and cost. Then they can negotiate from a better position.

Some clients will be inexperienced in the costs of multimedia projects, and will expect you to be able to give them an estimate during the first meeting. This is unfair, but it can help if you have ready some examples of the range of costs that can be incurred for projects of different length and different quality, to help them understand a top and bottom price.

You can't really work out an estimate unless the client has specified the size of the project and the expected media mix, and you know the usual production charges per minute of your company and can make a good guess at any extras such as the costs of rights clearances. Even then, considerations of content, existing assets and use will affect the costs, and we have gathered only first-level information about these. You need to explain why it is difficult to cost, and which factors affect the cost.

The people you are dealing with may not necessarily be the budget holder: they may have to refer the decisions on in the organization, and negotiate themselves in turn. It is important to know whether they have the authority to release the budget themselves, because if their decisions can be changed then you have to take this into account, for two reasons. First, you need to be talking directly to the top decision makers to keep the decision time and sign-off time as short as possible to avoid delays in the project, since end dates are rarely as flexible as start dates. Second, you need to find out whether the budget holder will have any authority over the content before he or she releases the budget. You do not want to work for agreement with your client only to have their boss make changes.

Organizations work in different ways, so you need to find out how the client's authorization to spend operates, and what controls are in place to stop it. This can affect the turn-around time for decision making throughout the project, and it will help if you sort out your approach to this as early as possible. If you are to propose costs for maintaining and updating the site, the person who has to accept the long-term budget costs may not be the same as the company project manager you are dealing with, so make sure the right information is passed to the right person, to save difficulties later.

Offline scoping questionnaire

Client's previous multimedia experience

Project name/no: _____

Contact details

Client/Organization name: _____

Address: _____
_____
_____
_____
_____

Tel: _____ Fax: _____ Email: _____

Web site: _____

Project contacts:

Name(s): _____ Position(s): _____

Direct line _____ Email: _____

Previous interactive media experience

Online

None ☐ A little ☐ Fair ☐ Good ☐ Experienced ☐

Offline

None ☐ A little ☐ Fair ☐ Good ☐ Experienced ☐

Experience description

Online

Products: _____ Producer: _____

Offline

Products: _____ Producer: _____

Refer to the online questionnaire analysis (page 37) for the reasons behind this set of questions. The rationale is the same for both categories of project.

Type of project

Project type

Commercial	☐	Corporate	☐	Government	☐
Presentation	☐	Point of information	☐		
Training	☐	Advertising	☐		
Point of sale	☐				
Publishing (specify)	☐	Hybrid CD/Web (specify)	☐	Other (specify)	☐
Education	☐				
Edutainment	☐				
Entertainment	☐				
Reference	☐				

Often clients have no understanding of the different categories that exist to describe a multimedia project. It will help them and you to shape their ideas if you can begin to categorize the type of information that they want to communicate.

There are many differences between working on commercial, corporate, international and government projects. The scale is different. The components and resources needed are different. The budgets are handled and reported in different ways. The way information is structured will be affected by a company culture and image, or by the specification that's worked out by the international partners. There will be conventions and controls in corporate work from other parts of the organization – corporate communications departments, also known as 'style police', for example. The administration involved for an international project is far greater than usual. You might be one of several project managers of various levels and with differing responsibilities in an international project.

We shall now look in some detail at the different types of project.

Multimedia presentation

Most presentations tend to be produced for large corporations, whose executives need to project an internationally competitive company image. Multimedia fits perfectly into the kind of conference presentation where large audiences watch the speakers on a projection TV screen as well as in the flesh.

The tools for computer-based presentations have made it possible for many to produce the lower-level forms of computer-based presentation, but when image, style and impact are expected, the higher end of animation, video and video graphics, and sound are important.

These tend to be quick, high-pressured projects because there is a definite immovable deadline – the day of the internal or external presentation. Also, decisions to use the more complex high-production multimedia elements – such as video graphics, animations or original video footage – are often taken late. The projects are of a shorter duration than many of the other projects, and are usually meant to last for approximately 20–30 minutes. They can be an aid to a speaker who talks to and around the visuals, but it is becoming increasingly common for them to form the basis of a standalone demonstrator for conference stands or general publicity as well. This would then give the project a dual status of *presentation* and *point of information*.

It is also increasingly common for the speaker to publish the presentation or aspects of it on the company intranet, or on the Internet for public access. You need to fully understand the exact uses of the end-product to understand the true costs and to design as economically as possible, across the various forms of delivery if necessary. You should tick the *hybrid* section here as well if the project will have a dual purpose that includes online aspects, and note the requirements necessary for the alternative delivery. Take time to use the relevant parts of the online questionnaire. A separate specification of the hybrid part will be necessary to make sure you know exactly what is wanted. If extra information for a different audience is needed for the hybrid part this will mean extra work for you, which needs to be costed.

These are not easy projects, but there is a tendency in the industry to give them less credence than the production of larger applications. The shorter time-scale increases the difficulty and the risks. They are harder to control, and there is little room – if any – for contingency. Also, since they often involve the projection of corporate image, the company's style guidelines have to be taken into account and this can be a cause of frustration for the graphic designer as well as causing delays on vital approval stages.

Because they are high-profile, high-pressure projects, you need to establish a strong, clear method of working and agreement procedures. Any delays are critical.

Training

Training applications can be either commercial or corporate. Some that start as a corporate product can later become commercial if they are offered for sale outside their original target company. Several of the larger organizations produce their own applications. Others commission multimedia companies to produce them for in-house use. If the training application goes on general sale through training distributors then it is a commercial venture. It is important to remember that a change such as this may affect the rights bought for the original project.

Training has its own methods of working. There is a strong emphasis on defining the expected changes in the user's behaviour as a result of using an application. Data collection for evaluation might form part of the specification. There are differences between structuring information for learning and structuring it for information transfer, and these differences need to be addressed. The techniques for ensuring cognitive retention are different from those designed for immediate reaction to such things as strong visuals.

A recent major initiative in training has been the move towards accrediting work done in the workplace. This has meant defining skills and competences that underpin various roles in the workforce and then sorting them into hierarchical levels. Many vocational bodies have been involved in this definition, and their own qualifications have been restructured accordingly.

The trend towards doing more on-the-job and on-site training rather than sending staff away on courses opens opportunities for multimedia developers. Use of the Internet and company intranets for training is increasing. Companies that have invested in open learning or resource centres are used to the full multimedia experience in their products, so they find the transfer to Web-based courses, with their text bias, is equivalent to taking a step backwards. Others, who have not been used to multimedia CDs for training, are attracted by the convenience, access and costs of training via online delivery. This sector is tipped to expand rapidly. Companies that have had successful training CDs are converting them to online courses, and other companies are beginning to produce new courses offered for either delivery system. If you are going to produce a hybrid Web/CD follow the advice given above for hybrid Web/CD presentation.

Point of sale (POS)

These are retail projects where the application needs to sell products. Increasingly they are being moved online as the distribution and media capabilities expand. These projects are often confused with *point of information*, since the customer can usually get information on the products and then request the sale. The deciding factor will be whether the customer can buy the articles on the spot in some way. The goods may be ordered by credit card for later delivery or, in some cases, can be supplied to the customer there and then.

The home shopping concept is a possible market for the emerging on-demand systems. Trials on interactive TV have included home shopping, for example; so point of sale applications may take many forms.

Point of information (POI)

There are a wide range of applications that fit this category, from tourist information systems to applications in museums that give specific information about exhibits. They are often intended for use by the general public. Some are based in the reception areas of large corporate organizations, where a more specialist slant needs to be taken for the type of audience.

Kiosks, of which POS and POI are types, are a significant area for multimedia. The requirement for sophisticated and attractive user interfaces to encourage public use provide a good outlet for design skills. Since the kiosks are usually specially designed systems, the hardware configuration can be chosen to be the best for the task, with few constraints other than cost.

More and more of these systems are being networked to the client's databases so that information on relevant sections can be updated as often as needed.

Advertising

Advertising agencies are beginning to recognize the potential that multimedia might offer. Some are experimenting with prototypes, but most of the interest is still at a strategic level in the companies. This sector is likely to grow, but at the moment it is still an unknown quantity. Besides the question of making ads interactive themselves, which is possibly another version of POI/POS, there is the potentially fascinating issue of how an interactive audience treats advertising. A video-on-demand audience might pay differential rates for viewing, depending on whether they wanted (or would tolerate) advertising or not.

The Web has opened the floodgates to interactivity in advertising, although the boundary between, say, a sponsored game and a game based totally around a particular product is blurred. It has been felt in the past that interactivity is a barrier to advertising: a fear that assumes such things as people switching away from TV adverts with their remote control. This example has resulted in two features of UK television (and often elsewhere): a synchronizing of advertising breaks, and an increase in the entertainment quality of the ads themselves. Following this logic it seems inevitable that, as interactivity comes to media that traditionally carry advertising and as advertising comes to new media, the advertising creatives will rise to the challenge with gusto.

Publishing

Traditional publishers (which in this context includes record and audiovisual as well as book publishers) have been watching the multimedia market for several years. Many of them have experimented with projects, and some set up their own production facilities. However, the promise of the consumer market was not fulfilled, and there are fewer publishers involved at present. This makes it doubly important for a publisher to take market conditions as well as distribution channels into account, because the consumer has to have easy access to the products to be able to buy them.

Some multimedia companies set up their own publishing arms to try to reap the better returns that publishing could offer, especially as a long-term source of revenue. It makes business sense to invest in your own productions if you will get a better ongoing return than the profit made once on productions for a client. Ownership becomes an important issue. Audiovisual content development forms a major part of the cost of development, and the ability to reuse such assets in other forms or as the basis for new development depends on ownership. If you do not own the content, you have to start from scratch every time. This overlaps with rights management, which will be covered later. However, it is even more important for multimedia companies to have established distribution channels for their products, which is often a new consideration for them.

Education

This is a market that has increased in the past few years. The standardizing of curricula means that there is a potentially large market.

The popularity of the Internet as a multimedia information and reference source shared between millions of users was first spawned through its use in universities. Although it started as a text-driven method of communication, it has moved rapidly into a distributed multimedia channel throughout educational establishments. Because access to the Net is almost a matter of course, many of the education CDs are hybrid Web/CDs and need to be scoped as such. Follow the directions for hybrid scoping as outlined in multimedia presentations above.

Edutainment

Many of the titles that are being published fall into a category called Edutainment. These are meant to attract the home owners of computers to buy them for their children's general education but have enough general interest to be used in their own right by a wider age range. They can span both the consumer and education markets if they have been designed carefully, indicating which stages of the curriculum they cover or contribute towards as well as having wider appeal because of the subject matter. These increasingly have a hybrid component as well, via the publisher's Web site.

Entertainment

Entertainment is another category that is aimed at the home and business markets. Games, quizzes, titles built around celebrities such as pop stars or actors, and even television soaps would be examples from this section. Many of these now have hybrid components as well.

Reference titles such as atlases, road maps and encyclopedias have made their mark, and are popular. They obviously benefit from the users' being able to access the Web to update any volatile data or to have access to extra information on topics. These products can have quite extensive Web sites attached, so you need to understand how large these will be and exactly what data is expected on them. They need separate specification, and can be considered a separate project in terms of time, resource allocation and costing. Adapt the online questionnaire to help scope the hybrid Web aspects of the CD project.

International projects

These types of project, particularly if they are related to government research, demand a good deal more administration than others. Many extra levels of communication and documentation are built into the project plans to ensure that the progress of the project is monitored and recorded. These projects follow international project management principles, and as such are well structured and defined. The projects start with a specification stage, and then contracts and resources are allocated according to this.

In funded research projects, for example, there may be a process of external review where experts are called in at regular intervals to analyze and comment on progress. The funding and budgeting structures are very different from those for other multimedia projects as the funding organization may have its own conditions to be met. Your company may have to meet the equivalent of the money from the fund in money, or in time equivalent, or in the value of the assets you bring to the project.

Major international projects often break new ground, so developers can find themselves working with untried technology and software. This undoubtedly makes the projects higher risk, and contingency time has to increase because of the risks. This applies to any research project.

Technology doesn't stand still, so there is constant prototyping and trialling of new technology platforms and tools. In tool development it is common for the software to be tested by people outside the company that is writing it. The final stage of this is beta testing, when the writers think the software is finished and it is up to you to test this claim. There are very good reasons for wanting to build multimedia projects with beta versions of tools, not least because of the lead it might give you over your competitors. On the downside are the difficulties caused when the tools do not come up to expectations, or when bugs are found. As a developer you may be the first person to really try to build an application with this new tool, and it can be surprisingly easy to 'break' it.

Content (general statement)

Content (general statement)
What's the project about? Why multimedia?

Content (general statement) (cont)

Content suggestions

During the discussion about the type of project it is likely that you will have got a reasonable idea about the general content as well. It should enable you to complete this section and perhaps some of the others without taking too much time. Use the information you have had to reiterate the ideas as you fill in the categories to check that you have fully understood what the client has said.

Here is an imaginary example of what might be put in this category:

The project is to form part of the centenary celebrations of the museum. It will contain a brief history of its development from its founding till now. The local history connections, with the museum's original benefactor and architect together with its main achievements, have been suggested as contributing to the content.

The audience/users

Audience/Users

Commercial   Corporate

General public   In-house (all)

Specific market   Exec

Sectors (specify)   Managers

                                Sales force

                                Other   (specify)

The type of user will affect the style of the application more than any other factor, but it is easy for the self-interests of those involved in the development to become the dominant interests. A lot more information about users will be needed from subsequent meetings.

The combination of the numbers and type of user will affect decisions about which platform and tools will be needed. It is no good producing an application that won't reach users because they haven't got access to it. Quite often clients have not considered in enough detail how the product will be used.

This information gives you a good feel for the weighting of the project in terms of the size of the production team that will be needed. It is very important to have this information early and in writing because clients have a habit of trying to extend their intended audience to cover more groups. You must resist this once you are past the early stages of the project.

It is easy to make the mistake of thinking that a change in the number of users will merely mean that extra copies of the application will be needed. If this really is the case, then it is no problem if the client agrees to the extra duplication costs. However, it is rarely this straightforward. You need to recognize that any change in the size of audience may have an effect on the type of audience and so will have an impact on the range of content. This is not always evident when the change is requested, but as the detailed design takes shape the client will most likely ask you to split the information into specific sections for the types of user or extend the original content to cover more useful information. So the interactive structure could be affected as well as the amount of material. Then the number of media components needed to serve the information would increase.

All these factors change the scope of the project. You end up having to go back to the beginning with any budget agreements, or having to ask for sacrifices in the rest of the content for the programme. Once a client has agreed content it is hard for them to agree to cuts. If you agree to the extra users and later try to explain to the client that they are expanding the structure and content so the costs need to be reworked, you run the risk that they'll say you should have warned them and that they won't accept the extra costs.

This is one case where you must make an agreement that if the client tries to extend or alter the information later to suit the new users, and it has an impact on the time and budget, they will bear the extra costs or cut the material intended originally. You need to recognize the potential risk early and cover it.

We'll take an example from a corporate project to make the point. If the intended audience was originally the non-management sales force and it was then extended to include first-level management, it is easy to see that different messages will be needed for management and non-management. It is harder to recognize the risk if the intended audience was originally executives and then it becomes top management. The difference in messages would depend on the company and its way of working.

Estimated number of systems/location

Estimated number of users (approx.)

1–100		5000–10 000		
100–500		Other		(specify)
500–1000				
1000–5000				

Estimated number of systems   **Location:**

The number of users need not reflect the number of systems needed. If the systems are going to be put in open learning centres where a number of people will use one system in rotation, then knowing the number of users does not help you to specify the number of systems or the locations where the maximum projected use will be found. Similarly, if a project is classified as a consumer title (which means for sale to the general public), then this question may be irrelevant other than as an estimate of market size. But if you need to clear rights in materials used, the numbers of users will be important for the costs. The location of use can also affect costs. If the market for use is international, the rights clearances go up. See the contract and rights management chapters (Chapters 5, 10 and 17) for more details.

Benefits/achievements wanted

Often this section is one of the hardest to complete. If the client does not have a strong understanding of what they wish to achieve, they will keep changing the brief without even noticing it. As they move towards a stronger recognition during the project, they'll redefine what they want. This should be cautiously encouraged since, with careful handling, it will lead to a better result, and one that the client feels happier with. But remember the implications of late change.

It is worth putting in effort to get clear definitions, and it is advisable to send the client away to agree what they want for themselves and for the users. The definition takes quite a lot of discussion. It is easier for the client to be general than specific, so it takes skill to keep refining to clear statements. This is similar to the process of defining training objectives. The terminology you choose to use may depend on the client. If they are used to formulating objectives then this might be the best term.

Benefits/achievements wanted

Not applicable [   ]   (Reason) [   ]

[   ]

The organization will benefit by/objectives/wants:

1. _____
2. _____
3. _____
4. _____
5. _____
6. _____

The users will benefit by/objectives/needs:

1. _____
2. _____
3. _____
4. _____
5. _____
6. _____

Without this definition you won't get a feel for the amount of content, or how you might begin to treat it to achieve the results. If there is more than one contact in the organization, and they are divided in their vision of what each needs from the project, you will end up being pulled in different directions. You need a unified statement. The time spent working on this section pays dividends later. Do not proceed before it is completed satisfactorily.

The information defined now will affect how you devise your testing strategy during the next stages of the project. This is covered in detail in Chapter 18, *Testing*. The final sign-off will depend on your proving that you have achieved what has been specified. You will have to consider how you will demonstrate this in practice. If showing the benefits depends on feedback from the users, you might advise your client that they should have a prototype field test to allow the users the chance to influence the design, or it might be advisable to allow for usability testing at the end of the project. Both these forms of testing are time intensive and costly. If there is a definite time-span for the project, you will know if there is enough time to build in these tests. If not, and you explain their benefits to the client, they will make the decision to include them or not. Your client should make the decisions on which and how much testing they require, so that they recognize and accept the subsequent risk of quality loss. Refer to Chapter 18, *Testing*, to understand your responsibilities for testing.

Content (existing assets)

Content (existing assets)				
Written			Contact:	
Video footage		Spec:	Contact:	
Graphics/stills		Spec:	Contact:	
Audio		Spec:	Contact:	
Content experts			Contact:	

Because the creation of assets is costly and time consuming, it is wise to see if there are any suitable existing materials that could be used. The interactive scriptwriter will welcome any written materials and access to content experts. Any audio or visual materials need to be of a certain quality to make it viable to reuse them so the technical specification of their type is needed here. This will help to gauge a rough cost of development. If there are no suitable materials they will all have to be created, and this will affect both development time and cost.

A good provision of material from the clients will affect the costing process. But even if there are suitable existing materials they will need to be reworked and integrated. Beware of clients' overestimating the suitability of their existing material. Clients do not understand the various processes that are needed, and often argue that with the provision of materials the cost of development should be much less than you submit. How you can deal with this will be covered in the next chapter. Check also that clients have the copyright for use in an electronic form for all the materials they will submit to you, otherwise you could face a lengthy, costly clearance process, or have to produce new assets. See Chapter 10, *Contract issues 2*, for more on this.

Time for development

Time for development				
Client expectation		(months)	Start date	
			End date	
Any fixed dates (demos etc.)				
To be specified in proposal				

There is often a mismatch between clients and developers in expectations of the development time that is needed for a project. Clients do not usually appreciate the complexity of some of the processes involved. Their expectations may be impossible to achieve, and the scope of the project may have to be reduced to meet a definite time-scale.

You need to understand any factors that are driving the client in their decisions on the time-scale, to see if they might be negotiable. This is why any fixed dates become important. We've seen from a previous example how a fixed voice-over date had several knock-on implications. This is the right place to establish as much as you can about the client's needs for completion, because this will help you to determine the amount of content and the types of media that might be achievable. Be careful to check what deadlines really mean because you might find you lose a few days because of the need, for example, to ship the software to another country for a conference, or to allow time for rehearsals.

Platform

Platform

Existing platform(s)	Specification:	Nos:
	Location	
Client's suggestion	Specification:	Nos:
	Location	
	Reasons:	
To be specified in proposal	Factors to consider:	

This can be complicated. If there is an existing platform that you are expected to use it could impose limitations on the media and quality it will allow. Also, it may not be suitable for the intended audience to access correctly. The combination of the specification, location and numbers of machines is important to help you identify how the existing platform can be best utilized, or to suggest an alternative.

Sometimes there is no existing platform, but the client has a suggestion. This might happen when a competitor has used a platform and the client wants to compete with them. It is important that you know the reasons for the client's choice to see if there is room for negotiation, because there are many factors that can drive a decision in either the right or the wrong direction.

Quite often a client will expect you to suggest a platform based on the information that they have given about the users and content. It is a good idea to check whether the client's organization has any strategic plans or directions for technology, so that you can integrate your decisions into them if possible. Beware of hidden agendas, which can lead to clients' seeming open to suggestion but really wanting you to suggest something specific.

Media mix

Media mix

Expected length of programme/how long a user would take to complete (hrs/mins)

Client's media expectations	None, wants suggestions			Text		%
	Video		%	Graphics		%
	Audio		%	Animation		%

The length of time that it takes a user to complete a programme, combined with the type of medium, gives a good basis for costing. If the client has an idea of the total time needed for a user to cover all the components, this provides a yardstick to users how much of the space should be occupied and therefore how much of each medium might be possible. However, more often the client will expect you to specify how long the programme will be according to what is needed in the content. If the client does not give a figure, indicate that they don't know.

The same is true of media expectations. The client may have impossible expectations, because the amount of video that they want may not fit. The content may not lend itself to the mix they suggest. However, their expectations can help to shape the use of media and help with the costing. It is healthy to try to get the client to voice any expectations they may have, because it gives you more information to work from to make decisions or to negotiate.

Usually the client will not have thought about the project in these terms, but you should try to encourage them to answer the questions. The answers, whatever they are, give you an important starting point. Even if the client seems to have no idea, you can guide them by asking probing questions such as:

■ Do you expect any video footage?
■ Do you expect a lot of talking around one picture on the screen?
■ Do you expect screens that change often?
■ What do you think your audience will expect?

If the client really wants to leave the decisions to you, then once you have an impression of the content and the audience, it will help if you fill in the percentages and talk them through with the client. You can use them to set up common expectations for the cost you quote.

This percentage chart also proves useful if later the client starts asking for an increase in the use of one type of medium because during development they come to appreciate its potential. The percentage rating would help you win cost increases and de-scoping of other media because you could show that if one increases, others must decrease or the time must increase.

Budget

Budget		
		£/$ approx
Budget holder:		Position
Tel:		
Email:		
Cost to be proposed and negotiated		

The reaction of the client to on- and offline budget information tends to be the same and so the information is repeated here. In an ideal world (for the developer), projects would be scoped and specified and clients would then pay for work done on a time and materials basis. Unfortunately clients will usually want a fixed price up front, and will not want to change that even if circumstances change. Doubly unfortunate is the difficulty of accurately costing any software project, let alone one with as many constituent parts as multimedia. For the sake of this discussion we shall assume a fixed-quote budget.

This can turn into a see-saw battle. It is common for the client to withhold their actual budget figure because they know you will scope to the top of that budget. Many clients prefer you to draft a few alternatives with a range of costs so that they have an indication of the quality and cost. Then they can negotiate from a better position.

Some clients will be inexperienced in the costs of multimedia projects, and will expect you to be able to give them an estimate during the first meeting. This is unfair, but it can help if you have ready some examples of the range of costs that can be incurred for projects of different length and different quality, to help them understand a top and bottom price.

You can't really work out an estimate unless the client has specified the length of the programme and the expected media mix, and you know the usual production charges per minute of your company and can make a good guess at any extras such as the costs of rights clearances. Even then, considerations of content, existing assets and platform will affect the costs, and we have gathered only first-level information about these. You need to explain why it is difficult to cost, and which factors affect the cost.

The client may not necessarily be the budget holder. They may have to refer the decisions on in the organization, and negotiate themselves in turn. It is important to know whether they have the authority to release the budget themselves, because if their decisions can be changed then you have to take this into account, for two reasons. First, you need to be talking directly to the top decision makers to keep the decision time and sign-off time as short as possible to avoid delays in the project, since end dates are rarely as flexible as start dates. Second, you need to find out whether the budget holder will have any authority over the content before he or she releases the budget. You do not want to work for agreement with your client only to have their boss make changes.

Organizations work in different ways, so you need to find out how the client's authorization to spend operates, and what controls are in place to stop it. This can affect the turn-around time for decision making throughout the project, and it will help if you sort out your approach to this as early as possible.

Theory into practice 3

Look back over the scoping questionnaires. Would you be confident in using them with clients? Without looking at the text, can you give reasons why you need each category of information?

If you are not working with client-centred projects, what equivalent questions need to be answered to scope your project?

Post-meeting responsibilities

Clients may need to get back to you with some of the information you've requested – the benefits to the user, for example. Make sure you agree a time frame within which to receive the information. A lot of time can be wasted during these early stages, which can affect the start and end date of the project and therefore what you can produce.

If the client doesn't get back to you in the agreed time with the right information, take this as an indication of what they will be like to work with, and make a mental note that if the project goes ahead you will build in contingency time at points where the client needs to find information or give decisions. This may seem a harsh judgement, but you'll need to make many decisions on very limited information. As one of your main responsibilities you need to identify potential risk areas and start trying to minimize them. This type of decision making is characteristic of managing innovation.

You will have information to check out from the meeting as well. If the client has given any contact numbers for further information you need to pursue these to firm up on facts. The client may think there is little visual data available but the contact may be able to indicate that there is good source material of the right specification to help with the project.

Once the scoping questionnaire is complete, make a copy and send it to the client as a record of the meeting and of the information given. Get into the habit of dating the documents for the day of their dispatch as well as having the date of the original meeting. This can often prove important later in the project, particularly in corporate projects.

Organizations are changing their focus all the time, and staff changes occur during projects, so you can find yourself working with a new person who has a completely different perspective on what the organization wants in a particular area. From his or her perspective, the new person will be quite right to point out some fundamental changes that he or she was aware of at a particular date, but you will be able to show that this was not the information you had. If he or she wants major changes then the project has to be re-scoped at the client's expense.

Summary

- Establish the client's expectations and needs for the project in detail, what assets they can bring to the project, the audience profile, and the budget.

- Record the meeting clearly to form the basis of the proposal.

- Assess whether the brief is realistic in terms of development time, the use of media, and the client's expected outcomes.

- Give clear requests for further information from the client within a time frame.

- Follow up any information you need as soon as possible.

- Send a record of the meeting to the clients.

Online client-centred project scoping questionnaire

Project name/no:

Contact details

Client/Organization name:

Address:

Tel: Fax: Email:

Web site:

Project contacts:

Name(s):   Position(s):

Direct line   Email:

Previous interactive media experience

Online

None   A little   Fair   Good   Experienced

Offline

None   A little   Fair   Good   Experienced

Experience description

Online

Products: Producer:

Offline

Products: Producer:

Client's initial statement of what they want

_____

_____
_____
_____
_____

_____

Online project type

Internet ☐   Hybrid Web/CD ☐   Intranet ☐   Extranet ☐

Set up new facility ☐

(If yes, domain name suggestions?)

_____

_____
_____

Add/Change existing facility ☐

Market sector

Commercial ☐   Corporate ☐   Government ☐   Education ☐

Project bias

	Importance ranking	Size of section (large, medium, small)
Company profile	☐	☐	☐
Information gathering	☐	☐	☐
Information dissemination	☐	☐	☐
Retail (products or services)	☐	☐	☐
Marketing/advertising	☐	☐	☐
Redesign site	☐	☐	☐
Others (specify)	☐	☐	☐

_____

_____

Site maintenance

Client to maintain ☐

You to maintain ☐

Benefits/achievements wanted

Not applicable [ ] (Reason) [ ]

The organization will benefit by/objectives/wants:

1.
2.
3.
4.
5.
6.

The users will benefit by/objectives/needs:

1.
2.
3.
4.
5.
6.

Access and use

The audience/users   Access to what information

Internet [ ]

General public [ ]

Specific market sector(s) [ ]

(specify) [ ]

[ ]

Intranet [ ]

Corporate/government/
education/other: [ ]

In-house (all) [ ]

Exec [ ]

Managers [ ]

Sales force [ ]

Other [ ]

Access and use (cont)

Extranet

No. of sites to connect

Who will need access
(specify)

Media mix

Client's media   None, wants suggestions   Animation   %

expectations   Text   %   Audio   %

Graphics   %   Video   %

Content (existing assets)

Written   Contact:

Relevant databases   Spec: Contact:

Graphics/stills   Spec: Contact:

Audio   Spec: Contact:

Video footage   Spec: Contact:

Content experts   Contact:

Time for development

Client expectation   (months)   Start date

End date

Any fixed dates
(demos etc.)

To be specified in
proposal

Budget

£/$ approx

Budget holder: Position

Tel:

Email:

Project cost to be prepared and negotiated

Separate costs to be put forward for maintaining and updating

Offline client-centred project scoping questionnaire

Project name/no: _____

Contact details

Client/Organization name: _____

Address: _____

Tel: _____ Fax: _____ Email: _____

Web site: _____

Project contacts:

Name(s): _____ Position(s): _____

Direct line _____ Email: _____

Previous interactive media experience

Online

None ☐ A little ☐ Fair ☐ Good ☐ Experienced ☐

Offline

None ☐ A little ☐ Fair ☐ Good ☐ Experienced ☐

Experience description

Online

Products: _____ Producer: _____

Offline

Products: _____ Producer: _____

Project type

Commercial ☐   Corporate ☐   Government ☐

Presentation ☐   Point of information ☐

Training ☐   Advertising ☐

Point of sale ☐

Publishing ☐   Hybrid CD/Web ☐   Other _____
(specify)   (specify)   (specify)

Education ☐   _____   _____

Edutainment ☐   _____   _____

Entertainment ☐   _____   _____

Reference ☐   _____   _____

Content (general statement)

What's the project about? Why multimedia?

_____
_____
_____
_____
_____
_____
_____

Content suggestions

_____
_____
_____
_____
_____
_____
_____
_____

Audience/Users

Commercial		Corporate	
General public		In-house (all)	
Specific market		Exec	
Sectors (specify)		Managers	
		Sales force	
		Other	(specify)

Estimated number of users (approx.)

1–100		5000–10 000	
100–500		Other	(specify)
500–1000			
1000–5000			

Estimated number of systems   **Location:**

Benefits/achievements wanted

Not applicable   (Reason)

The organization will benefit by/objectives/wants:

1.
2.
3.
4.
5.
6.

Benefits/achievements wanted (cont)

The users will benefit by/objectives/needs:

1.
2.
3.
4.
5.
6.

Content (existing assets)

Written			Contact:	
Video footage		Spec:	Contact:	
Graphics/stills		Spec:	Contact:	
Audio		Spec:	Contact:	
Content experts			Contact:	

Time for development

Client expectation ___ (months)　Start date ___
End date ___

Any fixed dates ___
(demos etc.)

To be specified in ___
proposal

Platform

Existing platform(s) ___　Specification: ___　Nos: ___

Location

Platform (cont)

Client's suggestion ⬜ Specification: ⬜ Nos: ⬜
⬜
⬜
Location ⬜
⬜
⬜
Reasons: ⬜
⬜
⬜

To be specified ⬜
in proposal Factors to consider:
⬜
⬜
⬜

Media mix

Expected length of programme/how long a user would
take to complete (hrs/mins) ⬜

Client's media   None, wants suggestions ⬜   Text ⬜ %
expectations   Video ⬜ %   Graphics ⬜ %
                 Audio ⬜ %   Animation ⬜ %

Budget

⬜ £/$ approx

Budget holder: ⬜   Position ⬜

Tel: ⬜

Email: ⬜

Cost to be proposed and negotiated ⬜

Recommended reading

As this chapter was based on experience, there is no reading material recommended.

4

The Proposal

Project manager's responsibilities

- Given the brief, to offer a realistic, fair deal in the time-scale and budget for the client and the development team

- To make no false promises

- To make decisions based on the facts and your assessment of risks

The aim of the proposal

The proposal will summarize the development decisions, and these will be based on the information you have received from the client, on your experience, and on the discussions you have had with colleagues about the possible alternatives for the treatment.

The aim is to give the client a clear, high-level understanding of the approach. For online projects this needs to be linked to the plug-ins and browsers that will be used, and whether the nature of the site needs static pages, dynamic pages or a combination of them. (See Chapter 7, *Choosing the platform*, and Chapter 16, *Integration*, for more on these aspects.) For offline projects the approach needs to be linked to the platform that will be adopted and the reasons for the choice. The proposal should include a suggested schedule for development of the main stages, and the overall cost.

The client needs enough information from the document to make a decision on whether or not to continue. This will be based on how convincing and relevant your suggested treatment is for their needs.

They may have asked a few companies to tender for the project, so your treatment may be in competition with others. This often leads to pressure to offer more than is appropriate, and sets up risks for the development stages. You have to balance your responsibilities to the clients, to your company, and to the development team.

One way to do this is to reach a decision on what would be safe to offer for the time and cost, and what would be foolish to offer for the time and cost but would be exciting and innovative. You can then work out a range of best alternatives that would allow some shift from the safe baseline, but not too much. This keeps the project challenging without making it impossible. You may even find that one or two additions need to be put forward with some extra cost tags, but it is good for the client to be given some options to consider.

Offering alternatives.

The main difficulty should be obvious. You have to commit the company and team to a plan of work for a cost that is almost certainly based on incomplete information. A complete understanding of the amount and nature of the content is not reached until later in the development. You need to compensate for the unknown by building in a contingency over the development stages. You can build this contingency into the overall cost, or you can include it item by item. Alternatively, if the client accepts this, you can be specific about some areas and say that others contain unknown factors, which may affect the cost. This could be due to the need for research that is impractical before the project starts, or it might be because of third-party costs such as rights.

What it should contain

The proposal should not be a long document. It needs to make its impact quickly and clearly. You will not be able to go into great detail because so much of the content information is unstable. You should also indicate that the document, as its name implies, is suggestive not prescriptive. You will need to adjust some features as the amount and nature of the content become explicit, so you need to make sure that the client understands this, and that it may result in shifts in cost.

The proposal should cover the following:

- general introduction and executive summary,
- statement of what the client wants from the Web site or application,
- statement of what the users need from the site or application,
- description of the general treatment and reasons for choice,
- variations on the treatment that are possible,
- outline diagram of the proposed structure,
- description of the human resources needed,
- work breakdown and schedule,
- cost/payment structure,
- company statement of the limitations of the proposal.

Each of these will be explained in detail in the following section.

Description of the components

General introduction and executive summary

This will collate some of the data from the scoping questionnaire: the definition of the type of project, its purpose, a description of the numbers, and the type of audience. The decisions on the offline platform or the equivalent system for online could be included here. Give the reasons why multimedia was chosen as the vehicle for delivery. It is worth considering whether there should be an executive summary at the beginning of the proposal. This becomes more useful as the length of the document increases, and basically provides a resumé of the proposal. It is different from an introduction in that it will summarize the decisions and may even give a cost. The person who will find an executive summary useful is anyone you would expect to read the final part of the proposal – the budget – first.

Statement of what the client wants from the project

The statements that the client has given at the first meeting need to be shaped into a sharp, business-focused account. It is helpful if you can use phrases and terminology that reflect the business area of the client. If you have attuned yourself to their business approach during the first meeting you will find it easier to write to suit them.

You may not have attended the initial meeting with the client, because companies work in different ways. You may for example be verbally briefed, or passed notes from initial meetings conducted by others to work into a proposal. Some companies split the responsibilities between people who land the business and people who manage the development teams. Exactly who writes the proposal or equivalent may not be straightforward. However, if you have to write them, you have to work hard to understand the client's business and to show that you understand it. This can be as simple as realizing that people from an audiovisual background often find the term 'user' rather unfriendly and might prefer to think about 'viewers'. Those from a journalistic background might be more comfortable with 'the reader' for online projects.

It is useful if you can explain some of the positive factors that the interactive media environment will add to help the client achieve their needs.

Statement of what the user needs from the application

The client will have interpreted the needs of the users in the scoping questionnaire. You should reshape these, but you can also add your experience of the users of an application from a professional point of view. It is important to state that their experience of the application must be the focus of concern for all. You can predict the interactive level needed from the programme to suit the users. If there are examples of attributes from similar programmes that have appealed to this type of user, you should introduce these here.

Description of the general treatment and reasons for choice

There is no right or wrong answer to deciding on the treatment for the topic for your clients. It might help you to consider that, for the same project, different companies would suggest very different treatments for a variety of reasons. There are certain guiding principles, but the general treatment might be the combination of ideas from several strands of experience within a company or it might be up to an individual to define an overall approach. The ideas should reflect the aims of the client and the needs of the users, and it is important to explain why the suggested structure will achieve these.

There are differences in the treatment of the next few sections for on- and offline projects, and so they have been split out for clarity. The processes you should use are common to both, so they are then brought back together for consideration.

Online projects: treatment

Your experience will be influential when defining the treatment. It is a good idea to have walked your client through several sites at the initial meeting, noting their general reaction to structure and interface design. It helps to explain the reasoning behind some of the structure decisions and levels of interactivity and, most particularly, to begin to focus them on the needs of the users rather than on personal preference. See Chapter 9, *Interface design*, for more on this aspect. If you have managed to influence them with this exercise, then your proposed treatment will extract features they liked and ones you know will suit the needs of the users.

The home page is all important. It sets the expectations, structure and image for the rest of the site. It serves the purpose of giving a mission statement or an overview of what is on offer. The users want to have a quick, clear understanding of what is available. If they enter the site seeking specific information, then they want the categories to point to where they can find it. If they come to the site for entertainment or amusement, then the page set-up should reflect this. The home page also has a secondary function when the site is indexed by a Web search engine. Some engines index a site from hidden information in the page headers (called META tags); some work with the title and text in the page; some use both. The home page is also the starting point for a search engine working through the whole site, just as it is for a human visitor, and both need to be taken into account for the design.

Clients tend to underestimate how difficult it is to categorize and classify information and provide apposite summaries for people. Many want to put in too much inappropriate text, not understanding that users adopt different reading techniques for the Web. See Chapter 9, *Interface design*, for more on this.

For the proposal you may not have had time to prototype a home page completely, but it would be good to show the general structure and the number of elements that will be included for branching off to other pages. A diagrammatic representation of the branches is a good idea, with a statement of the reasons for them, and showing how their structure relates to the needs of the user and the wishes of the client.

Each section of the site should be mentioned in terms of its expected size, the media components and reasons for the media choices, and the estimated time needed to complete the content and design for each section. You will have to work hard to get a feel for the size and complexity of the sections because your cost quote will be linked to these.

At this stage it is impossible to know how long it will take to get the right information together for the respective sections, or how much there will be, but you'll have a better feel than the clients. It may well be easier for you to talk in terms of small, medium and large sections, representing each by a banding of pages and a complexity indicator:

- Small = 5–10 pages
- Medium = 10–20 pages
- Large = 20–30 pages
- Very large = 30+ pages

Pages here are taken to mean sub-menus and the content associated with each. There could be several levels in one section according to the split in information.

In the section audit table (Table 4.1), complexity can relate to the media production components, the content, the programming, or all three. You may rank each of them as low, medium or high. For example, a section that relied on pulling information from an existing database and adding a new front-end could be småll in size of pages displayed, medium in terms of complexity for media, and low in content production and programming because the database exists. However, later you may find that the database is relatively old and needs a complete overhaul to port it to the Web. Now the content would have to shift to high; the programming would increase and the cost would move accordingly.

When you have a good grasp of the complexity and size of the whole site, you are in a position to determine the resources you'll require and the time that they may need. This assessment can help you in costing the project.

Table 4.1 Section audit.

Section name	Size (pages)	Complexity			Development time + Testing + Rework	Cost
		Media	Content	Programming		

Different companies have different ways of costing. A lot depends on whether all the resources are in house or whether extras need to be sourced. Allow some contingency for flexibility to make the inevitable adjustments.

This analysis is based on static pages of HTML. If the information is volatile, and the clients want to be able to update it themselves, or if the site is exceptionally large, they may need to generate pages on the fly, to be dynamic. Many such Web sites are actually generated by purpose-built databases. If the site is both large and structured, with a large number of pages that contain similar layouts of differing information (such as a catalogue), then a purpose-built database should be considered, and your programmer needs to be involved to make a different form of analysis from the one shown here.

Rights clearances are generally fewer in number and involve fewer types of media for online than for offline, but they still need to be considered and costed accordingly. If you are reusing assets from the client's company, they need to have the right to reuse those assets in electronic form. It is prudent to ask the client to double-check this. See Chapters 10 and 17 for more on the legal considerations. New assets or ones that do not wholly belong to the client will need to be cleared and paid for. The number that require this will depend on the media mix you are using and on the size of the site.

In your time for development, consider the resources and time that will be used for production, but don't forget the time for testing and rework, and for trials with user groups if necessary. Testing and trials are often overlooked, but they can eat up time and resources. You should establish exactly how much of this the client requires and build it into the equation. It is common for clients to forget that you asked this. They often reject the idea at first but change their minds later. So keep good records of their response to this, and put it in writing to them confirming that they do not want user trials or extra testing apart from your own in-house verification. If they suddenly decide that they want to do an internal trial with colleagues, you'll then be in a position to negotiate for the time and rework that this always produces.

When drafting the proposal, refer back to the scoping questionnaire and list the client's wishes/objectives for the site and their user needs. Show how your company intends to achieve the objectives in the treatment of the content for each section (Table 4.2). This then links your decisions back to specifics that the client understands. They should recognize your concern for their needs and their own client's needs. This should help instil in them trust and confidence in you. It also provides guidelines for your decisions.

If there are any objectives for either client or user that are not met in the sections as agreed by you, you can either point this out to the client, asking for clarification of the content that might meet the need, or put forward a range of suggestions of what you could do to meet the needs. In this way you can spot gaps between the client needs and content areas. A similar process is explained for offline projects in more detail below, and it may help you to refer to that explanation.

For each section, as you describe the approach that will be used check the media list that the client may have given you in the scoping questionnaire.

Table 4.2 Section related to needs.

Content section	Client need satisfied	User need satisfied

You may not meet the expectations they had, if you have valid reasons. You should indicate your reasons for media choice for each section linking it to the objectives and user needs.

Offline projects: treatment

You should discuss the main areas of content, and indicate how they will be linked. A diagram, along the lines of a flow chart, would be useful here. The media selection for each area of content needs to be discussed and the reason for the choice of media explained. It helps at this stage to indicate the total number of minutes of material that each section will contain, as this will later provide the editorial control over the amount of information contained.

Content and media definition.

For example, if you promise 10 minutes of total audio and graphics and 3 minutes of video in one section, but as the detail comes to light it becomes clear that it will need 15 minutes of audio and graphics to do the topic justice, then you have the power to bargain for extra money for the extra time. Equally, if there is not enough to put in this section you might suggest cutting out the 3 minutes of video here but adding 3 minutes in a more suitable place.

The process outlined below might help you in your decision making for proposal treatments. It assumes that you have filled in the equivalent of a scoping questionnaire. The data used here is based on the museum example, found at the end of this chapter. You will need to refer to this in order to understand the incomplete chart (Table 4.3) and the analysis here.

There were a couple of definite suggestions for content and an overall indication of what was wanted from the client's and users' perspectives. So you can start by matching the suggested content against the needs to find out where the gaps are. Then it is easier to concentrate on filling the content gaps to fulfil all the needs. This type of exercise can focus creative brainstorming from your team to fulfil definite purposes rather than have complete free play with ideas. The aim is to suggest content and treatments that will cover all the wants and needs at some stage.

In the example, the client made two content suggestions, which are listed across the top. The first suggestion has been worked through the table for you with ticks and a suggested treatment. You and your team would need to decide whether the content could match the 'wants' of the client listed on the left. If the content can be valuable in fulfilling their wishes you need to suggest the treatment of the content that would suit these needs.

In the example, the portrait and records of the founder certainly form part of the history of the museum, and may help towards instilling local pride. The precise nature of the records and how they will be treated in detail could be focused this way if the scriptwriter/researcher is told to do so.

Once you have started to show how the content might suit the purpose, you should begin to get a feel for the best media to use. As a portrait is static rather than video, and the records will be text based, it would seem a good idea to suggest that a treatment using graphics and audio might serve the purpose. This has been filled in on the chart as an example.

As you decide on the treatment you should check the needs of the users, as this can influence your decision. The account here needs to be brief, not just because it is a requirement for the user but because the generation of new graphics to fit with audio is time consuming and therefore costly. Again, the directions to the graphics artist and scriptwriter could help to slant this section to be attractive and stimulating, so these could be ticked as responsibilities for the people who will produce the components. At this point you can suggest some timings and an overall duration for the section, but these will change as you work out costs later.

So the decisions about treatment can be influenced by, and need a balance between, the needs of the user, the type of materials available, the time to produce, and an appreciation of the cost. It is this simultaneous weighing of several factors that makes multimedia decisions a complex skill.

Table 4.3 Identify gaps in the content (museum POI example).

	Area 1	Area 2	Cont.
Content areas suggested	Portrait and records of founder	Museum records of special exhibitions	
Wants and needs			
Clients			
1. To inform about the history of the museum	✓	✓	
2. To be the centre point of a centenary exhibition			
3. To add a dimension to the exhibition			
4. To demonstrate the museum's contribution to the locality		✓	
5. To instill local pride	✓	✓	
6. To encourage people to come			
Treatment	Graphics and audio: about one a half minutes brief history – linear		
Users			
1. Ease of use	✓		
2. Attractive	✓		
3. Motivating			
4. Content brief but stimulating	✓		
5. Memorable			
6. Cater for all age ranges	Suit youth and adult		
Time			

Once the client's suggestions have been accounted for, you will be able to see where there are gaps in the needs and wants. These will require content to fill them. This is the most creative aspect of the decision making, and is where most of the risks are taken, because assumptions have to be made on availability of material, suitability of treatment, and reactions of the client.

A question of balance.

Remember to include built-in help and preference selection if these are appropriate. Help can either be general – ideally your functionality should be simple enough to require minimal extra help – or context specific. Preferences can be of varying complexity depending on the expectations of the user but, for the museum example, one consideration might be a choice of language.

Choose the media that you think would best suit the content you decide on. At this stage you should not worry too much about platform or media constraints. Add these onto the page or spreadsheet so that it is easy to change them later. It helps to differentiate the ones that originated with the client from those suggested by your company members.

Choosing media won't be as easy as it sounds, and it can help if you brainstorm with colleagues. One category of content should serve more than one requirement, so that you keep control of the amount of material even at this stage.

When you've got a feel for the content range, you need to look at the expected media mix if the client has stated one, and check it off against the treatment you've suggested. The platform decisions can affect media decisions, so take this into account now, changing the treatment accordingly. But keep a record of what you had intended, as you might find this can influence the client later. If a platform isn't stipulated, make your decision based on any strategy that the client has indicated and the needs of the users. Indicate the reasons behind your choice of platform.

Put a total time on each category, with the time for each media component broken down into constituent times. For example, you might have decided to set a scene with 2 minutes of video and then allow the user to choose between five points of view about this video. If each interview was $1\frac{1}{2}$ minutes with audio over graphics, the total for that category would be $9\frac{1}{2}$ minutes.

Then cost the media components. You need to refer to past experience – both your own and that of your colleagues – to do this. Companies work in different ways for costings, so you'll need to adjust this part accordingly.

Some will give estimates based on the combined staff and production costs related to media components. For example, a company might have tables of costs per half hour of different video formats – full drama production on location, full drama production in studio, studio interviews, location interviews – and you can cost each type of video production according to your estimates. Another set of tables might list the digital conversion costs and so on, so you gradually apply the tables to the components you have suggested to arrive at the total estimate. It is important for the tables to be current in this case.

Another way of costing starts with the staff and the time needed as shown (Table 4.4). Apply internal and external costing rates according to the roles and general salary levels for the role. The time for which the staff will be

Table 4.4 Identifying costs from staff, time and rights breakdown.

Internal	External	Time/weeks	Cost
Area 1			
Jake (graphics)		1	
Sue (")		1	
	Area 1		
	Phil (script)	¾	
	Phil (audio)	½	
Area 2			
		Total	

Rights clearances		
Category		**Cost**
Stills		
Music		
Voice-overs		
Video footage		
	Total	

needed depends on several factors – new material development, complexity of the graphics, use of animation and special techniques, and so on.

It helps if you look at the costs of a recent project to estimate an average time for production of graphics per day. This is an inaccurate rule of thumb since the difficulty of graphics production varies according to content, so take this inaccuracy into account in your estimate. Gradually build up the picture of how much time the content would take to research, process and produce.

Rights clearances can be very costly, so they need to be considered here and refined later. Work to an estimate of how many voice-over artists you might need, and for what length of material. They are costed per hour even if there is only 10 minutes' work. You also have to consider how much and what type of music – library, commissioned, recorded – as these have variable costs too. If you have to clear permissions from picture libraries or companies there will be costs attached. The same is true if you will be using existing footage from a film library. All these factors will affect the costs that you need to build in to arrive at a realistic offer to the clients. See Chapters 10, *Contract issues 2*, and Chapter 17, on *Rights, copyright and other intellectual property*, for more detailed information on rights.

On- and offline projects: common ground

Cost considerations vary.

Some companies work to a defined profit margin, which needs to be added to the staff and production costs. Other companies have built this into the daily rates that you apply, so you should understand how your company is working to make sure that you have accounted for all the factors.

When you have your total time and cost, go back and look at the time and budget that have been stipulated by the client. Then you can make editorial decisions on what to cut or add, depending on the match between the two. You should also assess how much of the cost is real external spending and how much is in overheads such as salaries and hardware amortization. The amount of money you actually have to spend to carry out the work should influence whether you ask for some of the money in advance.

Variations on the treatment

These will come to light as you apply the process described for defining the treatment for online and offline respectively. If you need to cut any major features to suit the budget, you could add them to the proposal as extras for consideration, suggesting to the client that these would offer value to the user, and the reasons for this. You would already have the extra time and budget implications worked out for the features so you could build these into the variations on offer – with their respective price tags.

Outline diagram of the structure

This is best placed at the beginning of the description of the treatment, but the best place to devise it is at this point to see if it is worth offering the variation diagrams as well. It is difficult for clients to understand the navigation routes through the content, so a diagram of the main categories and their interrelationships will help.

Description of the human resources

List and describe in general terms the roles that will be part of the project. You will probably have a core team, with extras to supplement it at key stages. Most clients are surprised at the numbers involved, and it shows the complexity of the project in terms they understand. You do not need to put in the time that the people will spend on the project at this point, even though you have had to do a rough estimate for the overall cost implications. The possibility of using multiskilled personnel for more than one task is something you should be aware of, but for the time being it should not be reflected in the proposal. The point of the proposal is to sell the ideas and suggested treatment to the client. You will be able to manoeuvre time and cost better later if you have not made strong commitments here. You will need this leeway because of the instability of the development process.

Work breakdown and schedule

Even if you have used a computer package to help with your scheduling and costing (see the example budget template on the CD), it is wise to leave the description of costs for the client to a minimum, for the reasons already stated. You, however, have to have as detailed a breakdown as possible for yourself and your management, to create whatever figures are given in the proposal. Remember, different companies have different policies on how to approach budgets. If you are a contract project manager, check that you understand how to work out your budget according to the company's template. Some will include stationery and couriers in their overheads, for example. Others will expect you to project figures for these specifically for the project. The way contingency costs and profit margins operate will be company specific as well.

For scheduling, it will be enough at this stage to state the start and end dates for each of the options, with general timing for research (outline and detailed documents dates) and key development stages, often called **milestones**. For more complex projects you might break the work down into work packages, each of which has a budget and timing and one or more deliverables.

Time and costs for testing

It is easy to forget to include phases for testing the application, but these can take a significant amount of time. You should take the lead here in specifying how much can be absorbed into the development time and what sorts of testing are recommended. It is important to establish this at this point and negotiate with the client so that a realistic level of performance is achieved for the time allowed. Chapter 18, *Testing*, describes how to devise a testing strategy, and how to explain the options and implications of decisions to the client.

Cost/payment

The total cost should be given, with indications of the company's payment policy. Most companies ask for staged payments to improve cash flow, and to cover themselves for unforeseen circumstances where the project might be stopped or delayed. The stages are often linked to key deliverables or milestones of production. Companies will define these in different ways but many link staged payments to:

- the phase or phases leading to the detailed agreement of content;
- the first working example of the code and navigation, sometimes called an alpha;
- the near-final stage, often called the beta;
- delivery of the final version of the project – a gold master for a CD-ROM, or a fully functioning site for online, for example.

Limitations of the proposal

Because the proposal is based on a limited understanding of the overall content, there need to be indications of this to allow for changes from the developers as their understanding deepens.

If you have based any of your decisions on material that will be supplied by the client you will need a proviso that this is subject to the material's being of the right type and quality. Otherwise you will need to revise your estimates of how much material will need to be produced.

Technology production is changing rapidly all the time so costs vary quickly. It is wise to put a time limit on the offer subject to costs being reworked. You need to point out that the start dates are dependent on the client's agreement to proceed in time and that any delay for the start would add time to the finish date. It is surprising how often clients return to you after the start date with agreement to proceed but still expect you to complete in the same time without cutting any of the production.

Conclusion

Proposals often need to be turned around quickly. They are difficult documents to draft, and there need to be clear guidelines to help with the drafting according to company practice. It is management's responsibility to ensure that these guidelines exist so that whoever writes a proposal for the company covers the scope in the way that serves the company best. Bias within the company towards any specific origin, such as video production, will affect the components in the proposal.

The principles that underlie a proposal are the same, however. The client will be looking for clear statements of what the company can offer for the time and price. Their attitude will be affected by their own bias towards media and the needs of the project. They can be influenced by good ideas that show value. To define the added value of one form of medium or treatment over another requires professional expertise and experience.

It is rare for the proposal to be accepted outright, and the client will negotiate on the range, type and composition of the content as well as debate costs. You face a problem if you give a more detailed breakdown of costs at this stage because you have been working from a hypothetical mix for the team. For example, you may have presumed that you could have an internal graphics resource at one cost, but until the project becomes a reality the allocation of resources is notional. It might transpire that all internal resources are booked on other projects for the period, and that a completely new freelance team needs to be formed.

Theory into practice 4

You have been asked to draft a proposal because there is a deadline and your colleague is sick. She attended the briefing meeting with the client, and all you have to work from is the completed scoping questionnaire. You have one working day to complete and fax it to the client while coping with your ongoing projects. This sort of time-scale is not unusual. Remember this next time you look at a programme and criticize the treatment.

You have a choice of two completed scoping questionnaires – one online and one offline. Using the information given, derive a proposal for one of them.

Online client-centred project scoping questionnaire

Project name/no:	Wrap-it Com/106
Contact details	Jeff Standing, President
Client/Organization name:	Wrap-it
Address:	29 Westbery Avenue
	Mission Quay
	ONTARIO K3X 4T5

Tel: (613) 555 7171 Fax: (613) 555 7289 Email: standing@wrap.intmail.com

Web site:

Project contacts:

Name(s):		Position(s):	
	Jeff Standing		President
	Stella Carpanini		Production Manager

Direct line: as above   Email: as above

Previous interactive media experience

Online

| None | ☐ | A little | ✓ | Fair | ☐ | Good | ☐ | Experienced | ☐ |

Offline

| None | ✓ | A little | ☐ | Fair | ☐ | Good | ☐ | Experienced | ☐ |

Experience description

Online

Products:	Producer:
Home page as part of trade	Small Business Alliance
association package. Standard	
Template, little feedback	

Offline

Products:	Producer:

Client's initial statement of what they want

This is a small firm specializing in all forms of wrapping paper/goods for crafts people/hobbyists. Some customers are now asking if they have a site and if they can order online. They feel this will grow, and want to build up the facility in stages to allow them to ease into an online culture. Don't want immediate ordering online but want to be able to upgrade to that once they get a better perspective from information on hits/enquiries. As the company is Canadian they need the site to be in both English and French. They will supply text and translations.

Online project type

Internet ✓　Hybrid Web/CD ☐　Intranet ☐　Extranet ☐

Set up new facility ✓

(If yes, domain name suggestions?)

Company name if available and appropriate but willing to listen to suggestions

Add/change existing facility ✓

Market sector

Commercial ✓　Corporate ☐　Government ☐　Education ☐

Project bias

	Importance ranking	Size of section (large, medium, small)
Company profile ✓	2	small
Information gathering ☐		
Information dissemination ✓	1	small
Retail (products or services) ✓	1	small, later medium
Marketing/advertising ☐		
Redesign site ☐		
Others (specify) ☐		
Image improvement through general look and feel ✓	1	

Site maintenance

Client to maintain ✓

You to maintain ☐

Benefits/achievements wanted

Not applicable [　　　　　　] (Reason) [　　　　　　]

[　　　　　　]

The organization will benefit by/objectives/wants:

1. Offering new service to customers
2. Increased enquiries about products
3. Increased sales
4. Enhanced image appropriate for niche market
5. Seen to keep up with competitors' Web presence
6. Platform for offering special deals cheaply and quickly
7. Profile of customers using new service

The users will benefit by/objectives/needs:

1. Up-to-date information on the company and products
2. Clear, fast access to information wanted
3. Access to new product details before other customers
4. Access to special deals advertised on Web only
5. Quick, easy enquiries via email
6. Fast response to enquiries

Access and use

The audience/users		Access to what information
Internet		
General public	✓	All
Specific market sector(s) (specify)	✓	All

Company traditionally deals with specialist craft packaging needs. Wins business on small runs others won't do. Could be useful to general public who have craft hobby/interest.

Note: the client liked the features and feel of our paint manufacturer site (Cozy Colour) best but could not afford the treatment once told the cost.

Intranet		
Corporate/government/ education/other:		
In-house (all)		
Exec		
Managers		
Sales force		
Other		

Access and use (cont)

Extranet

No. of sites to connect

Who will need access
(specify)

Media mix

Client's media	None, wants suggestions	✓		Animation		%
expectations	Text		%	Audio		%
	Graphics		%	Video		%

Content (existing assets)

Written	✓		Contact:	Nigel Benson
Relevant databases	✓	Spec:	Contact:	Lindy Cortez
Graphics/stills	✓	Spec:	Contact:	Nigel Benson
Audio		Spec:	Contact:	
Video footage		Spec:	Contact:	
Content experts	✓		Contact:	Nigel Benson

Time for development

| Client expectation | 1 | (months) | Start date: | January |
| | | | End date: | February |

Any fixed dates
(demos etc.)

To be specified in
proposal

Budget

£/$ approx

Budget holder:	Jeff Standing	Position	President
Tel:	see above		
Email:	see above		

Project cost to be prepared and negotiated ✓

Separate costs to be put forward for maintaining and updating

Offline client-centred project scoping questionnaire

Project name/no: SMCE / 67

Contact details

Client/Organization name: Brentfields Museum

Address: The Parade

Brentfields

Tel: 234 444   Fax: 234 445   Email: jane@brentfields.org.uk

Web site

Project contacts:

Name(s): Jane Morris   Positions: Exhibition Organizer

Libby Turner   History Curator

Direct line   Email:

Previous interactive media experience

Online

None [x]   A little [ ]   Fair [ ]   Good [ ]   Experienced [ ]

Offline

None [ ]   A little [ ]   Fair [ ]   Good [ ]   Experienced [ ]

Experience description

Online

Products: Producer:

Offline

Products: Producer:

Project type

Commercial	x	Corporate		Government	
Presentation		Point of information	x		
Training		Advertising			
Point of sale					
Publishing (specify)		Hybrid CD/Web (specify)		Other (specify)	

Education			
Edutainment			
Entertainment			
Reference			

Content (general statement)

What's the project about? Why multimedia?

As part of its centenary celebrations, the museum is putting on a special exhibition.
There will be five sections covering 20 years each. Each section will feature the five most
important acquisitions during the period and have mini exhibitions of work of two/three key
local people who won international fame during those times. The history of the museum will
run as the main theme throughout the sections.

The multimedia application is needed as a centre point for the exhibition area, which will
be shaped like a star. The client wants it to complement and extend the other exhibits

Content suggestions

There's a family portrait of the museum founder and records about the family, which they
feel could offer good background material. They have a full record of special exhibitions
held over the whole period with a copy of the accompanying catalogues, which Jane
thought might be useful

Audience/users

Commercial		Corporate	
General public	x	In-house (all)	
Specific market		Exec	
Sectors (specify)		Managers	
		Sales force	
		Other	(specify)

NOTE: More schools and retired people form the audiences. Also, tourists, surprising number of foreigners.

Estimated number of users (approx.)

1–100		5000–10 000	x
100–500		Other	(specify)
500–1000			
1000–5000			

Estimated number of systems   1   **Location:** At the museum in the centre of the exhibition

Benefits/achievements wanted

Not applicable   (Reason)

The organization wants the POI:

1. To inform people about the history of the museum
2. To be the centre point of their centenary exhibition
3. To add to the visitors' experience in some way
4. To demonstrate the museum's contribution to the locality
5. To instil local pride in the local visitors
6. To encourage people to come to the centenary exhibition.

Benefits/achievements wanted (cont)

The users need the POI to be:

1. Easy to use very quickly
2. Attractive
3. Motivating
4. Brief and to the point but stimulating
5. Memorable
6. Suitable content for all ages.

Content (existing assets)

Written	x		Contact:	John Barnes, Records
Video footage		Spec:	Contact:	
Graphics/stills	x	Spec: photos/slides (top quality).	Contact:	John Barnes
Audio		Spec:	Contact:	
Content experts	x		Contact:	Jane Morris, Libby Turner

Time for development

Client expectation	3.5	(months)	Start date	1/5/98
			End date	15/8/98

Any fixed dates   x
(demos etc.)

Exhibition opens   15/8/98

To be specified in
proposal

Platform

Existing platform(s)   Specification: none   Nos:

Location:

Platform (cont)

Client's suggestion [ ]   Specification: none   Nos: [ ]

Location:

Reasons:

To be specified   [x]
in proposal   Factors to consider:
Robustness, child-proof, vandal-proof, to fit in with
exhibition style and decor

Media mix

Expected length of programme/how long a user would
take to complete (hrs/mins)   50 mins

Client's media	None, wants suggestions			Text	5	%
expectations	Video	60	%	Graphics	10	%
	Audio	15	%	Animation	10	%

Budget

£40,000   £/$ approx

Budget holder: Mike Vincent   Position: Finance Director

Tel:

Email:

Cost to be proposed and negotiated [ ]

Summary

- From the information given, present an understanding of the approach, schedule and cost. If working on an offline project explain the platform choice.

- Work from the client's objectives for themselves and the users.

- Take into account any content suggestions from the client and match these to the objectives.

- Find the gaps left in the objectives, and devise content and treatment to fill them in the time allowed.

- For online projects, check that the media mix is suitable for the content, the users and the download time.

- For offline projects, check that the media mix is suitable for the content and the users.

- Check that the media mix can be achieved by the platform.

- Cost the proposed treatment, and refer back to the client's budget.

- Tailor the treatment to the budget. Don't forget to include a testing strategy, with options for clients to make decisions on.

- Define the resources that are needed.

- Explain any limitations of the proposal.

Recommended reading

As this chapter was based on experience, there is no recommended reading.

5

Contract issues 1

Project manager's responsibilities

■ To rework the proposal document's specifications, schedule and costs according to discussions until contractual agreement is reached

■ To elicit as much detail as possible to perform detailed costing on resources and clearances

■ To educate clients in ways of working together

What needs to be covered?

Benefit and burden.

A contract is an agreement between parties that defines the benefits and responsibilities for those concerned. Multimedia contracts will involve several documents and several parties. You will need agreements not only with the clients but with your staff and with any companies you work with during the project. In this book we shall cover contractual aspects in several chapters because we are following the stages of the project development, and the various issues have more relevance at certain times during development.

The chapters that will deal with specific contractual issues are: this one; Chapter 10, *Contract issues 2*; and Chapter 17; *Rights, copyright and other intellectual property*. In this chapter we shall refine the proposal into a contractual document, and suggest forms of agreement on how you and the clients should work together.

Background to multimedia contracts

The various industries involved with new media have their own ways of reaching contractual agreements. Publishing and computing are generally the most formalized. The arrangements in training vary according to company practice, and video production often still works on informal arrangements.

Multimedia development is a combination of stages from the different media production processes, and so it is difficult to apply one form of agreement that will satisfy all the stages. Your clients may well have background experience in commissioning some of the media components, and will have expectations from the previous work practices they have encountered.

It is difficult for a client to trust something that is expensive and unknown. Consequently, many clients feel they need to exert more control over multimedia projects than over other projects. They want to understand the processes that lie behind a project's development; they want to feel that they are getting their money's worth. As a result they query more, they hesitate to make decisions, and they want justification for actions. If they come from an audiovisual background they are also likely to take a detailed interest in the audiovisual content.

Because of this climate of uncertainty and apprehension, it is important to agree how to work together to help smooth the production path. Once you have set up a working relationship with a client, or if they understand multimedia production because they employ it themselves, this assumes less importance. Throughout the book we take inexperienced clients as the base because they have the most needs to consider and are the most likely to benefit from a set process. However, it is of course a mistake to underestimate the knowledge and experience of clients. Your way of working needs to be balanced against their experience.

Refining the proposal into a contract document

As soon as it becomes clear that the new client has not rejected your proposal out of hand, and wants further discussions, you need to listen carefully to their redefined needs, and then recost and refine your budget. The sooner you recognize any major differences between the initial proposal and the final work specification and costs, the better. If you are still at a negotiation stage, you can influence the budget. Once the amount and type of work has been agreed, you lose this facility, or at least make it much harder for yourself to justify more time and money.

In the rush to produce a proposal you are guided by the media components that are required and the amount of production that these will take. You may have applied a house formula for production costs, or have relied on your experience to quote a production figure. You may have defined the number of staff that would be needed and estimated the staff costs based on a split of some internal and external resources. You will have guessed at a figure that might be needed to clear rights from film or picture libraries, if necessary, and estimated voice-over costs, again if necessary. Many of the cost components would of necessity be vague at this stage. You wouldn't know exactly how many pictures of what type were needed or from where, for example, and this can affect the cost significantly.

However, as soon as the specifications and time-scale become tighter, you need to break down the costs so that you are sure that you can achieve the project according to time and budget. This means establishing how long and at what rate the staff will be paid, and the maximum that can be paid for each component to stay within budget. It also means refining the estimate of what rights might need to be cleared, how many stills to be cleared at what maximum rate, and so on.

You were asked to outline the major cost components in Chapter 4 to serve as a quick assessment of costs. Here, these will be expanded.

We left the proposal document at the point where it was handed to the client for the first time. In the first draft of the proposal, you may have offered the client a range of options and costs. If the client wishes to proceed, negotiations will then take place between you to refine the specifications of deliverables. You have to record all the changes from the meetings, and rework the costs and schedule accordingly until agreement is reached. The final proposal document will form a major part of the contractual agreements between you and the client because it will specify the work tasks, schedule and cost. The sign-offs are also contracts. They are agreements that demonstrate that certain parts of the work have been completed satisfactorily.

During the proposal refinement, you need to carry out a detailed budget breakdown based on resources, acquisitions and clearances. The client should need only the high-level summary that was contained in the original proposal, with milestones and sign-offs indicated in the schedule. But your estimation techniques should become firmer to allow you to feed better figures into the summary. (See the budget template example on the CD.)

The charts that we used in the first proposal document cover the right areas to prompt you to arrive at estimated figures, but Table 5.1 indicates the amount of detail that you should be aiming at in discussions with the clients, and provides a checklist to make sure you do not overlook anything. Your project may not need all of these resources, so you can cross them out. Alternatively, you may have special resource needs to add in.

Table 5.1 Multimedia project resource costs.

Resources	Initials	Internal/External	Rate per day	Days/weeks needed	Cost
Management/administration					
1. Project manager /Web manager					
2. Project assistant					
3. General production assistant					
4. Secretarial support					
				Subtotal	
Video production					
1. Director					
2. Producer					
3. Production assistant					
4. Camera					
5. Lights					
6. Sound					
7. Grips					
8. Make-up					
9. Continuity					
10. Logging					
11. Scriptwriter(s)					
12. Video graphics					

Table 5.1 (Cont)

Resources	Initials	Internal/External	Rate per day	Days/weeks needed	Cost
13. Offline editor					
14. Online editor					
15. Film/Picture research					
				Subtotal	
Audio production					
1. Production manager					
2. Scriptwriter(s)					
3. Editor					
4. Voice-over artist(s)					
5. Musicians					
				Subtotal	
Stills/graphics production					
1. Production manager					
2. Graphics production					
3. Picture researcher					
4. Animator					
5. Photographer					
6. Lighting					
7. 3-D modeller					
8. Graphic designer/Web designer					
9. Scanner/digitizer					
10. Art director					
11. Illustrator/artist					
12. Typographer					
				Subtotal	
Database development					
1. Data collection/management					
2. Integration/development					
3. Indexer					
				Subtotal	
Design/documentation					
1. Interactive designer					
2. Instructional designer					
3. Interface designer					
4. Web editor/Scriptwriter					
5. Subject matter experts					
				Subtotal	
Computing and integration					
1. Programmer/Web programmer Software engineer/Author					
2. Technical manager					
3. Network manager					
				Subtotal	
				Total	

There will be a wide range of rates that fluctuate according to the internal charge-out rates for company staff who work on the project and freelancers who are brought in to supplement them. You can't affect the internal rates, but the external ones can vary a good deal. As you gear up to start the project you should try to get a feel for which resources will operate as in-house ones and which you'll need to recruit. Take a near-top rate for any freelancers to give yourself some leeway when you are recruiting, because your recruitment decisions will be affected by the budget you've allocated to specific tasks, the skills of the people interviewed, and their rates. However, if cost was an issue with your client from the first round of the proposal, you may need to use a lower middle rate and cut the quality of the freelancers employed.

An explanation of how you arrive at your team mix, and the roles of the various people mentioned in the listings, is given in Chapter 11, *Selecting the team*.

It is important that all the new details in the specification are recorded in the refined proposal document so that the new agreements are clear. It is easy to confuse points that have been raised, discussed but rejected, and points that have been accepted at this stage. Good records need to be kept of the meetings during this time particularly.

The refined specification will help to determine better costs and scheduling than in the original document. Your objective is to get the client to sign the document understanding exactly what they will receive for the time and money. Both you and your team will benefit from a sound specification with clear deliverables.

Agreeing how to work together

If we examine the logic behind agreements – and contracts are agreements with responsibilities on both sides – then agreements are made on understanding, and understanding comes from knowledge. We should be asking ourselves how we can give the client knowledge about the working processes of multimedia development and their responsibilities in this. It is easier to reach an equitable agreement if both sides understand what is involved and what each one is expected to contribute.

The education of the client will continue throughout the project, but it is helpful to indicate what is going to happen at the beginning of the project. Once the project proposal has been accepted, the successful completion relies on both parties. At certain points the development company has to pass control to the client and cannot proceed without agreement and the subsequent handing back of control.

The real problems lie in the definition of a client's role. Clients hold the balance of power because they are paying for the service. The customer is always right from a retail perspective. But in a collaborative process, where you depend on the client to provide some of the materials and decisions according to a schedule, you should not be held responsible for deficiencies that originate with the client, nor for the impact these have on the development process. It is perfectly acceptable for the responsibilities of both sides to be agreed.

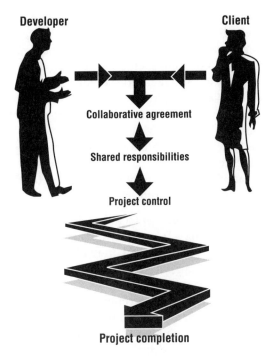

Developer

Client

Collaborative agreement

Shared responsibilities

Project control

Project completion

Working together.

The client's responsibilities need to be defined, and you should get their agreement that they will accept the consequences of time, cost and quality changes if they do not fulfil their side of the bargain. The converse is true, of course: the company and project manager also have to accept responsibility and liability for not fulfilling their own responsibilities.

There is one other aspect to take account of in a client relationship. Even if the client has agreed to the defined dates and processes, the project may be revised in terms of the priority level it receives from them because of other factors. Your contacts within the client company will be subject to their own pressures from their own organization, and internal matters will often be given higher priority than external projects. You need to understand the pressures they are under, because these will affect the project.

Every multimedia project is unique because the products are tailored to circumstances. Some may be similar to others, but they all have some aspects that are characteristic of the tailored approach. In principle, though, they all follow certain stages and rely on certain points of agreement or acceptance.

The way of working may not be defined in a company but it will help your role if you explain the way that you want to work with your client. A definition that is company based carries more weight, and it means that there are prior examples that you can use to show the client. It is in your interest to encourage the management to define the stages of documentation and the ways of working. As long as these remain defined at the level of guidelines, they will be flexible enough to allow the project manager to decide exactly which combination may be right for a particular project.

Some companies include aspects of these agreements between client and company in formal contracts, but they rarely explain in enough detail what the terms and conditions mean in actual practice. If there are formal contract terms you will need to check them to see if there is enough to help you in agreeing the precise way of working. More formal agreements are necessary to establish ownership and rights, for example, and these will be discussed further in Chapter 17.

You will find the following useful to give the client once there is agreement to proceed with the project:

■ Online – a short non-technical description of the platform that the client will be using – Internet, intranet, extranet – the range of possible media related to plug-ins and bandwidth, and the stages in producing these media components. A glossary of the more technical terms used within the description is also useful.
■ Offline – a short non-technical description of multimedia, its media components, the stages involved in producing and refining each component, and relevant platforms. A glossary of the more technical terms used within the description is also useful.
■ A short description of the stages that the projects go through, indicating where sign-off is needed. For online, this could be related to the stages of producing a small, medium or large site. The company's approach to changes needs to be stated clearly. The stages may vary in name according to the company or the nature of the project, but could include proposal, outline design, detailed design, testing, and so on. It is wise to break down the sign-off into component parts or you may find that disagreements arise about what a sign-off actually meant.
■ A general description of your responsibilities and the client's responsibilities to ensure a smooth project.
■ Sample copies of sign-off forms.

Change management

In the previous chapters we have seen examples of the impact that changes in the project can have. There are different causes of change, but one of the most common is an alteration to the work specification. The work specification is stated in the proposal, and once this is signed it is a contract. If a client asks for changes, they are asking for alterations to the contract. They need to recognize this. Agreement on ways of working together needs to address how any changes to the agreement should be handled.

The computer industry has had to develop some form of control to contain the impact of changes once production has begun. This is called

change control or **change management**. It is not commonly in use in new media companies, but all of them will recognize the recurring problems of changes and the consequences of the company's having to absorb overruns on budget.

Some argue that the agreement between client and company should be based on trust. These people would see change control as a mechanism that would interfere with the client relationship. Trust comes from understanding and respect, and as new media is not understood by the general public, there is little trust in the professionals. Mainstream computing still suffers from mistrust, but this has shifted towards better acceptance as the mystique has disappeared and its potential has become more widely accepted.

Software engineering has shown that any changes in a project need to be carefully controlled and monitored, because the consequences of changes can be disastrous. Several things can happen. If the change is not communicated to all of the team, people working on different parts will end up working in different directions. Then the pieces will not fit together, parts of the program that worked stop working correctly, and a lot of time is spent unravelling the problem. Version control is also used in software engineering so that everyone can check which version of the program they are using by looking at a version number and date. Version control helps to avoid wasted effort, but it is changes that drive the need for new versions, so change control precedes version control.

It is not always immediately obvious that a change will have spin-off consequences, even if the whole team is informed. With offline projects a change to some graphics may cause programming problems, extra audio or video may make the program too big for the disk or platform to run efficiently, and adding an extra section may cause stripping down of the code and rebuilding because a programmer plans coding based on an understanding of the total way the program needs to work. With online projects, many changes can usually be accommodated more easily than with offline, but they can still have ripple effects across work already completed, causing more rework than expected.

Communicating the change may seem trivial, but the team is usually an extended one in which some processes are performed off site. Contacting several people to communicate a change and then ensuring that they remember to carry it out is not trivial. Even identifying the change can be problematic unless each tiny component has a unique identification code of some sort.

Apart from informing everyone, any documentation will need to be revised and extra copies given out. This takes time in itself. Documentation for a multimedia project can run into several hundred pages, often with illustrative graphics. If individual sheets are sent out, it is easy for them to disappear in a paper chase, particularly if several changes are made per week. It is also common for changes to be made to previous changes as an original idea is refined. It should be obvious how easily chaos can occur.

Clients need to understand the possible consequences of changes and accept a procedure for implementing change. Software engineers recommend using a **change request form**, which would have the following features:

■ Project name
■ Date
■ Change initiated by
■ Change description
■ Requirements affected (with identifying numbers)
■ Other program effects
■ Other system effects
■ Planned start and completion
■ Resources affected (personnel and schedules)
■ Approvals (this could include the systems manager, development
   manager, configuration manager, quality manager, programme manager)

This makes it clear that any change needs to be considered by all involved for the possible impact and the time for implementing the change to be agreed. A similar process is needed in multimedia development.

At the moment, given the way multimedia is working, this level of what will be seen as bureaucracy would be totally unacceptable. The equivalent approvals needed might include: client, development company director/account manager/finance director, technical director, project manager, Web designer, programmer, graphics artist, video director, video graphics artist and so on.

Development time is always at a premium in projects, and administration suffers. Because the project manager's role is often split between developing part of the project according to a specialism and the overall management, any lengthy administration procedures would add to an already over-burdening workload. But without some form of change control, the project can quickly degenerate.

The form as described above does not work for a client-driven project, because if the client initiates a change they are not in a position to describe the change or its possible impact in ways that can be understood by the team. The project manager has to work with the client to derive a description, and then check out the consequences. In this way the communication time increases in a client-driven project.

The form also does not work for every multimedia project component. It has been drafted for changes to the code and structure of a program. Multimedia changes might affect these but there are also changes requested in graphics, audio scripts, video scripts, video graphics and text scripts.

In offline projects, if a careful object-oriented approach to the software design has been undertaken then quite a lot of the changes to the content will not impinge greatly on the software. The difficulties that changes cause are also related to the time in the project when they are made, and whether the components have been integrated with others.

With online projects, the impact of changes can be as great as in offline if the more complex coding – such as Java – is being used. Otherwise, changes to HTML code are comparatively straightforward. But asking for a few pages within a section that demand a new structure that has not featured before is a significant change even though the pages are part of a section.

If the client is made aware of the last opportunities to make changes for each of the components, the project can run more smoothly and truly trivial changes can be accepted willingly. It is right for clients to adjust components until they are satisfied with them or until the agreed time frame for adjustment has lapsed. If clients agree that after sign-off of each stage any changes will incur time and cost penalties, the developers have some form of control.

A compromise solution is needed. This is why it has been suggested that client education needs to address changes. If clients can understand the complications that can arise, they will be more disposed to stipulate their requirements carefully at the beginning and within the adjustment leeway. If they understand that, after sign-off, changes will be costly and time consuming, they will be more careful in suggesting changes.

Stages of a project

A project generally follows these stages of development:

(1) Agreement to the overall structure and major content areas (the proposal or sometimes the outline design should stipulate these). Sign-off stage 1 and 2.

(2) Agreement of platform for offline projects, the system's technical capabilities for online, and product specification for both types of project. These can be in Sign-off 1 or 2.

(3) Agreement to the detail of each component: text, navigation methods/ menus, audio, graphics, video. These can have individual sign-off stages if the scripts are produced separately.

(4) Agreement that the package operates as stipulated for Phase 1. This is the equivalent of the alpha test sign-off.

(5) Agreement that the product has fulfilled all specifications and is concluded. Final sign-off.

If sign-off dates are set within the schedule then last change dates can be set ahead of these to allow the last set of changes to be carried out and checked. The overall timing of the project will affect how much time is allowed in total for each stage.

The client needs to know how the project will develop and what they will be expected to do at each stage, so that they can plan their time and effort.

Responsibilities

If a list of responsibilities is agreed, this will give commitment to the project as well as educate the client in how it will progress. The list needs to be tailored to the type of project and company practice. Agreement to the responsibilities is best achieved formally, with signing and dating, rather than verbally.

The lists show the responsibilities for a project manager and a corporate client respectively. Although the project manager's list will remain relatively constant for client-driven projects, the client's responsibilities will need to be tailored to the specific project.

Project manager's responsibilities

- To work with the client to produce a mutually acceptable proposal that outlines the project content, timing and budget
- To produce a detailed work schedule consistent with agreed start and finish dates, which will map out phases of production
- To monitor and record time spent on the project
- To keep clients informed:
  - on general progress, e.g. a written summary every month
  - on any slippage as it occurs and actions to be taken to remedy it
  - on any suggested changes to the specification arising from technical or design factors as soon as these occur
  - on any other factors that affect the project as soon as they occur
- To ensure that each component part of the project is produced to the right technical specification
- To ensure that the structure and approach to the program are agreed and signed off by the named contact in the client organization
- To ensure that the content/script is agreed and signed off by the named contact in the client organization
- To agree the number of turn-around days for the client organization for any decisions/revisions on any of the parts of the project
- To provide deadlines for the client for:
  - the last round of changes on parts of the script (the number of times a client can make changes will depend on the overall time limit of the project and can vary accordingly)
  - the latest time that changes can be made to any graphics
  - the latest time that changes can be made to any video
  - the latest time that changes can be made to any text
- To get final sign-off for the completion of the project

The client's responsibilities

- To prepare a clear brief for the developers
- To work together on the detail of the specification
- To inform the project manager of any factors that will impinge on the project as soon as they occur
- To appoint one sign-off person in the organization who will be able to devote adequate time across the whole project and whose agreement will be binding
- To agree any subject matter with experts from the company who will need to be involved and ensure that they offer adequate time in accordance with the schedule
- To keep within the turn-around time agreed, or accept revised time, cost and quality penalties
- To agree that any changes made after deadline dates or sign-off will incur time, cost and quality penalties
- To agree that any slippage caused by delay of any type by the organization will incur time, cost and quality penalties
- To help the developer gain access to any people or materials in the organization who will aid the project

Does education work?

It works slowly, and a project operates better if the client has some under-standing than if they have none. However, there are several issues that will arise irrespective of setting up these measures of control.

The client will be anxious about sign-off points because they recognize that they are points of no return. (A sample sign-off form is provided for refer-ence.) They may delay signing because they say they are unsatisfied, but the longer the delay the more the end date will need to slip. The partnership aspect of working on a project needs to be made clear. The final product can only be finished on schedule if the components are produced according to schedule. Both of you may need to compromise on some aspects to achieve this, so that the components may not be the absolute best that could be achieved but they are the best in the time available. If you continue to strive for the best with refinement after refinement, the project is in danger of never being finished. To put this dilemma in perspective, the film director François Truffaut once said that he started every project wanting to make the best film ever made but that as the work progressed he ended up thinking himself lucky just to be able to finish it at all.

Project name:	Wrap-it
Project No:	Com/106
Client name:	Wrap-it

Components for sign-off:

Outline design including:
- Structure map with main content sections defined
- Overall treatment of each section
- Length for each section
- Schedule
- Sign-off authority

Signed on behalf of the company:	**Signed on behalf of the client:**
Name: (printed)	Name:
Signature:	Signature:
Date:	Date:

The client will be subjected to pressures for change from other factors. If their organization changes their approach or a key member of staff, the con-tent and structure of the original specification may become outdated. This is not a problem if extra time and costs can be established. But with corporate projects particularly, the release date is often linked to high-profile events, which cannot be changed. Your client has to produce something that is in tune with the tenor of the organization at that time. They get trapped politically, and you are ensnared in the consequences.

Another problem that still occurs with clients is the thorny problem of their agreeing to one thing on paper but imagining the end result will be visually different. The discrepancy between actual visuals and a text description of visuals, and the difference between static and moving items, always cause problems. This is the reason why prototyping parts of the project may be valuable.

With online projects, prototyping is quicker and easier, and really helps to smooth the process. With offline projects prototyping tools have improved, and it is easier than it was, but the process still takes enough time to need scheduling into the plan.

Clients will become suspicious if you make changes but prevent them from making changes without adjusting the time and cost. This is difficult to justify, but the only way to explain it is to refer to your proviso in the proposal and outline designs, where you reserve the right to adjust according to the detail that emerges. You need to remind the client that you have made provision for your changes in the estimate of time and cost based on the experience of the range and type of adjustments that occur as the content firms up from a development point of view. You have taken the risk in agreeing to produce a partially defined product to a fixed rate. You may be very wrong in the estimate and have to absorb far more than experience dictated. However, if the client asks for changes to the specification, then you have the right to revise the estimate. Of course you can always ask for more money if you have to make changes because of errors on your part, but you are unlikely to endear yourself to the client by doing so.

If a project has a short life span then some of the phases may well need to collapse or not occur. The tendency is to work according to verbal agreements during the project. Unfortunately, the tighter the project turn-around, the stronger the need for tight specification with no changes, and the client needs to be aware of this. It should be up to the management of the company to explain the risks to a client of undertaking a complex task with a short timescale and how it will affect quality and working practice. This rarely happens, because the thirst for business outweighs sense. It appears that multimedia development has not learnt from the software engineering experience.

There is one further issue to consider regarding the final sign-off: the completion of the project. With an offline project such as a CD-ROM there is a definite psychological point where a golden master is handed over to the client for replication. With a Web site this does not usually happen. The site may even have been visible on the Web, albeit hidden away, during the production process. In this case the client may not feel that the process of production is ever complete, and will continue to ask for small changes. (This is a totally different issue from maintainance of a site since, in essence, a Web site should continually evolve: we are considering the job you initially set out to do.) To help overcome this you may like to give your client a master copy of the Web site on a CD so that the psychological hand-over is actually carried out. Do this even if you have installed the site on the client's server.

Theory into practice 5

Choose one of the tasks outlined below. Select the one that suits your type of project best.

Online

Try writing a brief, non-technical account of online production for prospective clients. You will be trying to convey the differences between Internet, intranet and extranet without confusing the reader. You will need to indicate the possibilities of the use of different media, their advantages and disadvantages according to bandwidth available. Then cover the stages of development for each media component to explain what is involved for the prospective client.

Try out your account on a few members of the public who know nothing about online production and evaluate whether you have succeeded in improving their understanding in the ways you need.

Offline

Try writing a brief, non-technical account of multimedia for prospective clients. You will be trying to convey the complexity and interdependences of each of the media strands without confusing the reader. You will need to mention the stages of development of each component. Video production could include the following, for example: decisions on video quality and final digital type, research, script, storyboard, shoot, offline edit, online edit, digital conversion, integration.

Your purpose is to give the reader an appreciation of the number and type of stages that a multimedia application can have so that they can understand why it appears to take so long to produce.

Try out your account on a few members of the public who know nothing about multimedia and evaluate whether you have succeeded in improving their understanding in the ways you need.

Summary

- Clients often suggest changes to the proposal document, which means that the specifications, schedule and costs need to be reworked.

- The final agreed document forms part of the contractual agreement between you and the clients, as it states the work to be performed, the schedule and the costs.

- It is important to firm up the details so that you can refine the costs – particularly on the resources and rights clearances – if there are any.

- At this time it becomes more important to know which team members will be in house and which will be subcontractors, to cost more effectively.

- The lack of understanding about multimedia development leads to difficulties between the company and the client.

- Educating the client eases the difficulties. Successful development depends on a partnership in which each side contributes.

- Building in control mechanisms based on change management and sign-off points helps to achieve steady progress.

- Defining the responsibilities of work practice helps to achieve a smoother way of working together.

Recommended reading

Brooks F.P. Jr (1982). *The Mythical Man-Month. Essays on Software Engineering.* Reading, MA: Addison-Wesley

Humphrey W.S. (1990). *Managing the Software Process.* Reading, MA: Addison-Wesley

6

Agreeing the content

Project manager's responsibilities

- To ensure content integrity suitable for purpose and audience
- To establish time for market/content research, if necessary
- To influence the client's selection of content
- To guide the client on commenting on content
- To agree turn-around time and number of revision cycles
- To get sign-off on content scripts

The importance of content

It is a sad fact that there are many interactive products that leave both professionals and public wondering why they were developed. In Chapter 2 we saw that design quality is defined in terms of content and treatment, so if the programme causes a reaction of this type, the faults lie in the content, the treatment, or a combination of both.

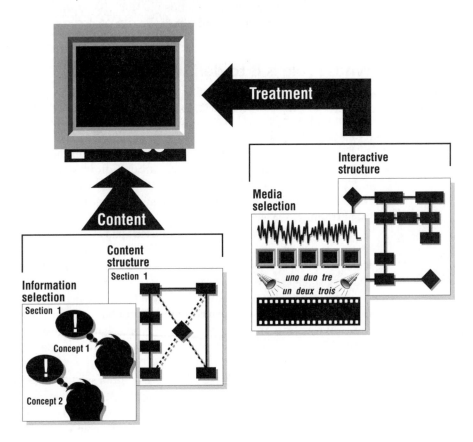

It is difficult to isolate content from its treatment, so we need to take the definitions further to help this process. Content means the messages or information contained in the product, and the way these are arranged. Treatment means the media, the techniques associated with the media, and the user interface that is chosen for the product. This is usually known as the **look and feel**. In some offline applications the treatment dominates because there is little or no content – games programs and some entertainment applications, for example, if they are activity or action based. This chapter does not apply to these kinds of application.

Despite its central role in most multimedia projects, the content is often neglected. More importance is given to the visual treatment than the messages – and since multimedia is about communication where exactly are we going wrong?

The quality of the content depends on a number of factors: the selection, breadth, depth, appropriateness for the audience, pace of delivery, and the sequence in which it is presented. The media techniques can only serve to help the content achieve its purpose better; they cannot make up for poor selection or lack of content integrity.

Whose role is it to define content?

In new media production there has been no specialist role devoted to defining the content of a project. In part this is because a lot of the content often came along with the brief.

The media industries, except graphics and computing, have evolved their own roles for defining content. The author, editor, scriptwriter and training analyst have fulfilled the function for print, video and training. Within these roles there have been further specialisms – comedy scriptwriting or management training, for example.

Graphics, whether video or print based, has always had a supportive role except in very specialist areas such as full film animation. As a result, graphics artists usually creatively interpret other people's scripts. They extend, shape and reshape the ideas, adding their dimension of visuals.

Computer programs often do not have the equivalent of scripts because the most widely used computer programs do not have content. The users provide their own scripts in word processing, spreadsheets, and presentation programs. The content has not been the important focus; the support structure and functionality have.

If computer programs have contained content – educational packages, and many entertainment programs, for example – then it has usually been determined by someone in the team who has taken on the role. However, as programs have become more complex and are designed for both experts and the general public, the 'help' content has expanded dramatically. It uses a variety of media to convey how to use the program. Technical writers have taken on the design of the electronic version as well as designing the paper manuals. Their skills have not often been used in new media applications yet, but this may change. The role of the Web editor is becoming established, particularly where a Web site is committed to daily updates, new stories and so on. The role is similar to that of a traditional editor because in many ways a Web site has much in common with traditional print-based media, especially magazines. This does not imply that the editor makes decisions on the structure of the Web site – although this may be a part of the role – but that the editor provides the content to drop into predefined sections. In offline applications, computer-based training (CBT) has come close to developing a recognizable role for definition of content and functionality in the person of the **interactive designer**.

The interactive designer works with the commissioner or nominated subject matter experts to define the scope of the content. He or she recommends an overall interactive structure for the main sections, and then works through each section defining the detailed content with its accompanying detailed interactivity.

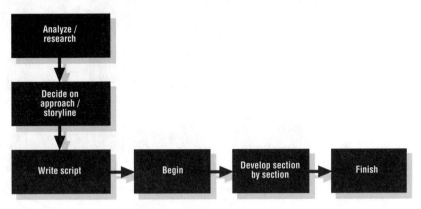

Scripting for linear media.

Perhaps the best way to describe the additional skills that are needed is to compare scripting for a linear media and for multiple media as the equivalent of working in one dimension or in 3-D. This is not meant to belittle the skills of working in one medium, which has its own complexities of selection, treatment and techniques, but rather to show the scope of the additional knowledge and skills needed. It is more like designing a relational database of knowledge on a subject suitable for different levels of ability and a range of audience profiles. (Compare this diagram with the next).

It is the appreciation of interactivity and how it affects content that is important, and is lacking in the traditional content definer's role. Competence in scripting in non-interactive media is a good base to start from, but it takes extra knowledge and skills to become a good interactive, all-media scriptwriter. In the past, multimedia scripting has relied on ad hoc solutions either from a person who has gradually acquired the skills through experience or from a team contribution from specialists of single media. There are courses now that are beginning to address interactive writing, and with the rapid progress of online materials plus the interest in interactive TV this role is beginning to get the recognition that has been denied until now.

The journalistic skills of a Web editor capitalize on skills used in print-based roles, but as more media become commonplace on sites the role will expand to cover the audio and video aspects of communication as well as print. The role will then need the wider skill set.

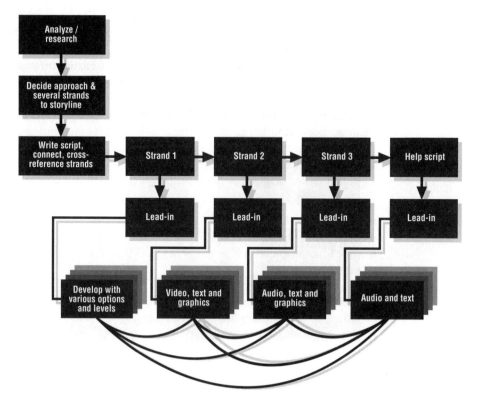

Scripting for multimedia.

Scripting for multimedia

The diagram demonstrates that scripting for multimedia needs a complete understanding of the component parts of the content, and the places where there may be occasion for the user to move sideways or diagonally through the content as well as up and down. It is also important to remember that an interactive viewer has control over the order in which the information is presented – there is no definite beginning, middle or end. Alternatively, the program might need to track what the user has done and tailor access to the rest of the information accordingly. The content is intertwined with media types and techniques because they affect each other, but the possible impact of media and techniques will be covered separately in Chapter 8.

The main sections of content in an application might involve the use of different media, and may well have had different people script them. This might mean that they have component integrity but not cross-component integrity. Another problem might be that each section has different weighting – one could be 2 minutes long, another 20 minutes long. Unless there is good reason, different treatment of the depth of the content risks leaving the user puzzled and dissatisfied.

The purpose of the communication affects the breadth and depth of the content. People absorb different types of information in different ways and for different reasons. It is no good people using a point of information tourist kiosk to find out the opening hours of a castle, for example, if they have to watch and listen to all the information on the castle before that information is given. This is acceptable for a television travel programme but not an interactive system. Interactivity is meant to enhance access to information, not hamper it. You may need to second-guess the user during the early design stages and, if you have the luxury, test your assumptions in user trials.

Multimedia scripting is complicated and demands a complex set of skills. These include:

- making decisions on what material is relevant,
- deciding which media would be right for the purpose,
- scripting various levels of materials in different media,
- providing the cohesion between the levels by providing navigation diagrams/flow charts,
- understanding the user and the implications of user choice on the structure of the material,
- being able to communicate with and instruct the programmer,
- keeping the vision of the whole while dissecting it into fragments,
- organizing the material into a detailed design document that the team can understand.

There are many ways of scripting projects, and it is beyond the scope of this book to cover the detail of how to script. The references at the end of the chapter will point you to several resources that do provide this. We are concerned here with identifying the driving background factors that affect content.

What affects content selection?

Influences on content: business and retail

From previous chapters we have seen that there are many factors that can affect the length of a programme and its media components. Most of these have been driven by business principles of scoping a solution according to time and cost. These undoubtedly constrain the amount of content and the way it might be presented. But the content still needs to have integrity and cohesion, whatever the length or treatment.

In Chapter 4, *The proposal*, the wishes of the client and their perception of the needs of the user were used to help make content decisions. Multimedia development is thought of as a service industry and is subject to the retail pressures of giving customer satisfaction and the retail premise that the customer is always right. Retail clients are, however, middlemen acting on behalf of the consumer, who is ultimately the customer for the product. The client should know more about the consumer's profile than the developer, so their perception can be useful. If the application is being developed for a retailer, their organization should have access to market research on their customers. Decisions on the content mix should reflect market trends and intelligence. Anyone making decisions on content for a retail product should try to tap into this research.

There's an obvious problem of the restriction of time between meeting with the client and completing a proposal. You should try to convince the client of the need to gather market intelligence to help with the decisions on the quality of the content and treatment that need to be settled in the proposal. If they don't grant this then you can only do what you can do in the time. Unfortunately clients will often think that the lack of knowledge at this point is due to your inadequacies rather than theirs. It should be their responsibility to state clearly what they want, and they should know what they are trying to achieve with the particular market and why.

Online customers/clients/users are a specialist section of a market by nature of their way of seeking information. Market sector research on online use will become increasingly important and will have a strong influence on what content is provided, its style, and its structure.

The client also has a responsibility for the level of quality in the programme, and if they choose to curtail quality of content selection because of time that is their prerogative and risk, but they need to recognize that this is what is happening. There are other occasions where the client dictates the content completely. They may insist on a body of content that is inappropriate for an interactive medium. They may insist that a large amount of information is covered when the user may be likely to spend relatively little time on the application. Content inadequacies are not always due to developers.

A few telephone interviews with relevant people from within and outside the organization may help to indicate trends in the customers' behaviour that can trigger thoughts about relevant content areas. Finding out what is irrelevant is equally useful because you can cut it out of the range. In the Brentfields Museum example (Chapter 4), the extra notes about the users' profile – age ranges, status, nationality – were gleaned from a two-minute conversation with the cloakroom attendant as the developer collected her coat and umbrella on the way out of the client meeting. The answer to the question 'What are the people like who come here then?' gave a short profile of potential users that should influence the content selection.

In the online example, Wrap-it, a few minutes spent checking on the range and type of enquiries that the receptionist or customer service desk gets might prove interesting. The answers might help to define categories of information that the Web site might cover initially until a profile of online use emerges.

Influences on content: training applications

The concern with cohesion and detail in training stems from the need to test the strength of the overall message and of each of its component concepts. It is likely that the users will be tested or have their performance evaluated after doing the programme and you can only test what has been taught. Care is taken in presentation of ideas to maximize comprehension and make tests fairer.

It becomes important to know the user's entry level of knowledge in the subject so that the interactive designer can make decisions on what to leave out as assumed prior knowledge. A thorough understanding of the audience is essential to keep the content relevant.

The structure of the content in this case is driven by theories of learning. The content needs to be assessed in terms of complexity, and the concepts need to be introduced in a sequence that aids retention. Reinforcement is important, as is the chance for the user to apply the knowledge in some way to make sure that it is retained in the longer term, not just stored temporarily in short-term memory.

The distinction of knowledge and skills is useful. Knowledge can be taught by sequential building of facts and concepts from easy to difficult, general to specific. Skills are acquired by the application of combined strands of knowledge to particular circumstances – knowledge in action, so to speak. Some techniques are better than others for demonstrating and explaining the different types, and these will be covered in Chapter 8, *Selecting the media and techniques*.

Lately, the emphasis on knowledge and skills has transferred to **competences**. This movement has taken place to help people achieve qualifications in the workplace. People naturally employ knowledge and skills to do their jobs. The definitions of the competence levels that are needed to do various jobs have been analyzed so that an employee can use examples of work and interpersonal skills to offer to an assessor to achieve a qualification.

This is a reversal of the ideas of traditional qualifications, where people are isolated to learn theoretical principles that are tested and then applied later. It is a recognition that application is the true test of worth and that many are already applying themselves in ways that demonstrate mastery of certain skills without traditional qualifications. The structure of the content of these qualifications depends much more on giving enough information for the learner to perform self-assessment of skill level and present themselves for independent assessment when they are ready.

The construction of educationally sound tests and assessments is complicated. The determination of the content and structure of tests has a wealth of professional experience in its own right. Because the content and assessment of a topic should be worked out simultaneously in a training or educational programme, it is important to have a training or educational professional involved when developing such a programme. A distance learning professional, instructional designer or interactive designer may well have a better appreciation of the interactive treatment of content and tests than a classroom professional in this case.

Limitations

Traditional learning theories do not link content to media use except to recognize that people learn in different ways so that using various alternatives will help. The areas that have tried to investigate which media is better than another for presenting information are **distance education** and **instructional design**. Instructional design has enjoyed more popularity in the USA than in Europe. Europeans often use the term **educational technology** rather than instructional design. These areas attempt to understand the way media stimulate reaction, and have value for interactive developers. The ideas behind instructional design and media will be covered in Chapter 8.

Although training and educational applications have principles that can be applied to guide content selection and structure, these principles do not transfer directly to other types of application. When the burden of proof for transfer of information is taken away there is more freedom. The principles of

- repetition,
- the use of remedial modules,
- ongoing checks for comprehension,
- setting up situations for the user to apply the knowledge,

do not have to be applied in non-training situations.

It should be evident that the content of training and education packages has recognized principles that should be applied to ensure content integrity for the purpose. Establishing content for other applications is not so clear cut, and there is the added difficulty that the strengths of interactivity are not currently understood in a consumer sense yet.

Yet unless content is taken more seriously, one part of the quality equation will continue to be neglected. Online training has its own considerations. There are many ways of structuring Web courses. Often the type of interaction online may be traditional distance media components: texts, videos or CDs mailed out to you, with the added bonus of emailing your tutor and contributing to discussion groups with other students on the course, for example. However, there are also complete Web-based courses constructed to be fully online where all content is transferred and tested via the Web or company intranet. In between, you can find all manner of combinations. The principles outlined above as considerations still apply, because they underpin all attempts to ensure transfer of knowledge and skills.

Theory into practice 6

Apply the content integrity test shown opposite to three new media products, both online and offline.

Content Integrity

Application/Site name _____

Online [ ]   Offline [ ]

Platform _____

Purpose of package   To inform [ ]
                       To entertain [ ]
                       To train [ ]
                       To educate [ ]
                       To sell [ ]

	Inappropriate			Appropriate	
	1	2	3	4	5
1. General coverage of subject matter	[ ]	[ ]	[ ]	[ ]	[ ]
2. Breadth	[ ]	[ ]	[ ]	[ ]	[ ]
3. Depth	[ ]	[ ]	[ ]	[ ]	[ ]
4. Suitability of content choice of major sections	[ ]	[ ]	[ ]	[ ]	[ ]
5. Suitability for audience	[ ]	[ ]	[ ]	[ ]	[ ]
6. Suitability for purpose	[ ]	[ ]	[ ]	[ ]	[ ]
7. Weighting for each section	[ ]	[ ]	[ ]	[ ]	[ ]
8. Access to information within sections	[ ]	[ ]	[ ]	[ ]	[ ]
9. Access to information across sections	[ ]	[ ]	[ ]	[ ]	[ ]

Training and education products only

By the end of the session:

	Yes	No	N/A
(a) Were you taught the necessary knowledge/skills?	[ ]	[ ]	[ ]
(b) Did you reach the required skill level?	[ ]	[ ]	[ ]
(c) Was there feedback to remedy poor performance?	[ ]	[ ]	[ ]
(d) Was the content offered in a variety of ways?	[ ]	[ ]	[ ]
(e) Was there extra information for remedial purposes?	[ ]	[ ]	[ ]
(f) Was there extra information for advanced learners?	[ ]	[ ]	[ ]
(g) Were there opportunities to apply the knowledge/skills?	[ ]	[ ]	[ ]
(h) Was the material motivating?			

All applications

	Yes	No
Would you recommend this application in terms of content integrity?	[ ]	[ ]

Why? _____

	Yes	No
Would you recommend this application overall – media, treatment, and so on?	[ ]	[ ]

Why? _____

How to get content agreed

There are stages of refinement in the production of content, and sign-off should follow these. The first stage is to agree the major sections or topics that will be addressed, and to indicate the volume of content for each section. This high-level agreement should set the scope and balance of the application. This usually happens at the proposal or outline agreement stages of the project, as explained in Chapter 5, *Contract issues 1*.

Some developers do not agree with this definition so early in the project. They say that the content evolves as the detail becomes clearer. This is true, but unless the client agrees to fund an analysis stage separately – which is common in training applications – there is a double dilemma: the developers have to quote a price for the project without creating some form of guidance for the price, and then the client is at liberty to change or add to the content specification.

The high-level agreement of topic names and volume does not mean that the content cannot be reshaped within the components, or that a topic cannot be scrapped and replaced with another, provided the changes are agreed and take place at a point in the project where the changes can be contained.

The developer is in the strongest position here, because many of the suggestions for changes from the development team are small but significant improvements – refinements rather than structural rework. Any experienced members of the team will share a common understanding of the shape of development and what can be suggested at which point to improve but not disrupt. Clients are not in this position and do not recognize which changes have structural implications and which do not, or why changes take on different significance depending on the point in the project development.

Stage 2 for content agreement occurs as each major section is drafted. Here there is another dilemma: the more clients see, the more they want to change or at least influence the development. There is also a strange but common reaction to make changes for the sake of change – perhaps to show that they have actually read the script!

New media scripting is not standardized. Some companies begin from a storyboard approach, emphasizing the visual and layout elements. Other companies use predominantly print to describe the content and interactive linking via a number system or other such denotation system. Both forms are professional forms of scripting, and often provoke the wrong responses from clients. The client may well end up focusing on details of the visual when they need to define the content. Or, with an interactive print script, they often get lost in the instructions, and may well end up rewording instructions to the programmer rather than editing the text relevant to the content. There are many ways to script, but it is wise to introduce your clients to your method and educate them in how to read and comment on scripts. The references at the end of the chapter cover techniques and specific ways of scripting. The subject is too large to cover here, as it needs a book in itself.

Another problem to watch out for is when clients rewrite scripts in an inappropriate way. With online text scripts they tend to want to put too much information in each section, and do not appreciate that the 'scan and dip' mentality of the Web affects the amount of information presented at any one time. Many people do not recognize how varied styles can be, or how the impact of the words is affected by this. The client may alter the tone or style so that it becomes inappropriate for the purpose. This is clearer when applied to other media scripts, as explained below, but the same is true for altering styles within text scripts.

With offline scripts, for example, the client might change short, informal audio scripts into formal speeches or text appropriate for business reports because they're used to that variety of English. Also, they are reading the script in a written form without projecting the script into its proper setting, and so they react to it as written English. If such changes were made, they would act as a good example of the style of English becoming inappropriate for its purpose. Its weighting would be affected as well, if the type of information was intended to motivate, not to inform.

You face the most difficult problems if the client does not approve the script. With offline they may react after the recording or video shoot has taken place, so control has to be established at script stage. You can take the risk of their not signing off, and minimize it by allowing only your one sign-off authority to make any comments or changes to the script. Do not allow your designated sign-off contact to hand it out to others as this starts a paper-chase reaction with people disagreeing with colleagues' suggestions as well as the original! This takes weeks to sort out for each piece of script, and involves rewrite after rewrite, because once people have been involved they want to stay involved. This is more characteristic of large corporate projects than others. This is why it is important to get as high a sign-off as possible from the client organization because others will tend not to disagree with the authority figure.

In a business application the sign-off authority may well insist on delegating someone with more expertise in the area to agree the script. This is fine as long as you get it in writing that this delegate has absolute authority in this case and that the main sign-off authority will not countermand any of the delegate's decisions. This might sound harsh, but once you have been involved in a script paper-chase, whether for on- or offline projects, you'll try anything to avoid it again. It is one of the major causes of slippage in projects, and one that is unstoppable once it is in motion.

A useful tip for audio and video is to keep the client away from scripts but do mock voice-over tapes without professional artistes. This helps to set the style and setting better for the client. It adds an interim stage but allows changes without too much time and expense.

Lastly, you can educate again. If there is a standard way of scripting for projects in house, you could arrange for a previous application demonstration with accompanying pieces of script. Then you could talk the client through the process of matching the paper to screens. This can prepare them for meeting their own paper script and attune them to what the different pieces mean, who they are aimed at in the team, and what their role is. Online projects are easier than offline in this respect because it is so much easier to make changes to text within Web sites.

You need to ensure that the client understands how many revisions they are allowed per script. Otherwise you can find that instead of the changes becoming fewer as revisions go on, they become more. This happens when the client gives more time to their script reading as the point of no return approaches. They need to understand that their time investment should actually diminish as the scripts progress, and that they should merely check that their requests have been complied with, not begin to read the whole script again. The project manager can influence clients by explaining how many revisions are allowed – dependent on the time available – and that the first reading should be the most thorough to set the conditions for changes that diminish through the revision cycle.

General principles for establishing content

- Irrespective of the project being on- or offline, the purpose drives the selection of content, whether in terms of education, information or entertainment.
- The age range of the intended audience can influence content selection.
- Market trends can influence content selection.
- If you are doing a project for a corporate, the company's culture can affect content selection. Sometimes the developer, despite trying, cannot influence this in order to achieve the best result.
- The purpose of the project will indicate the length of time the user is likely to spend on the system, and this determines the depth and breadth that the content needs to have.
- The length of the sections of the application and therefore the depth and breadth of the content should take access and attention span into consideration. This is particularly important in online, point-of-information and kiosk applications.
- Content that dates quickly should be avoided, or put in a format that is easily updatable, unless the client accepts the consequences.

Summary

- Content = the messages or information in the package.

  Treatment = the media selected, media techniques employed, and the interface.

- The quality of content = the selection, breadth, depth, appropriateness, pace and sequence of presentation.

- There is confusion over whose role it is to define content, content quality and integrity.

- Scripting for new media needs complex skills: the more media elements are used the more complex it becomes.

- The purpose of the project and the business sector it is being developed for influence content selection. The client may provide or influence the content.

- Get sign-off agreement to the content stage by stage.

- Control the sign-off process carefully – it is a high-risk area for project management.

Recommended reading

Boyle T. (1997). *Design for Multimedia Learning*. Englewood Cliffs, NJ: Prentice-Hall

Bonime A. and Pohlmana K.C. (1997). *Writing for New Media: The Essential Guide for Writing for Interactive Media, CD-ROMS and the Web*. New York: John Wiley & Sons.

Collis B. (1996). *Tele-learning in a Digital World: The Future of Distance Learning*. London: International Thomson Computer

Duffy T.M. and Jonassen D.H. (1992). *Constructivism and the Technology of Instruction: A Conversation*. Hillsdale, NJ: Lawrence Erlbaum Associates Inc.

Ellis J. (1992). *Visible Fictions. Cinema: Television: Video*. London: Routledge & Kegan Paul

Gagné R.M., Briggs L.J. and Wagner W.W. (1992). *Principles of Instructional Design*, 4th edn. Orlando, FL: Harcourt Brace Jovanovich

Garrond T. (1996). *Writing for Multimedia: Entertainment, Education, Training, Advertising and the World Wide Web*. Boston: Focal Press (This has script examples)

Korolenko M. (1997) *Writing for Multimedia: A Guide and Sourcebook for the Digital Writer*. Belmont, CA: Integrated Media Group

Naidu S. (1994). Applying learning and instructional strategies in open and distance learning. *Distance Education*, **15** (1), 23–41

7

Choosing the platform

Project manager's responsibilities

- To discuss the chosen delivery and development environment with the client and advise on the best choice for the particular application
- To similarly advise on delivery medium
- To understand the implications of platform choice

Introduction

The word 'platform' was traditionally associated with hardware: the computer platform. But a platform can also describe software as well as hardware, and it is increasingly used in this way. For an offline application this might mean the operating system, such as Windows NT, while for an online project it is more likely to refer to the browser, such as Netscape Navigator or Internet Explorer. A useful definition might be that the platform is whatever you have to specify in order to run the application. Often the specification will be extended to say what kind of display is needed, or how big a hard disk, or how fast an Internet connection. This chapter will use the word 'platform' in this broad sense.

There are three options that will be discussed in relation to platforms. The first is the most obvious, and is the delivery platform: what does your user have to use in order to see your application (or Web site)? Then we come to the delivery medium: how do you get the application to the user? Finally we shall discuss the development and testing platform: what do you need to use in order to make the application in the first place?

Delivery platforms

Sometimes a client will come to you with a project and they will know exactly what platform they want to use. This may be because they use a certain machine or browser in their business, or because the target market for the application has mostly machines of a particular type. Sometimes they will be a little more vague, and often they will ask for your advice. This chapter will not offer any advice for your particular project but it will help you to ask the right questions about the requirements, and to work out how to identify the positive and negative factors influencing the choice.

Delivery on the World Wide Web usually side-steps many issues of the delivery platform because Web browsers all take the HTML (and more) that makes up a Web page and display it on the user's computer. The Web is the multimedia delivery system that works on most computers because the browser takes care of the underlying operating system and hardware. It is an example of document-based programming, because the Web page is a document made to certain standards, which is displayed by any browser that adheres to those standards. For this reason we shall consider online mostly as a delivery medium rather than a delivery platform, so the next few sections relate more generally to offline than to online projects.

Computers and operating systems

As we have said, a platform is not just the microprocessor or operating system. For a mathematical calculation program it may be sufficient to name the operating system, but for multimedia there are issues of screen resolutions and bit depth, sound parameters, the speed of the CD-ROM drive, the way that video is handled, the amount of RAM and the size of the hard disk . . . at least. There may be issues of whether the system is capable of multitasking (doing more than one thing at once) and whether you should take account of that.

In an ideal world every computer program would run on every kind of computer hardware. However, there are serious differences even between the way the basic microprocessors work, let alone differences between operating systems. Fortunately there are also similarities.

The 'standard' computer for many years has been the PC. Although 'personal computer' is a generic term, the initials PC have come to refer to so-called IBM compatibles and clones, based on the Intel microprocessor family. This processor family, in conjunction with a disk operating system produced by Microsoft called DOS (for Disk Operating System), defined the basic platform. The kind of screen available has been the subject of separate 'standardization' starting with screens designed for use with American television sets. Ironically, a screen resolution of 640 by 480 pixels (this is the active size of an NTSC television picture, of which more is said in Chapter 14) used to be one of the most standard things about computing systems, although this is now changing as higher screen resolutions become commonplace.

PCs are made by a large number of companies, and it is this range of competing manufacturers that has led to the PC's becoming so inexpensive and widespread. Only UNIX is as successful, but it remains successful in a niche in education, science and technology rather than on the business desktop. In multimedia, UNIX has most impact in Web servers because many of the machines that run servers on wide area networks run UNIX, and if you are producing CGI (Common Gateway Interface) programs for Web sites, then you might come across UNIX.

With the introduction of Microsoft's Windows the PC found itself a more friendly face, and Windows itself became the defining factor for the platform, which was vital, as the underlying microprocessors became more powerful and part of the Multimedia PC (MPC) standard.

Competition for Windows came from the Apple Macintosh, which had adopted a friendly windows (with a small w) approach from its inception. Only programmers drove a Mac from a command line; the users moved a pointer about and pressed virtual buttons on the screen. In some other niche areas there were companies such as Commodore (with the Amiga) and Acorn (whose Archimedes machine is firmly lodged in British education, but boasted the most bangs for the buck of any desktop machine of its day and was the world's first RISC workstation).

Besides general-purpose computers there were games machines (from the likes of Sega, Nintendo, and Sony), short-lived home entertainment machines like CD-TV, 3-DO and CD-i, and (somewhat more in the future) set-top boxes for video-on-demand, Web-television and interactive television. As a multimedia developer your choice of platforms encompasses these and more.

Criteria for choice

It would be nice to be able to say that, as a multimedia developer, you have the freedom to choose the platform best suited to deliver your multimedia vision. In fact the market is more likely to drive your choice, and often that points to whichever machine is prevalent in your target sector. Businesses have business machines, often not suited to entertainment techniques even if those techniques are appropriate.

You will have to research your sector and find a lowest common denominator for the machinery your customers have. This relates to factors such as:

- manufacturer and machine type;
- type and speed of processor (and therefore performance);
- amount of memory (RAM);

- size of hard disk (speed is less important but should not be forgotten);
- operating system (don't forget which version);
- CD-ROM/DVD-ROM drive (speed and, in future, capacity);
- access to online systems (local networks, Internet, World Wide Web, and so on);
- speed of network connection;
- resolution of the screen;
- number of colours on the screen;
- ability to handle moving video, and the multimedia architecture;
- sound handling (8- or 16-bit, mono or stereo, what compression?).

In some cases you may need to find out how often your users actually make use of their machine. This could be especially true in a business or training situation, where machines may be shared between people. It would be awkward for your users to spend half a day using your training package if someone else needed to use it every two hours to read the electronic mail.

Cross-platform chameleons

An alternative to choosing a single platform for an offline project is to produce the application for a number of platforms. This can be done by using an authoring system that produces versions of the application for several platforms. Macromedia Director is such a package, which will produce files that will run on Windows and on Apple from the same 'source'. At a lower level, there are libraries for graphical user interfaces, which can be used with C or C++ to run on different platforms with separate compilation.

It is possible for one computer platform to emulate another. A fast processor can run a program that appears, to the application, to be another platform entirely. The more powerful the platform, the more easily it can do this. There are Mac emulators for the Sun and Windows emulators for the Mac, where one machine pretends to be the other. It can even be possible (if rather strange) to run a program under emulation where the emulator is itself running under emulation.

A further refinement of this technique is the **virtual machine**. Here the application code runs in a specified environment. That environment is provided by a program, the virtual machine, that itself runs on the host machine. To run the application on a new platform you need only a new virtual machine. The ancestor of C, BCPL, ran in this way, and used a compiled intermediate code (called CINT code), which then ran on the virtual machine. This technique has a new lease of life through Java.

This technique needs fast processors, otherwise it is best suited to low-interactivity applications. This is because interpreted software (interpreted by the virtual machine) runs more slowly than software compiled to run directly on the target machine. There is also the problem of the abilities and drawbacks of particular machines. A virtual machine has to have an audiovisual capability (since it is, to all intents and purposes, a platform in itself), and this will be the same as or less than the capabilities of its host.

If there is an incompatibility between the different platforms that can run the software then the software might have to run differently. A lesser platform may run the software in a less than optimum way. The way that the application (and possibly the virtual machine if there is one) copes with this is by degrading the performance of the application. Pictures may have fewer colours; movies may run more sluggishly. If this is done well, and possibly even invisibly to the user, it is called **graceful degradation**. Graceful degradation is inherent in the Web, and is relatively easily achieved by providing versions of Web pages for browsers with or without frames, with or without plug-ins, and so on. You add plug-ins, Javascript or Java if you think that your Web pages need them and your viewers have the motivation, but you can be sure they will see something even without them. Offline multimedia has no such guarantee, and graceful degradation has to be programmed specifically rather than assumed.

A classic example of graceful degradation is illustrated in basic HTML. The browsers that display HTML documents have differing abilities, and it is recommended that any graphics used in documents are supplemented by words that will be displayed on browsers that cannot display pictures: although these are rare they are still around. In this way the document display

Graceful degradation.

gracefully degrades from graphics down to text only. If you are designing multimedia applications that will run on networks you might have to account for extreme cases like this. Refer to the CD for an example of HTML document design for different browser capabilities.

Delivery medium

We have already defined the delivery medium as the means by which you get your application to the user. If it is a Web page then the World Wide Web is that medium, and we shall come to that in a moment. Let's start by considering offline delivery.

Besides deciding on what computer platform the end-user will actually view and use your production, there is the question of how you will actually distribute the end result. To a certain extent this will depend on the size of the application, and might even have been specified up front. It is not unknown for small multimedia presentations to be delivered on floppy disks, with a little help from compression.

Here are some of the options.

Floppy disk

Using a floppy has the advantage of using a standard medium, as you can assume your potential market has a floppy disk drive. However, the downsides are the capacity (1.4 megabytes is still the most common), the slow access times, and the relative difficulty of replicating in large numbers. Compressing the material on the disk means that it has to be decompressed onto the user's hard disk to run, but this also overcomes the slow speed of the floppy. It is, however, very easy to copy floppies to order if the quantities are small enough.

Compact disc and DVD

This medium has become so universal that it seems unlikely that it may ever lose its supremacy as a carrier. Currently it is splitting into an increasing number of different incarnations (Video CD, multi-session, CD-Plus, Photo-CD and the various formats of DVD). Back in 1984, when CD-ROM first appeared, it was touted as the data carrier to exceed all our requirements; but that was before digital video. DVD is a higher-density format for CDs; it makes use of a smaller physical structure on the disc and more layers of data to increase capacity, but otherwise it is just a 'turbocharged' CD. Replication in quantities is very cheap (almost down to pennies), and the discs are very robust.

Conventional CDs (as distinct from DVDs) adhere to a group of standards called the **coloured books**. The original one is the Red Book, which defines the physical disc and the original CD for digital audio. The Yellow Book defines CD-ROM, and has an extension for CD-ROM XA (Extended

Architecture), which provided a bridge across to CD-i (defined in the Green Book). The Orange Book defines magneto-optical discs such as the Mini-Disk, and the format for writeable CDs. This writeable format also recognized that such a disc could be written in several sessions rather than all at once – hence the multi-session disc. The White Book specifies the Video-CD using MPEG digital video with the option of simple interactivity. The Blue Book defines a multimedia extension to audio CDs known as CD+ or Extended CD. Refer to the CD for information on how these coloured books relate to each other.

A related standard is **ISO 9660**, which specifies file structures. It is based on DOS but has extensions to cover other filing systems. Importantly, an ISO 9660 CD-ROM can be read on a large number of computers. This means that the computers can access the data on the CD: they cannot necessarily do anything with that data unless they have the appropriate application. DVD-ROM uses a system called **universal disk format** (UDF) to give multi-platform compatability in the same way.

DVD discs are still, at the time of writing, in their infancy, but the video versions of their discs, and presumably the CD-ROM equivalents, will have either one or two sides and each side will have either one or two layers. A disc side can have two layers because the laser beam that reads the data on the disc can be focused at different depths in the transparent surface of the disc and so read two different layers. It is theoretically possible to produce a disc that has a CD-ROM upper layer with a DVD-ROM lower layer and so is backwards compatible. The variants of DVD are numbered after their approximate capacity in gigabytes: so we have DVD-5 with one side and one layer, DVD-9 with one side and two layers, DVD-10 with two sides and one layer, and DVD-18 with two sides and two layers. Each layer has a capacity of 4.7 gigabytes.

Disk-based multimedia has been overshadowed by online systems in recent years. In future we have the influence of DVD and interactive broadcasting and cable to consider, and this makes it uncertain as to what delivery platform will dominate. In practice it is likely that evolution will find favour over revolution, and on- and offline systems will coexist. DVD-ROM will evolve from CD-ROM, and broadcasting and the Internet will find that they have much in common. Added to this are mobile offline systems. Within the individual formats there will be evolutionary developments, just as CD-ROM drives became faster and faster.

Online delivery

The philosophy behind providing multimedia applications online is somewhat different from that for offline ones. There are four main issues: speed of access, updating, security/payment, and the 'unlimited' size of the data space that can be provided online. You can restrict access, charge your users for access, and even keep track of who has accessed your information and when. Some of these techniques have spread themselves to CD-ROM, with software and fonts being sold by giving away encrypted versions and then charging for decryption.

The speed with which your potential users can access your application is unpredictable. If you find yourself frustrated by the access times of a compact disc then the access speed of the Internet will frustrate you further. Unfortunately, speeding up the local link between the user and the network will not necessarily resolve the problem, because other links in the system will in themselves be unpredictable, with speeds depending on the bandwidth of the link itself (colloquially 'how fat is the pipe') and on how much other traffic there is on it. Also, the fatter the pipes become, the more data people want to pass down them.

On the Web, problems of download times for audio and video have been addressed by **streaming** the data for audio and video rather than copying it and playing it later. Streaming is the method whereby a steady stream of data is expected from the data source, and it is processed and displayed as it arrives (on the fly). The classic example of this is digital audio from a compact disc. The 16-bit digital audio data arrives at the decoder chips and is converted into analogue audio immediately. There is no storage of the data. If for some reason the stream of data is disturbed then you hear either clicks, where a single sample is misplaced, or pauses and hiccuping.

A way around this problem is buffering and/or caching. For **buffering**, the data from the source is read into memory at the rate at which it arrives, and is read out of memory at the rate at which it is needed. In this way small discontinuities can be removed. With a **cache** the data is read completely into the cache memory and, once it has all arrived, the application accesses it. The disadvantage of a cache is that the application has to wait for all the data to arrive, although once the data is in the cache it can be accessed many times. The program can be designed to allow the data to be both streamed and cached, of course, but that is practical only if the data stream is fast enough.

In general, the use of a network implies that people other than your intended user can access the data. If this is a concern then security systems have to be built in, ranging from password protection and access from selected terminals only to full encryption. In a networked environment it is possible to log the amount of data that a user accesses, whether the data is stock market prices or clips of video. If necessary, the user can be charged accordingly, and any royalties required by the data owner can be paid from that money.

A final benefit of the network is the huge data space that can potentially be presented to the user. The 650 megabytes of a Yellow Book CD-ROM and even the gigabytes of DVD are not a limiting factor. The likely size of your Web site is a crucial factor in one part of your choices over its platform. Web sites that consist of static pages, handwritten in HTML and updated occasionally by rewriting, will usually consist of a few dozen pages at most. Admittedly, sites can grow over time with new static pages being added, so this is not a hard and fast rule. A large static site can be difficult to maintain; in any case, you can reach a point where it is impractical to hard code all your pages and your HTML will no longer be handwritten but will be generated on demand – dynamically – by programs running on the server. In an extreme case, a very large site will be generated from a database. We shall come back to this issue in a moment.

Video on demand (VOD) may provide another market for interactive services, and if so it will provide a potential market for multimedia developers. At the time of writing VOD has gone into a limbo after the heady days of the initial user trials, and some observers say that the economics of it will preclude VOD's ever becoming commercially viable. That aside, the way in which VOD develops as a platform will depend on which of the two proposed models for it is used and where. You can say that in one model the VOD server pushes the application for display in the home on a television linked to the service by a **set-top box**. In the other model the set-top box itself pulls the application from the server.

The 'push' model works like this: the set-top box functions as an audiovisual version of the dumb terminal and basically passes user commands down the line to the server, takes the data the server sends, and displays it. This means that the application itself, usually something to run a movie, is actually being run in the server and not in the set-top box. This can be a crucial situation for the developer because the servers are often going to be very powerful processors running real-time operating systems totally unlike those you would usually find in multimedia. This is unless the servers are set up to run virtual machines that emulate other platforms. Since the set-top boxes are operating only as dumb terminals, including MPEG decoders, there is relatively free reign for potential manufacturers as only the display and communications need to be standardized, not the application environment because that is in the server.

The 'pull' model has the server operating as a data source, whether for downloaded data or for streamed data, and the downloaded application runs in the set-top box, which therefore has to be more than a dumb terminal. This raises a different problem both for the developer of applications and for the service provider. Since the set-top boxes are likely to be from more than one manufacturer, compatability between the boxes and the applications is in question. In practice this can be overcome by offering only applications that the server knows the set-top box can support or that the set-top box itself knows it can support.

Hybrid delivery

Sometimes you can make use of both on- and offline delivery. The two classic examples of this, using the World Wide Web, are to have a CD-ROM that is updated from a Web site, and splitting your data between the CD and Web depending on how big it is.

Updating a CD from the Web allows a publisher to keep a product up to date between editions. Many CD-ROM encyclopedias do this. Sometimes the application will update the CD-ROM data so that the updates are seamless; sometimes the application displays the new data in its own right as an addendum. This kind of application becomes less necessary as more users of the application are able to read all the data from the Internet.

Splitting data provides a good way of holding big assets such as movies but also allowing volatile information to be available from the Web site. This is easily achieved because Web browsers will happily read files from hard disks or CD-ROM as long as the Web pages are written with relative file paths or addresses. If you study the file structure of the Web pages on the CD-ROM with this book you will see that it is arranged this way, and it accesses the book's Web site from a link on the home page.

Web sites and server/browser balance

On a network, where there is software running on the user's local computer (the client) and it is working closely with software running on a server, the platform issues can become more complex. For the purposes of our discussion here we shall be dealing only with the Web, but sometimes similar issues can develop in any client/server application.

There are four software components in the Web page chain: the page itself, the browser, the gateway software (CGI), and the server. The Web page runs on the browser, and the CGIs run on the server. HTML, Java, JavaScript and plug-ins are part of the page/browser combination.

When a Web page is requested by a browser a set of http (hypertext transfer protocol) requests are sent to the server. Each request is totally independent of any other and, besides the information about the requested page or asset, the browser will pass information to the server telling it such things as the type of browser and platform, the referring page (where you clicked), the network address of the browser's machine, and possibly a string called the environment variable, which is passed to a CGI program.

Sometimes you will need to decide whether a particular task is best handled by HTML or a server program. On the author's infrared photography site, Invisible Light at http://www.atsf.co.uk/ilight, there are a number of photographs that are displayed in individual Web pages. When a viewer clicks on a link to display one of these pages a CGI program (written in Perl) is executed, which takes as its input the picture name that is passed in the http request as a parameter. You will see that the URL requested has the extension .pl at the end rather than .html. In this way there is no need to have a separate HTML document for each page: the page is generated by the Perl script on demand. So the gateway program removes the need to have a lot of HTML documents on the site, and this is the essence of dynamic Web design. As has already been mentioned, a very large site with hundreds of pages or more will almost certainly have to be generated by a database in order to be maintained and updated – in other words, dynamic.

You should not confuse the size of the design task with the number of pages on a Web site. Database-driven Web sites may have hundreds of pages, but those pages will have a small number of different layout templates into which the database 'pours' the content. For example, the author maintains a casting directory on the Internet for the UK company The Spotlight (the CD-ROM version is illustrated in the colour section). Although there are over

20 000 possible pages available – one for each actor – there are actually only four different Web page layouts used: one for the home page, one for the search card, one for the list of hits from a search, and one for the individual actor's information and photograph. A relational database generates all the pages except the home page based on HTML templates.

Another decision is whether a particular task can be carried out at the client side or the server side. For example, if you want to modify the Web page according to the browser being used you can do this either by using JavaScript (for example, and if the browser supports it) or by using a CGI program. The advantage of JavaScript is that the load on the server is lighter, but the disadvantage is that the HTML is larger because of the JavaScript embedded in it. The advantage of CGI is that some browsers do not run JavaScript, and so the solution is more reliable. However, running a lot of CGI programs can be a problem if the site is heavily visited.

Sometimes the choice is made for you. If you want the Web page to reflect the time of day where the user is situated – remember they could be anywhere in the world – then only the browser knows this, and so client-side is your only option. Conversely, if you want to show visitors what number visitor they are then this has to be done at the server because only the server can keep a count of all visitors. There are also many Web surfers who do not enable JavaScript or Java, or who are prohibited from using them on a business network.

CGI programs can be written in any language that runs on the server, and databases are a common form of CGI. In practice, server owners may restrict you to using interpreted languages such as Perl rather than running compiled C code because this dramatically reduces the risk of accidental damage to the server.

Platforms for development and testing

So far, this chapter has dealt with the delivery of your application to the end-user: your customer. You will also be making choices about the platform or platforms you use to design and build your application or your Web pages and to test it.

You do not have to develop your application on the delivery platform. This is especially true for a cross-platform offline application, since the usual practice would be to develop the application on one of the group of delivery platforms and test it on them all. Even low-level code can be produced on a different computer using a cross-compiler.

It is more likely that you will use one consistent platform for your asset creation and manipulation for every application. Even though the IBM PC 'standard' has been the most common delivery platform for multimedia, many multimedia developers have used Apple Macintoshes for their asset work and have moved the assets across to their delivery platform during integration. The reason for this approach is that the best tools tended to appear first on the Macintosh and that, for the graphically minded, the Mac was already the platform of choice.

Moving assets between platforms needs to be done with some care and attention to quality and parameters. Even though PCs and Macs both have a 'standard' audio sample rate of 22 kHz the actual sampling rates are very slightly different at 22.254 and 22.050 kHz. The screen gamma is different as well: the same image looks lighter on a Mac than on a PC. This and other asset formats will need to be checked and tested on both platforms. If you are producing an application for more than one platform, especially if you store your assets in a single common format, this will be even more important.

In fact it does not matter whether you are a Mac fan or a PC fan or whatever. The point is that you can retain your platform of choice for asset creation and manipulation even if your client or market wants a particular application delivered on something else. The only limiting factor is that the asset creation platform must have a display that matches or exceeds that of the delivery platform. It is clearly no use whatsoever to try to do colour graphics on a black and white machine, or to use an 8-bit system to produce sound for a system with CD quality 16-bit sound.

Similarly, you should create and manipulate your assets in the highest convenient standard and convert down, if necessary, at the last moment. This will not only give you the option of porting the assets to other delivery platforms if required, but will actually help you to keep the quality as high as possible.

For online authoring you can use almost any computer since an HTML page is simply a text file. But just as any browser should be able to read the Web pages, so you have a choice of the ways you author them. Some people like to handcraft the HTML in a word processor, while others use one or more of the many WYSIWYG packages for Web page layout. The production of Web page assets is very much like offline work. The same packages can be used to produce the images, sounds and movies, and even animations and interactive mini-applications. Again, you can choose to produce your HTML and assets on whatever platform you can use.

It is certainly true that your design platforms have to include your delivery platform so that you can, at the very least, test the performance and carry out debugging. This can mean that you have to have access to every possible configuration of platform that your customers will have. This is no trivial task. With a Web site you can test with a package like WebLint to make sure that your HTML is correct, but you should also look at the pages on as many combinations of browser and computer as you can.

With an offline application the problem can be significantly worse because you are likely to make more direct use of the computer's facilities. To show the magnitude of this problem, let's consider variations of a computer:

- different models
- different amounts of RAM
- different screens and numbers of screens
- different sizes of hard disk
- common extensions to the basic system
- different versions of the system software
- different CD-ROM drives
- different network configurations.

With that list, and assuming five possible options for each category, the number of possible configurations is $5 \times 5 \times 5 \times 5 \times 5 \times 5 \times 5 \times 5$, which is 390 625. This is not really practical, and you will test for the most likely problem areas such as system software versions and amounts of RAM.

Theory into practice 7

Experience is the best teacher on moving applications from one delivery platform to another. You can learn a lot by talking to people you know who have direct experience of this and by discussing the detailed problems they may have encountered.

For offline, look at a multimedia application that is available on more than one platform and compare the versions.

For online, set up as many computer/browser configurations as you can and look at some Web sites with them to compare the results. If you have PCs, Macs and Web-capable televisions you should also compare the brightness of the screen images.

Summary

- The choice of delivery platform will usually be decided by either your client or your target market.

- You do not have to do all your development on the delivery platform, especially when it comes to working with your assets.

- It is possible to develop an application that will work on more than one platform, but moving from one platform to another can lead to changes in performance, and you should be aware of what is likely to happen.

- When planning Web gateway programs you should consider the balance between the browser and the server.

Recommended reading

December J., Ginsburg M. et al. (1995). *HTML and CGI Unleashed*. Indianapolis IN: Sams.net Publishing
Siegel D. (1997). *Creating Killer Web Sites*, 2nd edn. Indianapolis IN: Hayden Books
Vaughan T. (1994). *Multimedia: Making it Work*. Berkeley CA: Osborne McGraw-Hill

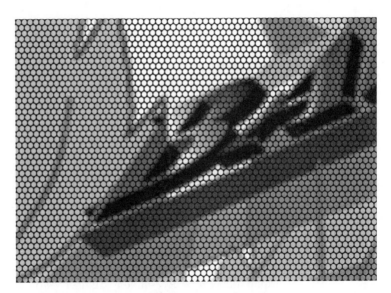

8

Selecting the media and techniques: the treatment

Project manager's responsibilities

- To define the project constraints that affect the use of media and techniques
- To understand the strengths and weaknesses of each medium
- To involve experts from each medium for the detailed treatments, if possible
- To keep the focus on interactive use of media and the needs of the user
- To keep abreast of research because this area has few guidelines to date

Constraints

Online or offline platform

It may seem to be counter-intuitive and negative to start from the constraints that affect the development team, but in reality this is usually what happens. For online projects you need to understand what specification of machine the users are likely to have and perhaps more importantly which browsers they have or want to work with, and start from there. With intranets and extranets you will be able to get a fair idea of the machine's capabilities from the client. Someone in the organization – usually the IT department – will have a profile of capabilities within the company. If they do not, you'll have to balance the time to find out against a good guess based on what information the company can provide you with. You are trying to understand what media components will be accessible to all users and design the site accordingly. It is no good producing a high-end Java-based Web site with RealAudio, for example, if no one can access it.

Make it part of your task to get sign-off for the base range of machine and browser capabilities you will design for, as this will pay dividends later when complaints start coming in. For example, you might be told about hundreds of people not being able to read the new corporate mission statement from the CEO as the text disappears on the right-hand side on the intranet. Your client might have insisted on a graphics banner at the top of the page that suited a 17 inch screen despite your best endeavours to persuade them to design for 14 inch. So their wishes overrode your experience, and the result appears to be bad design.

If you are designing a general Web site, you need to make your decisions based on the type of information you are trying to convey, the purpose of the information, the image your client wants to project, and the profile of the users. Added to this, you need to keep in mind the market information about the best fit of target machines, browser use, and your audience.

For offline projects, if a client specifies a platform you need to find out as much as you can about it quickly, because many organizations will customize standard computer set-ups. This will affect your decisions about what is possible, what is likely, and what is impractical, because of the platform's capabilities and limitations. This is especially true for the range and technical quality of the media components that it is able to support.

If the platform is already in place – perhaps in hundreds of installations – then you may find that you have no leeway and will have to work with the hardware provided. This could be equipment that is several years old. As technology advances quickly, this can mean that the team has to work to a much lower specification than they would like. With this situation, if there is a possibility that the client would upgrade their systems to allow better use, the arguments need to be made early for them to find the extra budget. They need to understand the factors that have driven the decisions for your solutions so that they recognize the constraints their systems might be imposing and the benefits that a better system would bring.

For both types of project (online and offline), if you demonstrate examples of previous work to a client you should exercise care. If there are features and quality levels that are not possible for them to have with their online connections or their offline equipment, this needs to be made very clear indeed. It is difficult for anyone, let alone the client, to see some stimulating demonstrations that imprint themselves on the memory while listening to passing remarks about why some of these features will not be possible. They will often hark back to these features later and comment on the difference in quality that they are getting. They will have forgotten that it is the constraints you have identified that cause the restrictions.

Another problem occurs if clients see or read about the latest developments in technology and expect to be able to have them when you are already halfway into the project. Clear, straight talking backed up with written records is the only way to cope with the change in expectations as clients become more versed in multimedia and its possibilities. This change is healthy for the next project because specifications will be clearer, cleaner and faster.

It is more useful if you can show a client examples of the range and type of features that their particular circumstances can handle.

Budget

Online projects

The more media you use, the more production costs increase. Your client may want a full range of audio, video and graphics, but expect not to pay a lot more for the higher production values. One of the problems of online productions is that clients expect production to be fast and cheap. They are fooled into equating ease of access with ease of production. If this is the case then an explanation of the production processes and relative costs of a few minutes of audio, video and a range of graphics from animation to stills will be invaluable to shape the client's expectations. See Table 8.1.

Offline projects

The biggest constraint on the selection of media and techniques is the budget. Many clients do not have systems already in place so the outlay for both the platform and the application is expensive. Many projects of this nature are pilot projects, and so clients want them done cheaply even though their purpose is important. Pilots are used to impress the organization to move towards using multimedia. The purpose and budget do not match well, so you have to work hard to compensate.

Resources

Within each kind of medium there are a range of possibilities that affect the cost. You therefore need to decide the best for the purpose, platform, price

Table 8.1 Media components.

Component	Type (Q = quality)	Cost	Production time	Notes
Video	Drama	High	Long	Rights and clearances
	Interviews	Low to medium	Short to medium	can be costly and
	Location 'documentary'	Low to medium	Medium	time consuming
Audio	Drama	Medium	Long	Good voice-over
	Interviews	Low	Short	narrators and actors for
	Narration	Low	Short	drama can be expensive
	Music	Low to medium	Can be off the shelf	
Video graphics	3-D animation (Hi-Q)	High	Short to medium	Treat as video when
(graphics as found	Animation (Hi-Q)	High	Short to medium	transferring to computer.
in video facilities)	Sophisticated tricks (Hi-Q)	High	Short	Usually transferred in the
	Static graphics (Hi-Q)	High	Short	same facility
Computer graphics	3-D animation (Hi-Q)	High	Long	Production time longer
	3-D animation (Med-Q)	Medium	Long	than video graphics but
	3-D animation (Low-Q)	Medium	Long	usually better value for
	Static graphics (Hi-Q)	Low to medium	Medium	large number of graphics
	Static graphics (Med-Q)	Low to medium	Short	
	Static graphics (Low-Q)	Low	Short	
Photographs	Film-based	Low to medium	Short to medium	Wide choice of libraries
	Digital	Low to medium	Short	at varying costs. Do-it-
	Library	Low to medium	Can be off the shelf	yourself an option
Text		Low	Fast	Can sometimes be costly
				if licensed or needing
				special fonts (in offline)
Translations	Video soundtrack (timed)	Medium	Medium	Check results with
	Narration (timed)	Medium	Medium	subject expert if
	Narration (not timed)	Medium	Short to medium	possible. Remember
	Text (constrained to space)	Medium	Short to medium	different languages
	Text	Medium	Short to medium	take different space/time

and user. The costs are not straightforward, since they depend on other factors: for example, access to the right equipment at the development site, the need to hire facilities, whether the right expertise is in house or if there is a need to hire it. Your resources can constrain you to work in certain ways.

Table 8.1 gives guidance on some of the media components, their major categories, and the relative development times and costs for any project. This presents them in general terms, and the time and costs need to be considered in a work context to refine the generalizations.

Once you understand the constraints you are working with, the challenge is to produce the best within them. Constraints do not stifle creativity: they shape the way it can contribute. Each combination of media, message, techniques and interface can have unique features that are suitable for the content and the users.

Matching the media to the message

Media and message.

If the developer has complete freedom, there are definite occasions when one medium will convey some concepts better than others, and there would be a natural selection – video for coverage of action-based events, for example.

The power of a medium does not just lie in the way it offers us messages – audio, visual, text, or combinations of these. It is also dependent on the techniques that have evolved in each medium – sequencing, ways of editing, morphing, time-lapse photography and so on. This power is difficult to analyze, because it is very subjective and difficult to identify which techniques or which combination of them have caused a reaction. The power of the media, messages and techniques is released only when the person receiving the messages interprets them, so we need to consider the skill level of the recipient as well as the impact of the techniques themselves. Basically, the ease with which viewers 'read' the grammar and syntax of media changes. It becomes more sophisticated as the media develop. However, this interpretation is not a conscious activity. The techniques have symbolic significance and influence the viewer's interpretation in this way. This is why the change in speed and quality between audio/video and higher-end graphics through the distribution capabilities of online need to be considered carefully, since the consequences can affect how the users receive your messages.

The impact of each media component depends on a combination of the quality of the content, the medium itself, and the techniques employed by the media specialists. For example, a great deal of research has been done with printed text. Specialist techniques would include decisions on layout, use of space, length of sentence, readability, style and tone among others. These fine details all contribute to the quality of the product and to increased reception of the messages by the reader. Some of these can be useful for screen-based text, but the size of the screen and the electronic nature of the environment mean that parameters that work on the page have to be adjusted. Web pages have already changed their style several times as more has been learned about how readers are utilizing the variety of features presented to them on screen.

There are two problems with making recommendations for use of media components. The first is that new forms or new quality levels of display are constantly emerging, and these evolve quickly, particularly for online projects. The second is that research into different forms of media and their relative merits for imparting similar information has been inconclusive. As there is conflicting information on the 'right' use of single media, decisions on the use of multiple media or combinations of them remain subjective, based on experience.

In view of this we shall present the individual media and discuss their strengths and techniques. We shall indicate wherever possible where the context and platform may influence use, and how multimedia may cause extra considerations.

Video: background factors

As video becomes easier to use and control in digital form, its use in general multimedia applications is increasing. Developers find it as liberating as digital audio, but its use needs to be considered wisely within the constraints that still operate. Online use depends heavily on the bandwidth available (either for downloading or for streaming) as well as on the characteristics of the intended audience. With offline projects, not all systems allow full-screen video, and the size permitted affects the type of content that should be communicated. Even the term 'full screen' can be misleading, since the video often fills the screen only because it has been expanded to do so. MPEG-1 as used in Video-CD is a case in point, since the real resolution of MPEG-1 is only a quarter of the area of a standard screen. When a Video-CD is displayed, the pixels of the digital image are blown up to four times their original area. With DVD and MPEG-2 the picture is already big enough to fill, or nearly fill, most computer screens, and can actually exceed 640 by 480 pixels.

It is easy to demonstrate the size versus content issue when you consider the inappropriate use of video for a well-known theatre drama that was transferred to CD-ROM and shown in an inch-square box! At the time of development that was the technological constraint for video on the system. With online projects you have to consider whether the size of the video materials, the speed of transfer, and the quality really achieve what is wanted.

Remember that users are familiar with good-quality visuals because of television. Their expectations are high, and they will be critical of poor quality, as will your clients. Any undue waiting during the use of the system also causes universal annoyance, so this needs to be avoided or made explicit to the client from the beginning. If you remember the example of 'Just a small change' in Chapter 2, it is easy to get carried away once the project is under way and agree to what appears to be a small change. It would be tempting to include extra minutes of video because the material that is shot is so good, but the repercussions need to be thought through from every angle – space, speed of interaction, sacrifice of other material.

Drama needs to be displayed in a size that is large enough for detail to be visible. This would seem to be a self-evident guideline, but sometimes the drive to try out what is possible with technology seems to blunt common sense. A talking head, shown in close-up, is likely to be satisfactory in a small window, but the same could not be said of a group of actors in a dramatic scene, or several people in a discussion. Anything that relies on wide shots of detailed scenes will suffer in such circumstances. The video needs to be big enough to suit the circumstances for the user. This is true for both on- and offline projects.

Video of this type in a kiosk, for example, should be at least half-screen since the user tends to stand further back from the screen than if sitting at a system: usually at arm's length. Kiosks also tend to be used for communal viewing because people commonly share the interaction.

Online and CD-ROM users tend to operate on a one-to-one basis with the application and sit very close to the screen, so there is a case for the video to be smaller. However, this should not affect the size to the extent that the video cannot be viewed adequately. An option for offline is to allow the user to choose whether to view the video in a window with other screen components around it, or to see it blown up to fill the screen. Blowing up video to fill the screen does not increase its resolution; it merely makes each pixel bigger, so the image will look 'blocky', and it is possible that the computer will not be able to play the expanded video smoothly.

From these few examples it should be evident that the strengths of a medium are affected by the total context in which it is used. The guidelines for the use of media that will be cited here need to be adapted to the context of platform, the needs of the user, and interrelation with the other components. Many of the existing general guidelines do not indicate that these factors affect the decisions for use. A lot of the educational research guidelines do not recognize that their own context and purpose affect the validity of the findings for other types of media use. For example, a completely incongruous use of sound effects juxtaposed with weird graphics that make no sense would break all the rules for design, but it could also be very powerful in an entertainment application for that very reason. This type of use would fall foul of guidelines for both general and instructional use of media, however.

Video

Video is already a combined medium because it generally uses sound to accompany the pictures in some form. It is the current medium that gets closest to reality, since our lives are full of moving images and sounds. (Immersive virtual reality is another contender, but the image quality is not yet realistic.) Watching and listening are the natural way we process our understanding of the world, and we are comfortable with this realistic medium.

Film and television have developed some interesting techniques that relate to the treatment of information and its sequence of presentation according to time. Our own perception of time in the form of days, months and years is always linear and, to start with, the so-called grammar of film making followed this convention. But over time, as audiences grew accustomed to watching movies, film makers began to change the grammar to enhance the story-telling abilities of the medium. Time becomes non-linear and therefore closer to being interactive. The use of flashbacks or parallel action, for example, allows a non-linear progression through information so that the viewer gradually builds up a complete picture. Action replays allow a concentrated focus on particular events. These non-linear techniques provide a basis for helping people to relate to other non-linear techniques that come under their control as computer interactivity is added to sound and motion. It is interesting to note how these techniques have also infiltrated written literature.

Video can be used for a whole spectrum of purposes – explanation, humour, demonstration, exposition, fiction. In general it is used for appealing rapidly to the senses and transferring impressionistic information very quickly. Viewers cannot absorb and retain all the information that passes, so they filter it according to their preferences and prior understanding. This happens internally as the video passes across viewers' consciousness, but computer control will allow a greater manual selection of preference within a topic. Viewers will be able to preselect pieces to view. This is a proactive filter of information, although they will continue to filter the detail of the information even as it is delivered.

This control that the computer element allows when added to sound and motion means that information can be marked unobtrusively into smaller units of meaning than usual, so that each piece can be searched and selected. This might mean in practice that the equivalent of a 20-minute video programme could be classified into themes or sections, and viewers might select to see two or three minutes of the material most relevant to them rather than watch the whole programme.

Of course this level of control will be more useful for some forms of information than for others. Drama needs to develop and the story needs to resolve over a period of time, for example, so tiny pieces might be disconcerting, even frustrating. But put in a learning context where, for example, specific use of gesture or look is being studied by actors and actresses, such fragmentation can still be very useful.

The type of application will govern the amount of control and the size of the pieces of information. Kiosks, for example, will need to offer people fast, interesting information. Advertisers are used to getting their messages across quickly but powerfully, so developers could learn a lot from their techniques. Advertisers are the masters of short sequences of video, and they innovate continually to motivate people.

Because of the constraints of the delivery system, online projects for the Internet generally use video for short, high-impact sequences. This keeps transfer time down. The messages tend to follow precepts from advertising so that entertainment is the prevalent style.

The combination of sound and vision can appeal to people's logic, imagination and feelings. But sound and static visuals can do the same, so what is the difference? The difference lies in how much viewers bring to the interpretation of the content and how much they have to do to construct meaning. The combination of sound and moving images is easier to process because viewers' senses are fed with stimuli that are realistic and are absorbed effortlessly and almost unconsciously. Static images and sound require viewers to contribute more to their interpretation.

In the extreme case, when only text is used, readers have to consciously apply decoding techniques to extract meaning from the letters. The skills of reading take several years to learn because the information is removed from reality into a complete system of symbols. There are various levels of symbolism used throughout the mix of media but there is a gradual move from the realistic to the symbolic as you move from video to text. When the mixture uses more symbolic than realistic elements the viewer needs to decipher more, and this takes more effort.

Viewing and listening are not passive processes, and this is often forgotten. The combination of vision and sound is more powerful for most people because they stimulate reaction more easily. They appeal to a larger range of possible reactions. Stimulation and motivation are closely linked, so it is easier to motivate the viewer to respond to an appropriate mix of sound and vision.

Appropriate use is the key factor, and the more media that are combined the harder it is to keep all the factors appropriate. For example, an historical video needs to ensure historical accuracy to be convincing. This includes location, location detail, dress, accents, type of language used, type of music used, and so on. Exactly the same criteria need to be applied to interactive video sequences. Details such as the tone and look of the presenter need to be be appropriate for the purpose or the audience. Carefully and correctly chosen, they can be the making of the application. Any music used can motivate, can be ignored, or can actually demotivate the audience.

Most people are used to controlling videos in a limited interactive manner on their VCRs. The controls allow a combination of forward, back, search, play, stop and perhaps slow motion. Viewers cannot jump around the video following links or backtracking to the point they started from. They are used to a semi-interactive environment within the one medium, and this limited control has become standard in interactive systems as well.

A few finer points of visual grammar

When film was invented it was believed that the camera had to remain static. The action was framed as if it were on a stage and the film frame was the proscenium arch. In time, directors and cameramen developed the techniques of framing, moving the camera and editing and, as they did so, the audiences learned with them. Today an audience is sophisticated enough to know that if the film shows a car drawing up at a building, the camera looks up to zoom in on a window, we cut to inside a room, and two people walk through the door, then those people were in the car and the room is the one we looked up at. The film is edited to remove time and so speed up the action.

At a simpler level the very way in which a shot is framed can convey information. If, during an interview, the camera gradually moves close in to the speaker, then the impression is of sharing in a secret or of some momentously important point that is being made. Often this visual metaphor will override anything that is actually being said.

The way a face is framed in a picture is important. This is true for stills as well as for movies. The face should have space to look into, otherwise the effect will be unnatural. The strongest points in an image are a third of the way across or up and down the image. You can increase the impact of an object by framing it to make use of this rule of thirds.

Of course, there are more straightforward ways of drawing a viewer's attention to something, such as zooming in on it or panning to follow it, and viewers now know these conventions. You might, if you are feeling devious, actually distract the viewer by using the visual grammar to draw attention to

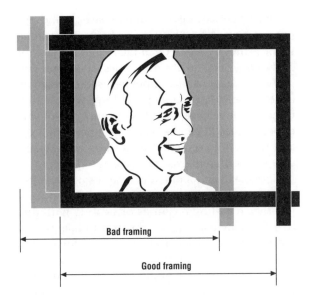

Bad framing

Good framing

something completely inconsequential so as to hide the real action, which can be revealed later. This technique was used to great effect by Alfred Hitchcock in his films, and if done well, as he did it, can completely unnerve the viewer. There is the way the viewer is made to identify with first the girl and then the private eye in *Psycho*, only to have them both killed. In *The Birds*, there appears to be something significant about the two lovebirds that the hero and heroine are carrying, but in fact they are another of Hitchcock's McGuffins, as he called them.

However, the quality and size of video sequences in online projects should affect the filming effects. Using close-up shots has already been mentioned, but with the extreme data compression used for video on the Web it usually pays to avoid fast smooth action or combined pans and zooms since they tax video compression algorithms. The alternative is to accept that movement may be jerky.

Video and applications for education and training

It may seem odd to single out training and the use of video but there are many factors that make the imparting of information for learning different from its use for other purposes.

As explained in Chapter 6, *Agreeing the content*, if the user is going to be tested on the knowledge and skills covered in the application then the information needs to employ certain structures and techniques to aid this. One of the strengths of video in other contexts – the ability to cover a great deal in a short time – is not necessarily a strength in a training context because the user needs to absorb more of the detail. This explains why there appear to be inconsistencies between educational research findings and general practice in the use of video. When the viewers have no control over the medium – as in television – they cannot look at the material again for revision. They have the one chance to listen and absorb – unless they have taped the material, of course.

Video players and computer-based interactive materials offer the means to control the video and so provide viewers with the opportunity to revise the information if necessary. Computer control can offer more than just replay opportunities. It can be used to pinpoint the concepts the user finds difficult and re-route to remedial material where the concepts are offered in a new way with different explanations.

Role plays and simulations are recognized as good techniques for demonstrating skills in action. Video is very good for showing interpersonal skills, whether handling meetings or dealing with difficult customers. An interactive role-play could allow the user to take one side of the role-play while the video character asks or answers questions accordingly via prompts through the computer. This is an example of the combination of video with computer control and text with audio serving the educational purpose possibly better than a linear video. The other obvious advantage is the use of the computer for testing the transfer of knowledge during and at the end of the application. A computer mixture of media-based information can also provide a superb reference set of materials where the learner is asked to research or discover information.

There are several defined approaches to the way people learn. People have preferential learning styles – the way they prefer to absorb, process and classify information so that it makes best sense to them. Educationalists can choose to present information based on a progression from easy parts to more difficult ones. Alternatively, it can be left to learners to impose a structure on the information through discovering links themselves. This is called **discovery learning**. The only problem is that discovery learning takes longer, and there is no guarantee that what is discovered covers the whole range that

Structured learning/discovery learning.

would be appropriate. Luckily, multimedia can be set up to cover both approaches with the same data, depending on the requirements.

There has recently been a large expansion of the use of online for education and training. This market will continue to grow. Traditionally the education market lags behind commercial markets in terms of its access to high tech equipment because of the costs involved. Developers of online materials need to consider their specialized market and the restrictions on higher-level access.

It is difficult to make a case for using video at the moment because of the special needs. The sequences may need to be longer to explain processes and other concepts in a variety of ways to suit various learners. Length of sequence is a problem online. Also, the attention to detail is important. Any decline in quality makes it harder for learners to discriminate specific meaning if it is tied to the visual. Furthermore, the size of the video window becomes crucial because there may well be more than one viewer in an educational group – more like the parameters that drive kiosk layout as mentioned earlier rather than the one-to-one use where smaller visuals are acceptable.

The development of online training courses may well have different considerations, particularly if you are developing for corporate rather than for public use. The firm may have better faster online connections on their intranet, which might release more opportunities for using video effectively in the course.

Hybrid use has become a bridge when online access is limited. Any video might have been put on the CD so that the user can refer to it efficiently without the fear of delays in downloading or corruption in transfer. However, the production and distribution costs of the associated CD will push budgets up. In this way it is noticeable that decisions on when and how to include video in projects are driven by a complex set of interrelated factors.

Audio

Audio is a very versatile medium, which will usually be an integral part of any video but can be used alone or to accompany graphics, text, or both simultaneously. In offline projects, it uses relatively little space so can be used quite freely. The space it consumes depends on the quality level that is used but the levels are easy to choose because there are guidelines on matching the types of audio information to the quality level. These are explained fully in Chapter 13. Audio is, as yet, a slow starter in online projects. Background audio, either as a digital audio file or as MIDI, is possible with some browsers but the general reaction to background sounds has been negative. Audio clips, especially RealAudio® streamed sound (both live and recorded), is quite common and is even used by 'radio' stations that exist only on the Web. The quality is poor compared with broadcasting, but the attraction of listening to radio from the other side of the world has always attracted enthusiasts. Perhaps Web radio is the new short wave experience.

In offline projects, before audio was common in digital form, text and graphics had to be used for all information. This made explanations onerous. Screen after screen had to be used for the main content and all the help explanations. Access to relevant pieces of the information became problematic because there was so much of it. Applications tended to be tedious and linear.

Audio liberated developers from lengthy text explanations. The main problem is overuse because audio is cheap and efficient. Its efficiency fails when too much information is given too quickly for the user to absorb and there is no opportunity to repeat it. Its effectiveness is increased when it supports text and graphics appropriately so that the information, like video, addresses both sight and sound senses for better reception by the user. The use of audio feedback for help in offline applications has increased, mainly because it can be played at the point in the programme where the user needs it. This means that users do not lose their place in the programme, and the audio supports the visuals that are on screen with extra explanation. It can be repeated easily. The alternative used to be endless scrolling text boxes, which took the user away from the main program and could cause disorientation.

Audio includes speech, music and sounds. Both radio and television have developed techniques to use with sound that make it a sophisticated medium, but as it is so easy to listen to, the sophistication is not appreciated. The sympathetic blend of music and speech with variations in pitch, volume and style can add greatly to static pictures and text. These can be effective alone, of course. But it is precisely because listening is effortless that the subtleties of its qualities have been almost completely ignored in projects, to their detriment.

It is no accident that both radio and television choose to introduce many programmes with a signature tune. It identifies the programme (a form of branding), and it settles the listener and viewer to be receptive to what is coming next – or brings them in from the next room. It emphasizes the end of the programme. During the programme it can form part of the continuity strategy to blend segments together when there may be little overt connection. In a non-broadcast context such as video or multimedia some music at the front end also helps the viewer to adjust the sound volume and even check that the sound is getting through.

Sound can be evocative. It can appeal to emotions and in this way influence the reactions of the listener. It can set an atmosphere. These are good points for applications that need to persuade, such as presentations, demonstrations and point of sale. Equally, it can jar and demotivate when used wrongly.

Most applications fall in a neutral middle ground in their use of sound. They have missed opportunities – but the opportunities are difficult to spot. Few recognize the full potential of a well-planned and well-executed sound track. The extra effort means extra money and time for something that is intangible. It is hard to prove its real worth until you compare one that has professional touches and another that does not. Listen to the examples and explanations on the CD to improve your appreciation of sound quality for on- and offline.

Sound has its own techniques to appeal to the listener. A fade-up implies that the listener is eavesdropping on something already under way, and a fade-out signifies that we are moving on and leaving them to it. Sound effects can be humorous, intriguing or realistic. Ironically, sound effects are not always what they seem. You can try this experiment. Take a piece of paper and crunch it up into a ball. Open it out and gently manipulate it. The sound is not unlike the crackle of a fire. Crunching quarter-inch audio tape could sound like walking through grass, and we all know about horses and coconut shells.

Interactive sound does have differences for developers to consider. Sound used on computer systems to attract passers-by irritates other people who might have to stay in the vicinity. Kiosks and demonstration programmes can be prone to this misuse. A phrase becomes annoying if it is repeated often as the user navigates around the system. Developers need to consider how sound can have a good initial impact but then becomes irritating. They might need to consider giving control to the user so they can switch it off when they want. Alternatively developers can build in control themselves where repetitive audio turns itself off after a couple of times of use by the same person.

Another problem with kiosks, and any other installation in a busy area, comes from high levels of background noise. Any sound needs to be carefully manipulated to make sure that it is still audible over any extraneous noise without sounding distressingly loud.

The use of sound in a Web site can be unpredictable. Sounds that play when the user clicks on a link are straightforward: because the user selects them, the user wants to listen. As has been mentioned, background sounds can be an irritant, especially when what might be precious bandwidth is being used for sound that is arguably superfluous. For this reason, users sometimes configure their browsers to turn sounds off just as at one time many people surfed the Web with images turned off so that the pages loaded faster. This means that you cannot guarantee that the viewers of a Web page will hear the sounds.

Computer and video graphics

Computer graphics systems, whether they are on desktop machines or on dedicated sophisticated television or video graphics machines, are capable of very impressive results. Desktop computer graphics are very versatile, and can range from simple line drawings to 3-D animations. More than any of the other components, they can be manipulated to suit the budget allowance. However, many of the specialist skills within graphics are still needed. Original material might need to be created, such as cartoons for example, before it is processed and integrated into an application. The manipulation of source materials and their successful integration are the two computer graphic processes that figure most in multimedia. Their quality can be affected by the platform and software.

The strength of graphics is to provide a visual stimulus that can trigger reaction in the user. It can be the prime source of the reaction, or can offer support for other media components so that their impact is improved. In offline projects systems have become more sophisticated and have more memory, and so it is easier to use many high-quality graphics. This has changed the look and feel of applications considerably away from a text, menu-driven approach to a visual selection in the form of icons.

The use of graphics has grown quickly for online applications, but the restrictions on access because of the need for plug-ins and extended download times still mean that care and thought should be given to the size and complexity of the graphics, balanced against their real value for the site. There has been a move away from using large image maps as first pages because many users wouldn't wait for them to download. Their use demonstrates a mismatch between their potential for visual impact and ease of navigation around the site and the time it took for them to download, demotivating the user to the point of not waiting to access the site. Some sites also had no text information at all on the first page – it was all in the image map – and this made it difficult for Web search engines to index the site.

Even though graphics can be realistic – as realistic as photographs – their advantage over video stills lies in their ability to be representational in a symbolic sense. This can add a dimension, a unique style and feel to an application or site. The style is often set by the home page for online and the first main selection screen or menu for offline. It usually is the key feature, the hallmark of a program, and one that is used the most and seen the most by the users. (Check out the colour section, where you can see examples of online and offline graphic styles. There's an example main menu for an offline application discussed on the CD.)

Sophisticated graphics allow superimposition of one picture on a representation of itself and animation could add to the understanding of transformation. For example, this technique can be very effective when there are layers of visual material like the bones, muscle, tissues and skin of a person or animal that need to be shown or even the relationship between the outside of a machine and its internal parts. This type of technique is found useful in developing analytical and discrimination skills, and so can be extremely useful for educational purposes. However, these considerations may work well for offline but not for online for the reasons stated before. The delivery system needs to be capable of utilizing the features of graphics that are educational.

The expense of dedicated video graphics has meant that they have been used very little in online or interactive programmes, except for developers with a broadcast video connection. However, this kind of equipment has special hardware, which allows for very fast working, and video graphics can offer high-quality animation faster than most computer-generated animations. So in offline projects when time is crucial and there is enough budget, video graphic sequences could provide an answer. Also, for offline projects if an application has video as part of it, the use of video offcuts from the main sequences to construct video graphic images can offer a continuity of style and quality through the application. A lot of these decisions can only be made once the size of the project and content treatment have been established, because video graphics sequences, like video, eat up space. A lot of small sequences can be too costly and space intensive for an application once they are added together.

Ironically, many high-powered special effects in feature films and television are now being produced using desktop compositing software: After Effects is an example of this kind of package.

The use of graphics in education and training applications

As with the use of video, there is research that applies particularly to the use of graphics for instructional purposes. The choice of a particular type and style of graphic still lies in the joint decisions of designer/producer (or whoever takes this role) and the graphics artist, but they can both be served in making a selection by some of the insights from this research.

Instructional graphics have been categorized into representational, analogical and logical:

■ **Representational graphics** share a physical resemblance with the object or concept that is portrayed. An example of this might be a picture of a particular style of architecture that demonstrates the points that are being addressed. A photograph of machinery, for example, would also be representational.
■ **Analogical graphics** display something that has similarities with the issue under discussion but in an abstract way that uses analogy to help convey meaning. An example would be a time-lapsed video graphic that used a leaf decaying as an analogy to the decline of a dynasty, corporation or whatever, as shown here.

- **Logical graphics** are symbolic representations in the form of flow charts, graphs and charts. The flow charts describing linear and multimedia scriptwriting in Chapter 6 are examples of logical graphics.

It was found that although learning theory recommends the use of graphics to support and extend text to aid comprehension, this was being ignored in computer-based courses. Representational graphics were used the most, and analogical the least. This may be related to the history of education and training, where text has played the dominant role. The visual side of communication needs to be recognized in those teams involved with developing interactive education and training so that the effort put into defining well-structured content achieves better success with a balanced use of media. This might be achieved by making sure that a graphics specialist works closely with the person whose role it is to define the content.

The instructional use of animations has also been researched, and these findings can be applied across different types of applications. It was found that users can be easily distracted by other factors, so that the relevance of the animation is only partially understood. This is particularly true when the users are inexperienced in the subject matter.

The guidelines recommend that animations are kept simple enough to be understood, but sufficiently complex to convey the important information. Users can fail to notice aspects if too much happens at once. Because of this, the use of cueing strategies such as narration and the use of colour becomes important. They help to direct attention to salient parts of the animation at the right time. It is recommended that users should be given control of parts of the animation such as the speed, triggering factors and so on, as this involves and focuses them. Animations were found to be good for representing motion, trajectory, spatial organization, and otherwise invisible events, but their overuse can be distracting.

For online projects, though, the use of all forms of graphics has to be balanced against the most likely configuration and speed of transfer as discussed earlier, together with their educational impact. The impact can range from motivational to instructional, and the range of type of instruction is diverse, as noted above. There are ways to juggle the size, quality and speed of download of graphics, and these techniques can be particularly valuable in instructional materials.

Text

The value of text tends to be overlooked by multimedia specialists, but it is an integral part of any application and needs to be thought through as carefully as the other media components. Strangely enough, the treatment of text in online and offline projects displays the most difference between the delivery systems. Whereas a few years ago text used in offline applications was a dominant feature on screens, the amount and function of text has changed as the other media components have come to the fore. Many of the problems that made it difficult to integrate all the offline media components in a digital domain have now been solved. Previously, text had to bear most of the communication load, aided with some graphics. Even the graphics were limited, since they took up a seemingly enormous amount of disk space. Now, although space can still be an issue, things are easier because the storage capacities of disks have increased dramatically. The opposite is true of online projects. Text still dominates here, and although the barriers for using other media are being eradicated, the biggest one – that of the configuration of the most common base system – is holding progress back.

In offline applications, the function of text information in multimedia has become supportive rather than dominant. It is used most for help explanations, reinforcement or summary information, summaries of decisions made by the user, titles, names of hot-spots, and quick-scan information such as opening times and admission charges in a tourist application.

Poor typography is immediately evident beside the quality of the other media components. For an application to have integrity, its components need to blend into one another without any noticeable drops in quality. This may not be easy. If text has been added to the video at the video edit, other text added over computer graphics, and some screens are text screens alone, the difference between them can be very great.

This is because the final integration process can affect each component in slightly different ways, and can have a knock-on effect. Text is one element that suffers in video encoding, for example, because its sharp edges do not respond well to the compression and often become fuzzy. Of course, if text has been added into each component, control over font use, characteristics and size needs to be consistent across all and has to be established early. It may be better to generate all the text with the computer to maintain stricter control, but decisions such as this have to be made by the core team members.

When text is a dominant media component, as in current online Web sites, it is important to pay a good deal of attention to screen layout, readability and legibility. This mirrors the problems that offline had a few years ago. While the cascading style sheets that are part of dynamic HTML allow greater control over typographical and other layout, the best current way of presenting a controlled typographical style for a document on the Web is by means of the portable document format used in Adobe Acrobat. This format now also supports dynamic media types and hyperlinking.

Making text easy to read is more complex than many imagine. Readers are adept at deciphering text, but their job can be simplified or complicated by the techniques employed in the layout of the text. The users of the application will have certain objectives once they see text, because they will make the decision whether to read it thoroughly or not. They will employ their own reading strategies of skimming and scanning the information to appraise it. It surprises a lot of people to find that many readers of Western languages do not start to read at the top left of the screen. They may not scan the text from left to right until the bottom right piece of text. Instead, they may skim the headings to get the gist of the material; they may scan the material looking for a key word that could indicate that the information they require is in the vicinity.

These types of strategy are used more often when the text is giving information, as opposed to text that narrates or explains. In sound there is a phenomenon called the **cocktail party effect**, whereby listeners will clearly hear a word across a noisy room just because the word has a special meaning for them, such as their name. When a viewer picks out a word from text, a similar phenomenon is occurring. Of course, the word may be misread, or hyphenation may result in anomalous groups of letters being at the start of lines.

The layout can help the reader by having clear headings or markers of some type. Line length is also important, as the comfort of eye span across words is linked to the length of a line: you will notice how many Web pages now set the length of lines or use multiple columns. Because screens are generally small, it is tempting to cram as much text as possible into the space. However, this will not necessarily help readability. Because of the limited space, it seems logical to have a small font size and as many words to the line as can fit, but this will only increase the difficulty of reading. The size of the font will also affect the legibility of the text. You need to consider the distance of the viewer from the screen when making decisions on how large and how much text will be viable.

The use of space helps reading because the reader needs natural prompts to understand how much concentration and attention to give to the information. If there are few or no paragraphs, the reader quickly reaches overload. Headings stand out if there is space around them, but if you need to sacrifice space, other cues can help. The use of bolding, colour and size can help to establish the importance of some parts of the text over others.

See the CD-ROM for examples of readability and legibility.

The use of colour alone to distinguish some text from others should be handled carefully, because a sizeable minority of the general public suffers from colour blindness – particularly red and green tones. It is also wise to remember that not all cultures share the same reading pattern of left to right, top to bottom. If the text is going to be translated there is more to consider than whether the translations will fit into the same space: English is substantially shorter than any translations into most other languages. The block of text may be better placed in a completely different part of the screen according to the reading conventions of the country.

Text is still a powerful way to communicate. It allows readers a lot more control than the other media components because they control their pace of reading. They decide how and when to assimilate the information. They can re-read and pause, if necessary, to think things through. It is a versatile medium, which has changed with the times.

The use of computers has changed the way that text is organized, and this in turn affects the way people relate to it. They need new reading strategies to suit the new types of organization. Developers need to understand that just because reading printed matter can be taken for granted, reading on computer screens cannot. The use of layers of text instead of pages, as used in hypertext and Windows for example, represents a different form of structure for text. The stacking of related and unrelated information needs readers to develop new reading strategies. They are expected to keep track of detailed lines of investigation across time and space instead of reading sequential text that has been pre-ordered in logical patterns that they recognize.

The research on hyperdocuments and the confusion that they can cause in readers is fascinating. Readers can easily get carried away when they select link after link across cross-referenced text until they lose sight of their original line of investigation. Worse than this, they find they are lost in the depths of a seemingly never-ending document.

The Internet is a case in point. Unless a site is carefully designed and has good 'signposts' (either visual or text) to remind people where they have come from, and where it is logical to move next, they can get lost in the maze. The 'back' tracking facility that is now a feature of the World Wide Web stemmed from the unreliability of the human mind to keep track. There have been several attempts to build three-dimensional 'worlds' that mirror the structure of a Web site and assist navigation around it. This may not be a big issue for many designers, working on Web sites with simple structures and only a few dozen pages, but for the Microsofts and Sonys of this world the Web presence is substantial, and great care is taken in helping visitors to find their way around.

Overlapping windows that have many selection possibilities can present a daunting image for newcomers. They forget what they have opened, forget where a particular function is hidden, and may never be able to find something because they do not know what it is called. With the spread of interactivity to television there will be many potential users with little or no experience of computer desktops, and for them overlapping windows on screen are unfamiliar.

These initial problems will multiply as text documents themselves become multimedia documents. In multimedia documents a piece of sound information will be cross-referenced to a bit of video, which will be cross-referenced to other sound, text and video components. Multimedia archiving and office automation are accelerating, so this scenario is no fantasy. (See more on archiving in Chapter 19.) There is much to learn from the analysis of reactions of users to the new forms of structuring information on computers.

Overview maps of multimedia applications are becoming common; when users complete a section, the map indicates that this has been done. The concept of a bookmark is also being used more frequently. This records how much of an application users have completed and what remains to be seen so that when they return to the application they can continue where they left off. The bookmark or favourites facility of a Web browser can serve much the same function.

Theory into practice 8

Getting lost with associative logic is easily demonstrated if you play a game of verbal associations for a minute with a friend. One person starts with a word and the other has to reply immediately with the first word that comes to mind. At times this can operate like a trapdoor, where the association works in one direction but becomes virtually impossible to trace backwards. It is difficult to retain the thread of connections for long unless they are recorded.

Look at the following example and try to guess the flow of logic of the blank spaces. The answer is provided underneath the diagram.

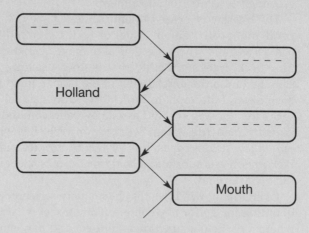

Lost in hyperspace

Answer: Light, Bulb, Holland, Cheese, Food, Mouth

If you think that was difficult, remember that in hypermedia there would be multiple choices at each point.

The difficulty for the developer is to decide how computer literate the audience will be, and how much guidance will be needed in the form of help explanations or aids such as route maps. These are aspects of the computer interface, and will be dealt with in the next chapter.

Where does this leave us?

Media selection will remain complicated because of the constraints, whether these are mechanical or influenced by humans. It is a complex subject, which needs much more attention, but because multimedia is still embryonic there are no set answers yet. We can only try to understand where and why one combination succeeds while other combinations fail. There needs to be broader research that crosses the traditional media demarcation zones so that interdisciplinary insights can emerge.

Theory into practice 9

Try to write a text set of instructions to go with these graphics for a Web page for a motor parts company. Think your way carefully through the diagrams, imagining you are carrying them out, or ask a friend who has never changed a windscreen wiper to read them to see if the instructions are clear.

After completing this, go to the CD, Chapter 8 Support Material, Windscreen wiper example 1. What difference does the sound commentary make to your understanding?

Finally, look at the CD example 2. What difference does the movement make? Is animation more effective than video would be in this case?

All information can be represented in text, sound or visuals, or a combination of these. Media selection means making the best choices given the limitations of the distribution system, the audience attributes, the purpose of the work, and the time and cost.

Windscreen wiper instructions.

Summary

■ Understand your constraints and work within them.

■ Research offers few conclusive principles to help match media and message in specific multimedia contexts.

■ Video:
  – The display size of any video needs to be appropriate for the content, the needs of the viewer, and the method of distribution.

  – Video uses more space and/or bandwidth than other media, and may affect the interaction speed.

  – Video use for education and training has extra considerations from research.

■ Audio:
  – Audio is a versatile medium, which is cost effective.

  – It can save the overuse of text when this is an option.

  – It appeals to the emotions.

  – Its range and scope are unappreciated to date.

  – Care is needed to avoid sounds that become irritating when repeated in an interactive environment.

■ Computer graphics:
  – These are versatile and have a wide range of quality.

  – They can offer realistic and symbolic representations.

  – Educational research findings have value for all applications.

  – They handle transformations between layers of visuals well: for example, skin and bones.

  – The use of video and computer graphics needs to be related to the delivery channel limitations.

■ Text:
  – This is used extensively in online but less so in offline; care should be taken to keep its quality in line with other media components.

  – It can be difficult to integrate text and maintain its quality in offline projects.

  – Layout, size and legibility are always important.

  – The new ways of organizing text in interactive environments can pose problems for readers. Ensure that help and aids are provided.

Recommended reading

Bordwell D. and Thompson K. (1993). *Film Art: An Introduction*. New York: McGraw-Hill

Boyle T. (1997). *Design for Multimedia Learning*. Englewood Cliffs: Prentice-Hall.

Clarke A. (1992). How are graphics used in computer-based learning? *British Journal of Educational Technology*, **23** (3), 228–33

Clarke A. (1994). *Human Factors Guidelines for Multimedia*. European Commission RACE ISSUE Project 1065, HUSAT Research Institute, Loughborough University of Technology, UK

Collis B. (1996). *Tele-learning in a Digital World: The Future of Distance Learning*. International Thomson Publishing

Ellis J. (1992). *Visible Fictions. Cinema: Television: Video*. London: Routledge & Kegan Paul

Foley J.D., van Dam A., Feiner S.K. and Hughes J.F. (1990). *Computer Graphics, Principles and Practice*. Reading, MA: Addison-Wesley

Gagné R.M., Briggs L.J. and Wagner W.W. (1992). Selecting and using media. In *Principles of Instructional Design* (Gagné R.M., ed.), 4th edn, pp. 205–23. Orlando, FL: Harcourt Brace Jovanovich

Jonassen D.H., ed. (1982). *The Technology of Text*, 2nd edn. Englewood Cliffs, NJ: Educational Technology Publications

Koumi J. (1994). Media comparison and deployment: a practitioner's view. *British Journal of Educational Technology*, **25** (1), 41–57

Leher R. (1993). Patterns of hypermedia design. In *Computers as Cognitive Tools* (Lajoie S.P. and Derry S.S., eds), pp. 197–228. Mahwah, NJ: Lawrence Erlbaum Associates Inc.

Lowe R. (1993). *Successful Instructional Diagrams*. London: Kogan Page

Milheim W.D. (1993). How to use animation in computer assisted learning. British Journal of Educational Technology, **24** (3), 17–8

Monaco J. (1981). *How to Read a Film. The Art, Technology, Language, History, and Theory of Film and Media*. New York: Oxford University Press

Neilsen J. (1990). *Hypertext and Hypermedia*. New York: Academic Press

Preece J., ed. (1994). *Human–Computer Interaction*. Wokingham, England: Addison-Wesley

Watson R. (1990). *Film and Television in Education*. London: The Falmer Press

9

Interface design

Project manager's responsibilities

- To recognize that different types of interfaces are needed for different types of application whether on- or offline
- To understand the components of an interface and their significance for users
- To analyze the target audience to find possible problems with the symbolic meanings embedded in the interface
- To test the elements of the interface early with the target audience if at all possible

What is an interface?

All online and offline Web sites and applications have an infrastructure that links the component parts together so that users understand what is contained in them, how the information is organized, and what they need to do to activate the separate pieces. An analogy that is often used refers to navigation within the application and the routes that the users can explore.

The interface is this structure. At a detailed level it means the selection screens where choices are given to the user, the style with which the selections are denoted, the transitions from one part of the application to another, how options are linked or cross-referenced, and the method of input for any data the user needs to give. Offline applications have evolved their interface style from text to icons or visual markers. Online is following the same evolution as visuals become easier to transfer and download. Initially, the interface of a Web page was defined by the browser, and often consisted of little more than underlined links between pages. Sites now include features such as drop-down menus and roll-over buttons that were once the preserve of offline applications.

Since online design is becoming more able to match many of the capabilities of offline we shall use the word 'application' in this chapter to include Web sites as well as disk-based projects; and the issues will be just as important for interactive television and other developments.

Interface design

If you glance back at Chapter 4, *The proposal*, you will see that the foundations for the interface needed to be laid then. The main content sections were suggested and agreed. This gives a shape to the intentions of what the site or application will contain. The decisions about the content will indicate the best way of organizing the information, and will take the audience and platform capabilities into account. Even at the proposal stage the decisions will be shaping the interface in an irreversible way, since the amount of material and the number of sections it will have tends to govern the style of the interface.

When text is the dominant medium, applications have tended to be structured through menus. The user makes a choice that leads to another text menu and so on. The user goes down through the levels and returns by selecting Exit or the equivalent. This leads the user back through the levels to the top menu. This type of structure is known as a **tree structure**. Many Web sites follow this basic pattern.

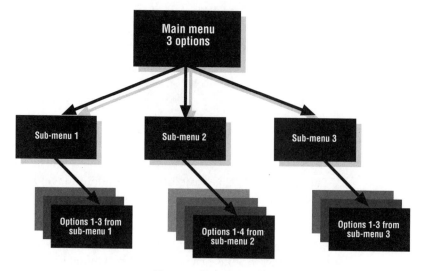

Diagram of tree structure.

There can be variations on this structure, in which the user can select other routes to return to the top level instead of the reverse decision mode. It all depends on the links between the content areas and the options the users are given to move around the program. The tree structure has survived text menus, and can now be identified with icons instead of text on the menus.

As it became easier to have graphics, **icon-driven menus** started to become common. Icons have certain advantages over text. They can take up less space. They are not language specific. They're more aesthetic and appealing. They can make access through an application easier. However, the research on the use of icons has inconsistencies. Sometimes they're good and sometimes they're bad.

What are icons?

The research on icons can be linked with that on signs and symbols. In multimedia any pictorial representation that a user can select is called an **icon**. But in the theory of signs, icons are images that are readily recognizable. They are not symbolic; they are realistic to the extent that they are recognizable without explanation. Commonly, icons in multimedia encompass the complete range of images from abstract symbols to realistic representations. The user quite often has to learn what the symbols mean to be able to use the icons effectively. One distinction that is sometimes made in multimedia relates to the use of high-quality graphics that are so realistic they are like small photographs on the screen, and these are called **picons**. If there are the equivalent of icons with moving images that can be selected, these are sometimes referred to as **micons**. (Examples of icons, picons and micons can be viewed on the CD.)

In the theory of signs, icons can be classified into iconograms, pictograms, cartograms, and diagrams to help define their individual functions. Iconograms are like picons – realistic pictures. Pictograms are equivalent to icons, and so are related to more symbolic, abstract images. There is no equivalent of the miniature moving image in sign theory as by nature it is a study of static images.

Considerations for designing icons

Interactive media permit the combination and manipulation of information in new ways. Icons form part of the new vocabulary. They show that the user has choices, and try to indicate what sort of information can be activated if the icon is selected. However, current interface research could learn from past research. This has shown what happens when new techniques that are symbolic are used when the user does not have the ability to decode the meaning.

There are classic examples of cross-cultural misinterpretation that it would be wise to note as new forms of structuring information emerge on interactive platforms. Health educationalists in developing countries found that commonly understood visual techniques used in Western communication were completely misunderstood. In Peru, when demonstrating how to identify and eradicate lice, they used magnification to show the insects in detail. This only served to distract the viewers. They did not link the enlarged visual image to any insect they understood and so did not think the information relevant to them. The modern equivalent may relate to the use of new techniques for manipulating information, such as the use of icons. The use of a trash can icon to represent getting rid of unwanted files has been noted as culturally unsound for many countries that do not share this method of disposal.

As soon as you begin to design an interface it becomes obvious that some concepts will be difficult to encapsulate into an icon. Even something as simple as Exit is not that simple. There may be several forms of the concept 'to leave' in the program. Users may need to leave a section but stay in the application, they may want to leave the application completely or they may want to leave a screen, check something and return to the same screen.

The functions have similarities, and so any icons used to represent these functions might need to have similarities. But as there would be different results when using these icons, they would need some differences as well to indicate the different consequences of use. First, this example shows that an application can need many icons to indicate the functionality. Second, it shows that it can be difficult to choose symbolic pictures that demonstrate the functionality clearly. Designers also need to take into account that there will be a saturation point for the number of icons a screen can support, even though icons take up less space than text.

If there are many icons, users will take longer to learn their meaning. In some multimedia examples, especially where users are not expected to spend much time on the system – kiosks, for example – it is best to limit the number of icons to the minimum. Users will want quick access to information.

Some concepts are by their nature more abstract than others and are difficult to represent visually. In packages where the concept 'save' has been needed to indicate the transfer of work to disk for storing, various icons have been used to indicate this meaning. Many have tried to follow the principle of relating icon use to everyday objects, but this can lead to strange anomalies. The 'save' icon has been represented by a piggy bank and a monetary symbol. There is a link between save and money, but the money-saving metaphor is out of context in an application for storing information.

Using everyday metaphors helps people to remember icons if and when the set of icons relate to an overall metaphor. The overall metaphor of a book or an office has been used successfully, with individual icons relating to specific details consistent with the metaphor, for example. But some of the concepts of dealing with information electronically, such as Undo, are new, and these pose problems for relating to everyday items in ways that will make sense. A compromise solution seems to be more common now, where an icon is used and its text name is either written underneath or appears when a cursor is placed over the icon.

This technique will provide answers for some of the problems, but not for all. Guidelines for international use advise against the use of text names in

These *Information* kiosks in the London Science Museum provide a quick and easy way for visitors to orient themselves and find their way around the vast collection.

An attractor loop runs when the kiosk is not being used and the kiosks are networked to allow centralized daily updating.

Graphics by Nykris Digital Design. Courtesy of the Science Museum.

The 'Fight Racism' Web Site (www.fight-racism.org) is aimed at a young age range and this is reflected in the animated nature of the site and the lively typographical style.

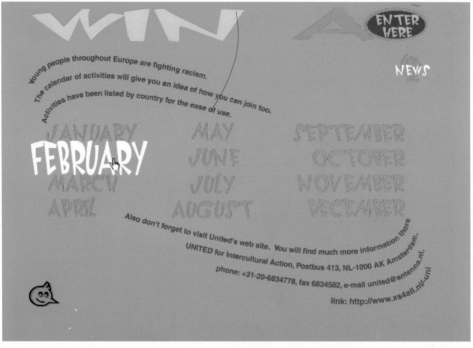

Produced by Nykris Digital Design. Courtesy of Solidar.

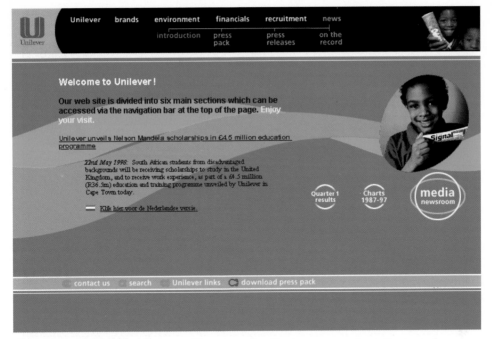

The Unilever Web Site (www.unilever.com) reflects a range of products and markets. This is again designed by Nykris and has some common ground with the Fight-Racism site, particularly in the strong use of colour, but it clearly appeals to a different readership.

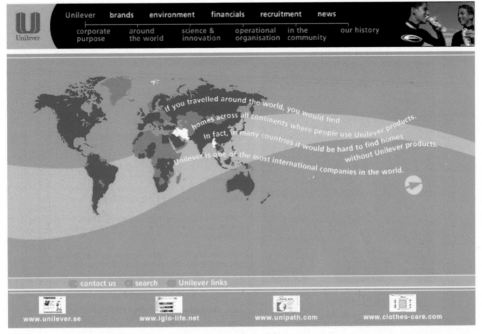

Produced by Nykris Digital Design. Courtesy of Unilever plc.

The Spotlight Casting Directory CD-ROM and its associated Web Site are aimed at a dedicated business readership who make regular use of them in their work. This market is also less computer-literate than many and so this design is simple and 'obvious' so users rarely need to be told how it works. Basically you fill in a form.

Produced by Independent Multimedia. Courtesy of The Spotlight.

this way because they cause problems in translation. Often translations cannot be fitted into the same space.

The arguments about interface design seem to lead you round in circles. The guidelines can seem inconsistent. However, a lot of progress has been made because of the use of icons. Their use has widened the use of computers from specialists to the general public. Overall they do provide better access to the functionality despite their limitations. Instead of having to remember sets of symbols and codes, such as computer languages, icons provide prompts to help anyone activate the power hidden in applications.

Web design has gone through phases. As it is primarily a text-driven medium – but evolving as rapidly as the access and bandwidth allows – icons tend to be collected together in a bar at the top or left of the screen. For a time, image maps that used visuals to give an impression of the range of the whole site were popular. But the users were not happy with the amount of time it took for the maps to download, and the danger was that they did not wait and went on to another site. Micons are appearing in the form of flashing, rolling adverts or banners within the general layout of the screen.

Get to know your target audience

The more you understand your target audience, the better your design will be. At present the hardest audience to design for is the public because, in general, their use of interactive media is so limited. There is little profile of use for different types of application, and until the market increases this will not improve.

However, if and when your application is tied to a specific target group you need to spend time building up a profile of them, their multimedia literacy level, what they would like from the application, and their expectations of what information/results they want from the interactive application.

Let us take the set of icons used in this book as an example. Their design was influenced by the need for them to be used in black-and-white text. Gary Weston, the designer, decided to emphasize the black-and-white medium by using the strength of contrast of the colours, and by using strong clear lines. The size of the image affects the amount of detail used as well as the concern with the possible deterioration of detail in the printing process. This approach was carried through all the illustrations, and provides a cohesion in look and feel throughout the book. This consistency is a factor that needs to be achieved in electronic applications as well, because it helps users to identify the application and recognize the navigation paths faster, and provides a sense of harmony that contributes to a feeling of satisfaction for the user.

If you look at the transfer of these icons to the CD, where they are in colour, you should be able to assess how Gary has maintained the continuity of feel in their design by maintaining a colour hue and strength to give consistency once again. The strong, stylized lines and shapes also maintain their original purpose. However, if the icons had been needed only for the CD, or if the book had used colour, the whole conceptualization would have had a very different starting point and the icons would have looked different as a result. If the designs had been for a Web site, the icons might not have retained the bevelled borders and might have blended in more subtly with the overall page design. Coloured print layouts, more like that of magazines than of books set a common style for Web pages, where the strength and strong colour acceptable for offline may not suit.

As depicted here, the stylization in the icons shows the identification with you, the readers, as a specialist audience. Some presuppose in subtle ways that you have a certain level of computer literacy, and think in certain ways. The *Summary* icon not only stylizes bullet points but also changes their usual horizontal position. This presupposes that you are comfortable with the link between summaries being denoted by bullets or the equivalent, and that you are sufficiently familiar with them to compensate for the angle shift in perception. The *Responsibilities* icon links the concept of someone having a finger on the button with the implication of having the knowledge and responsibility to make decisions. This is particularly true with interactive media, where the user has control to access or even delete information, for example. *The Theory into practice* icon uses an arrow to denote direction, and the split format of the icon enhances the concept of change from one stance to another, representing the transfer of theory into practice. The arrows also reinforce the idea that this is not a linear action. There is an interplay between theory and practice as people move back and forth between them – referring to the book and trying something out then referring back to the book or CD again.

These icons had to represent more abstract points than the others, but they needed concrete clues within their stylization to help establish their meaning for the reader and to re-establish the meaning every time they are seen.

All the icons are based on the design of buttons, as denoted by the frame around them, and this gives them their integrity as well as reinforcing the subject matter of interactive media. The diagonal split between the reversed images will trigger some people to think of negative images and therefore photography – this has yet another level of meaning of a medium that is used in multimedia. So, there are various triggers within the design to consciously and subconsciously link the icons to their overall purpose as well as their specific one.

Hopefully, this analysis of the way in which the design of some of the features of an interface assigns meaning to a particular audience will indicate the complexity of maintaining integrity of look, feel and sense in an interface. It is not an easy task, but it does provide the key to good application design. You need to build up an empathy with your audience, and there are several ways to do this. Some of these are outlined below.

Needs analysis was introduced in Chapter 3, *Scoping a project*. Task analysis forms part of needs analysis. This is particularly important if the application is going to form part of the workplace as a job aid, or offer an alternative service to a human one outside normal work hours. Task analysis is the study of how a set of actions are carried out, what processes/procedures and questions need to be followed to achieve a satisfactory result, and what results match which set of circumstances. The analysis is usually carried out early in the project so that all decisions can be based on the findings.

If the type of application does not warrant task analysis then concept testing may help to give a profile of expectations and preferences from the target audience. In **concept testing**, also called **focus groups**, people are told what the application will do and what it will provide. Their reactions are monitored to see whether the design principles have predicted their needs/wishes accurately or whether they have common agreement on suggestions that arise during the discussion. These may be used to tailor the design so that the application matches the user profile better than before. Concept testing takes place at a stage when there is a very limited prototype or no working prototype of the application. It is not to be confused with **usability testing**, which takes place later in the project when a good working model is available. The target group in this case actually uses the application instead of reacting to the ideas that will be embodied in it.

Testing interface design

If there is any way to get the budget to build a prototype application that would include usability testing of the interface, then go for it. Experience can help to predict certain problems with a certain audience but you learn more with every application you work on. There are always a few aspects that do not work out in the way that was planned, but by the time the team has spotted the deficiencies there is often no way back. Usability tests provide a wealth of information, but they are of little use unless they are carried out methodically and professionally. Unless this happens, conflicting results and recommendations will be made.

The theory and practice of usability testing is too great to go into here, but its principles are important, and so some of the insights will be mentioned briefly to encourage you to look into this further.

It is too easy to base interface decisions on your experience rather than on the experience of the target audience. This does not mean that insights gained from experience are not valuable. Nor does it mean that you have to suppress any creative ideas about interface design. It is an evolving area, so there is scope for flexibility and experimentation as long as these are recognized as such, and tried out with the intended audience. It may be that they will experience some difficulties with the interface design. But the important aspect is that you notice where and why there are problems and reach some decisions on (a) how to eradicate them or (b) adding help to educate the users into using the new aspects successfully.

One of the misconceptions about usability tests is that you need a large number of people to produce valid results. More recent research has shown that up to 80% of the problems were found with between 4 and 5 participants and that 90% were detected with 10 users.

This needs to be put in context, however. It is important that:

■ the selection of the participants has been made according to a predetermined profile of user groups;
■ the environment for the test has been carefully prepared;
■ the participants have been inducted into the test environment and know their rights;
■ the tasks to be performed have been created to mirror the aims of the product and the needs of the users;
■ the ways of collecting quantitative and qualitative data have been agreed;
■ the testing team have been thoroughly prepared and tried out in a pilot test;
■ the ways to organize and communicate the data have been agreed.

See Chapter 18, *Testing*, for more information on these and other forms of testing.

The interactive environment

If the purpose of the interface is to make the interaction smooth then this is the criterion that needs to be applied for quality. The users' levels of competence and understanding need to shape the design of the interface. The project manager takes on responsibility for acting on behalf of the users. The biggest problem is deciding what can be assumed as prior understanding of the interactive techniques. This is harder for the general public than for other groups since the application would have to appeal to the naive and experienced user simultaneously.

Any interactive communicator aims to trigger the user's interpretation of the messages embedded in the content. This ability holds the key to good communication with media. But if techniques are used that are alien to the users, they may miss the point completely. If they do not understand the symbolism of the techniques that are used, they will not reap the full benefit from the content. The new forms of interactive structuring employ techniques that take time for users to understand – just as using magnification was outside the comprehension of the tribe in Peru. Understanding, in this sense, is not an innate ability; it has to be acquired. Media techniques are culturally based and depend upon shared experience. The shared experience can be part of a subcultural group or cross-cultural group. The Internet would be a good example of a cross-cultural group that shares common understanding of particular symbolic codes and techniques.

Just as icons are part of the new vocabulary of multimedia, the layering of information associated with Apple Mac and Windows has become a common technique. Windowing with option bars and icons has proliferated. The techniques associated with the use of a mouse (point and click) free users from typing in their selections. It becomes easier to organize access to information with small drop-down menus. This approach lends itself to structuring access to a mass of information by splitting it into small pieces. But does your audience have the experience to use this structure efficiently? Will you need to train them in it? Should you stick with established conventions or break them? Should you take some things for granted?

Many multimedia applications fall in between tree and window structuring, and it is common to have picons arranged on a screen. Picons often reveal the text names of the content section they represent as the mouse pointer passes over them. These are called **hot-spots**. Other applications have scrolling graphical menus in which the screen width and/or height extends as the mouse pointer reaches the edge of the screen.

All of these share the same purpose; they show the scope of the program. The initial selection screen is very important. It sets the expectations and understanding of the user. It gives an indication of the scope of the content and the techniques needed to navigate through it. It establishes whether there is help available at all times or whether the user needs to discover aspects about the program. It should set the example of:

(1) how users are to select an option – find the hot-spot and select, click on an icon which expands into a menu, and so on;

(2) how they will know if they have made the selection. For example, you may use a sound to show that something has been successfully selected, or the button/hot-spot/picon may change shape, size, colour or stay in a depressed position.

Once users have started the program you need to establish how they can move around in it. Do they have an option to select to return to the main selection screen? Do they have a map to show them an overview of where they are? Are they allowed to go up, down, sideways, forwards and backwards, and if so how do they know this? Do they have to complete certain sections before others? How will they know this?

Once certain ways of working have been established, these need to be consistent within the application. The interface and its working needs as much integrity as the other factors we've looked at. If users become confused, lost or irritated by the operational side of the program, their concentration on the content will suffer. They will become demotivated. They will tend to leave the

Interface antics.

program before they have found what they wanted or before they've explored all the possibilities.

Designing an interface that helps people to reach all the application information effortlessly is far from easy. It usually provides the longest discussions between the graphics artists, programmers and producers. The high-level structure will affect how the programmers set up their code. They need to be clear how it is meant to work to ensure that they construct an adequate frame for the application. They will have opinions on what functionality the platform can support, and because they have studied interface design as part of their courses, they often feel that it is their role to design it. The graphics artists feel exactly the same. The interface graphics are one of the prime ways they can exert their creativity and style.

The project manager will have the best understanding of the scope of the content and the client. These have an effect on the interface design. There may be corporate conventions that irk the programmers and graphics artists, but they will have to prevail. There may be special considerations for the intended audience – poor second-language speakers, for example.

Your research on the intended audience and their multimedia literacy level is crucial. It will help to determine the best methods of interaction, their prior experience, whether they will be receptive to innovation, and how many levels of help they might need.

Sometimes, as with games and activity-based entertainment programs, the consideration is not to make the interaction too easy, as this is not the purpose of the interface. With these the purpose is to excite, surprise, demand attention, and to use fast reactions to interpret a changing environment. These types of application need different considerations for their interface, and many of the guidelines covered in this chapter will not apply.

Online interfaces share more common features than offline. The proliferation of sites a user can access means that there is competition to attract viewers, but at the same time there is recognition that the viewer can move on quickly to a lot of other offerings. Site designs influence each other, so that features that work and make sense – such as the control to go back, and a selection bar on one side of the screen with a block of text on the other that allows easier scanning of the text than long lines – become commonplace. If a site is difficult to navigate, you will lose your user to other sites; if the site is easy to navigate but has boring content, you will also lose them. The balance between the user's needs, the content and the style is as true for online as it is for offline.

The use of sound

Sound means any type of audio use. This can include speech, warning bleeps, alarm bells and so on.

When sound became easier to digitize and store on CDs, it became apparent that overuse was unwise. People become irritated by repeated sounds. Some sounds that are initially attractive or entertaining pall quickly. You need to guard against inappropriate use of sounds at the planning stage, which is difficult, because it is easier to react with your mind than with your ears at this time.

It helps if you take time to look at the use of sound independently of the other factors and see how likely it is for the sounds to be repeated inadvertently. The prime example is the use of audio to state the function of a picon. The sound occurs even when the users are trying to move to a picon in a different part of the screen. The information is useful at the beginning but annoys users after that. As indicated in Chapter 8 on media selection, you need to consider giving control of volume and silence to the users, as is now more apparent in the inclusion of a control bar linked with the sound (and video) allowing the user to control the volume, pause, repeat, move forwards and backwards, and so on. Control of these could help make the application more versatile for people with hearing difficulties. These users might form a strong subgroup of the audience profile, and if that were the case, their needs would drive the total interface design, not just the use of sound.

The use of colour

Because the use of high-quality colour is easier and more common in applications, and the resolution of screens has increased, the concern with the general use of colour has diminished. Prior to this, the use of background colours, the colour of text against a coloured background, colour linked with layout, and the awareness of colour-blindness in a percentage of the audience were all factors that were researched. The major problems were poor selection of colours in relation to each other, causing difficulties in readability and legibility. A screen is still not as easy to read as print because of screen glare and the nature of electronic text. Because text is prevalent in Web sites, the lessons learnt in offline production can benefit Web designers. Tiled images are often used in the background of Web pages without enough thought for legibility.

Graphics artists are important members of the team. They bring their knowledge and skills to bear on the problems of style, design, consistency of visual approach, layout, legibility, and readability. Their training in making the best combinations of colour is invaluable. There can be several uses for colour – attention cue, aesthetic, styling, and branding. As with the use of sound, colour can please initially, then become annoying for users. In online projects, if colour is used badly, then all the factors that applied for offline projects remain true.

One of the problems that still prevail for offline projects is the changes that occur in colours depending on their origins, the platform, the software, and the encoding processes. So even with good planning, colour shifts can occur. It is a good idea for the project manager of offline projects to get the graphics artist to check the effect of the varying processes and to tap into contacts who have used the combinations before to see if there are any adverse but unrecorded reactions. With some applications, colour consistency is vital – medical applications, for example, are notoriously difficult for colour integrity, and can need special processes to ensure accuracy.

Finally, another problem associated with colour remains. There are cross-cultural associations in the use of colour. This is part of the aesthetic appeal of colours, but it may become more important as applications need to reach international audiences. The retail sector has noted the variations in response to combinations of colour. They sometimes adjust the packaging of products for various countries. Some cultures respond better to bright, strong, primary colours, while other cultures prefer pastels. For applications that need to sell, this could be more of a factor than in other types of application. Common examples of Western colour psychology are:

Red   = stop, danger, heat, appliance is on
Blue = cold, water, sky
Green = go, environmentally friendly

There is little research in this area at present.

Packaging and related materials

It is easy to forget that hybrid and offline applications need to be packaged, and that this forms part of the interface; in fact, it can help to set expectations before the users actually begin the interactive part. The attention given to book covers, record labels and music CD cases shows the importance of the initial impression. The consistency of design in the applications needs to carry over into the packaging and labelling to give a professional stamp to the materials. Although unusual a couple of years ago, additional printed materials and even videos can sometimes be part of a total package that includes some interactive multimedia material. All extras need the same attention to their design as the multimedia component. If it is the dominant part of the package, then elements of its design should be carried through to the other materials. This might include colour combinations, layout, montages of graphics from the application, and so on.

The planning and budgeting of any such extras need to be linked to the multimedia production phases to ensure that they are all ready simultane-

Theory into practice 10

Use the interface assessment form that follows the Summary to assess your next interface after discussions and initial decisions have been made in the team but before the client has been given the decisions. Use your appraisal to go back to the team if necessary for rethinking any issues.

Use it also to appraise any interactive materials you look at to help focus on their true strengths and weaknesses.

ously for release.

Summary

- The interface is the infrastructure of the application.

- The use of icons and the method of organization – tree, windows, hypertext – are symbolic, so the users' correct interpretation of their meaning is the key to good design.

- These need special care, explanation and possibly training, when the target audience has little exposure to such symbolic structures.

- Usually, the aim of the interface is to provide smooth, easy access to any part of the program the user wishes, but games or activity entertainment titles can have different aims.

- The use of sound and colours in the interface also needs attention to ensure

Tick as appropriate

Application profile	General interface assessment

1. User profile

	Inappropriate			Appropriate	

a. Naive ☐   Specialist ☐   Mixed range ☐   Match to users   1   2   3   4   5
General public ☐   Other ☐ [____]

b. Application use   Match to use   1   2   3   4   5
National ☐   International ☐

2. Proposed style of use

Disagree ... Agree

Functionality
Sustained/regular use by people ☐   matches use   1   2   3   4   5
Simple functionality
Brief/occasional use ☐   matches use   1   2   3   4   5
Range of levels
Mixed usage ☐   match mixed use   1   2   3   4   5

3. Application purpose   Style suits purpose

To inform ☐   To sell ☐   1   2   3   4   5
To entertain ☐   For reference ☐
To train ☐   To educate ☐
Other ☐ [____]

4. Overall marks for: General impression

Poor ... Excellent

a. Ease of use   1 2 3 4 5 6 7 8 9 10
b. Design style   1 2 3 4 5 6 7 8 9 10
c. Consistency of selection methods   1 2 3 4 5 6 7 8 9 10
d. Consistency of functionality   1 2 3 4 5 6 7 8 9 10
e. Consistency of visual design   1 2 3 4 5 6 7 8 9 10

5.   Inappropriate ... Appropriate

a. Use of colour in interface   1   2   3   4   5   n/a
b. Use of sound in interface   1   2   3   4   5   n/a
c. Use of moving image/animation in interface   1   2   3   4   5   n/a

6. Help

a. Suitability for user profile   1   2   3   4   5   n/a
b. Amount of detail   1   2   3   4   5   n/a
c. Tone   1   2   3   4   5   n/a
d. Effectiveness   1   2   3   4   5   n/a

best use.

■ Materials that form part of the total package are part of the interface 'look', and need to be treated accordingly.

Recommended reading

Clarke A. (1994). *Human Factors Guidelines for Multimedia*. European Commission RACE ISSUE Project 1065, HUSAT Research Institute, Loughborough Institute of Technology, UK

Del Galdo E. (1990). Internationalisation and translation: Some guidelines for the design of human computer interfaces. In *Advances in Human Factors/Ergonomics 13, Designing User Interfaces for International Use* (Nielson J., ed.), pp. 1–11. Amsterdam: Elsevier

Deregowski J.B. (1980). *Illusions, Patterns and Pictures. A Cross-Cultural Perspective*. London: Academic Press

Dumas J.S. and Redish J.C. (1994). *A Practical Guide to Usability Testing*. Norwood, NJ: Ablex Publishing Corporation

Jonassen D.H., ed. (1982). *The Technology of Text*. Englewood Cliffs, NJ: Educational Technology Publications

Kennedy J.M. (1982). Metaphor in pictures. *Perception*, **11**, 589–605

Maissel J. (1990). *Development of a Methodology for Icon Evaluation*. National Physical Laboratory Report DITC 159/90, Teddington, UK

Marcus A. (1992). *Graphic Design for Electronic Documents and User Interfaces*. New York: ACM Press; Reading MA: Addison-Wesley

Salomon G. (1979). Media and symbol systems as related to cognition and learning. *Journal of Educational Psychology*, **71**, 131–48

Shneiderman B. (1992). *Designing the User Interface: Strategies for Effective Human–Computer Interaction*, 2nd edn. Reading, MA: Addison-Wesley

Siegal D. (1997). *Creating Killer Web Sites*, 2nd edn. Indianapolis: Hayden Books.

UNESCO (1976). Cross-cultural broadcasting: psychological effects.

UNESCO Press Reports & Papers on Mass Communication, No. 77.

10

Contract issues 2

Project manager's responsibilities

- To understand legal issues that can affect multimedia contracts
- To carry out the company's policy for binding clients and subcontractors to its terms and conditions

Introduction

In *Contract issues 1* (Chapter 5) we concentrated on establishing ways of working between you and the client. Without these agreements, your work could be affected by hold-ups out of your control, which would impact on your deadlines. We recommended you control these risks by defining the work flow responsibilities between you and the client. Change management principles were also explained, and it was suggested that they were included in the agreement for the way of working.

In this chapter, we shall return to the process of developing more detailed costing that should form part of your background estimates for the final proposal document. After all, you are in business to make a profit, so you have to predict the costs as accurately as possible to stand a chance of coming out on top. Secondly, we shall note the more formal legal details that may need to be addressed.

Costing rights and clearances

This is a complex area. The background to the types and the processes involved in rights is covered in Chapter 17, *Rights, copyright and other intellectual property*. If you are not experienced with these, you might benefit from reading that chapter first. Here we're concerned with approximating the numbers involved and their costs to help stipulate a workable budget. Rights and clearances are a good example of knowledge that applies across many stages of development. The project manager needs the knowledge here to define the budget. Whoever takes on the role of rights clearer needs a good grasp of the varieties to be able to negotiate the best deal from owners of materials across media during development. The factors that influence clearance costs are similar for most kinds of asset, and you should bear in mind that a clearance for the Web is a clearance for the world.

Still pictures

Any reuse of an existing photograph, picture or slide, or even extracted details from any of these for which neither you nor the client has copyright, will incur costs to clear permission for use. The amount charged varies according to the location of the visual – museum, picture library, for example – who owns it, the purpose for your use, where it will be seen, and how long your programme or site will be in use. This list does not cover all the variables, so you can begin to get a feel for how problematic this is. Unlike Europe, the USA has a tradition of freedom of information that leads to a large number of free sources of assets. NASA is the best known example. There are also many sources of clip art for which no royalties are payable. It would help if your company found out about free and royalty-free sources, as you never know when they will come in handy.

Scanning and rights.

Music

This is the most complex part of rights and clearances. Conditions change depending on the artistes, the length of the music, whether it loops (is played repeatedly), the publisher, and whether it is an original work, library music or a commercial recording. The costs change accordingly.

Voice-overs

These are usually cleared through the voice-over's agent. Rates vary according to the artiste, the length of time spent recording, the type of use, the length of the clearance, and the number of countries.

Video footage

This is rather like stills clearance, and depends on the owner. Costs may depend on the length of the footage, and if the videos come from different sources and have to be edited together you may have to convert them to a common format, which will affect quality and cost. Video footage, if it is being licensed from a television programme, can sometimes contain material with many secondary rights implications including stills, music, artistes and scripts. This can contribute to the clearance costs significantly, and it is vital that the rights situation is known comprehensively.

Table 10.1 gives an indication of some of the variables that can occur, and some examples have been given to demonstrate the variation in costing across the range of media. There isn't a standard rate per photo from museums, for example, so you may be negotiating individual rates from different museums depending on where the originals are kept. Rates vary from country to country.

Table 10.1 Rights and clearance costing.

Category	Clearance type	Numbers/length	Market covered	Time cleared	Other factors	Ball-park rate	Total
Stills	Photos from museums	approx. 60	Commercial/world	3 years		£75–100 B&W £100–150 colour	
Video footage	Library	10 minutes	Commercial/world	3 years	Technical costs can be high	£250–1000 per minute + rights	
Music	Commissioned Title music	3 musicians 3 minute piece	Commercial/world	Indefinitely	Buy-out on rights One single payment	£1000 upwards	
	Library (background in 2 sections)	approx. 15 mins	Commercial/world	3 years	MPCS negotiation	£100 per 30 seconds	
Voice-overs	Professional artistes	2 artistes 1 approx. 35 mins 1 approx. 15 mins	Commercial/world	3 years	2 payments, one for recording, one for rights	£150 per hour +100% for rights	

You should make your client aware of the problems of costing clearances, and stress the estimated cost. You will really only know the true figure once the job is completed; so it may be wise to negotiate an estimate for this part, which you will confirm and renegotiate during the project as you become clearer about the numbers involved.

The nature of the task should now be clearer. The complexity should show that a person who will research, negotiate rights, keep accurate records, and keep track of the assets to send back is not performing a trivial task, especially when different types of assets are involved. It may be as well to mention that you are charged penalty payments by some libraries if you do not send the original photo or slide back by a stipulated date. These unknown costs that can occur should be covered by having some of the budget defined for contingency. Also, you should remember that courier companies such as FedEx and DHL may be used to carry the assets, and the cost of shipping is not insignificant. Consider whether your researcher has to travel to look at images.

The legal issues

There are a surprising number of multimedia projects that are undertaken on little more than a handshake and often on simple letters of agreement. Also, of course, legal aspects would indicate access to lawyers, preferably specializing in multimedia, and they are expensive professionals. It is true that in most cases projects progress with some hiccups but these are resolved amicably. In cases where things go wrong they tend to go horribly wrong, and people end up saying 'If only we'd . . .'. Conversely, if the project is very successful, this can also lead to queries of who can exploit it and how, and who should be getting what from the sales!

The major problem lies in the uncertainty of how to treat multimedia in a legal sense, because it is still emerging as a delivery medium. In mature delivery media such as broadcasting, music and film the issues of primary rights in materials and the use of the materials for secondary purposes have been sorted out. So, for example, a contract to write and record a talk for BBC Radio will include several clauses explaining in detail what the residual payments are, as percentages of the original fee, for such things as repeats, translations, printing in publications, and sales to foreign broadcasters. See Chapter 17 for more details.

We shall look at several key areas and highlight why some formal agreements might help, but each company has to take responsibility for its own terms and conditions.

Rights and clearances of assets: liabilities

The methods to use when clearing rights are addressed in Chapter 17. Here we shall be concerned with establishing and agreeing which rights and clearances need to be addressed. Your client may give you permission to reproduce, edit and reuse many of the visual assets they have, but they may not own the copyright to be able to give you permission. They may believe they own the images, but ownership of visual images is not straightforward. Visuals prepared for a company brochure may have been given solely for that purpose and no other. So reuse would constitute a breach of conditions from a former contract. Originators of work have particular rights that protect them from other people editing their original work. It is a difficult area, which changes according to country. The client may own copyright for the original purpose of the materials but not have the electronic rights that are required for multimedia.

So it is in your interests to get written agreement, called an **indemnity**, that the clients own the electronic copyright in all the assets they provide to you, as a safeguard in case of any future dispute over the rights.

Other assets you may have to find and clear for the purpose of the project – music, for example. You will be asked for the purpose, audience type, and countries where you want permission to use the application. These are known as the **markets and territories** you want covered. This is not as simple as it sounds. Many applications begin with one purpose but evolve into others. Material licensed for a CD-ROM in one country may be moved to a Web site, which is accessible across the whole world. If the rights were originally cleared only nationally, they would have to be renegotiated. An in-house training application may be released on the consumer market after a period of time in the company. The market would have changed, and the necessary rights and clearances may need revision. It is cheaper to negotiate once than have to renegotiate later. For any who still doubt this, consider the possible reclearance costs of the film below.

It has been recognized that reuse of some of the best film footage from television programmes in interactive programs would seem sensible, but many that have proposed this have fallen by the wayside once the cost of re-clearing electronic rights with all those who took part was worked out.

The duration of rights is also established at the time of negotiation, so you need a good idea of the life span of the product to determine how many years to ask for, or you may consider 'buy-outs'. These mean paying a once-only payment by which you get agreement to use the material indefinitely.

You need a clear directive from the client on their short- and long-term plans for the site or application. You should state what markets and territories you will cover when clearing rights for offline, and how long the clearances will be valid for any project. If you put this in writing and have their agreement to this formally, there can be no confusion as to who should have done what and when, if circumstances change.

If you intend to remake the application or Web site in another language then you must have obtained clearance for such use. In some cases a rights owner will count a direct translation as part of the original agreement, but in others they will not. It will be easier to cover multiple languages if your agreement provides royalties because an increased number of languages attracts more sales. For a buy-out this argument does not work. A similar situation occurs when an update of the application is required, to change information that has become outdated. The extreme situation in this chain is the derivative, which is another project based on the first.

Other liabilities to note

You will be using other companies' code in the form of libraries, tools and authoring packages under licence to develop your project, as well as producing your own code as and when necessary. You cannot guarantee that bugs from these will not affect the performance of the end-product. This is not as uncommon as it sounds, since multimedia is an experimental environment and code gets used in circumstances that were not originally envisaged, and may therefore fall over. You do not want to be held responsible for problems originating with other people's software, so you should include clauses to cover for this. The same is true of hardware, which can have unforeseen and unstated idiosyncrasies. On a Web site you may be using CGI programs from other sources including ones in the public domain, and in some cases the licences for these place you under obligations.

Payment structure

You can see that your company will have put in quite a significant investment in terms of time to reach the agreed proposal stage. All this has been unpaid. On a large project, you might be working for a year or more to completion. Even smaller projects can mean considerable outlay of money during the production stages. The company needs to define a payment structure so that payments are staggered according to specific points in the project.

Sign-offs are well defined and represent agreement points, so these might be linked to staged payments. Others follow the computing model and define milestones that represent phases of the project. Payment could be linked to achievement of these. Alternatively, payment stages could be linked to calendar months and achievement of schedule to dates. Yet others ask for a certain amount up front, staged payments through the project, and final payment of the remainder at completion. Whatever option is chosen, some form of phased payment would help your cash flow.

Your client, however, will be interested in containing the costs. This is why they begin by trying to get an estimate from you and then haggle about the fine details of the deliverables to get the best deal for the money. Effectively, you are signing a **fixed-term contract** when you agree to the final proposal. It states what you will produce in the time for the money. Your only safeguard in a fixed contract is agreed, comprehensive specifications with as detailed costing as possible done up front; so you have to be confident in your costings.

The alternative to fixed-price contracts, which are notoriously difficult to achieve in any ill-specified projects, is a **time and materials contract**. This means that you indicate what you expect the cost might be, but that you will keep strict records and bill according to the actual amount it takes. You should be able to see that clearances are so difficult to predict accurately that this approach makes sense. Unfortunately, as time and materials are more open-ended, clients are not receptive to this model although it may be fairer on the developer.

There is another model, which is a shared development where the client clears the rights in the content but the developer undertakes all other work to a budget. This is a likely model where the client is a publisher or asset holder.

Ownership of code and other assets generated

Part of the way developers survive is to build up a stock of code or libraries that help them in the production of other projects. This does not mean that they will produce an application that looks and behaves exactly the same as the original product for which the code was generated. Most often the code is adapted to fit the new requirements but forms some of the building blocks. If your client is not a computer company or a developer they will probably not have any use for the source code that underlies their application. It is best to try to retain copyright in the code but issue a free licence to the client for its use.

The company needs to establish where it stands on this issue so that it will not infringe any rights in reuse of the code later. There is an added problem in that the code used may well be a combination of third-party code as well as its own. This makes it problematic to identify exactly which new code might belong to the client and which you would not have the right to sign away anyway as it belongs to the third party.

Many clients are reasonable once they realize the lack of value to themselves in having the copyright in the code. You might have to agree to provide access to source codes under extreme circumstances, such as your company ceasing to do business.

If clients have been used to commissioning video productions then this will seem a new concept for them. They would never expect a video production facility to retain rights in what they do. It will help if you explain that this is usually the case with software. It is common practice for application software never to be sold but only licensed, with restrictive conditions on usage, copying or decompiling.

Establish your right to demonstrate and promote the product

It is important for winning new business that, as a developer, you are able to demonstrate your capabilities to new clients. Some clients will bind you to confidentiality agreements, and you need to recognize the effect this might have for demonstrating the program after completion. Some clients will not grant permission for competitors to see the product but may be happy for non-competitors to see it. There are several ways to approach this to establish limited demonstrations with the company's permission, but this will be onerous on you.

If the client will be demonstrating some aspects publicly, there should be no reason for their stopping you doing the same. Often confidentiality agreements have a proviso or time limit whereby once the information is in the public domain, then the clause no longer applies. However, it is one more aspect that needs a clear statement, or your company may find that it cannot use the application as part of a repertoire to show at exhibitions or to prospective clients.

Similarly, you should consider what happens if you wish to publicize a project by advertising it or getting editorial coverage in a magazine or on television. Can you show any of it under these conditions?

Moral rights

As developer, your company can ask for a right of paternity to be included in the contract. This will allow your company and its members who worked on the project to have a credit; otherwise, no one is obliged to recognize your involvement once the product is released. See Chapter 17 for more details on moral rights.

Severance

Problems can arise from many quarters that may make it important for your company to extricate itself from any agreement, mainly to protect it from further damage. If your client's company is taken over and you hear that they will be closed down as part of an inevitable downsizing operation, then you may wish to pull out earlier rather than later. Make sure that you still get paid for work done if the project is stopped. Alternatively, if the key person in the client organization leaves and the new person makes it impossible to continue with the project as previously specified, you may wish to terminate the contract.

A severance clause works both ways, so that clients can extricate themselves as well if they have cause.

Force majeure

This refers to the situation where a major unforeseen disaster such as an earthquake or terrorist bomb stops your company fulfilling the contract. Although unlikely, major catastrophes do happen, and then you want your liability to complete the contract to be contained. This avoids your company being sued for non-completion when it was no fault of your own that you were unable to do so. It costs very little to include in an agreement, but a lot if you don't and you need it.

Which law?

If there is any need for legal action to be taken – over non-payment, for example – then it is to your company's advantage to state which country's law your agreement complies with, and which country's law any proceedings will comply with, since the law on certain points varies around the world. Also, your costs will be easier if the hearings are in your own country. So, again, it is easy to stipulate up front which country's law is to be used, but possibly very costly if you do not.

These are a few of the main considerations, but it is in your interest to establish your terms and conditions and ways of working so that you can capitalize from your time and effort. It should not be the role of the project manager to draft the legal clauses in the agreement, but just to know enough to make sure that the main risks are covered. Each company will have its own way of drafting, issuing and checking agreements: some will do it through the legal section, some with a contracts manager, and some – after guidance from lawyers – will do it on their own behalf.

It is the company's responsibility to have enough support for the project manager to ensure that agreements conform to their requirements.

Freelancer and contractor contracts

When you need to recruit extra people for the team, you also make agreements with them. These will have separate issues that need to be covered, or you may find for example that your graphics artist's company owns the copyright in the visuals that are developed, not your company. Employees are different from contractors as long as it has been established that all work that is created in the course of their work belongs to the company, and this would be stated in their contract of employment. Any of the team, whether in house or external, has the same moral rights as the company does in relation to the work and the client. So the company may need to establish an overall policy for themselves and employees, depending on how moral rights are treated in their country – if at all. Note that in some countries moral rights cannot be signed away.

The company may be comfortable with employing a contractor who then subcontracts the work, but it may not. Clauses indicating who is responsible for the work and if and how subcontracting can be done are necessary to cover the type and quality of the work. If you have agreed any confidentiality clauses with the client, these usually put the onus on the developer to bind any staff to the agreements, so you might need to be very clear who is working on the project to comply with your confidentiality undertaking.

Again, it should not be the project manager's role to draft the contract agreements, but only to agree the work tasks, the length of the contract, the rate of pay, and possibly payment terms. It is the company's responsibility to provide the standard contract where the project manager completes the relevant parts.

Conclusion

The project manager needs to understand the background to many issues about rights, clearances and legal obligations to reach a well-defined contractual agreement with the client. The proposal document becomes part of the agreement, which contains the detailed specification of the work to be done, the time and costs. The more detailed the understanding of what rights and how many will need to be cleared, the better. It can have a big impact on the costs, so it is in the project manager's interest to define this, particularly before work begins. Finally, there are legal issues that are more the responsibility of the company to determine for each project, but knowledge of them is in the project manager's interest to ensure that the project fulfils both the clients' and the company's interests.

Theory into practice 11

Improve your ability to predict costs on projects.

There are hidden problems that arise with most projects where you need to have allocated a percentage of your budget for contingency purposes. Your company may have a percentage that it recommends that you add on to the cost figure. You need to build up your knowledge about hidden factors to help you predict that your project is likely to run into them. Ask as many colleagues as you can about any overruns on time – remember that time means paying more for your resources and so is an extra cost – and extra hidden costs that they have encountered on projects. Check the percentage of the total budget that these factors cost. Build up a profile of factors related to type of project to define the risk factors and the percentage contingency to cover risks. You may find that some are not risks, but rather costs or tasks that were overlooked. In this case you can detail these into the true costing rather than the contingency.

Summary

■ Clearances can be complex depending on the nature of the assets and the owners. It will be impossible to cost accurately because there are so many variables. You either need to get the client to agree to an estimated price, which will be firmed as the project proceeds, or work from the top rates that you know to cover yourself.

■ Anything used on a Web site should be cleared for the world.

■ There are legal issues that you should understand, although it is the company's responsibility to determine its terms and conditions.

■ Apart from clearing rights in assets you acquire from sources other than the clients, you need to avoid liability if your client gives you assets but does not own the electronic copyright.

■ You need to establish ownership in any new assets created by the project – code, pictures, and so on – and where you stand in development of any derivatives from the project.

■ Other aspects for attention include your right to demonstrate the application, moral rights, severance clauses, force majeure, and which country's law will apply in any proceedings.

■ You are not only involved with contractual agreements with the client. Some of these issues carry over into the contracts needed for subcontractors.

Recommended reading

See the reading list for Chapter 17, *Rights, copyright and other intellectual property*.

11

Selecting the team

Project manager's responsibilities

- To match the skills needed to the project requirements
- To check the in-house resource availability – align the requirements
- To determine the roles and responsibilities of the core and extended team
- To interview and select all key team members
- To establish a list of criteria for each role
- To ensure that the company's policies on contract terms and conditions are carried out
- To ensure that the correct rights and clearances are made
- To provide clear and detailed briefs to those employed

Introduction

Although the selection of staff was touched on in Chapter 3, *Scoping a project*, the consideration there was to demonstrate how to assess the cost of the project rather than the skills, but these two happen in unison. The aim of this chapter is to give a more detailed account of the staffing decisions, and to demonstrate the complexity of the process. You need an appreciation of skill sets across several disciplines to be able to match your project needs to personnel requirements, while balancing the cost of the resources against the needs.

Identifying the skills needed

The mix of skills needed for any project depends on its content, use of media components, size, platform, and amount of administration. As project manager, it is your responsibility to ensure that resources are available at the right time to keep the project on track. This means that you plan who you need at which points of the project, and then ensure that:

- these resources are on hand,
- they are properly inducted into the project,
- they have been contracted under the right terms and conditions,
- they have the right skills for the job,
- they have the right tools for the job,
- they have a good working environment.

Because of the nature of multimedia, there is often a core team who work together for the majority of the project and then an extended team who are brought in for particular tasks – a video editor or a specialist in CGI programming, for example. The core team may well be full-time staff members from the company, but because the workload fluctuates according to demand, or projects can be long and complicated and therefore lock people into a time frame, quite often it is necessary to contract-in people to form part of the core team.

According to the company you work for, you may be expected to carry out the interviewing process or there may be a specific personnel role in the company to take care of the search and selection process. In either case it will pay you to define the skills and experience level you need to make sure that you staff the project correctly.

Once you have a feel for the scope of the project and the expectations of the client, you should be in a position to identify the staff needed. Your decisions at this point affect the budget decisions and the costs. You need to assess the position for a core team first by matching the core skills you need with the availability of the nearest match to these in house.

Once the client has agreed to the proposal, you have to move fast to assemble the team. Situations change quickly. Even though a few of the core team appeared to be available at the time the project was scoped, they might have been placed on another project if the go-ahead for that came first. This can leave you with the difficult task of recruiting very quickly to ensure that the project begins on time. Any delay can be vital to achieving the deadlines, so this is another dangerous time for the project manager – the time between a proposal and confirmation – because some of the circumstances may have changed.

Many companies try to build some flexibility into their organization by having a list of independent contractors that can be brought in for specific projects. A project manager needs to work up a good set of contacts across all the multimedia sectors to help the recruitment process. There are agencies that specialize in multimedia and/or Web design recruitment, and some companies use these to help construct teams. Remember that if you will be using an agency to help, you need to budget for their fees as well as for the staff costs.

Whatever way your company works to solve its staffing needs, someone has to do the interviewing and make the final decision. It is wise to become involved in this process to build up your own skill set. It is not an easy task, and is very time consuming, but unless it is carried out effectively you could be landed with a poor team for a difficult project.

For an online project your core team will probably comprise the following:

■ one or more graphics artists,
■ one or more HTML authors (often the graphics artists also do this),
■ yourself as a producer/project manager.

Similarly for an offline project:

■ one or more programmers,
■ one or more graphics artists,
■ yourself as a producer/project manager.

Your extended team might include:

■ CGI programmer (for online projects)
■ video personnel
   – a video director/producer
   – an assistant producer
   – a production assistant
   – a video editor
   – a video journalist
   – a video graphics artist
   – actors/actresses
■ sound personnel
   – voice-over artistes
   – sound editor
■ general support
   – a personal assistant
   – secretarial support
■ specialist support
   – technical support
   – scriptwriters
   – a training specialist
   – an instructional designer/interactive designer
   – subject matter experts.

Because some multimedia specialists have built up experience across a range of skill sets, one person might be able to take on a couple of roles. But when exactly do you need any of these roles, and how do you assess whether you need them? The profile of each skill set and the type of project that warrants their use will be defined to help decision making about resources.

Considerations for interviews: general

It is as well to remember that interviews are a two-way process: you are assessing the candidates, but they are also assessing you and the organization. It is better if a couple of people can attend the interview so that impressions can be consolidated through discussion and comparison. Those interviewing should have:

■ established what to say about the company and the project to introduce the candidate to the set of circumstances, the requirements and the set-up;
■ established a set list of questions to ask all candidates;
■ established the skill criteria needed, and have thought of ways to assess whether the skill set is present at the levels required;
■ defined the role needed with the level of responsibility;
■ gained an impression of the candidate from pre-reading a CV;
■ formulated extra questions specific to the information contained in the CV to ascertain:
   – the accuracy of the information,
   – the reasons for any apparent discrepancies or breaks in employment,
   – the strengths and weaknesses of the candidate;

- put a time-scale on the number of minutes to be given to each section of the interview and have appointed a person to be timekeeper;
- allowed a few minutes between candidates to discuss reactions and findings and make notes.

The interviews should start on time, and should progress according to plan. If the plan overruns, any waiting candidates should be kept informed of progress. Some people have the same reaction to interviews as they do to examinations, and it is not an ideal way to form solid impressions. Some larger companies use group interviews for full-time jobs, where the candidates are set tasks to assess their abilities in a range of factors such as leadership, teamwork, and so on.

However, this is not a practice that prevails in multimedia at present, mainly because the majority of workers are employed on an ad hoc basis. It is a good idea to allow members of the core team to meet candidates for other core team roles because they will need to work together. This can be done after the formal interview while the next candidate is being interviewed. The project manager should then collect any additional comments from the other core team members prior to making decisions.

Skill set profiles: core team

Computer graphics artists

Quite often the HTML authoring for a Web site is done by the graphics artist rather than by a programmer, largely because the layout of the page is defined by the HTML. For this reason we do not separately discuss the selection of HTML authors.

Web sites and applications can demand a certain style because of the content, and ideally a graphics artist should be selected to bring the best to the content and to the interactive environment. The development platform and the delivery platform will dictate the level and skill set that are needed for the graphics artist. In the same way, these will affect the skill set needed for the programmer, as we shall see in the next section. The artists will come from either a PC or a Mac background and will have experience in the respective graphics packages and, if appropriate, in Web page design.

The artist needs to be both creative and technically minded, since creative ideas in multimedia graphics have to be achieved through technical means. Many adjustments have to be made because the graphics process is not straightforward. Colours can shift quite often as the graphic moves through its various stages to the final image, and for applications where accuracy of colour is needed – selling items that have a range of colour options, for example – this can be a major problem.

The sizing and placement of images cause other problems. Text often becomes corrupted at the last stage. It is difficult for the client to realize how much rework is needed because the graphic may have to be taken back through numerous stages to correct such problems. The technicalities and inconsistencies mean that the graphics artist needs patience and logical, analytical thinking as well as creative flair. Your application may require more of one of these attributes than the others.

The programmer or HTML author and graphics artist have to work closely together. The graphics person constructs the images to a certain stage and then passes them to the programmer or author to integrate them with all the other pieces – sound files, text, position in the program, the means of access to the image, and so on. They work out together exactly how to produce and transfer the images between them. In offline projects particularly, there are often hundreds of images and pieces of images that have to be assembled, so the naming convention for the assets and the version control between them is important.

Online projects make demands on the artists because they have to balance the size and quality of the graphics against the download times. They have to learn tricks of the trade to compress graphics with as little drop in quality as possible but with speed of transfer.

Because people may have worked in various companies with diverse approaches to working, and have different ways of expressing concepts, bringing the core team together can be problematic. Some of the skills overlap, and the graphics artist might have been used to taking the image process further than the programmer expects, or might be used to liaising with clients directly when the project manager wants to avoid this. There may be a strong split between the technical and creative skills. A technical artist may depend on the source images' being produced by conventional means and then they scan, adjust, assemble and integrate ready for the programmer. This will always be true for specialist areas such as cartoon images, for example. But if the artist has a strong technical bias, it will affect the resources and costs of the project if you do not recognize that one graphics resource will not suffice. Often this is the case where there is one main artist and input from others as and when needed.

You may find you have to work with an artist who is available in house but who doesn't have the full skill set you need. The erratic availability of contractors can also mean that you may have to select a person who displays many but not all of the attributes you need. Then you will face decisions of how to build up the balance of skills according to budget.

The project may form part of a set of projects so several artists with a variety of skills might be needed. If there are several people they need to be managed, and a senior graphics artist could be appointed to take on this role, or an art director might be considered.

An art director is usually employed by larger graphics studios as the creative ideas person who is responsible for managing the overall style of projects. You may have a set of projects that need to show continuity of graphic style – a certain look and feel. Also, if you have several computer graphics and video graphics artists involved in your project, someone needs to coordinate the artistic direction and personalities. Although the role of art director is unusual for multimedia projects at present, it may develop as the number of projects increases. At present a senior graphics designer usually takes on the responsibilities of the art director, but whether the person should come from a video graphics or computer graphics background will change according to the bias of the company and its production routes.

Pre-interview

Although there is usually one main artist for the project, you may need several for different functions during the development, particularly with offline projects. You'll need to define exactly how you intend the project to run with any split of work needed between graphics artists, for example, so that there are no misconceptions about what type of work each artist will be doing. Some tasks are more laborious than creative, and tensions can occur if an artist thinks he or she will be doing creative new work rather than repetitive conversions from source materials. The size of the project will determine whether these tasks are combined for one person to do or whether the tasks are split. Also, one person needs to have responsibility for artistic direction, otherwise clashes in opinions, style and approach will show up in the application.

At interview

The definition of roles is easy to state but difficult to achieve because you will be working blind until the fine detail of the project is teased out: so you can explain to candidates how the graphics appear to split but remind them that the circumstances may change once the project is under way.

It is important to see examples of the candidates' work and understand exactly their role in the production process, whether technical, creative, managerial, or all three. Graphics artists will be happy to discuss their preferences and styles, and might be able to come up with a feel for some treatments for the project once they understand its scope and their expected role. Because interactive graphics production is not straightforward it is a good idea to probe where the candidates have experienced problems and how these were solved. This will give you a feel for the depth of experience and knowledge of the idiosyncrasies of the graphics packages.

You may be working on a project that has a 'house style', and this might mean that the artists will need to adapt their style appropriately. Some find this easier than others, so you should check their disposition for this.

Because the synergy between the programmers or authors and graphics artists is important, it is good to allow them to meet if possible and get their reactions. If the contractors have worked for the company before, it is also wise to gather informal feedback from those that worked with them.

Programmers

This section applies to both programmers as members of the core team for offline production and their role in the extended team for online production.

The skill set of programmers is wide ranging. As project manager, your programming resource will be affected by decisions on:

- the development platform;
- the software that will be used for development (authoring, scripting or computer language);
- the delivery platform considerations.

You need to understand what hardware and software you will use in the project to help pinpoint the exact skill set needed in your programmers.

The first major decision will be the development platform that your project will use – Mac or PC, for example. Programmers specialize at this level and then have specialisms within these main groups. There are other development platforms, such as Sun and UNIX, but these are less common apart from CGI development for Web sites. Often the company will decide which development platform is used. Under the Mac and PC categories there are different sets of authoring tools. These packages allow programmers, and non-specialists who have programming aptitude, to develop straightforward applications. You need to have a good understanding of what the tools allow, or take advice from your technical support, to decide whether the tools can fit all the project requirements.

Authoring tools have become much more sophisticated over the past few years, and can cope with far more than they used to, but you need to become informed of their limitations and nuances. Some authoring packages have their own scripting languages. These allow the tailoring of the package to specific needs but add a level of complexity to the skill set needed. Scripting languages bridge the gap between authoring tools and computer languages. The difference in the levels is equivalent to prefabricated house segments (authoring languages), prefabricated building blocks (scripting languages), and constructing your own bricks (computer languages).

A further category of programmer is an analyst or systems analyst. This group have experience in defining the requirements for projects. They are the most likely to convert into project managers since they deal with clients and supervise other programmers to deliver the specification as well as having programming ability themselves. They will have been trained in using structured methods to specify and document computer projects. There are differences in the skill sets required for managing computer projects and multimedia projects, but this group will have a better starting point. The very formal approach to defining requirements by using a functional and technical specification as well as having a user requirements study is seen as over-complex and off-putting for many clients in the business sector. The principles are sound, but the methods have to be adapted and extended for multimedia.

The application platform does not necessarily dictate the development platform, so a PC application may be authored in a Mac tool set, for example. Sometimes applications need to work across platforms, and this is where wider expertise is needed to ensure that the development takes account of the cross-platform restraints. Of course, developing for the World Wide Web is

Cross-platform.

inherently multi-platform, as different browsers running on a variety of computers have to be catered for. You have to be confident that the right decisions have been made about the choice of development hardware and software to fit the delivery platform requirements. If you are non-technical, you need to have complete confidence in the technical support staff and/or programmers who make the decisions on your behalf.

If the application cannot be developed in an authoring environment, a programming language will be needed. Although there are exceptions, non-specialists have not got enough experience and training to use computer languages so usually a specialist will be needed. Different languages suit different purposes and accomplish certain tasks better than others. This is why your technical support needs to understand the whole scope of the project to make an informed decision as to what combination of hardware and software will be needed.

Programmers can apply past experience to learn new languages/packages as they work. Some packages share similarities in approach so that the learning curve is relatively fast; others have a totally different approach to their logic, so they take longer to learn if the past experience is not compatible. Quite often the programmers you employ will have to learn as they go along, and you need to be aware of how much extra time to build in to allow for their learning. This might sound like poor project management – to employ the wrong skill level – but several circumstances can lead to this. First, you may have to use full-time members of staff with a lower skill level for your project because they are available and therefore it is cheaper for the company to use them than employ contractors. Second, some specialisms within programming are harder to find, and you may not be able to find contractors with the right skills. Third, when skills are scarce they become expensive, so even if you find the right contractors you may not be able to afford them within the budget. In this case you have to gamble on the extra time for someone to gain the knowledge against the speed of experience. This would tend to mean the lower cost for longer or a higher cost for a shorter period of time.

This is a difficult decision, since estimating the time it takes for programming is not an accurate art, particularly in interactive media development.

Considerations for interviews: programmers

Pre-interview

You need to have worked out the skills you want, the skill level you would be willing to accept and 'grow', the length of time necessary to complete the project, and the cost range you could work with within your budget. Ask candidates to bring examples of their work.

At interview

There are good and bad traits within professions that are part of their 'folklore'. Programmers can be creative, versatile, act on initiative, quick thinking, adaptable, precise, accurate, work to time-scales, and reliable. However, the profession suffers from labels from the business world that indicate erratic timekeeping (both personal and project specific), poor communication skills, stubbornness, a wish to fulfil themselves rather than the project in hand, and a tendency to be wilful, seeming to live in a world of their own. The problem is that some of the best programmers are not easy to manage.

You have to decide whether solidity or finesse is needed more in the particular project if you end up with a choice of candidates who display different traits, and you need to recognize your own strengths and weaknesses in your management style to assess a fit within your team that you can manage successfully.

If you are technical, you could conduct the interview to assess the technical ability of the candidate. You also need to assess the candidate as a project member. You may well be looking for different attributes than in a full-time employee. Project-specific work can make it easier to manage a more diverse range of people than those you need to work alongside continuously. In a project-specific situation, the expectations are different for all involved.

The extended team: skill sets

Video personnel

The use of video in online applications is growing. When a company's image or the information about a key product – a new car, for example – warrants high exposure, or indeed needs to match the exposure level employed in other media, then the pressure mounts to include video despite the restrictions of quality and download times.

At present the shooting of video specifically for online use alone is unusual, and so video production follows offline production paths, and extracts might be used online as well as for other purposes. Another scenario where video plays a part is when a Web site precipitates alternative media arising from it. So a marketing CD might well use extracts from the existing Web site, but because CDs set up expectations in the users for audio and video, extras might need to be produced for the CD. In the case of hybrid Web/CDs the strengths of each medium are utilized, since the volatile data is kept online for ease of updating while the rest is encapsulated on the CD using an appropriate media mix.

What does this mean in terms of the skill level needed for video online production? It may mean that you need only the expertise to edit and compress extracts of material already produced, to provide online pieces of the best possible quality. Alternatively, you may need to employ a crew to produce major pieces for a hybrid Web/CD, where stills might be used on the Web site for continuity of style between the Web and the CD. In between these, you might decide that a video journalist who shoots directly with a digital camera, records commentary and edits items on computer would have all the right skills you need to produce pieces for a particular site. This all-in-one approach is common only for news at the moment but may develop into use in other sectors.

The variety of video that can be appropriate means that you have to recognize and set the quality level of production and the attendant skills needed carefully or your budget can quickly go astray.

If your offline application is going to include video footage, you might need to use a video director/producer, an editor, and perhaps a video graphics artist too. The directors/producers will have contacts and preferences for using certain facility houses, editors and video graphics people, so it may save you some effort if you trust your main video contractor to organize the other video needs. Again, depending on the company bias, you may have access to all the video personnel you need in house.

The difference between a video director and a producer is not straightforward until you define the roles for a full feature film, where the director has the creative role and the producer is more of an administrator. For shorter pieces of work you need to check what a person will be prepared to do if you interview directors and producers, so that you are aware whether they will collapse the roles together, or whether they expect support themselves. A lot will depend on the amount and type of video footage you require.

As video has become more of a key component in applications, the traditional roles from video production will figure more in multimedia teams. Production assistants have had a key role in video productions, helping the director and producer. The role involves organizing and administration, but can extend to supervising edits, directing part of the shoot, clearing rights,

Use of video is increasing.

organizing facility houses, and editing scripts. A good production assistant is well organized, used to troubleshooting, well skilled in audio and video production, and has a useful range of contacts.

Personnel with a video background find the seeming disintegration of pieces of a script and the lack of control over the user's sequence of using the material an anathema. Their backgrounds have prepared them for continuity, flow, strong storylines, methods of story development, build-up, characterization and unity of a whole. They lead the viewer through the material. Interactivity destroys this to a certain extent, and it takes time for traditional directors and assistants to come to terms with the changes that are needed in material development. They have a tendency to be critical about the technical quality and the structure of interactive programmes that they have seen because they compare them with video programmes.

Although the addition of interactivity and working with programmers is a new area, video personnel are used to dealing with a mix of materials and people. It is possibly a little harder for those coming from a programming background to pick up the creative aspects of audio and video production than it is for video personnel to adjust to interactivity; but it is easier for them to learn the technicalities of audio and video production than it is for video personnel to understand computer graphics and programming technicalities. This might mean that some personnel from a computing or graphics background will claim to have audio and video production skills. You need to decide whether these people have full creative, administrative and technical skills or whether audio and video specialists are needed.

Assistant producers help the producers with the creative direction of the video footage. The producer may delegate some of the responsibility for shots and edits to an assistant but still maintain a strong directional line. This means that some assistants have a wide range of skills and are capable of directing smaller projects. You may decide that an assistant producer could fulfil the role you need, depending on their experience. It would be rare in multimedia to need both producer/director and assistant producer.

Production assistants can be invaluable when a project needs video footage, photos or pictures from picture libraries, clearance of video, sound and graphics rights, or if several strands of the project need to be completed simultaneously because of the time-scales. They have an administrative role supporting the director and producer.

The casting and directing of actors and actresses might form part of your overall responsibility. If your footage needs extensive detail such as external locations or studio sets you will need a full production team. This is why and where video footage is expensive and might take up a good portion of your budget. The producer would usually coordinate, recruit and manage the video team, and take care of casting, but you may have to sit in with the client to check that the actors and actresses fulfil their expectations and needs.

So much depends on the scope of the project and the budget that the number of people involved and their roles is difficult to quantify. Multimedia at present tends to expect people to collapse a few roles and responsibilities together because the amount filmed is generally shorter and less complex than for videos and films.

Sometimes, and this is true for on- and offline projects, you might find yourself in the position of selecting and organizing facilities houses and personnel, such as video editors, to work on pre-shot footage. Your need for a producer or director diminishes in this case, but you still have to clear the rights and re-edit the material to suit the purpose.

Video editors work to directions, so if your application needs existing footage reworked you need to consider whether you can handle the direction or whether you need help. This could depend on your own background and experience and whether the scripts are straightforward. Alternatively, the editor might be prepared to work with the scripts without direction. The range of possibilities within video production and the variety and level of skills within the personnel mean that identification of which personnel are needed and recruitment are much easier with someone who has been part of the industry.

Increasingly, video footage for multimedia is edited on a computer desktop, and even in broadcast production desktop systems are used for the early offline stage of editing. You might produce your video using broadcast facilities, in which case you will hire these facilities complete with their personnel, and the editing is not really a team-recruitment issue. If you are going to make use of desktop editing for your production then you will need to have a team member who is able to do the work. This might be something that a graphic designer can do, especially if the video editing is combined with compositing work, where moving sequences are combined together. Your decision whether to use an edit suite or your own computer could be influenced by cost, personnel abilities, time-scale, and the complexity of the editing. However, the creative processes involved with the choice of which edits and video effects will suit the material best are skills that still reside more with video personnel than with computer personnel, although the skill sets are converging.

Sound personnel

The production of audio for a Web site is basically the same as for an offline application.

If you are using audio with graphics and text, you will need to:

■ book a studio with a sound editor,
■ select and book your voice-over artistes,
■ select any music needed,
■ have all the scripts ready and signed off,
■ specify exactly the format in which you will need the material.

You will be asked how long you'll need the studio and editor for, so you have to make sure that you know how much work is involved in the scripts and estimate the amount of time needed to edit the material afterwards. You have to work out the timing sequence of all these aspects so that they come together at the studio. Selecting the voice-over artistes is no trivial task. You'll more than likely have to go through an agency. Your company may hold banks of voice-over tapes from different agencies that you can browse, you may have a voice in mind and need to find out the agent, or you may have specific requirements for voice qualities and need to match them to people. You can phone agencies and put your specifications to them; they will suggest some alternatives, and then send through some demo tapes.

The voice-over industry is well structured, and is used to responding quickly to enquiries. The agencies have several questions about use of the voice-over that determine the basic rate for the artiste and any clearance and rights fees. For non-interactive productions the negotiations are straightforward and clear. They are based on the type of use, type of audience, period of time, and countries for clearance. However, the industry has begun to come to terms with offline but not online interactive media, and so you'll meet a range of prices from different agencies for the same result.

One of the standard categories that's been used – number of times for broadcast or use – is impossible to predict for interactive media, since the user

Different prices from different agencies.

may or may not access the particular voice-over every time. However, rights owners are becoming increasingly familiar with the nature of interactive applications and Web sites, and in many cases will now quote rates. Production music recorded specifically for use in film, television and multimedia is available from many sources, and in some cases it is royalty free.

If you are employing production assistants, it is invaluable if they have had prior experience with clearing multimedia rights. As it is an area that is constantly shifting, and the regulators are trying to address the problems, you need to keep up to date with the changes either through them or by yourself.

Voice-over artistes work quickly. They often have sessions before and after yours, so if you have miscalculated the amount of material, or there are too many changes, you will be looking at the hire of all concerned again. The artistes usually charge a minimum of an hour however little they say.

The sound editors will use a variety of techniques to deal with any retakes that are necessary because of mispronunciation, wrong intonation or whatever. The way they choose to operate depends on the sophistication of the equipment they are using. Some studios are tape based; some record direct to a computer file. If there are very specific subject terms, it is wise to have a representative from the client at the recording to check the pronunciation.

The artistes should have the script a couple of days before the recording so that they can prepare, although many are excellent sight-readers. The scripts need to have been signed off by the client prior to the recording. The editor will mark up the script to show where there were retakes, but you or your delegate should also keep check and decide which out of any that are disputed should be used. The client or their representative might prefer to make these decisions, but they have to be made then and there.

It is important that the editor knows what the tracks will be used for, and the quality level needs to be stated clearly.

Multimedia applications have underestimated the importance of the use of sound, as discussed in Chapter 8. This starts at the script stage, when speech and stills are often put together without the atmospheric use of music and sound effects. However, until the clearance and rights problems are sorted, the expense of quality audio might be too much for many projects, and it is easier to compromise on its quality than on many of the other components.

Audio production is a large administrative, creative and technical part of the project and carries its own risks, which the project manager needs to understand and control. A video producer or experienced assistant producer would have the skills to manage and coordinate the audio production as well as the video if necessary, but they would have to be made aware of the technical specification for the audio so that the next stage – encoding for the Web site or CD – can proceed smoothly.

The audio and video move to the next stage in preparation for integration. Because the tools have matured quickly, it is becoming easier to encode them. It is so much easier now that graphics artists and programmers can shoot and record pieces of material, then integrate them without the need for all the personnel, studios and facilities houses. If your application needs only this level of quality, there is no reason to go to the expense of full-blown audio and video production. You still need to clear all rights and ensure that there are no accidental infringements such as advertisements on a wall used as a background in the video, or uncleared use of any music. There are lots of traps to avoid when this in-house approach is taken, and the creative personnel are often not aware of all the administrative angles that need to be covered for legal reasons. If this is the right approach for your project, you have to take full responsibility for ensuring that all the administrative procedures are carried out and recorded correctly.

General support

Personal assistant

If the administration in the project is going to be heavy, you may well need a personal assistant instead of or as well as a production assistant. The skills of organizing are parallel, but personal assistants will not get involved with the audio and video production to the same extent. They may book facilities, and arrange and clear rights under your direction if you will be performing these tasks. They should possess secretarial skills so that they can assist in documenting the project and collating scripts as well as contributing to the general communication with the client and team.

If the project is an international one, with all the administrative extras that this entails, a personal assistant may be the answer. If the project involves details of the client's products – a kiosk or a full online retail site, for example – it can be a large task to ensure that the information is accurate and in a form that will facilitate integration.

Clients will be used to changing their details on a daily basis until the products are on sale, and it is difficult to keep track of the current situation on prices, colour descriptions, product dimensions, product specifications, and so on. Unless the application links online to the client database as part of the project specification, you will most likely need to reproduce the details and get sign-off on a version at the time you need to do final integration. You will have to build up the relevant details and keep updating until the last moment.

This is one of those grey tasks that several people might do or share: an instructional or interactive designer might see it as a task to ensure the quality of data and be prepared to take this on; programmers might be persuaded to have this as part of their role, particularly if the technicalities of merging data from the sources can be streamlined; you might see it as part of your liaison and sign-off role; or you may set up a process between companies where your personal assistant will liaise with the appropriate people to maintain the records. A lot will depend on exactly how much data there is, how unstable it is, and how it will be integrated into the application.

The role tends to evolve according to circumstances and the aptitude of the people involved.

Secretarial support

All projects generate a good deal of general administration, and some level of secretarial support is always needed. If you have to type and produce all the documents and letters yourself, make all phone calls to book facility houses, and contact the various contractors, clients and officials, you need to block out at least half of your time for this and have other forms of backup support for the other functions to compensate. Lack of administrative backup is one of the most common causes of problems in multimedia projects, because the amount of time it takes is underestimated and undervalued by managers. This is not a major problem if you do not have to perform several of the core tasks yourself on the project, but if you are expected to do part of the programming, perhaps produce a prototype with an authoring tool, cover all the liaising with the client, and maybe write a script or two while recruiting and managing all the other staff, then the day-to-day administration becomes problematic. This is where the value of being multiskilled can become diminished because it is considered the norm rather than the exception.

If you need to have support, you may be able to identify the busy administrative periods and survive with temporary secretaries. However, inducting people often eats up vital time, and so continuity of personnel across a project needs to be carefully weighed against other factors.

Project managers in other business spheres are not expected to perform any of the core tasks themselves. In many ways, the practical skills are seen as non-management functions and therefore not part of the role. Multimedia is still embryonic so the boundaries are not as defined. Also, the skills are not as plentiful because of this, so doubling-up is natural at this stage. This may change as the profession matures.

Specialist support

Technical support

The day-to-day running of the technical side of the project can range from straightforward to very complex depending on the mixture of hardware and software that will be used. In some research and international projects your partners might be producing the hardware and software as part of the project, and you may be dependent upon their meeting their deadlines and testing the efficiency of the tools, prior to you using them. Inevitably with new hardware and software the unexpected happens, and it is at this stage that good technical backup is essential.

The company may have a technical director, a production manager, a network manager, a webmaster and technical assistants, or it may not. It is essential that any work on the project is properly backed up. The administration for the technical side of the project, such as registering software licences, general maintenance, chasing parts and creating backups, can be onerous.

You cannot assume that graphics artists and programmers will perform any administrative aspects unless these responsibilities are defined as part of their role. Depending on where they have worked, this might be considered normal or highly irregular. This is where a good definition of roles, responsibilities and general work practice pays off, because then no-one makes any assumption. Very often, it is the assumption that someone else is doing something that suddenly provokes a crisis for the project manager.

The amount of technical support should increase according to the number and type of projects that the company has. If, however, your project warrants extra for the whole period or part of the time, this is yet another resource to nominate and budget for.

Scriptwriters

Many scriptwriters could form part of the video personnel team if their experience lies in writing video scripts. If video scriptwriters are employed, they tend to work with the director or producer. But multimedia scripts, as we have seen, can combine any variety of audio, video, interactive instructions, interactive design, and text. You might find one person to write all the scripts for the project, or you might have to employ several for the different parts. Your prime concerns are to:

- maintain quality across the scripts so that every media attribute is used to best effect;
- ensure consistency of style;
- check that there is correct adherence to the overall interactive design;
- keep the scriptwriters on track;
- make sure the scripts keep to the size and specifications worked out for each section;
- determine that each script is technically achievable in the time and budget.

The precise content can take time to determine, and this can sometimes form part of the writer's brief; at other times the subject experts, interactive designers and/or training analysts will work to decide which issues need to be addressed and then work with writers to achieve the scripts. The whole area of scriptwriting is one of the least defined in multimedia and therefore one of the hardest tasks to control for the project manager. As each piece of script is addressed, there is a tendency for the writers to want to add and expand the original ideas beyond the scope of the budget or beyond the space allocated for the section, and this needs to be contained. Experience of working with interactive scripts helps writers to understand the new constraints that have to be taken into account, but if they have little experience you need to monitor them closely.

Prior to interview, you need to define a brief to direct the writers. The brief needs to cover the content treatment needed, the scope, style considerations, the audience profile, the company profile, and the time-scales. The briefing documents should be written and include as much detail as possible so that there is no misunderstanding later. If there is an overall interactive design, sometimes called the **high-level design**, the writers should be briefed to explain where and how their piece fits into the overall design. A structure diagram proves invaluable when discussing the project with most of the personnel involved, and always helps scriptwriters. They will have a different approach if they know that they are not responsible for the whole programmes and will want to ensure that their piece fits the overall specification as well as the individual section brief.

If the writer is meant to take on a fuller role and produce the interactive design as well as the detailed scripts your brief will be different, and you will be checking for a more complex skill set. The type of application will direct the needs for designers and scriptwriters and the precise skills they should have. The script for an advertising agency's Web site, for example, would need to be very different from a medical education CD.

Training specialist

As already discussed, training has its own approach to defining content and scripts, so if the project is a training application you need to make sure that it conforms to the principles of the discipline. The training specialists you recruit would need to have had experience in training needs analysis if you expect them to define the overall scope of the content. Their role may stop there and the scriptwriters could take over; or, if the training specialists have interactive experience, they may be able to take the project through the next stage of high-level design. They may possibly be capable of writing some or all of the scripts themselves. A lot depends on the application and the experience of the training specialist. So-called 'soft skills' such as assertiveness, leadership and counselling are harder to recruit for than other training areas. You should be looking for a fit in experience of the content, a match with experience in training analysis for a similar audience, and experience in developing interactive or distance learning materials.

You may find that you need to pair a training specialist with an interactive designer, subject matter experts and scriptwriters at different stages of the content development. If the application is an in-house training programme for a large firm, this mix of people would be quite common. If the training specialists were from the client company, and you had to utilize their skills, they might have little or no interactive experience. Then your role would be to recruit enough support staff around the training specialists to help achieve the right mix of skills needed for this part of the project.

In developing intranet, Internet and/or hybrid Web/CDs for training, the appreciation of the strengths and weaknesses of the media plus the attributes of the different levels of interactivity that figure in each delivery platform are paramount. The purpose of the training has to be balanced with the way the information is structured. The range and structure of the training information will be affected by considerations such as whether tutor support is built into the package via email, video conferencing or whatever.

You need to select people for your team who have worked across all forms of training so that they appreciate how to use each element best in the delivery mix. The breadth of skill is difficult to find, and so more than one training specialist might be needed; or a mix of training specialist with instructional designer/interactive designer – as defined below – might provide the solution.

Instructional/interactive designer

One of the key skills you are trying to cover is that of interactive design. Because this is bound up with defining the sections of the content, the interface, and the routing or navigation paths through the material, it spans several of the roles: programming, graphics, scriptwriting, producer, and interactive design. Your programmer or graphics artist may well be experienced in producing the equivalent of a high-level design but not scripts

Interactive design.

to support it. They may on the other hand not be very experienced or happy in liaising with clients to extract the salient information, and prefer building to a specification that they are given.

An interactive designer takes on some or all of the responsibility of defining content plus specifying the high-level design, and probably can write some or all of the scripts. The fine detail of the interactive design has to be negotiated between all the core team members because they all have relevant input to help shape the decisions. In this way, an interactive designer might sometimes be part of the core team.

If one of your core team, including yourself, cannot fulfil the functions of interactive design, you should consider recruiting an instructional/interactive designer. Other roles will be able to script for text, audio and video, but the 'help' script for an offline application, which explains how the program works, may also include text, audio and video. This is often forgotten but is vital. It is unlike the other scripts in style and tone. It can be the key to a successful application. As applications are now more complex, the help script is growing in size and importance. You need to determine whose responsibility it is to take care of this. Online applications can offer direct contact with people for support via the medium, but how this is set up and maintained can be a key decision for the content of the application.

Subject matter experts/personalities

Commercial applications tend to use a public figure because the name helps to sell the product. They may be experts in the field or have strong links to the subject. Sometimes, the experts will take an active part in the programme by being in the video or doing some of the voice-over. Sometimes they might just endorse the application. On other occasions, they might help to define the content and check the scripts. There can be a pairing between training analysts, subject experts and instructional designers or combinations of these, as and when the project needs it.

It is important that you and your client are confident about the integrity of the content, so it is useful to tap into subject expertise. However, the more people that are involved in vetting scripts, the more problematic it becomes to stabilize them. The subject experts have to be given a clear brief of their roles and responsibilities in the project. If the experts are from the client company, they can influence the project strongly. They can cause havoc if they begin to stray out of their area of expertise into criticizing the interactive structure or the interface, for example.

Their advisory and critical role has to have strong boundaries drawn around it to allow the rest of the 'experts', the core team, to do their job effectively. You need to explain to the client that the experts' advice has to be put into the complete interactive context, and that when this happens some compromises may have to be made. This is more of a problem when the experts suggest complete new areas that need to be incorporated into the application too late for you to reconcile with time and cost.

Subject matter experts and personalities are quite easy to locate and recruit but their guaranteed allocation of time to the project is more of a problem. Your clients will often recommend their preferred experts. It is important that you explain how time critical their input will be, and get a signed commitment. This applies for all types of project, on- and offline.

Theory into practice 12

Allocating roles and responsibilities

The check-list at the end of the chapter covers many of the tasks that need to be performed during the interactive media project cycle.

Apply the list to your present or a past project by inserting the team's initials into the relevant boxes to see how the roles and responsibilities pan out. Put 'not applicable (n/a)' where appropriate. Beware any gaps, and ensure they are covered next time.

The listing can be useful during your pre-interview and interview stage. If you are going to use in-house resources, then you can map out their roles and responsibilities, indicate where 'not applicable' applies, and from the gaps that are left get a feel for the personnel you need to recruit and the tasks they will need to perform. You can then make a note of the skills that lie behind the tasks to get a skill profile for the people you need. This check-list would not be comprehensive for international projects where more tasks are used, but it could serve as a starting point for you to adapt if necessary. The check-list can also be found on the CD.

Summary

- The project manager needs to identify the mix of skills necessary for the project and then assemble an appropriate core and extended team.

- Recruitment is not an easy exercise. It should be handled professionally with good preparation, briefing and role definitions.

- Knowledge of what roles exist and the contribution each can make to the project is important to help in decision making.

- Each role has its own range of skills and considerations. Careful assessment of the skill level needed has to be balanced with the project needs, budget constraints and management style.

- Clear assignment of responsibilities is necessary to ensure that all project tasks are covered. It is a good idea to list all the tasks and assign the person responsible for each as a check that all aspects have been covered.

Table 11.1 Project task and skill set check-list.

Client liaison	Initial	Recruitment/selection general	Initial	Video production	Initial
1. Attend meetings		1. Identify resource needs		1. Direction/production manager	
2. Write up meetings		2. Cost resources, align to budget		2. Identify resources needed	
3. Be the main telephone/fax/email contact		3. Organize deskspace, equipment etc.		3. Cost resources, align to budget	
4. Respond to queries		4. Organize appropriate CVs		4. Organize recruitment	
5. Organize sign-offs – proposal, contract, content, scripts, database		5. Select interviewees		5. Select interviewees	
		6. Define roles and responsibilities		6. Define roles and responsibilities	
6. Handle scheduling		7. Write job descriptions/criteria		7. Interview	
7. Monitor budget		8. Define skill mix needed		8. Recruit or delegate recruitment	
8. Handle disputes		9. Interview		9. Recruit: scriptwriters, camera, lights, sound, grips, make-up, continuity, catering, communications, logging etc.	
9. Inform of project status		10. Select appointees			
10. Negotiate changes in time and cost		11. Negotiate contracts			
		12. Negotiate with agencies		10. Negotiate contracts	
		13. Induct new recruits to company		11. Negotiate with agents	
		14. Induct new recruits to project		12. Organize shoot (locations, props etc.)	
				13. Clear locations, liaise with police	
				14. Cast artists	
				15. Organize facility houses/edits	
				16. Recruit video graphics: 3-D animator, computer compositor, Harry operator, etc.	
				17. Direct edits	
				18. Edit offline	
				19. Edit online	
				20. Approve edits	
				21. Film/picture research	
				22. Clearances and rights (footage, pictures, music, voice-overs etc.)	
				23. Liaise with programmers/technical quality assurance	
				24. Monitor and approve costs	
				25. Organize video encoding	
				26. Encode video	

Table 11.1 (Cont)

Audio production	Initial	Stills/graphics production	Initial	Database development	Initial
1. Direction/production manager		1. Direction/production manager		1. Identification of data fields	
2. Scripts (main and help)		2. Graphics production		2. Collation of data	
3. Organize studio facility		3. Picture researcher		3. Verification of data	
4. Organize recording/edit		4. Rights and clearances		4. Liaison with clients	
5. Organize translations		5. Electronic asset management		5. Integration into project	
6. Direct edit		6. Animation production		6. Indexer	
7. Select voice-overs		7. Photographer		7. Help script	
8. Select/commission music		8. Lighting		8. Spell check and editing	
9. Negotiate rights and clearances		9. 3-D modeller			
10. Liaise with programmers/technical quality assurance, formats		10. Computer graphics			
11. Organize M & E tracks		11. Paintbox operator			
12. Organize encoding		12. Scanner/digitizer			
13. Encode		13. Art director			
14. Monitor and approve costs		14. Illustrator/artist			
		15. Text/page layout			
		16. Typography			

Design and documentation	Initial	Computer and integration	Initial	Administration	Initial
1. Produce final contract agreement		1. Programmer/software engineer		1. Typing	
2. Produce technical specification		2. Technical manager		2. Filing	
3. Product outline/high-level specification		3. Network manager/webmaster		3. Answering/making phone calls	
4. Research and define content sections		4. Maintenance		4. Collating personnel and project documentation	
5. Research and define detailed content		5. Backup/archiving		5. Sending and distributing faxes/messages	
6. Produce interactive script – interface functions, help script		6. Software librarian		6. Organize meetings, book rooms	
7. Liaise with subject experts				7. Organize couriers, cars, post etc.	
				8. Photocopying	
				9. Collect time sheets	

Recommended reading

Belbin R.M. (1981). *Management Teams: Why They Succeed or Fail*. Oxford: Butterworth-Heinemann Ltd

Belbin R.M. (1993). *Team Roles at Work*. Oxford: Butterworth-Heinemann Ltd

De Marco T. and Lister T. (1987). *Peopleware: Productive Projects and Teams*. New York: Dorset House Publishing Co.

Honey P. (1988). *Improve Your People Skills*. London: Institute of Personnel Management

Katzenbach J.R. and Smith D.K. (1993). *The Wisdom of Teams: Creating the High-Performance Organization*. Boston, MA: Harvard Business School Press

Phillips N. (1992). *Managing International Teams*. London: Pitman Publishing

Raudsepp E. (1963). *Managing Creative Scientists and Engineers*. New York: The Macmillan Company

Tjosvold D. (1991). *Team Organisation: An Enduring Competitive Advantage*. Chichester: Wiley.

12

Team management principles

Project manager's responsibilities

- To negotiate with higher management on behalf of the team
- To motivate the team and set the direction for them
- To create good communication between the team members
- To employ a variety of management styles appropriate for the occasion
- To identify and remedy any deficiencies in the team in functional, decision-making and interpersonal skills
- To resolve problems occurring in the teams
- To recognize and address environmental factors affecting the team

The project manager and team culture

Most multimedia projects take place in a team culture. A good team culture can be defined as having the following characteristics:

■ everyone pulling together to achieve well-defined tasks
■ respect for each other's skills
■ a sharing of success and failures
■ mutual support when needed.

The team will be affected by outside conditions such as recognition within the organization, being valued, being treated fairly, receiving support, and receiving adequate resources. A team culture will often take its lead from the organization culture but it can develop its own. So the manager has a dual role: to try to provide the conditions that will help to motivate the team to work well together, and to create an open, constructive working atmosphere to allow the individuals to achieve their best in a way that also serves the project best.

Project manager's position.

To provide good conditions, the manager has to negotiate with higher management for the necessary resources. You may need to justify how they will improve the success criteria of the project. As the team's representative to higher management, the manager takes the lead on their behalf. For many, this representation role appears a contradiction of the idea of leadership. Leadership seems to imply being in front of others, being ahead of them, making the decisions for them, but this is true only in some cases. Team leadership is also about being the representative of the team's needs, views and skills.

It is not easy to create an open, constructive working atmosphere. Individuals have their own aspirations, their own personality traits, their own strengths and weaknesses, their own defence mechanisms, and their own ways of interacting with other people. It might seem impossible to unify a disparate group who come from different disciplines, with different skills and different ways of describing multimedia. However, the team will respond to the tone and form of interaction you set. You can be the catalyst by being open and informative, supportive and straight-talking.

Team leadership is also about giving direction, but this should not be confused with being directive. Setting the direction in a multimedia project means performing all the background tasks that have been described in the preceding chapters and help define exactly what each member needs to achieve and how each task relates to the whole project. The administrative tasks, such as defining everyone's role and responsibilities, in themselves set a working direction, and this in turn gives unity of purpose. Maintaining the overall vision of the application also helps to set a direction. Individuals can become too involved with their own particular pieces to maintain the overview. Constant focusing on the needs of the user also sets a unifying direction for all concerned.

As discussed in Chapter 2, project management principles were generally derived from engineering projects. The background to the general management concepts of 'a manager' or a 'a leader' has been based on historical models with some insights coming from military models, and others from hierarchical business models. Just as the engineering derivatives for project management needed adjusting for multimedia project management, so the traditional principles underlying concepts of managers and leaders cannot be transferred directly to multimedia management. The difference that has been identified is one of managing creative teams. The research concerning successful multimedia managers has not been applied directly to multimedia teams, but roles such as theatre director, conductor of orchestras, and TV programme production have now been studied, and provide a contrast with other management models.

The main differences between traditional managers and managers of creative teams seem to relate to the dynamics of interaction with team members. For successful creative team managers, the old authoritarian role of manager appears to change to more of a collaborative role. The manager also retains more of a 'hands-on' approach to the task in hand, whereas previous models have stressed leaving one's specialism behind, trading it for new management and administrative functions. They are also more part of the team than removed from it, spotting role gaps and filling them. It is a more fluid role in concept than previously.

More of these emerging principles will be covered later in the chapter. The key point being made here is that we cannot blindly apply previous concepts about team management to teams working in emerging media sectors. The introduction to management styles that follows is presented in this spirit. It appears that the successful creative team manager shifts styles and this is reflected in the scenarios covered below.

Management styles

Setting a direction for the team means encouraging them to share the vision of the end-product. Being directive, on the other hand, is linked to management style. There are many ways of defining management styles but we'll concentrate on directive, consultative, collaborative, and delegation. Good managers employ a mixture of styles appropriate for the occasion and circumstances. The hard part is recognizing which to use, and when.

Management style: directive.

The **directive** style is appropriate when you have the knowledge and experience to make the necessary decision, you have to accept the responsibility for your decision, and the decision is needed quickly. Under these circumstances, you make the decision and then direct the team members to carry it out. If you communicate this to the team in an open manner, you can be directive without making them feel manipulated. They may challenge the decision from their perspective and experience. You should see this as a chance to broaden them by giving an explanation, rather than as a challenge to your authority – as long as you are confident that you are right.

If, for example, your client phones you to request an immediate demo of work in progress because a new divisional manager has been appointed who is re-prioritizing the workload and the whole project might be in jeopardy, you would be justified in directing the team to stop work and pull a demo together. This may well affect their schedule and cause rework later. However, faced with the alternatives of no project or some downtime, you have no choice. The important thing for the team to recognize is that your use of authority is not arbitrary.

You can employ a **consultative** style when you need to make a decision and you are fairly confident about it but you have some time to check the views of team members. They may influence you or they may not. You have

Management style: consultative.

the time to think things through and take all aspects into consideration before reaching a decision.

Collaborative decisions occur when you recognize that you do not have the right knowledge, skill and experience to come to a conclusion yourself, so you seek the team's views to pool experience and take a decision based on the majority view.

Management style: collaborative.

Collaborative decisions may not involve the whole team. You may seek the views of some of the team who have the relevant skills, and take the decision based on their expertise.

In multimedia management, where there are so many strands of expertise, often you do not have the same level of knowledge and experience in specific areas as members of the team, so you will need to collaborate with them often.

However, sometimes you will be forced into making decisions in time-critical circumstances where you cannot contact the right team members. Both sides need to recognize the constraints and accept that some decisions may not always be the best. They can be the best for the time and the circumstances, which may be your only consolation. You will maintain an open and honest atmosphere by admitting that the decision was forced and that you were aware of the risks but that you were left with no choice.

This can happen, for example, at a meeting with the client very late into the project, where they suddenly include an important visitor from their head office who states an opinion contrary to the one your client has stated in a video presentation in the project. You can see that they are as surprised as you, but they agree with the visitor wholeheartedly. You are placed in a very unfortunate position. You cannot embarrass your main client in front of their visitor by explaining that they have already stated their original position on camera and signed off the video, which has been encoded and integrated into the relevant section.

But once the visitor departs you have to address the situation. You recognize that there is no way that you can now keep that opinion in the section but also you cannot rework it in the time and money even if the clients agrees. There is little else to do but suggest that you'll look at the section and try to edit the offending part, or cut it out. The client insists that the new position has to be included. You know that a new video clip is impossible, and that the client will not move from their demand. The stakes are too high for them. You appreciate their circumstances. At the same time, you realize that your knowledge of the specific content is not accurate. The scriptwriters would be the ones to comment on the impact, and usually you'd have telephoned them. But as their work was finished a few weeks earlier, their contracts have ended and they are no longer around. With a public launch in a few days, you decide to go for the lowest common denominator – to cut out the old message and then insert the new one with text and graphics, knowing that this is against the design continuity of the application but is achievable.

When you and the team fully analyze the situation back at work, the new slant actually has much more of an impact than imagined because several of the associated ideas are affected as well. The whole section needs rework rather than one contained piece. So much is affected that it becomes better to scrap the video and reform the section into text, some saved audio, and new graphics. Your team are furious with you, and your client is furious – more with themselves and their top management for not communicating changes in policy faster to them – but they take it out on you. However, a decision had to be taken and the consequences accepted as part of your responsibility.

With hindsight, there might have been alternatives if you could have thought things through and talked things through. But with other pressing points on the meeting agenda, you needed many decisions and agreements, not just to fire-fight with that one. Your only consolation might be that other project managers would understand, and if you'd warned the client not to include time-sensitive information in a video, they had ignored the advice!

Management style: delegation.

Delegation means that you transfer the powers of decision making on some matters to members of the team. But you must meet certain conditions to be seen to delegate otherwise this can be abdication not delegation. If you delegate, you need to make clear:

■ how far the delegation is allowed;
■ that you delegate with complete authority within the limits set;
■ that you will support all decisions made on your behalf.

If you fail any of these criteria, you have not delegated effectively. There is nothing worse than a manager who confuses delegation with abdication. This can lead to unclear ideas of how far, when, and to what level the other people can make decisions. With no clear boundaries and with a confusing brief, it is easy to make mistakes. If your own manager has abdicated not delegated, you'll quickly find that there will only be support as long as you are right!

For example, you may decide to delegate the video production to a video director who would take care of the casting, the shoot and the edits, and hand you a master tape. You could allocate a budget from your budget for the completed tape and then monitor the spend. You might prefer to take over at the encoding stage so that the key points for you to monitor would be the quality of the content, the technical quality, and the compatibility of the tape source. This would then be delegation. The video director would know the precise tasks, the authority limits of the budget, where you would want sign-off, where you would take over, and the criteria for acceptance of the tape.

This has been a quick overview of some of the styles that have been identified. It is impossible to cover this area in greater depth here but it is important to introduce it as a topic because your performance as a project manager can be affected by your management style. Many multimedia project managers do not recognize the extent to which good people management contributes to successful projects.

It would be a good idea to include some more reading on management styles in your own development plan for the next year to get a better appreciation of the insights that can help with managing people.

Teams: lessons learnt so far

From the last chapter, we understand how to identify the technical or specialist skills needed for a particular project and recruit accordingly to make sure all the tasks are covered. But this is not the complete recipe for success. A project needs enough people in the team with a capacity to bond the individual pieces together. This means that they are willing to attend to detail and compromise their individual professional drive for the sake of the total project performance. The project manager needs to take the lead in this. A good team needs the complete set of technical or functional expertise, problem-solving and decision-making skills, creative skills, and interpersonal skills.

The problems of managing talented specialists have been recognized in investigations into teamwork. As indicated earlier in the chapter, research is beginning to recognize that traditional models of manager, leader – or whatever title is applied to the project manager of teams where creativity is necessary – need modifying.

We'll look at two approaches here. The first looks at managers of creative teams. The second is based on insights from managing IT teams. Interactive media development has elements of both, and so both are seen to have relevant contributions to make.

Successful managers of creative teams

Effective team leaders and successful teams: is there a formula?

John Whatmore has studied creative teams and has found the following elements of successful leaders:

- Strong experienced leadership. This was equated with experience in the design domain, with strength of personality and a democratic style.
- Leaders as part of the team. They used an empathetic approach to motivate the team. They immersed themselves in problems and helped the team to cooperate towards mutual goals.
- Care in selecting the team. The manager takes responsibility for selecting the team and defines their role in achieving the project goals.
- Provision of freedom and trust. Effective managers set realistic parameters whilst giving freedom of expression and trust to the individuals to 'produce the goods'.
- Encouragement of collective working. The work process is transcultural and transdisciplinary, and the project manager needs to be right on top of the progress to understand whether to swing the balance at a particular point or task, and if so, when.
- Support and protection for the team. Because the creative members of the team have skills that are hard to define and defend, the project manager creates a shield from outside influences to allow the creativity to flourish. They champion the team's beliefs outside the group.
- Being there and being sensitive. Effective leaders of creative teams exert influence more by what they do than by what they say. They are there when needed for support of any kind. They relate sensitively to the individual as well as to team needs.

These key points represent a shift from how traditional management effectiveness is perceived, and pave the way for new models to emerge. Far more has to be done in this area, and initiatives are under way. If you are heading up teams of multimedia educational or training projects, the *Skills for the Missing Industry* report listed in the references at the end of the chapter is particularly interesting.

Characteristics of successful teams

Another approach to defining the characteristics of successful teams has been taken by Meredith Belbin, who offers detailed insight into personality mixes, teamwork, success and failure. Personality attributes and behaviour characteristics can account for the success or failure of projects. Interaction skills within the project team can make or break it. Although Belbin's experiments were conducted with management teams selected on the basis of extensive psychometric testing, the personality attributes could be applied to any set of individuals who need to work in a team setting.

The use of psychometric testing as part of multimedia recruitment would not fit into the way the industry works at present. It is difficult enough to find the right technical and creative skill mix. But the project manager can benefit from understanding group dynamics, and may use the knowledge wisely to help in difficult situations.

Belbin's findings that appear to have relevance for multimedia will be summarized in the following paragraphs.

The premise that very high levels of mental ability in all team members make the best combination proved disappointing. It appeared that critical debate was a characteristic of these teams, and that there were difficulties in their reaching coherent decisions. They were difficult to manage. The emphasis within teams of high mental ability was analysis not synthesis, and in teamwork the analysis needs to be synthesized to move the ideas to tangible development. The teams performed best if there were one or two people of high mental ability and worst if there were none. The profile for teams from high-technology areas was one of high mental ability, and so there could be correlations between multimedia teams and these findings.

There is little that the project manager can do, as many of the necessary skills for a multimedia team warrant high mental ability. Critical debate is necessary in a creative, high-tech field, and specialists thrive on it. It forms part of their drive and motivation, both of which you need in the project. But if you recognize that the avenues explored lack cohesion, and no one else in the team provides a unifying stance, it becomes your responsibility. There will be a balance between allowing constructive debate and letting it run away with itself.

High-tech teams also portrayed the inability to have a rounded approach to viewing problems. This is a weakness associated with teams that have a concentration of specialists. Specialists were often found to have anxious-introverted personalities, and this was also noted as a cultural prevalence in high-tech companies. If the specialists had risen to management levels, they continued to display specialist tendencies. This also showed in the types of project that they selected. The projects tended to aim high within the specialisms rather than consolidating and refining known techniques.

There is a dilemma here because the literature has also shown that every project needs to be personally challenging for the team to give their best, otherwise they become bored or indifferent. The specialists may only be employing these principles, but because they are specialists they aim higher than others would. Again, you have to find the balance between personal challenge and achieving the project within time and budget. The business principles will help give the rounded perspective needed, or you might opt to invite a business specialist into some of the initial meetings to add balance.

The other option might be to share the criticisms of high-tech teams with your team as part of the critical debate. People can learn. They can begin to recognize when the team displays these tendencies and can move towards accepting the need to balance them. They may come up with some surprising strategies to compensate for them.

This would seem to leave multimedia project managers themselves in a vulnerable position. As indicated in earlier chapters, they often still carry a split role within the project, acting as specialist in one area and general project manager in the others. It is important that your own specialist views, as well as those of the other specialists, are considered within the business context of the application so that the criticism of narrowness in the team vision is avoided.

There are some points in favour of the project manager's being a specialist where other specialists are present in the team. They are difficult to manage but they are more predisposed to respect people who are achievers within a related specialism. It will not make the role easier necessarily, but it will be easier to voice your opinion with confidence.

Belbin noted that if teams were composed around those who showed creative criteria, there appeared to be weakness of follow-through. There was an abundance of ideas but they were not utilized effectively. A team needed a creative source, but also needed the backup of people who would create the opportunity for the ideas to move into action. There are by definition many creative people as part of the multimedia team, and so this might present possible difficulties.

From Belbin's research, the team leaders who were most effective with computer application development teams were selected not for their experience and seniority in the field but for 'chairmanship' qualities. These were defined as the ability to recognize the strengths of the others in the team, to explore options that were raised, to back the right person at the right time, and to obtain good results. This does not, and could not, define how the leaders knew who to back or when and therefore influence the final decision. The data seems to support the thesis that the leader should not be the cleverest person in the team but should appreciate the strength in others, help them communicate in ways appropriate for the whole group to understand, and keep them focused on the objectives. However, the tasks that the team need to perform can also define the type of leader that is needed. If the team has been in a rut, someone who is extrovert can galvanize it into action and drive it forward, and therefore might be more appropriate than the 'chairman' character.

Eight role types were defined as necessary for potential management team excellence:

- a solid organizer;
- a catalyst who would draw the best from other members;
- someone with drive and a readiness to challenge;
- a creative, imaginative person;
- someone with the capacity to shape the ideas into action by using contacts and resources outside the team;
- a hard-headed judgemental figure;
- a person who responded well to people and situations and who would engender team spirit;
- someone with the capacity to follow through.

These roles represent the concept of an 'ideal' team mix where there is balance for the variety of management tasks that could arise. Often, each team member may have to fill a few roles as and when they arise. The dynamic nature of teamwork means that the needs shift, and therefore team members adjust their roles to cover the needs.

Theory into practice 13

If you are working in a team at present, put the initials of the team members most likely to fulfil the role types into Table 12.1. The names are shorthand for the roles described above, so refer to that paragraph for confirmation of the role types. They are not the original names used by Belbin, and have been adapted to suit a multimedia audience, but the role types conform to the original research.

Remember, one person can switch between several roles over the course of a project if necessary, although one role tends to dominate. If there are any gaps left, what are you going to suggest to try to achieve a balance for the team?

Table 12.1 Team role profile.

Role type	Team member's initials
Solid organizer	
Catalyst	
Driver	
Creative	
Explorer	
Judge	
Carer	
Completer	

It was very difficult to find the last type of team member – the one who would finish the task and follow through on the detail. Many managers admitted that they lost enthusiasm for the tasks once the exciting and challenging first phase of definition had passed. This dwindling of interest is unfortunately characteristic of multimedia projects and project managers. The production phase is often beset with numerous adjustments after adjustments for a variety of reasons, and this is wearing for the team.

The end of the project spins out. Everyone wants to reach the final sign-off but it is the hardest to get. There is also a problem of reallocation of energy and resources from the team onto new projects, as these are phased in while the old ones are phased out. The team members are invigorated with the new, exciting challenges. The old project's appeal becomes stale.

This, one of the hardest phases for project managers, is made worse if the lack of finishing power is part of their own weakness. If the team members lack the will to complete tasks, and this is more characteristic of creative and analytical personalities, there is a problem in keeping the team on track to the end. It becomes the project manager's responsibility to get the project finished. The management of the company needs to recognize these problems, which are inherent in this type of teamwork, and back the project manager in the allocation of enough time and resources, as well as giving encouragement to the team to finish.

The other role that is a problem to fill in a team is the one of handling conflict or difficult situations. There is a tendency for the team members to opt out of this and leave it up to you even if the cause is related to a particular team member. The move between a hierarchical system where the team leader is accepted as the one who is directive, and the open team structure where whoever has the best fit of skills for the task takes the lead, is a strange feature of team interaction. There will be situations during the course of the project that need strong, hard decisions.

Take for example a graphics artist who likes working at night and so ends up arriving for work late in the afternoon. This becomes the norm. It is true that in multimedia there is tolerance for erratic hours, because the team will work hard and long to reach a milestone. But if the work habit of one member means that the rest of the team find it very difficult to communicate the necessary tasks, then some action has to be taken. The behaviour increases the time taken to complete a phase, and the error rate for the work is likely to increase because of the miscommunication. You will have to decide the course of action. If, after explaining the reason for the request, the team member fails to rectify the situation, what are your options?

You will need the backing of the rest of the team to take further action or you risk alienating them, but if they agree with the problems it is causing, and that the member's actions are detrimental to the project, you have the backing to become more formal with the treatment, which could lead to a change of staff for the sake of the project. The main problem lies in getting a replacement up to speed versus the disruption caused by the present situation, but the longer the situation remains unresolved, the more unsettling will be the effect on the team. You will need to take the lead in these situations because you have the nominal authority and the links to higher management. The main problem is the switch between the open, less formal management style that you need to adopt to allow the ideas to flow within the team and the traditional role of a strong director.

The only other way that these tough team problems are resolved is by getting the core team to commit themselves to mutual accountability for the project. If your company employs performance monitoring, there could be scope for doing this so that team objectives are set rather than individual ones. This might exert more influence over the team needing to work together and accept mutual responsibility for achieving the total project rather than expecting to fulfil the specialist role only.

If the team is performance driven and the tasks have been determined and agreed between all, then this should help keep the group working towards common goals and feeling mutually responsible for achieving them. Then the team itself should help to coerce errant members, because everyone's work is interdependent.

How the organization can affect team management

Because it is hard enough to recruit the functional skills for the core team, balancing the interpersonal skills so that there is a blend that will cover the eight role types may be like looking for needles in a haystack. The mental ability, creativity, and personality factors needed for multimedia development almost seem to work against teamwork and project management.

But an understanding of the blend that can provide a good team mix is a tool in itself that should help you to analyze some of the problems you'll experience better than before. It may provide some answers to the need for key extra resources that might have to be brought in at various stages as cement, for example.

In Chapter 2 specific examples were given to show how the structure of the organization you work for can affect your role as project manager. It can influence your team management if the in-house team members report to a functional boss as well as to yourself. The team members can have split loyalties, which may affect their work on the project. They may be pulled to work in different directions by both of you and find it difficult to reconcile their duties to the project and to the company at large. The company management needs to recognize this potential conflict and define the respective roles for the functional manager and the project manager so that the team is clear how they should relate to both.

The team will need frequent meetings to communicate how individual parts of the project are progressing and for you to pass on detailed information of the client's latest reactions. The organization can facilitate these meetings by having meeting rooms that are accessible and well laid out. People can take communication seriously or not, but the environment can help to provide the right stimulus for good communication. There is nothing as frustrating as holding a team meeting in the corridor or in part of an open-plan space with the constant noise of telephones ringing, copying machines, and interruptions from other people. Clear communication in a pleasant room takes a shorter time and causes less disruption of not only your own team's work but also that of other people, than the disorganized, patchy communication that takes place in crowded environments.

The layout of a meeting room can influence contributions from the team, so you need to recognize this and organize the room accordingly. A round table or a circle of chairs gives the best non-hierarchical feel to a meeting and encourages everyone to contribute. If you are trying to engender an open, constructive team culture, the circle will help. An oblong table encourages a hierarchical feel, particularly if you sit at the head of it in the traditional leader position. If you have no choice in this, at least sit on one side instead of at the top of the table.

Pointing out environmental factors is not popular with companies, although they are one of the few factors they can control or influence. Take the previous example of the graphics artist who had antisocial hours, which made it difficult for the rest of the team. The artist may well have said that the reason for the hours was that he or she was more productive when it was quiet in the office than when it was hectic. In this case, how would you deal with the situation?

Open-plan offices are common in multimedia companies, and the variety of tasks and people needed creates a busy, communication-rich environment. This in turn creates noise. The type of task that people have to complete affects the level of concentration. Multimedia is characterized by specialists' constructing pieces of the project. Concentration is needed here. There is also a good deal of demonstration and discussion to refine the parts as they are integrated, as well as general meetings to communicate both inside the team and to a larger group of company management and clients. It seems self-evident that the environment needs to support contemplative work and communication.

If environmental problems are genuinely affecting the performance of your team, the least you can do is voice your concerns to company management with any suggestions that could help in the short term. Perhaps working from home for a number of days with definite meetings in the office on regular occasions might suit some parts of the project. Perhaps reallocation of members of the team within the building or rooms could help. Perhaps the team themselves could come up with some suggestions.

De Marco and Lister correlated environmental factors with best programming performance in their surveys of programming projects. If the space was quiet, private, large and protected from interruptions, performance was on average 2.6 times better. Of course, this was part of a larger context of research, and the ability of the programmers was also taken into account. De Marco and Lister's description of how interruptions affect concentration flow is interesting. It takes about 15 minutes for someone to focus at the right level of concentration for intellectual work to flow. If they are interrupted it takes another 15 minutes to settle back into the same level. This means that phones ringing, colleagues interacting, and enquiries can be extremely disruptive for productivity. This can certainly affect your project. If there are any strategies that you can use to influence environmental factors, use them.

There are laws governing the ergonomic layout for workstations, the amount of space, lighting conditions, and the amount of use of screens. These vary from country to country. There are concerns over issues of eye strain, repetitive strain injury, and the effect of emissions on skin diseases and on pregnant women. As project manager it is in your interest to keep abreast of the regulations to ensure conformity. The health and safety aspects of the environment are the employer's responsibilities, but the welfare of your team is yours for the duration of the project.

Theory into practice 14

Think of the project manager or manager you have admired most to use as your role model.

Using John Whatmore's elements of the successful creative team leader as a check-list, how does your manager line up? Do the criteria work for your role model? Are there any noticeable omissions? Would you add any extra criteria? How would you measure up if your team was asked to do this exercise?

List the functional/technical, decision-making/problem-solving and interpersonal skills for your role model. List any weaknesses. Then list your skills in these areas together with your weaknesses.

Finally, draft the same list again but write it from the perspectives of your team members or colleagues, or, even better, ask them to fill the list in for you. What would they consider your strengths and weaknesses in a management role?

Compare the lists and decide on your own development needs from them.

Summary

- The aim is to create a good team culture of cooperation and effectiveness.

- Team leadership means representing the team to management as well as setting the direction for the project.

- As project manager you'll need to employ a variety of management styles to suit different circumstances.

- Effective managers of creative teams exhibit behaviour that is different from traditionally accepted models of management.

- Personality traits of multimedia teams can cause problems for performance management.

- The environment can affect the team's performance.

Recommended reading

Belbin R.M. (1981). *Management Teams: Why They Succeed or Fail*. Oxford: Butterworth-Heinemann Ltd
Belbin R.M. (1993). *Team Roles at Work*. Oxford: Butterworth-Heinemann
De Marco T. and Lister T. (1987). *Peopleware: Productive Projects and Teams*. New York: Dorset House Publishing Co.

Honey P. (1988). *Improve Your People Skills*. London: Institute of Personnel Management

Katzenbach J.R. and Smith D.K. (1993). *The Wisdom of Teams: Creating the High-Performance Organization*. Boston, MA: Harvard Business School Press

Phillips N. (1992). *Managing International Teams*. London: Pitman Publishing

Speake T. and Powell J. (1997) *Skills for the Missing Industry: An Exploratory Study*. Sheffield: DFEE

Tjosvold D. (1991). *Team Organization: An Enduring Competitive Advantage*. Chichester: Wiley

Whatmore J. (1997) *Managing Creative Groups: What Makes People Good At It*. Horsham, West Sussex: Roffey Park Management Institute report.

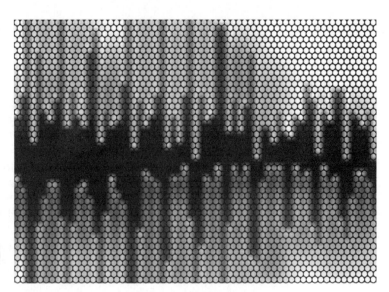

13

Audio asset production

Project manager's responsibilities

■ To book the studio and the artiste

■ To make sure scripts are ready

■ To make sure that the recording session is successful

■ To ensure that the material is prepared to the correct specification

■ To understand the processes involved in producing this kind of asset

Managing asset production

There is some debate about the amount of detail that a manager needs to understand in order to manage the production of assets – and by assets we mean the content of a Web site or CD such as text, graphics, photographs, sound and video. In conventional media areas, managers often come up 'through the ranks' and have done the job of the people they manage. In Web design and multimedia this is less likely to happen simply because of the newness of this medium and its multidisciplinary nature. A project manager might have worked as a television producer, a journalist, a trainer, a graphics artist or a computer programmer rather than as all of these. So a detailed knowledge of one area under your control could be counterbalanced by complete ignorance of another. Multimedia production not only integrates these disciplines, it also has to balance them.

When you manage the production of assets, and of the Web pages or computer software that make use of the assets, you could be working with people in the core team for your whole project, or you could be hiring in people or facilities for only a relatively small part of it. Your responsibility includes fitting their work into the whole project. This extended team will be less aware of your overall plan, and may be less involved and committed. In some cases, such as if you were to hire a photographer for a single day's shoot or book a sound studio for a voice recording, they may have very little knowledge of multimedia and its special requirements and idiosyncrasies. Because multimedia involves slightly different technologies from mainstream media there will be occasions when normal practices will not be exactly right, and a knowledge – or access to knowledge – of both will make it easier for you to explain your requirements and concerns.

If you, as project manager, know something of the processes involved in creating and manipulating the assets for your project, you are in a much better position to help the asset creator to achieve the result you want. In some cases you might need to be able to unravel technical jargon to do so, and you will often find that the level of respect that specialists have for you, and their willingness to go that extra mile for you, is influenced by how well you communicate with them and how well they think you understand their point of view. Sometimes you will need simply to point people in the right direction, but in other cases you may need to direct them specifically to do what you want. It will depend on their abilities, how well you share ideas and how flexible your vision of the result can be. Experience will make this easier, but background knowledge will help you on your way.

In the course of the technically oriented chapters of this book you will be introduced to some of the basic principles and terminologies so that you will be better equipped to achieve what you want. Although it is impossible to cover everything, the aim of these chapters includes pointers to those vital differences inherent in multimedia and, in some cases, to where assets for online projects differ from those for offline ones. However, the production of assets for use on a Web site or on a CD-ROM is very similar for both methods of distribution: it is at the final stages of preparation that the differences will become important.

Managing audio

During the course of making an offline multimedia production there will be, by definition, assets to be created or manipulated that make use of time-based media such as sound and video. Increasingly, Web pages are incorporating such things, as the bandwidth of Internet connections steadily goes up. Unlike text and graphics, you are likely to make use of specialist facilities with personnel that you hire to work on your assets. Video will be discussed in the next chapter; this chapter describes the processes involved in dealing with audio from a practical point of view.

The basic idea behind this chapter (and the other practical/technical ones) is to provide you, as a producer or project manager, with enough background on the technical processes to enable you to hold your own in discussions with experts. It will also make your use of specialized facilities more interesting and rewarding. Of course, depending on your background, you might already be an expert in one of these fields. It may also be the case that, in a small development company, you will have the opportunity to 'be' the expert and carry out some of the audiovisual manipulation yourself. So treat our use of the word 'you' lightly, since if you hire an external facility to record, mix or edit, it will be an engineer that actually carries out these tasks.

The aim in writing these chapters will be achieved if, next time you go into a sound suite and the engineer asks if you want the sound limited, or what sample rate you want, you can tell him or her, or even discuss it, with confidence. If you hire a facility and an engineer, make use of their knowledge and do not be self-conscious about asking advice.

Before the session

It is most likely that your first use of a sound studio will be to record a narration voice-over for your project. This might be for the soundtrack of a movie or to accompany an animation or group of stills. Music and drama are other possible kinds of material you might record, but this chapter will concentrate on recording a single voice. The basic principles are the same, but music and drama have the bells, the whistles and the fairy dust. When you decide to record a voice you need three things: the script, the voice, and the studio. You will also have thought about how you want the voice to sound, and this will have influenced your choice of voice-over talent.

Incidentally, do you have to use a studio for this, or could you record in the office or at home? If you or a member of your team have a background in sound recording and have the equipment then of course you have that option. But it can become very frustrating when you begin to notice all the extraneous sounds, such as aircraft and motor cars and sometimes even birdsong, that are so much part of our background sounds that we often forget they are there. Being in a studio can actually be more relaxing since the voice-over artiste can concentrate on the performance rather than worry about yet another passing motorcycle.

When choosing a voice-over artiste you might have decided to use a famous actor or actress, and would like to include their name on the cover of the CD or on the home page of the Web site. Alternatively your voice-over artiste might be a person who specializes in being a voice. In some circumstances you might do it yourself, or use a friend or someone in your company who has experience, perhaps as a radio presenter. For the first stages of a project it is not unusual to make a guide voice track yourself, which will be replaced with a professional one later. You might even record this guide track at home or in the office.

Unless you know someone already, your route to your voice will be through an agency. There are many who specialize in providing voices, usually for radio advertising, and they will have both famous actors and professional voices on their books.

The voice-over artiste will like to have a clean script, probably double spaced so that changes can be made clearly. The artiste will often mark in the emphasis to be used when reading. You should send the script to the artiste a few days before the recording if you can. The script should be printed out so as to avoid paragraphs going over a page boundary. The paper should be stiff so that it does not rustle. You should check pronunciations of any unusual words, especially proper names, and if you are producing the session you should be sure about every word in the script. Be prepared to make changes to make the script easier to read. Often the voice-over artiste will make very useful suggestions about this. Besides the possible direct benefit, you will be helping to create a good working atmosphere, and that will help the artiste to perform better.

With any luck you will find that your voice-over talent can read virtually anything you put before him or her. Many of these people spend the whole day reading one kind of script or another and can cope with most things. Interactive media may be so different from their usual work of advertising and corporate videos that telling them a little about the project will pay dividends.

You can work out the timings for the speech yourself before you go into the studio. All you need to do is read it at about the right pace, and time yourself. A rough guide is about 200 words a minute.

You can find your studio either by asking a professional studio body (in the UK this is the Association of Professional Recording Studios) or from a yearbook or even the *Yellow Pages*. Word-of-mouth recommendation or a studio you saw credited on another product is also a useful guide. When you book the studio, as with any outside facility, you will need to agree the rate, how overruns are charged, what happens if you underrun, and the arrangements for paying. You need to tell them the format that you want to take the recording away on, and whether you will edit the recording yourself (if you have the technology to do so) or will ask the facility to do it.

The background

The processes for recording sound date back over a century. Sound is the result of fluctuations in air pressure, which cause our ear drums to vibrate. If the frequency is right these vibrations get passed to the brain and are heard as sounds. In the earliest kinds of recorders you spoke, or rather shouted, into a horn, and the power of your voice caused a diaphragm to vibrate. A stylus was connected to the diaphragm, and this distorted a metal or wax surface over which it moved. To play the sound back you reversed the process and listened to sound coming out of the horn.

The microphone (usually just called a mic or mike and always pronounced 'mike') and loudspeaker (usually just called speakers or monitors) are still the mechanical components of sound reproduction. They work by detecting or creating the movement of air.

In the studio

You will find that a recording studio will almost always be in two parts: the control room and the studio itself. The studio may be called the **booth** if it is small and used only for recording voices. There will usually be a glass window between the two rooms.

Recording studios are strange places. You might find that no two surfaces are parallel because this stops sounds bouncing between the walls and setting up resonances and standing waves (where the room acts like a big organ pipe). Legend has it that some enthusiastic builders once thought that the plans for a sound studio were wrong because the corners were not right angles. So they kindly corrected the error.

The windows, while not being parallel either, will have double or even triple glazing, and the walls, doors and even the furniture will look as if they are either carpeted or designed by someone who likes to hang boxes on the wall. This is to reduce the reflections (for which read **echo** or **reverberation**) in the room. The difference between echo and reverberation (reverb) is simply in the time between the echoes. Reverb sounds smooth and continuous because the echoes are too close together for us to distinguish them. Unless you want to remake 'Heartbreak Hotel' you are unlikely to use echo as such. If there is no reverberation around a sound then we say the recording (or the room) is 'dead' as opposed to 'live'. In fact a room with absolutely no reverberation (called an **anechoic chamber**) is very uncomfortable to talk in, because we need something of the sound of our own voice to help us speak and some room reverberation around a recording to make it seem natural. With music, especially popular music, this reverb is normally added afterwards using reverb units (the modern electronic version of the echo chamber – which was simply a room with hard walls). This reverb should not favour some frequencies of sound over others. Reverb that does is called **coloured** and sounds unnatural. The natural small amount of reverberation in a room, together with any other background sounds, is sometimes called **ambience** or **ambient noise**.

To record a voice the microphone is usually placed about 18 inches to 2 feet (45–60 cm) in front of the speaker's mouth in a reasonably dead room. If the mic is too close it will pick up lip smacks and other bodily noises. If the mic is too far away the sound will be too live, which means there will be too much reverberation.

When you get close to some kinds of mic you suffer from a phenomenon called **bass tip-up** or **proximity effect**. This is, as the name suggests, an increase in the bass sounds in the voice, and it is caused by cancellation of high frequencies when the source of the sound (your mouth) is too close to the diaphragm of the microphone.

In general, the positioning of the mic in front of the speaker is crucial in getting a good sound, and an experienced engineer will know where to move the mic to avoid popping, breath noises and sibilance. **Popping**, as the name suggests, is the effect caused by blasts of air from the mouth hitting the microphone. In fact it is sometimes also called **blasting**. This is at its worst with the letter P, and a good test is the old tongue twister 'Peter Piper'. If the mic is very close, just breathing out may cause a noise. Most studios will put a wind shield in front of mics to stop this. To a large extent these problems can be reduced by having the mic slightly to one side rather than straight in front, and this is called being **off-axis**. Sibilance is more difficult to control; it is an unnatural whistle in any S sounds.

The mic will probably be on a stand with a gallows arm or boom suspending it over the table – assuming your speaker is sitting at a table. Some people will sound better, and project more, if they stand up. If the speaker is using a table then be careful about where he or she puts the script. It will probably be under the mic and so you could hear the paper rustling. Less obviously, the relatively hard surface of the paper will affect the acoustic around the voice. The movement of paper, and the movement of the speaker's head as he or she reads, can change the high-frequency component of the voice.

There are basically three types of microphone, and their names come from the shape of their sensitivity, or polar response curves, as the following diagrams show. The further the curve is from the mic, the more sensitive the mic is in that direction. The reasons for the names will soon be apparent. In most cases you can assume that this curve is the same in three dimensions: a shape turned on the axis of the microphone. The exception is the bidirectional mic.

A **cardioid** mic will pick up more sound from in front than anywhere else. It is called cardioid because the polar response curve is shaped like a heart.

A **bi-directional** mic is sensitive on two sides, and this is often called a **figure of eight**.

Finally there is the **omnidirectional** mic, which is equally sensitive all around. You should be able to speak closer to an omni mic than you would with a cardioid without bass tip-up and risk of popping. Some microphones

A cardioid microphone.

A figure of eight microphone.

An omnidirectional microphone.

can be switched between all these response types. To record a voice any of these microphone types can be used. A cardioid will have less pick-up from the room but may suffer from popping.

During the recording you, as producer, will be in the control room. The speaker may, or may not, be listening to the sound of his or her own voice in the headphones. Different people will want to hear themselves at different volumes (also called **levels**), and this can be critical to their ability to read well if they are inexperienced. Giving the speaker a volume control for the headphones is a good idea.

Most people's speaking voices will have quite a wide range between the quietest and loudest sounds. This is called the **dynamic range**. The engineer can control this dynamic range manually, by adjusting the volume control fader in the control room, or by using electronics to automatically compress or limit the signal.

Although the same word is used, audio **compression** is totally different from and unconnected with data compression. To avoid confusion, the term **bit-rate reduction** is often used instead of data compression. Compressors and limiters reduce the dynamic range of a sound. They are a sophisticated version of an automatic volume control in a tape recorder. A limiter is set to tightly control the volume of sounds that exceed a certain value, whereas a compressor operates over a wider range of levels but more gently. It is difficult to describe the effect of using these devices, but you will find some examples on the CD-ROM.

You would choose to limit or compress a voice, and therefore reduce its dynamic range, for a number of reasons. You are most likely to choose to make the master recording with compression or limiting that is inaudible to the listener, and most often limiting is used to catch and reduce a few bursts of the loudest moments in the speech. In this way you can bring up the level of the whole speech (that is, make it louder) without the few high points causing problems by overloading the electronics. With a digital signal, for which overloading causes more distortion than with analogue, limiting is useful as a back-stop to prevent accidental overload, especially if you can do only one take.

Both devices, but especially compression, can be used for effect. Because our ear's response to sound is not linear we tend to hear loud sounds with less dynamic range than quiet ones. You can fool the ear into thinking something is louder than it really is by compressing the sound. This is also useful if you want to put speech over some music and it is important that the speech is heard all the time without sounding shouted. However, remember to keep (and archive) a 'clean' copy of your master recording before you start to process it for delivery on your Web site or CD.

If your sound is finally going to be played on an 8-bit system (or less) then processing it to reduce the dynamic range of the recording will make the playback sound better because there will be fewer quiet parts to disappear into the noise. For similar reasons, anything that will be played in a noisy environment, such as a point-of-information kiosk at a trade show, should be compressed to make it easier to hear. With sounds on a Web site, which are usually bit-rate-reduced so they can be streamed or downloaded easily, audio limiting and compression will almost certainly be essential.

If you are in doubt about using limiters or compressors, a basic recommendation is to use a little limiting to catch the loudest peaks. If the recording is quiet, with no background hiss or reverb, you can always compress it afterwards. However, you should remember that compression tends to exaggerate reverberation, and you have to be wary of this. If there is a high amount of background noise then compression and limiting will noticeably affect this, leading to an effect called **pumping**. An example of this is also on the CD. If the response time of the compressor/limiter is too slow, you will hear it pushing and pulling the sound as the amplification goes up and down. If it is too fast, it will distort the waveform of the sound.

Volume, otherwise known as level, has been mentioned already, but how do you measure it? There are two kinds of meters in use: **VUs** and **PPMs**. VU (pronounced vee-you) stands for volume unit, and PPM stands for peak programme meter. VUs are the most common although they do not really tell you anything exact about the signal. However, an experienced engineer can judge the level of something very well with a VU, and it arguably gives a good representation of the loudness of the sound. A VU meter will move around very quickly. Even though a VU has a red band at the top (especially if it is a real moving-pointer type of meter) you will quite often see it running into the red. This is not necessarily an indication of overload, especially in an analogue system.

A PPM is a more exact kind of meter, and was developed by the BBC to control levels being fed into transmitters, although it is also used in recording. What a PPM does tell you is the actual peak signal going onto the tape or into the transmitter. PPMs are designed to have a fast rise time and a slower release. This helps you to read them. BBC PPMs also have an integration time (in other words they are not measuring the instantaneous level but an average over a small fraction of a second), which means that they will not detect very short peaks. This could be a problem for digital systems, but in practice, even though a short peak may be distorted if you look at the waveform, it will often sound fine because the ear may not hear a very short burst of distortion.

VU meter

PPM meter

VU and PPM level meters.

It is more usual to find VU meters and PPMs that use lights to show levels, but some would argue that a meter with a needle is easier to read. A particularly useful type of PPM is the dual stereo PPM, which has two meters side by side, each with two needles. One shows the left and right channels on two coincident needles while the other shows the sum and difference signals for stereo.

Besides level meters and a compressor/limiter, there will be equalization (usually just called EQ) in the channel of the desk through which the voice passes. This is a glorified bass and treble control, and will help the engineer to get a suitable sound out of the voice. Because of the ear's sensitivity you can often make a voice sound closer, have more 'presence', by slightly boosting frequencies around 2 kHz.

Working with your voice-over artiste

Your recording might be used against a video, a sequence of still images, or in isolation. If you are recording a voice track that goes with a sequence of stills or even over a single image then there will be no problem in recording the voice without any reference to the sequence. This is sometimes called recording **wild**. In this case you can work your way through the script, one discrete section at a time, rehearsing and then recording. If the artiste makes a mistake (fluffs), all you need do is ask him or her to go back a sentence and read it again. This is best done as you go along rather than at the end. Anything that will be heard in a continuous sequence should be recorded as nearly as possible in that sequence so as to avoid subtle changes in tone or speed, which would be very apparent over an edit. You can mark up your copy of the script with timings for paragraphs, and you should also note where any fluffs occur and how many takes it took to get things right.

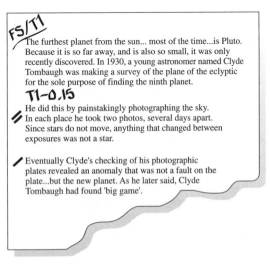

Marking a script.

You can mark takes by using a diagonal line like this /, which you mark in at the point you will probably use for an edit, or the beginning of the sentence. If there are two takes you can put in two lines //, and you may also need to note timings by the lines. You can get timings from a stopwatch, or better still from the timer on the tape machine or digital recording system. DAT machines and hard-disk recorders have a built-in time code that is recorded on the tape or disk (optionally with professional machines), and this is very useful for finding takes. A take that gets through only a few words and then falters is known as a **false start** (FS) and is not usually marked as a take. To assist editing, you should always record a few words in advance of where you know you will want to edit, to allow the speaker to get up to speed.

There is another way of dealing with takes, and that is to roll the tape back, play the preceding sentence and switch into record as the artiste speaks the lines again. This method avoids editing afterwards.

You might be recording a narration that has to be timed to a moving picture. In these cases you could bring in the computer and run the movie or animation or whatever, but an alternative is to record the movie onto a videocassette. In this way you can make use of a facility that has recording and mix-to-picture capability for TV or films so that the narrator can watch the movie as the recording is made.

Other things to remember about the session: check the spelling of the artistes' names for the credits and make sure that you have agreed the appropriate rights. If you have to go back to the artistes later to sort out rights you are at a disadvantage, and you cannot assume that because they came to the recording they have granted you the use of the material you require.

What can I ask the studio to do for me?

A recording studio will be able to do far more than just record your voice-over. If you want them to do so they can edit the takes together under your direction (and sometimes without) to produce a finished master. They can take your voice, script and music tracks and mix them together to produce a finished track for your application. Some facilities can even digitally compress the track into RealAudio® or MPEG audio for you, but remember not to confuse audio dynamic range compression with data compression. It is your choice as to how much you ask the facility to do, and how much you do yourself. This will depend on factors such as your ability and your budget, because the facility will need to be paid, and this is an above-the-line cost.

Mono, stereo and surround sound

A lot of sound in multimedia is mono, which means single channel. This is because mono sound, by definition, takes up half the space of stereo sound. If you have the capability, stereo will be useful to you because, rather like moving images, it helps you build up the effect you want to convey in your application. If you decide to make your application with stereo sound you will need to know whether it might also be used in mono: if in doubt assume it will. This is because a little care needs to be taken to make sure that stereo recordings are mono compatible and still sound correct when the left and right channels are added together to make mono.

Stereophonic sound means two speakers. We allocate a position to a sound by a combination of time delay – the sound reaching one ear before the other – and level. Using level to give positioning is by far the most common way, and in mixing (which we will come on to later) the balance engineer will position sounds between the speakers by changing the amount of the sound fed to the left and right channels. This is known as **panning**, and the control on a mixing desk that does it is called a **pan pot** (for panning potentiometer). Most of the time this simple panning of sounds will work perfectly. Incidentally, we get our directional information at high frequencies rather than at low ones.

When recording a real sound in stereo things are a little different. There are three main ways of recording in stereo. They are called the spaced pair, the crossed pair and the M and S pair. The pair refers to a pair of microphones.

A **spaced pair** will be two omnidirectional microphones positioned several feet apart. For distant sounds, such as a crowd at a sports event, this will be fine, but the sound will tend to have a hole in the middle since, confusingly, a sound close to the microphones but between them is probably not close enough to either. (This kind of set-up sounds particularly good if you listen using headphones, but strictly speaking this then makes it a binaural sound system, not a stereo one.)

A **crossed pair** is also known as a **Blumlein pair**, after the EMI engineer who invented the technique. You take two cardioid directional microphones and place them as close together as you can but pointing 90° apart. This gives

A spaced pair.

A crossed pair.

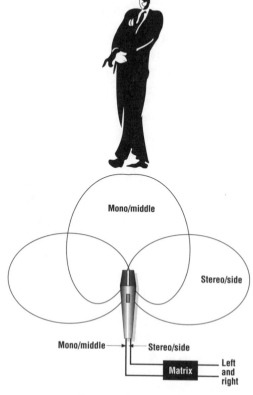

The M and S method.

a good stereo image and no hole in the middle. For the best results the microphones need to have identical responses.

You can do a simple calculation to show that M (which is mono, left + right) and S (stereo, left − right) can be combined, or matrixed, back to left and right. Left is M plus S and right is M minus S: you can ignore the factor of two here. This method combines a cardioid microphone pointing forwards and a figure of eight microphone pointing sideways. This system has several advantages: mono compatibility is assured; good stereo can be obtained at a distance using a rifle mic for the M channel; and the stereo image is very good, especially at the centre. The microphones do not have to have an exactly matched response. You can in fact buy single microphones that use this technique and yet give left and right outputs as in the diagram.

One additional factor to consider is that, strictly speaking, a sound in the centre will sound twice as loud as one at the extreme left or right when the channels are combined into mono. This should be a factor in the mixing, and most panning controls compensate for this. If you want to position a voice off to one side for effect, or to have two voices discussing something, then the best position in the stereo sound field is halfway between the centre and a loudspeaker. This will also give you a good mono signal.

Although quadraphonic sound on record, with four channels, came and went in the mid-1970s, multichannel sound is making a comeback thanks to surround sound movies. This is because such sound systems are being used on the soundtracks of movies to enhance the cinematic experience. More than four speakers are used. Originally, a speaker at the centre-front position was added to improve the stereo positioning for a cinema audience, since very few of them sit in the right place for good stereo sound when only two speakers are used, i.e. the middle. Basically a cinema audience is too big for conventional stereo. Having started with three speakers at the front and adding two at the back left and right to give a surround sound field, you can add what is called a subwoofer, which gives out only very low-frequency sounds, and possibly two extra front speakers at the mid-left and right positions. This gives either a 5+1 or 7+1 surround sound field (usually referred to as 5.1 and 7.1), as used in the cinema and DVD. It is also possible to encode a version of surround sound into two channels, and this legacy of quadraphonic sound is still found in surround sound on TV and video.

Recording surround sound is best done using a double-crossed pair with four cardioid mics facing in four directions 90° apart: double stereo. Otherwise a pan pot can be made that moves a sound source around a surround sound field, and some of the digital audio editing and mixing systems allow you to do this.

Tricks with sounds

There is a wide range of what are called **psycho-acoustical effects** that affect the way we hear sound, but it might be useful to describe a few potentially useful, or awkward, ones.

The ear's sensitivity to high and low frequencies diminishes at low volume levels. The 'loudness' button on your hi-fi amplifier takes account of this and lifts treble and bass to make it easier to listen at low levels. Another effect of this phenomenon is that if you take a recording and then attenuate (drop the volume of) it, it will seem to lose top, or high, frequencies.

If you want to give a cheap imitation of a sound coming from behind the listener then it can be done by making the sound to the two loudspeakers out of phase. It might be that because we cannot detect a position for an out-of-phase sound, many people think it is coming from behind them. This is nothing like as good as real surround sound, of course. 'Out of phase' is the exact electrical opposite of mono, and is actually difficult to achieve except in a professional sound system. The CD includes an example of in- and out-of-phase sound so that you can compare them.

You may be tempted to work with headphones rather than speakers in order to cut down noise leakage and avoid irritating other people, especially if you are carrying out editing yourself in the office. Beware, however, that when it comes to judging sound quality and the balance of a mix, headphones are notoriously unreliable.

One way in which we detect the loudness of a sound in the real world is by feeling the pressure of air on our bodies. For this reason it is dangerous to listen to sound loudly in headphones. The air pressure clue to loudness will not be there, and there is a tendency to turn up the volume to the ears to compensate.

A detailed knowledge of psycho-acoustics has led to high-quality and efficient ways of reducing the bit rate of digital audio files in systems such as MPEG. Sounds that we do not hear because they are, for example, masked by other sounds can be removed from a recording without noticeable effect.

Digital basics

Digital technology has entered most aspects of sound recording and editing. The basics of digitization are that the continuously varying sound waveform (the electrical representation of the vibrating microphone diaphragm) is **sampled**. This means that many times a second the instantaneous voltage of the waveform is measured. Audio is usually sampled at 44.1 kHz, which is the sample rate for compact disc. For reference, middle A on a piano is currently standardized at 440 Hz, and when you double the frequency of a sound its pitch goes up an octave. (This standard has changed gradually; in Mozart's time middle A was 430 Hz.) So a single cycle of a 440 Hz sound will be sampled in about one hundred places.

The highest frequency of sound that can be faithfully reproduced by a particular sample rate is just under half that sample rate (as discovered by a Swedish scientist named Nyquist), so the range of frequencies, called the bandwidth, of a compact disc is 22 kHz.

The 22 kHz bandwidth of a compact disc should be enough to reproduce all the frequencies you could hear. However, some people say that this is not the case, but in multimedia you are unlikely to have a better delivery sample rate to play with. Incidentally, DAT has 48 kHz as its standard sample rate, but most DAT machines can also record at 44.1 (after a while you stop saying kHz every time), and, if you have a choice, this is the better sample rate because any compact discs that you include in your mixes will have to be at 44.1 and ought to stay that way.

This relatively simple sample rate picture is becoming more complex as more digital formats enter the professional market. Some professional audio is now being sampled at 88.2 and 96 (twice 44.1 and 48) to give a cleaner sound for reasons too esoteric to debate here. Video formats with digital audio may use sample rates of 48 or even 32.

CDs and DAT share a bit depth of 16 bits. This means that the sound can, in theory, be digitized with a precision of 16 bits, or 65 536 levels. Again, with the exception of the usual sceptics, this will allow you to hear the sound without errors. You can work out the background noise of a digital signal from the bit depth, since the maximum error between the 'real' sound and the digitized version of it is half the minimum step in the digitization. Since 16 bit has 65 536 steps and 8 bit has only 255 you can see that 8 bit will be 256 times as noisy as 16 bit. You can hear examples of the difference that is caused by different sample rates and bit depth on the CD.

Fortunately our ears do not respond to sound levels in a linear fashion, which is why a logarithmic measurement, the **decibel** or dB, is used to measure it. This means that we do not actually hear 256 times more noise. In fact the signal-to-noise ratio of a 16-bit system is 98 dB (which basically means you will never usually hear it) whereas for an 8-bit one it is 50 dB. Since every 6 dB increment makes a sound twice as loud this means that 8-bit is eight times as noisy as 16-bit. Also, the noise only occurs in the sound, not in the silences (unlike analogue hiss), but it will be very noticeable on slight noises like rustles, so these should be removed from any recording destined for 8-bit.

With digital audio recording a balance has to be struck between recording at so high a level that you risk overloading, which means clipping the waveform and producing distortion, and recording so quietly that noise becomes noticeable. As a result, the reference level at which audio is recorded on professional digital audio and video tape machines is set so as to give plenty of leeway for loud sounds. This is called headroom and usually means that the peak audio levels may be as much as 10 dB below the maximum possible. Increasing the audio level in post-production to maximize the level, so that the loudest peak fills all the bits of the sample, is called **normalizing**. Professional systems have now started to record sound with 20 or even 24 bits (24 bits means that the noise is 150 dB down), which gives the engineers the freedom to record at a safe level without noise. For distribution the sound will be converted back to 16-bit.

To convert from 16 to 8 bits the procedure is simply to divide each sample value by 256 and round the errors to the nearest whole number. To convert from 8 to 16 you multiply the sample value by 256. This will, unfortunately, also multiply the errors that cause noise, so your 16-bit version will not sound any better than the 8-bit original.

To get the best level out of a digital audio recording you should normalize it. This means finding the loudest part and adjusting the level of the whole file so that the loudest part fills all 16 bits of the sample. Most audio CDs have been normalized. However, professional audio source tapes may not have been, and this could be a problem for you if you are sending a digital video-tape off to be encoded into MPEG, for example. The standard peak level for professional videotape is about 12 dB below the normalized maximum. If your other audio has been normalized then this will result in a level difference between different files.

In principle you should make sure that digital audio is normalized before encoding, although there are some exceptions. Some Web compression systems for audio will distort with a normalized file, so setting the maximum a little lower, say 3dB down, would avoid this. Also, files with the same levels can sound louder or softer since loudness does not completely depend on level. There is no hard-and-fast rule about this, especially when a user can choose the order in which things are heard. Perhaps the best approach is to normalize to 3 dB below peak, which will give a little leeway to boost quieter sounding sounds.

The sample rate of a recording can be changed by recalculating the samples, and most audio editing and processing software will allow you to do this. There are professional boxes that will do this as well. Reducing the sample rate of a file will reduce its frequency response.

For reference, here are bit depths and sample rates that you might come across and where you might find them. This list is not exhaustive.

- 44.1 kHz 16-bit – CD, DAT and digital audio editing systems. As a rule of thumb this kind of digitized audio takes up 10 megabytes per minute. It is also known as Red Book after the name of the standard for compact discs.
- 48 kHz 16-bit – digital videotape formats, DAT, digital tracks on LaserDisks and some digital audio editing systems.
- 22 kHz 8-bit (or lower) – personal computer sound and streamed audio on the Internet.
- 44.1 or 48 kHz 20-bit (or more) – some professional audio systems and digital videotape recorders.
- 32 kHz 12-bit – long-play DAT and consumer DV.

There are what are termed DASH systems (digital audio stationary head), which you might come across in a recording studio, but these also use either 32, 44.1 or 48 for their sampling rate. Variants of DAT and hard-disk systems are now also using sample rates of 88.2 or 96. Sony used to sell a digital audio add-on for their Betamax video recorders called the F1. This was a 44.1 kHz 12-bit system. Other digital audio formats you may come across include: μ-law (used in telecommunications); NICAM (a 14-bit system used for stereo television sound); MPEG/ISO layers 1, 2 and 3 (layer 1 is very similar to

PASC, which was used in Digital Compact Cassette; layer 2 is also called MUSICAM, and is used with MPEG-1 video and digital broadcasting; layer 3 is used for telecommunications such as radio contribution links down ISDN lines); ATRAC (used in MiniDisc); and Dolby AC-3 (of which more in a moment). MPEG audio, layer 3, which is sometimes confusingly and incorrectly known as MPEG-3, is the most efficient of the MPEG audio compressions, and is sometimes used on the Web as a high-quality compression format for audio files. In this case the files have to be downloaded (i.e. copied) across the Internet, but it is possible to stream audio on the Web using such formats as RealAudio. Streamed audio and streamed video are played in real time as the data arrives over the Internet. It is more like broadcasting than file transfer, and has the advantage (for rights owners) that a copy of the file is not usually left on the listener's computer. The encoding for streamed audio over a modem is very efficient but results in an audio file with a very small audio bandwidth – as low as 4 kHz in the case of RealAudio® for a 14.4 kBit modem – and high background noise levels. However, if you have two ISDN lines you can receive streamed audio of very high quality.

With the advent of DVD you will come across the two main standards for audio on the new digital video disks. Dolby AC-3 is the surround sound format used for most DVDs, but a surround sound version of MPEG audio (layer 2) is also possible. Although the MPEG audio is supposed to be a standard on the European disks it is likely that it will lose favour to Dolby. Unless you are producing disks for consumer DVD players (rather than DVD-ROM disks for computers) this is not likely to be an issue for you in the near future.

Aliasing

The Nyquist theorem says that in order to accurately digitize a sound of frequency n you must sample at a frequency of at least $2n$. If this rule is not followed strange results can occur. The phenomenon is called **aliasing**, and the result of this is that the digital signal does not accurately represent the analogue original. If there are frequencies higher than n in the signal that you digitize with frequency $2n$ there will be spurious samples in the result, which will usually sound like squeaking, and the signal should be filtered to remove such high frequencies before digitizing. Aliasing is a common problem in digital systems but it can occur in analogue systems as well. A popular example of the effect is seen on film and video when the wheels of a wagon appear to move backwards, and this also underlies the principle of using a stroboscope (regular flashing light) to 'freeze' fast regular motion.

This aliasing is a particular problem if you down-sample, which is where you take a sound digitized at, say, 22 kHz and shift it down to 11 kHz. You will think you can hear sounds of higher frequency than 5.5 kHz in the result, but they are not genuine sounds from the input but aliasing artefacts. For this reason you need to filter before you down-sample. Not all software does this, and you will hear the distortion that results. Down-sampling and aliasing can also introduce other sounds. One instance is if the original recording contains a small amount of television line whistle at around 15 kHz. This will be almost inaudible, but if it is shifted down by aliasing to around 7 kHz, which can happen in a 22 kHz down-sampled sound, it will suddenly become audible because the ear is more sensitive at 7 kHz than at 15 kHz.

Doing it on hard disk

Tapeless recording and editing systems are now common in audio, and systems are even available for desktop computers. It is possible to record straight onto hard disk, and some audio facilities will do just that for you. These same facilities will edit your audio and prepare the tracks for use in a computer system by compressing them to RealAudio or MPEG audio (or whatever is appropriate).

Where the hard-disk systems come into their own is for editing. The general principles are the same as tape-based editing but some things are easier and more versatile in a digital system.

Editing

Tape editing used to be done by physically cutting the tape with scissors or a razor blade. This process cannot be done with audio cassettes because the tape is not accessible in the machine, but quarter-inch tape can more easily be handled. If you are editing yourself then you rock and roll the tape backwards and forwards across the playback head in order to locate exactly the point at which you wish to cut. This is sometimes called **scrubbing**. Then you mark the back of the tape with a chinagraph pencil and slice the tape with a blade or scissors. You join the bits you want together with adhesive tape. The adhesive tape is slightly narrower than the recording tape and has a non-leaking adhesive. A specially machined block is used to align the tape.

In a hard-disk-based digital system the sound is usually manipulated by working with a representation of the audio waveform on the computer screen. The sound is cut and pasted in much the same way as text in a word processor. One useful feature of professional digital systems is the ability to do a mix across the joins, which can be used to make an otherwise impossible edit work.

Some places are easier to cut than others. You can fool the ear by cutting into a sharp sound, a transient such as a bang or a drum sound. By doing this you do not usually notice any cutting off of the preceding sound. In fact the incoming sound is more critical than the outgoing in most edits. For speech some sounds make for better cuts than others; 'p', 'k' and 't' work well, whereas vowels and the 's' sound are quite difficult.

You should listen to speech patterns to help with your editing. Many people miss out letters from their speech. If you were to say 'next time' you would probably not pronounce both 't' sounds, but would actually say 'nextime'. You can take advantage of these truncations to find places to join speech together. You will even find that just looking at the waveform will help you to find places because you can easily identify pauses and consonants by the shape of the waveform.

Rhythm is important in speech, and your edits should respect that rhythm and not cut across it. Although people do shift the rhythm of their speech, most of the time an edit will feel more natural if a speech rhythm is preserved. Rhythm obviously is very important in editing music, and some of the same rules apply to both music and speech. A few milliseconds can make all the difference to a music edit. You can hear an example of 'good' and 'bad' editing on the CD.

It is not true to say that a good edit is a joy to hear – because you will not hear a good edit.

Judging quality

Sometimes you will be required to produce assets to a certain quality. This might be specifically mentioned in a contract. It is difficult to define the quality of audio in objective terms. You could say that the frequency response will be one thing and the signal-to-noise ratio another, but these facts will not cover how well a presenter reads a script or how well mixed is a piece of music. The best course, should this issue arise, is to say that you will apply 'appropriate' standards or even 'broadcast' standards. You, and your clients or customers, will be able to compare with what you hear on radio and on CDs. It is important for clients to realize, however, that sound heard on a computer and on the Internet will often be of poorer quality than broadcast simply because the computer or the method of distribution is not capable of that quality of reproduction, no matter how well the material is prepared. On the bright side, you will usually find that the quality issue can be handled by comparing your results with other similar applications.

Theory into practice 15

Take the editing practice recording on the CD and, in whatever editing tool you have, try to make the speaker say the opposite of what he originally said. Listen to see how natural this sounds.

Listen to the examples of audio with different sample rates and bit depths and see if you can recognize any undesirable effects that result from them. This includes loss of high frequencies and addition of noise.

Search out some freely available encoders for MPEG audio and RealAudio and whatever you can find. Take a sound file and encode it with the different systems and compare the results.

Summary

- This chapter has looked at the background to sound recording, and has explained what you should expect when using a professional audio facility to record voices for your multimedia application. It has outlined the preparation you need to make to prepare for the session.

- The kind of microphone used, the way it is positioned and how the sound is treated will affect the way your recording sounds.

- Stereo and multichannel positioning is usually achieved by adjusting loudness between the channels.

- During recording, scripts should be marked up for later editing.

- Keep an archive master copy of any audio that you process for inclusion on a Web site or CD-ROM.

- In digitizing, the highest frequency that can be digitized with a sample rate of $2n$ is n.

Recommended reading

Bordwell D. and Thompson K. (1993). *Film Art: An Introduction*. New York: McGraw-Hill

Moore B.C.J. (1977). *Introduction to the Psychology of Hearing*. London: Macmillan

Pohlman K.C. (1989). *Principles of Digital Audio*. Indianapolis: Howard H. Sams

Watkinson J. (1988). *Art of Digital Audio*. London: Focal Press

Watkinson J. (1995). *Compression in Video and Audio*. London: Focal Press

Information on RealAudio encoding is available at their Web site: www.real.com

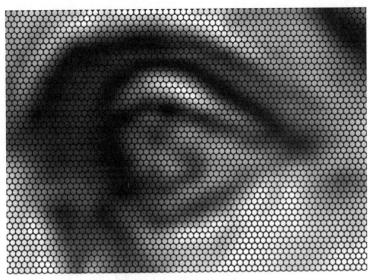

14

Video asset production

Project manager's responsibilities

■ To book crews and subjects for recording interviews

■ To explain to clients what quality of result to expect on the desktop

■ To make sure that the recording session is successful

■ To make sure tapes are logged and prepared for editing

■ To ensure that the material is prepared to the correct specification

■ To choose the most appropriate way of compressing video for the application and make sure it is done to an appropriate standard

■ To understand the processes involved in producing this kind of asset

Managing asset production

The previous chapter has explored the production of sound in multimedia, paying special attention to the use of external facilities. For video, similar arrangements are likely to be made. It is possible that the video content of a multimedia application will be shot using a domestic camcorder and edited on the desktop, but in many cases the budget will allow a professional facility to be used and the production values will require it. As with audio, Web sites currently make less use of video than CD-ROMs do, but as bandwidth increases this will change. This is especially true as systems appear that allow Web surfing from the home TV set.

One crucial aspect of video production is the amount of preparation required. While for sound it is quite feasible for the producer to turn up to interview someone having made the arrangements by telephone a few hours before, for video there is much more that needs to be done and more people to involve. This chapter concentrates on the set-up for an interview because that is the most straightforward and arguably the most common use of video in multimedia. You might wish to shoot drama, or work on location, but unless you already have experience in these areas you are advised to hire specialist help to direct the shoot and therefore to manage it. Location work is particularly difficult because of the range of permissions you need from people such as the police and local authority and because of the vagaries of the weather.

One managerial issue that rears its head in video more than in audio is the question of whether the client should attend the shoot or the edit. There is no simple answer to this but your relationship with the client should influence you. The main reason why the client should attend is to avoid arguments about changes later, since changes in a video edited at a facility house are probably the most expensive to fix. This, of course, is a strong argument for making an offline edit and letting the client see it, or for editing on your desktop. If you are completely confident that the client respects your abilities then you might not need to involve them, but if you think that later changes are likely, and if you have agreed a fixed price for the project, then invite them. You should emphasize the costs associated with changing video after the edit.

Moving pictures are a recent entrant into computing, although computers have long been a part of video, at least on the professional and broadcast television side. Engineers have for a long time been devising ways to manipulate and create images for broadcast television, starting with graphics and control of equipment. Today computers play a part in every aspect of broadcast television production.

Just as video is starting to take over as the dominant medium in the multimedia mix, so multimedia is beginning tentatively to make its way into television. Video on demand is essentially a multimedia database system for the home; prime-time television programmes are using desktop computers to generate graphics as part of the editing process; and digital television is now being broadcast by satellite and terrestrial transmitters to some home consumers.

Television itself dates back to the 1920s, and moving film goes back into the 19th century. John Logie Baird devised a mechanical system of sending moving pictures down a wire and through the airwaves, at a time when radio itself was in its infancy. Electronic scanning took over from his wheels and cogs, and the BBC launched the world's first regular scheduled television service in 1936 to a handful of very rich viewers in the southern part of England. A television set then cost more than a family car, and not many people had either.

This chapter deals with the way in which a television picture is made and how you might record and manipulate it on its way into the computer. Some background on the way a video signal is built up, and the differences between the various formats and standards, will help you work with video. As with the last chapter on audio it will concentrate on the kind of equipment and techniques that you, as a multimedia professional and practitioner, will come across when you make use of video.

Basic principles of video

Because our brains are easily fooled, we see a rapid succession of still images as a continuous stream, and, with the right images, we see movement. The movies work like this, by showing us tiny slices of reality 24 or 25 times per second. The frames of a movie are those slices of reality. Television slices the reality a slightly different way because each of the frames in a TV signal is made up of hundreds of lines.

As a compromise between resolution (in pixels), the rate of change of the picture (in frames per second), and the amount of radio waves that a television signal would occupy (bandwidth), the engineers who designed television made each frame out of two fields. The first field covers only half the picture by missing out alternate lines of the image as it scans down the screen. The second field fills in the gaps.

The beam that 'paints' the picture on the television screen starts at the top and scans from left to right at a very slight angle downwards. For the first line only, the beam starts in the middle rather than at the left. When it reaches the right it flies back to the left-hand side and starts again, a bit lower down. Eventually, after doing this a few hundred times, the beam reaches the bottom right of the screen and promptly flies back up to the top left and starts all over again. This time it will be scanning in between the lines it laid down last time; eventually it will reach the middle of the bottom line and fly back up to the middle of the top line, and the whole process starts again.

So there are two comb-like scans, interleaved with each other, making up each frame, with each consisting of half the number of lines in the whole picture. Each is called a **field**. The complete picture will be refreshed only 30 or 25 times per second, which keeps the bandwidth down, while the apparent flicker of the picture is at the rate of the fields, which is twice as high and so is less noticeable. This is a neat trick; but, as will be shown later, this system of interlaced fields causes no end of problems when we get onto the computer because computers use a non-interlaced display, in which the lines are written in turn, left to right, from top to bottom of the screen. This is called **progressive scan**, and one of the fiercest debates going on between broadcasters and the computing fraternity is about whether future television systems should, or should not, have interlaced displays.

Composite video television standards

Composite video television standards

These are the three main systems of broadcast colour television. They are known as **composite video** because the brightness and colour information is mixed together into a single signal. The oldest still in use is NTSC, which is used mostly in North America and Japan. The main European system is PAL, also used in places such as Australia and South Africa, and there is also SECAM, used in France (from whence it came), Eastern Europe and the Middle East.

For **NTSC** a constant-frequency signal at 3.58 MHz, called the **colour subcarrier**, is superimposed on the picture to carry the colour information. At the start of each line of the picture there is a short burst of the colour subcarrier. The colour at any point in the line (this is analogue so the concept of a pixel is not strictly valid) is determined by the relationship between the superimposed subcarrier at that point and the reference burst.

There are 525 lines per frame in NTSC. In broadcast 487 lines have picture on them: half in each field. In multimedia practice NTSC is considered to have 480 active lines rather than 487. In its earlier black-and-white incarnation, US television used 30 frames per second, but for colour this changed to 29.97. It was supposed to be 30, but obscure technical reasons to do with the subcarrier frequency changed all that.

PAL has a subtle, but significant, difference from NTSC in the way that the colour information in the subcarrier is encoded. NTSC suffers from colour shifts due to minute timing changes during a line. PAL compensates for this by switching the colour encoding between alternate lines and so 'averaging' out the errors. PAL also has a higher-frequency subcarrier, at 4.43 MHz, and has 625 lines in a frame, of which 576 have picture on them: half in each field. PAL shows 25 frames per second exactly.

SECAM, the French-devised third system, uses a totally different method for transmitting the colour (it sends the two colour components alternately with each line) but is otherwise the same as PAL, so if you fed a SECAM signal into a PAL monitor you would see a black-and-white picture. SECAM means 'Système en couleur avec mémoire' although it is reputed to really mean 'System essentially contrary to the American method'. Although SECAM is still used as a transmission system, and gives very good results, it has problems for production, mainly because you cannot mix or fade a SECAM signal out because of the way the colour is encoded. Incidentally, NTSC is reputed to stand for 'Never twice the same colour', but actually it is National Television Standards Committee.

There are some variations, particularly a South American variation of PAL called PAL-M, which is basically NTSC timing with PAL colour. You will sometimes see PAL-I and PAL-BG referred to, but these are different only in the way they are transmitted; the videotapes are compatible even though the televisions and VCRs are not, mainly because the sound is transmitted on a slightly different frequency, and that is why a European PAL television will not usually work in the UK and vice versa.

On European videocassette machines you may see a form of NTSC called NTSC 4.43 or Modified NTSC. This is a special version of NTSC, and it happens because the colour information on the videocassette is stored in a different way from the original composite signal: it is basically PAL with NTSC timings. When the VCR plays back the tape the colour signal is put back in its 'proper' place. On some PAL machines, NTSC is rebuilt with the subcarrier at the PAL frequency. This saves having two sets of circuits for the colour in the VCR and the monitor. However, this modified NTSC will appear as black and white if you feed it into a real NTSC monitor, or a digitizer card that expects real NTSC. This can also happen with formats such as S-VHS and Hi8, which, although they separate the brightness and colour information, still use a subcarrier to encode the colour information. You will not come across this problem with broadcast videotape machines, and it is not applicable to the component systems we come on to next, but it is the most likely cause of mystery colour disappearances when using NTSC videocassettes on multistandard VCRs.

A single video cable can be used to carry a composite video signal since the colour information is encoded in with the luminance and the synchronization pulses are usually kept together with the picture information. Some equipment labels composite video CVBS.

Component video

In recent years professional colour videotape has become either digital or component, or both. Component video means that the colour (**chrominance or chroma**) and brightness (**luminance**) information are kept separate, having been mathematically derived from the red, green and blue (RGB) signals received from the camera imaging tube or chip.

The luminance part of a component signal is referred to as Y. The true colour components are red-Y and blue-Y. Red and blue signals are smaller in value than green so they make for larger (and therefore less noisy) components. Often the components are referred to as YIQ (in NTSC) and YUV (in PAL), but these are not strictly equivalent and are often misused. Strictly speaking there is no such thing as an NTSC or PAL component but people do sometimes refer to component systems by their related composite system names in this way. PAL and SECAM tapes are the same.

Using colour components this way is useful for TV for two reasons. First, the luminance signal is exactly the same as the old black-and-white signal, and so the video is backwards compatible and easy to view on a monochrome monitor. Second, because we do not see as much detail in colour as we do in brightness, there is no need to have as high a definition for the chroma as for the luminance. This saves bandwidth, and is one of the two forms of data compression used in analogue TV: interlace is the other.

Component video offers better quality than composite because the colour information is kept separate from the luminance. It is possible for a colour television decoder to mistake some of the fine detail in the luminance information in a composite signal for colour, causing spurious coloured patterning. This means that luminance information of similar frequency to the colour subcarrier will be missing from the composite picture.

Connectors for component analogue video are the same as for professional composite, only there are three of them: one for luminance (Y) and two for colour. The sync pulses are usually carried on the Y line.

Halfway between composite and component video is S-Video as used in Hi8 and SVHS. This has two signals, one being the Y and the other a combination of U and V usually referred to as C. So a connector for S-Video might have Y/C written on it. An S-Video connector is made either from two BNC or phono connectors or from a four-pin mini-D type, like the Apple desktop bus connector. Sync pulses are carried on the Y line. There are only two forms of S-Video since, once again, PAL and SECAM are the same at this level.

Blanking and time code

Besides the image information, making up the visible part of the lines, there are elements of the analogue television signal that tell a television monitor, and other equipment, where the lines, fields and frames begin and end, and provide reference information about the colour. The places in the television signal where the picture does not exist, but these signals do, are called **horizontal** (for lines) and **vertical** (for fields) **blanking**. This is because they are blank, although the vertical blanking interval (VBI) has become home to such things as Teletext, vertical interval time code (VITC, pronounced vit-see) and test signals.

Time code is very likely to be useful to you. When you look at a videotape to select extracts for digitizing, time code is the way to specify the sections you want. Every frame of a television signal can be allocated a unique number divided into hours, minutes, seconds and frames (of the form hh:mm:ss:ff, for example 05:46:35:19). This time code signal is recorded on the tape along with the video and audio.

Time code is sometimes referred to as SMPTE (Society of Motion Picture and Television Engineers, pronounced 'sempty') although, strictly speaking, SMPTE time code is for NTSC video only, and the PAL/SECAM version is EBU (European Broadcasting Union).

Burned in time code (BITC) or **time code in vision** is a system whereby a character generator superimposes the numbers of the time code on the frames to which it refers. This is invaluable in choosing extracts and editing. Since a time code number can refer to either field in a frame, some readers will add a field indication to the number you see, because most videotape machines show you a field rather than the whole frame when the tape is in still 'frame'.

With NTSC time code you will see the term **drop frame** used. Because NTSC does not have a whole number of frames every second the time code has to be adjusted every so often to keep it in step with real time. This is just like the extra day in February in leap years. In the case of NTSC a frame is dropped, hence the term. This is fine when it is important for the time code to show time-of-day, as it is called, or to know exactly how long a programme is, but you need to remember that some time code numbers will be skipped. For everyday video editing it is more straightforward to use non-drop-frame time code. You should know which type of time code your NTSC tapes have otherwise you will miscalculate the actual duration of your video. In PAL there is no need for drop-frame time code as PAL has exactly 25 frames per second.

In the studio and on location

You might use only a small amount of video in an interactive application but its use can be very powerful and effective. One common form is known as a **talking head**. This is where all you see on the screen is a single person talking. If you have a famous presenter for your application then you might see him or her a few times like this. Even if most of the time you only hear the voice, it is nice to show your viewers what the face behind the voice looks like.

The talking head might be recorded in a studio or on location (meaning not in a studio), and he or she might be positioned in front of a real scene (a bookshelf is a common one for a subject expert) or against a single colour. A single colour is useful because, in some circumstances, you can decide on the background later and add it in the edit suite or on your computer.

Since a human face does not contain any blue, blue is commonly used. Television people call this **chroma-key** or **colour separation overlay** (CSO – hence CSO blue to denote the colour). Film people call it a **matte** (if it moves it is called a travelling matte – and yes, it was used for flying carpets in Arabian Nights films – and now you know the origin of the name of that character in *Fraggle Rock*). Another name for this technique is **blue screen**, although other colours can be used: broadcasters often use green, and the traditional colour for movies was the yellow light of a sodium discharge lamp.

Although in film-making a travelling matte works using totally film-based methods and some clever work at the time of printing, in television an electronic circuit detects the blue and switches the signal to another source wherever there is blue. This substitutes the other image for the blue.

Common problems occur due to spillage of the blue light onto the person's face, shadows on the blue backcloth, and difficulties in coping with the fine detail in hair and with shadows. The most sophisticated colour separation systems, such as Ultimatte, can solve these difficulties but, in any case, good lighting helps to avoid them.

Sometimes it pays to shoot against black. This can be very effective to isolate the person speaking and emphasize their role as a specialist, and it

Colour separation overlay.

can be less distracting than the ubiquitous rows of books. Black does not spill onto faces and, if you are careful, you can overlay onto black just like blue or green. In this case you need to watch out for shadows, especially under the eyebrows.

Although these are film and television techniques, the use of colour separation overlay extends easily onto the desktop, and video editing and manipulation programs usually allow you to clean up and replace coloured backgrounds in this way. When the video is digitized and compressed, a static background will compress very efficiently. This is especially true if it is free of noise, so it is common to shoot the interview against black and then replace the black with 'digital' black.

The simplest way of lighting a single person uses three lights: one will be a spotlight on the face, one will flood the scene to lighten the shadows, and the third will be positioned behind to both light the blue screen (if you have one) and backlight the person to help lift them from the surroundings and give the scene a three-dimensional look. The spotlight in front needs to be high enough so as not to make your speaker screw up his or her eyes but not so high as to cast shadows in the eye sockets. As usual, good lighting will look so natural on the screen that you will wonder just what you have paid for. The lights have names, and a redhead refers to a one-kilowatt lamp while a blonde is a two-kilowatt one. The lights will need to be set up, but it is bad manners to inflict this on the speaker, who will be under the lights for long enough later. One of the crew will stand (or sit) in for the speaker while the lights are moved and adjusted. Find someone the same height as the speaker. Also, you should make sure that the speaker does not wear clothing containing the colour of the background, if you are using overlay.

For a professional and hassle-free video shoot you should avail yourself of an experienced cameraman and crew. The smallest crew will be one that consists only of a cameraman and you, the director (so get yourself a chair and a megaphone). You should seriously consider having a sound recordist, who will also help the cameraman to set things up, and a PA (production assistant), who will take notes and carry out the little administrative chores and free the director to ... direct. You can reasonably expect the crew to bring their own equipment and videotape (referred to as 'stock').

If your application needs more substantial shooting, such as some drama or location documentary filming, then you will probably need to bring in a specialist director. If you have the experience to direct this kind of material, you probably do not need to read this chapter anyway. Crews for drama shoots can be very large, and include workers with colourful names such as the gaffer, best boy and grips.

The kind of camera used for professional video is similar to a domestic video camcorder, but it is physically bigger with a better lens and will give a much better picture. The cameraman will probably connect up a monitor for you to see the picture. For an interview, don't put the monitor where the speaker can see the picture.

Your speaker will need a microphone, and you will probably not want to see it. For this reason a common microphone used in filming is called a **rifle mic**, or **hypercardioid**. This is a long and thin microphone, although you will usually see it in a wind shield or wind sock. This makes it look like a big furry hot-dog held on the end of a pole by the sound recordist. Alternatively a very small microphone can be clipped to the person's tie or jacket collar. These are usually omnidirectional, and it is not unusual to position them upside down to avoid blasts of breath.

Shooting an interview

Although an interview seems to be one of the simplest forms of television shooting it is still difficult to direct well. Part of the problem is that you will want to edit what you record for inclusion in the finished application. With a sound interview you can cut almost anywhere as long as it makes sense, but with video you have the added difficulty of having the picture to cut along with the sound. It is highly unlikely that two similar pictures will cut together. In the case of a person speaking you will see the join as a jump, which is quite disconcerting. To hide the jumps you can do one of two things but you need to have recorded the material to do so. First, you can cut to a different view of the person who is speaking, known as **changing the angle**, or zoom or move closer (in) or further away (out). To disguise a cut, a zoom will work better than a simple change of angle, but ideally you should combine both.

Changing the size of the shot has a curious side effect. Zooming in on a person speaking, either as a real zoom or as a cut to a closer shot, makes what he or she says seem very dramatic, as if confiding in the viewer. Zooming out has the opposite effect.

The second method of covering an edit is known as the **cutaway**. You can cut away to anything relevant. This might be some footage of whatever the person is describing. Alternatively the cutaway can be to something as simple as a shot of the person's hands as they move to emphasize a point. Of course, while you are cutting away from the speaker's face you can edit the sound to your heart's content.

The shorthand for describing the amount of the speaker you can see in a shot is roughly like this:

(1) **Long shot** – you can see the whole person and maybe enough of the surroundings to see where you are.

(2) **Mid-shot** – you can see most of the person speaking, including his or her hands.

(3) **Medium close-up (MCU)** – you can see the top of the person, from the middle of the chest upwards. This is sometimes called a 'head and shoulders' shot, and is the basic shot for an interview or statement to camera.

(4) **Close-up** – you can see little more than the head.

(5) **Big close-up** – very close (tight) on the head, cutting off the forehead.

Incidentally, women who wear strapless dresses are difficult in interviews because the MCUs and close-ups make them look naked. This may not be the effect you want.

A very useful technique for interviews is to turn them into statements. This is used a lot in television documentaries, and basically means that the interviewer is neither seen nor heard in the edited result. This means, of course, that one place to which you cannot cut away is a picture of the interviewer nodding sagely (these shots are known as noddies). In this case it is important that the speaker never actually answers a question directly, and you should ask the interviewer to say things like 'tell me about your adventures up the Limpopo river' rather than saying 'was it fun up the Limpopo?' A common tactic is to ask the interviewee to repeat the question as the first thing he or she says in reply.

It is possible that you might be conducting the interview yourself, especially if you are not including the interviewer in the final edited footage. Part of your role is therefore as much to put the speaker at his or her ease as it is to ask anything meaningful. You will nod encouragingly, but never say anything while the interviewee is speaking. Some subject experts are so used to appearing in front of a camera that they will respond accurately to a request like 'tell me about Jupiter's red spot in 30 seconds' with consummate ease. Subject experts like that can be worth their weight in gold.

For the speaker, it is possible to work from a script but not appear to be reading. This kind of technique with half-silvered mirrors has been of benefit to politicians everywhere since Ronald Reagan showed it to Margaret Thatcher, but in television it has been in use for decades. It is used extensively in news and current affairs programmes where the presenter has little opportunity to learn a script. Almost as useful is to photocopy the script, blown up to a large size, and tape it just below the camera lens. This obviously works best with short scripts.

Prior to the interview you should run through the topics you want to cover, and you should have given the speaker time to research the answers, even if it is his or her specialist field. Rehearsing can reduce spontaneity, but retakes are always a possibility. You can change the shot for retakes to make editing between them possible.

If you have a PA with you, he or she can make notes of questions to set against the time code, which can usually be read on the side of the camcorder. You should resist the temptation to use time-of-day time code or drop-frame time code in NTSC, and you should start each new roll at a new hour on the time code. This way you can easily judge which roll is which (they are still called rolls even though they may be videocassettes) from the time code numbers. So the time code 04:23:01:10 is on roll 4 and 13:21:10:00 is on roll 13. It is vitally important that the time code always goes forwards as you work through a tape and that the code never passes through midnight. This is simply to make it possible for the editing system to know which way to spool a tape to find a number, and unfortunately 23:59:59:24 reads as being after 00:00:00:00.

Preparing for editing

The tapes from your recording are known as **rushes**, from the time when they were shot on film and were rush-processed so that you could see the results the next morning. They will be dubbed onto videocassette, usually VHS, with burned-in time code (BITC) so that you can equate the time code to the parts of the material you are viewing. A time-coded transcript of the rushes is a useful first step in editing, and can help you to choose which parts of the interview you want to use.

There are usually three stages of videotape editing, although in the multimedia world you may not actually do any of them in a dedicated facility since more and more video processes can be carried out on the desktop. The first stage of the process is to prepare for the edit. This will involve looking through the recording in the cold light of day and choosing which parts of it to use. The odds are that you will have recorded much more than you need for the final application. The result of this stage is a list of extracts, probably marked on the transcript with their time code numbers.

Offline

The second stage is the offline edit. Offline editing was originally introduced because of the high cost of editing equipment. Early offline systems used videocassettes, but offline editing was the first application of non-linear desktop video. The offline session is like a rehearsal for the online. Edits would be tried out, again and again, until the editor and the director settled on the ones that worked. The result of this stage was a list of the edit decisions.

The edit decision list can be taken into a 'real' edit suite and the edits carried out on the tapes. If this process is done automatically it is called **auto-conforming**, and this technique came back into fashion in the early days of digital video tape machines because of their high cost.

Today an offline session is as likely to take place on a computer, using a system like AVID or Lightworks, although the basic principle is the same. Quite a substantial industry has grown up around these **non-linear systems**, as they are called. Non-linear is another way of saying random access. Some non-linear editing systems are designed to seem familiar to video professionals, while other systems are more computer-like and so are not as popular with video editors but have their fans in the multimedia community because they feel familiar to them. Non-linear systems started as offline edit systems, although they are migrating upwards in quality, and have passed through news broadcasting on their way to full acceptability as a high-quality editing medium.

Online

A professional edit suite, like the sound studio, was likely to be in two parts. The videotape machines, with their whirring motors and fans, were kept in a separate room, called the **machine room**. This is sometimes still the case, but with the quieter videocassette-based systems used today the machines are now often kept in a rack next to the desk. In some facilities it is common practice to have a central pool of machines and allocate them to suites as required, rather than having machines dedicated to a particular suite. So you may not even see the machines being used for your session.

You, as the client, will be in the control room of the edit suite. There will be a bank of television monitors in front of you, with a control desk and a vision mixer. It is one of the standing jokes of the video industry that in *Star Wars*, when the denizens of the Death Star zapped a planet, they controlled the destructor beam with a Grass Valley vision mixer, common to many videotape editing suites around the world. (Computer people get their laughs from Scottie trying to use a Mac Plus in the *Star Trek* movie about saving the whale.) The staff of the suite will probably be two people: the editor and the tape operator, also known as the tape-op. Almost without fail a character known as a runner will come in from time to time and offer you coffee or toast.

The editor's skill is in working out how to cut your material, to your specification, so that it flows and so that the edits do not jar. There are little tricks, such as cutting just before a movement in the incoming picture, which

An edit control room. (Photo by Vassilis Skopelitis courtesy of JCA Facilities in London)

distract the viewer's attention momentarily and can be used to disguise the cut. With an edit, the material you have before the edit is called the **outgoing shot**, and that after the edit is called the **incoming shot**. The edit is adjusted by tightening it (making it happen earlier) or loosening it (making it happen later).

The editor will be editing sound and video. Often the sound will be mixed across an edit even if the video is cut. This is done to soften the impact of the cut. If the sound is heard before the vision cut it is said to be leading it. An edit where sound and video are cut at different points is said to be **split** (a split A/V). Sometimes you will continue the sound and come back to drop a short cutaway shot to replace some of the video.

Online videotape editing, in a broadcast suite, is often still a linear process. You start at the beginning of the programme material, edit shot onto shot, and finally reach the end. This means that you need to be satisfied with each edit as you do it, since you do not have much option for changing it. Hard-disk systems allow you to edit in any order, and you can go back to an earlier edit to change it if you want to. Eventually this method of editing will be the prevalent one. It is important that you are satisfied with the edited material when you leave the edit. The last thing you do should be to view the material all the way through to make sure it is cut to your satisfaction. Then you can arrange for a high-quality safety copy to be made and for a viewing cassette to show, perhaps, to your client. Do not transport the main and safety copies together. The idea is that the safety copy can be used if the main copy is lost or damaged.

Just as audio studios have signal processing equipment for echo and delay, so a videotape edit suite will have its equivalent. The computer graphic and compositing software used in multimedia have their equivalent in such devices as the Quantel Paintbox, for television still graphics. One very common piece of equipment is the digital video effects unit, or DVE. With a DVE attached to the vision mixer, the video can be processed to make it change size, appear to move with 3-D perspective, and even be wrapped around shapes. Such devices have a variety of names and manufacturers, but one legendary name was for a piece of BBC hardware, never marketed, which was called TIPSE. This stood for Technical Investigations Picture Shuffling Engine.

One important thing to remember about digital processing of television pictures is that, without exception, the picture will be delayed as it passes through the device. Usually it will be delayed by one frame, which in NTSC is just over 33 milliseconds and in PAL is exactly 40 milliseconds. This delaying of the picture will eventually make the sound lose its synchronism, so it is usual to delay the audio to match, and edit suites have audio delay lines for this purpose. There are many opportunities for sound and vision to lose synchronization so this is something you should watch for. If the slip is constant, it can easily be fixed by re-editing the audio onto the videotape in a slightly different place.

Videotape machines

It is possible that you will come across a variety of videotape formats, depending on the kind of work you are doing. Some of them will only be used now for archive footage, but it may be useful to know what the terms mean. Unless otherwise stated these machines can be found in NTSC and PAL formats, although component formats should be referred to as 525/60 and 625/50 (for lines and fields) or simply 525 or 625. SECAM and PAL are the same at a component level so there is no difference between a Betacam-SP tape recorded in France and one recorded in Germany or the UK. Similarly SECAM SVHS is the same as PAL SVHS as far as the recording on the tape is concerned.

The oldest tape format still used, even if only for archive material, is 2-inch Quad. Originally the American company Ampex developed a system called Quadraplex, which used 2-inch tape, in 1956. Other companies also made 2-inch machines for this format. Long-established broadcasters such as the BBC have archive material on 2-inch, and it was in regular use until the 1970s, so it includes colour. Some stock deteriorated over time because of physical problems with the tape itself, and the Quadraplex system was relatively violent, spinning four heads rapidly across the width of the tape, so it is possible when playing a 2-inch tape to damage the tape, especially if the edge of the tape is already damaged a little. If the owners will still let you use this material, and they allow it to be played despite the risk, then it should be copied onto a more recent format as it is first played. Oxide from the tape can easily clog up the tape heads, and sometimes engineers will use a piece of card or even their thumbnail to remove oxide from the heads as the tape plays. The basic rule is to leave 2-inch to the specialists, and, in any case, very few facilities will handle it these days.

There was a 2-inch helical scan system that was used by a few broadcasters. This is incompatible with the 2-inch quadraplex machines. A well-aligned 2-inch recording can be of extremely high quality with a sharper signal than later analogue formats.

After 2-inch came 1-inch. This was a helical scan format, which means that the tape heads are on a drum that moves in almost the same plane as the tape path. Videocassettes are helical scan as well. The main manufacturers of 1-inch machines were Ampex and Sony (who made C format machines) and Bosch (who made B format machines). Almost all 1-inch tapes in the UK and USA will be C format but some countries, like Germany and Austria, used B format. The essential thing to know is that the two are incompatible.

The 1-inch tape was in use from the early 1980s until the early 1990s, by which time cassette-based formats like Betacam-SP had replaced it. Sony developed Betacam as a derivative of their ill-fated Betamax VCR system. There is a difference between Betacam and Betacam-SP, and although most engineers will use the words interchangeably (or just say 'Beta') you should always specify Betacam-SP if you mean Betacam-SP just in case the video library also handles the older Betacam format. This is mainly a problem in the USA rather than Europe, where PAL Betacam never really caught on.

Betacam-SP is still very much in use. It is a very handy system to use, with small cassettes being used in camcorders (with 20 or 30 minutes of tape time) and larger tapes in console machines. Video quality is good, and as it is a component system unlike 1-inch or 2-inch, the pictures are better suited to digitization. There is another component cassette format competing with Betacam-SP, and that is M-II (M-Two). Beta machines come from Sony, Ampex and Thomson and M-II from JVC and Panasonic.

As far as sound goes, 2-inch tape carried a single mono track with reasonable quality, although it suffered from high-pitched whine caused by the video tracks, which lie at right angles to the sound track. The orientation of the tape oxide was also suited to video and so was in the wrong direction for audio. The 1-inch C format has either three or four tracks, depending on configuration. The performance is good, but Dolby noise reduction was often used to improve the signal-to-noise ratio.

Betacam-SP has four sound tracks. Two are very high quality but cannot be used during editing since they use the video track. So in practice the other two lower (but still good) quality tracks are used most.

Cassettes

Although virtually all professional videotape formats are now cassette based rather than reel to reel (also known as open reel), there are videocassette formats that are regarded as domestic or industrial. There had been domestic and industrial open-reel videotape formats, notably from Philips and Ampex, which became available in the late 1960s, but the price was far too high for domestic use.

Videocassettes first came onto the market in the 1970s with the 1500 format from Philips and U-Matic from Sony. U-Matic is still with us, and has high-quality (Hi-Band and SP) versions. It is also used for digital audio as the Sony 1630 format. However, you are unlikely to find U-Matic tapes used in high-quality video today since variants of Betacam-SP, digital video cassette (DVC) and S-VHS/Hi8 have taken that niche. U-Matic cassettes use $\frac{3}{4}$-inch tape, and are sometimes referred to as the $\frac{3}{4}$-inch format. One serious disadvantage of U-Matic is that the maximum tape length is 74 minutes. (Coincidentally this is the supposed maximum duration of a compact disc.)

The most common videocassette format for domestic and industrial use is VHS. The picture quality of VHS is relatively poor, with particularly fuzzy colour performance. Hi-fi sound tracks have recently been added to VHS, and achieve very high quality even though they are analogue. S-VHS uses cassettes of the same size as VHS but with different tape. S-VHS gives much better results with higher bandwidth, resulting in sharper pictures and better colour. S-VHS machines can usually play and record VHS but not vice versa, and both systems use half-inch tape. JVC developed a higher-quality version called Professional-S.

Video-8 is Sony's successor to Betamax, and boasts the smallest analogue cassettes in video. There is a high-quality version, analogous to S-VHS, called Hi8. These formats sometimes have digital sound. The tape width is 8 mm – hence the 8 in the names.

There are industrial versions of Betacam-SP with a lower price and a lower, but still very good, quality. The gap between S-VHS and Betacam-SP is also narrowed by the high-quality version of S-VHS available from JVC. One advantage of the industrial Beta systems is that they are compatible with the full spec. version.

Videodisks

John Logie Baird actually sold 78 rpm videodisks in the 1920s, but it was not until the 1980s that commercially viable videodisk machines came onto the domestic market. In Europe the domestic market for videodisks never really caught on, although there is a niche for film fans and classical music enthusiasts. Even this market is likely to disappear when high-quality digital video from a DVD arrives.

Interactive video, which uses videodisks with computer control, was the precursor of multimedia, and you are unlikely to be working with videodisks (in any case that is outside the scope of this book). However, you might use videodisks as a source for video and audio for multimedia, and there are a few points to bear in mind.

PAL LaserDisks can, if they are older, have analogue soundtracks. In any case PAL disks can have only two tracks, analogue or digital but not both, whereas NTSC disks can have both and often do. If you are trying to digitize from an NTSC videodisk, check whether your player outputs real or modified NTSC.

There are two types of recordable videodisk in use today. Like the older recordable disks they are incompatible with each other, but they are nonetheless interesting and may be useful for time-lapse photography or animations.

Sony produced a WORM videodisk that records component and is considered to be of broadcast quality. This system is used by some television stations to hold station identification sequences because of the random access and lack of deterioration (unlike tape).

Pioneer produced a magneto-optical recordable/erasable videodisk that also has two separate head assemblies, which can be used independently for playback. This is also a component system.

Both these machines exist in PAL and NTSC versions.

Digital formats

In the 1990s digital tape formats began to replace analogue ones. First there were D1 and D2. D1 is a very high-quality component digital system developed by Sony, but unfortunately the cost of machinery and tape stock made it popular only with advertising agencies, film companies and video research. D2 was a derivative system, which recorded digitized composite signals (PAL or NTSC). As a result it could be easily integrated into existing systems, and was more popular. Neither D1 nor D2 compressed the data used to record the video or audio. However, it was the advent of half-inch digital systems that brought digital video within the cost range of the majority of broadcasters.

D3 is a composite digital system, D4 does not exist, and D5 is a component digital system without compression. There is a mode for D5 that supports high definition pictures with some compression. Digital Betacam is from Sony (of course) and uses a little compression in the signal. Some Digi-Beta machines can play Betacam-SP tapes, which makes for versatility in editing. It is also possible to get Betacam-SP machines with digital inputs and outputs, but these are not Digital Betacam.

Even though there is a digital output from these tape formats, the usual way of copying the pictures into a multimedia system is by digitizing or grabbing the analogue output. This is partly because of the high data rate of professional digital video (270 megabits/second) and partly because of incompatibilities in the shape of the pixels between computers and the international standard for digital television.

A consumer digital videocassette format using 6 mm tapes, called DVC or DV, is becoming popular for industrial and even some broadcasting applications, especially in news. Two semi-compatible professional derivatives, DVCAM and DVCPRO (which also has a derivative high-quality version), together with a long-play derivative of basic DV, are also available. DV machines are now made by all the major camcorder manufacturers, and at its best with a three-chip camera and good lighting DV produces results that are hard to distinguish from broadcast equipment. Some of the manufacturers provide a digital connection (using the new IEEE-1394 standard, better known as FireWire) with which video can be copied to and from a computer. This system provides a very cost-effective way of shooting and preparing video for multimedia on a Web site or CD-ROM. There is a limited interoperability between these formats, which mainly means that the professional formats can play back the domestic tapes.

JVC have introduced a further broadcast digital cassette system called Digital-S, and have announced D-VHS as a time-shifting format for the home market. Sony have an industrial/news-gathering digital version of Betacam, Betacam-SX. An SX machine can play SP (i.e. analogue) tapes, and so an SX machine offers an upgrade option for anyone with a large archive of SP material. It is interesting to see how many competing digital videotape formats have been introduced in the past few years. The market is obviously now large enough for the manufacturers to try to shake out standards in a way that was not really possible 20 years ago. The most interesting aspect of these new formats for multimedia is that the inherent quality even of the consumer DV format is so high that the tape format is not the limiting factor: the lens and camera chip (CCD) have the most effect.

Copying tapes for use in multimedia

Since it is extremely unlikely that you will be allowed direct access to a master videotape it will be useful to outline some suggestions for formats.

If the master is composite then your working copy can be either composite or component. Since, as we shall explain in a moment, it is better to digitize from a component source, in most cases you will want to ask for a component dub of the master. If you can work with a digital source then you should ask for a component digital copy.

It is possible that you will be editing and possibly processing the video to make a new master tape. This might happen if you were to be encoding material for MPEG and wanted to prepare a master of your own first. This might include video noise reduction and re-editing. In this case a digital composite dub would be recommended (such as D2 or, more likely, D3). In this way the decoding of the composite video to component can be done as part of your processing, and you will have more control over it.

Film should be dubbed from telecine onto a component format. Under no circumstances should you get a composite dub of a component tape; neither should you digitize from a dub on videocassette such as VHS, S-VHS or Hi8 unless you really have no alternative. Incidentally, you can save money by asking the facility house to dub a VHS with burned-in time code in vision, for your viewing, as they dub the master.

For distribution on the desktop, and for MPEG-1, you can work from DV, especially if you have a FireWire interface for your computer. The lack of tape noise on DV makes it especially attractive for compression, assuming the lighting was sufficient and did not lead to noise from the camera circuitry.

Finally you should not standards-convert a tape between PAL/SECAM and NTSC or vice versa. Your copy should be in the same standard as the original, assuming you can digitize from the format of course.

Digitizing video for multimedia

Digital video in multimedia can mean partial screen or full screen, full motion (that is, 25 or 30 frames per second) or partial motion (down to 10 or fewer frames per second). The details of digitizing from a video source are very much down to the particular equipment in use, but there are some general principles.

'Recording' the video into the computer is called **frame grabbing**, and this grabbing should, if at all possible, be done at full frame and full frame rate. It is possible to frame grab uncompressed, but this requires very fast digitizing hardware and local storage. The kind of hard disk used in a desktop computer cannot work this fast unless several are joined together in an array. It is now possible to directly copy DV video from a camcorder using a FireWire interface connection: as this video is already compressed most hard disks can cope with it.

The pixels of a television picture and the pixels on a computer screen are not actually the same shape. This affects 525 and 625 line pictures differently, but essentially means that when copying a digital TV signal to the desktop, such as DV via FireWire, the aspect ratio of the image changes slightly. If you are editing on the computer and copying the finished video data back to the DV machine then this is not a big problem, but if you are going to distribute the video on a computer then you need to correct the aspect ratio change at some point.

In order to play the video back on the computer it will have to be compressed and probably shrunk in size, but this is better done 'at leisure' rather than in real time. From a practical point of view high-quality JPEG can be used during the grabbing process to save disk space and to reduce the cost of the necessary hardware. The results from this will usually look very good.

One important point about frame grabbing is that the frames you store on your hard disk will be either component or RGB; they will not be composite. This means that if you are grabbing from a composite source the grabbing board will need to convert (decode) NTSC or PAL into component or RGB. This will involve filtering the incoming signal to separate out the colour from the luminance. Unfortunately, the cost of a good filter to do this would be much higher than the cost of the rest of the equipment put together, so the filtering in a commercially viable grabber board has to compromise on quality, and some artefacts may be noticeable.

First, the luminance bandwidth may be compromised by the filtering out of the colour subcarrier if the video input is a composite one. Many filters (including those in most television sets) remove the higher frequencies of the luminance signal, those above the subcarrier, as well as the subcarrier itself.

Ringing.

Second, filters 'ring' and this has an effect on vertical edges in the picture. A sharp vertical edge has high frequencies in it: the sharper the edge, the higher the frequencies involved. Passing such a signal through a filter can have a detrimental effect on the shape of the edge, and the signal can overshoot and ring (just like a bell). What you see is a dark band between a bright and a dark part of the picture, darker than the dark part. Now if the dark part is black this results in a small part of the picture that is blacker than black, which is possible in an analogue television signal. For this reason, amongst others, black and white in a digital television signal are not set at 0 and 255.

A good filter can avoid these kinds of problems, but a better way is to avoid filtering altogether and always digitize from a component source, such as Betacam-SP. If the signal has to be converted from composite, because it was originally recorded that way, then a high-quality broadcast filter can be used during a dub from the original tape or a digital composite copy of the original tape to a component tape.

Taking a movie film and recording it onto videotape uses a machine called a **telecine** and the process of putting the film onto tape is called a **transfer**. For digital video in multimedia this telecine transfer should be done into a component videotape, and preferably a digital one. The film should be clean to avoid dust, and for top-quality transfer the imaging gate on the telecine machine can be submerged in a liquid with the same refractive index as the film base. This is called a **wet gate**, and produces excellent results. Many telecine facilities also have digital noise reducer, which make use of the similarity between frames to 'remove' dust and scratches.

Video digitization should be done from the original television standard and not from a standards-converted videotape. This is because standards conversion changes the image, even if only slightly. In any case, for digital video, the computer controlling the playback is generating frames at its own rate, and the system will cope automatically with the input frame rate. Unfortunately it will do this by attempting to read out a frame when it needs one, even if there is not a new frame available. In this case it repeats the last frame. (The opposite may occur where frames are dropped.) There is nothing you can do about this, but you would make it worse by digitizing from a standards-converted source where this process, or a sophisticated version of it, has been carried out already.

A television standards converter will interpolate new frames, or combine old frames, in order to avoid the jerkiness that this basic 5–6 conversion has, but a computer display does not do this. This may suggest that, if you have the freedom of choice, you might actually use NTSC rather than PAL for your video in Europe, because the NTSC frame rate is more like that on the computer.

Another set of problems is caused by the television signal being interlaced. When a television camera captures motion during a frame it does so in two separate slices of time, a 50th or 60th of a second apart. The moving object will have changed position between those two slices, the fields. When this is played back on an interlaced television screen there is no problem because the output display is interlaced with two fields per frame in the same way as the input camera. This does not happen when the full frame is displayed on a computer screen because a computer screen is not interlaced, but writes the picture in one sweep from top to bottom, left to right. The result is that horizontally moving

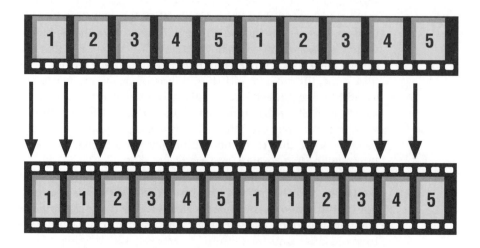

To read out six frames where five are available means that one frame is repeated.

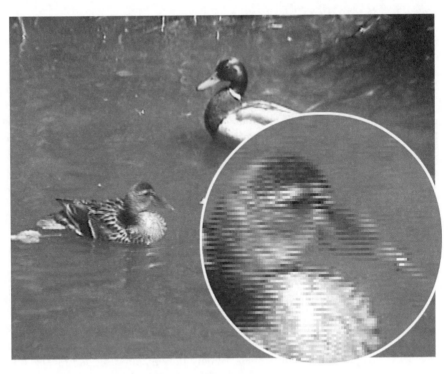

Combing.

objects can appear to break up like a comb. Vertical filtering, also known as convolution, can be used to correct this fault. It does not occur when the camera was a film camera because a film camera exposes the whole frame at once.

This situation will also only occur if the video on the computer screen is the same size (has the same number of pixels) as the original video grabbed. If it has been shrunk to half size, for example, to make a quarter-screen image of 320 by 240 pixels, then the result will be a slight horizontal blurring or a double image rather than a comb effect.

Some computer systems will allow the computer display to be set up to be interlaced, but use of this is rare unless the application is going to be shown on a television monitor. Using an interlaced display with a computer causes flickering of fine detail in the picture (called **twitter**), and filtering this out reduces the effective resolution of the image.

When shrinking an image (it does not matter whether it is movie or still), new pixels should be calculated from combinations of the old ones, rather than by sub-sampling (that is, only selecting some of) the old pixels. If this is not done then near-horizontal lines will 'staircase' and also appear and disappear with movement of the picture, as they go from 'visible' pixels to 'no longer visible' pixels and back again. This process is called **filtering**, and vertical filtering (to blend together information from the fields) is very important when dealing with television pictures in the digital domain.

Compression

Video in multimedia is, by definition, digital. For practical reasons it also has to be compressed, because it is impractical to handle the high data rate used by raw video. Broadcast technology is able to handle this, but at a price. For multimedia we have a choice of various 'standard' methods of compression, and the choice available increases as time goes by. These standards use compression and decompression software or hardware called **codecs**.

Two of the international standards that are applied to video compression are JPEG and MPEG. JPEG, which is discussed in the chapter on graphics, is a compression system used for still images. JPEG is attuned to work with photographic images, which have smooth gradations of tone rather than sharp lines. JPEG works in only two dimensions: the height and the width of a frame. MPEG adds further data reduction by comparing groups of successive frames. Since not all of an image changes – frame by frame – in a movie, this redundancy can be used in the compression.

With sufficient data bandwidth available, from a fast hard disk for example, JPEG images can be displayed fast enough to become a movie, and this is a pseudo-standard called M-JPEG. MPEG uses less data but is more difficult to decompress (and compress). Both of these standards, when used for movies, require hardware or a very fast processor. MPEG actually encompasses three variations, with MPEG-1 being the version designed for use on compact disc at 1.5 megabits per second. MPEG-2 is a higher-quality, higher-bandwidth version, which is used for digital television and DVD, and MPEG-4 (currently under discussion) is aimed at low-bandwidth applications and interactivity.

Several software video compression systems exist, making use of operating system architectures such as Video for Windows (particularly Intel's Indeo) and QuickTime (with Cinepak). Although these give poorer quality for their bandwidth than MPEG-1 they need no hardware to display, and will run on medium-powered processors. For use on the Internet the issue is how the systems will perform with a low bandwidth, and at the time of writing the de facto standard is RealVideo®, which is designed to cope with modem or ISDN data rates. In this case the video is streamed across the Internet, rather like broadcasting, instead of being copied to the user's computer. The CD includes some examples of video compression, of various qualities.

As a general rule, video codecs that give good results at one data rate will not perform as well at a very different one. This is called **scaleability**, and means that increasing the data rate will not allow an increase in quality because the codec has a quality ceiling. Cinepak is a codec that behaves in this way and is being replaced by the Sorensen codec, which can also work at higher rates.

In fitting movies into an operating system environment, the manufacturers (such as Apple and Microsoft) define standard interfaces for control of the movie with VCR-like controls for play and fast forward and rewind. A progress bar, to show how far through a movie you are at any moment, is also a standard part of such an interface.

QuickTime and Video for Windows both can work transparently with a range of video compression systems, since the operating systems present a consistent interface to your application. This means that you can switch from using, say, Indeo to using MPEG-1 without changing the application as long as the two videos have the same resolution and share the necessary control parameters.

With the movie come sound and stills, since an audio file is basically a movie with no pictures and a still is a movie consisting of only one frame. It is MPEG that currently offers the best set of these features since MPEG audio and MPEG stills are of extremely high quality and are very efficiently compressed.

Judging quality

The points outlined in the previous chapter on quality as it applies to sound also apply to video. However, it is usually very difficult to achieve broadcast quality with video on a multimedia system (if not currently impossible on a Web site), and your client should be aware of this. Again, use of the term 'appropriate' to describe the quality may be the best option. Some of the quality issues are less tangible. The quality of editing and the camerawork are independent of the technical quality of the desktop video, and in these cases you should aim for a quality threshold similar to that of broadcast television. Explaining early on that the multimedia video will not look as good as TV, and showing the client some examples, will avoid this becoming an issue, but you should be prepared to explain why, especially to a client who has experience of corporate video or broadcasting.

Theory into practice 16

One of the ways of building video skills is by watching. Look carefully at what you see on television. See how people are framed by the camera, and watch particularly how faces usually look into space within a frame. Look at how a movie is cut, and think about why a cut might occur in a particular place. Watch for the way the incoming shot often starts with an action that will distract your attention from the edit itself.

Summary

■ Moving pictures are a very effective way of conveying information in multimedia.

■ You need to be aware of the different broadcast television standards that you might encounter and of the difference between composite and component video. NTSC and PAL are the main forms of composite video, and each has a component equivalent.

■ For a variety of reasons component video offers better quality than composite and is more suited to multimedia digitizing.

■ Time code is a numbering system used in videotape recording that will also be useful to you. You can use it to show tape numbers as well as time.

■ Shooting a video interview is one of the most likely kinds of video you will undertake. The subject can be separated from the background by shooting against blue or black.

■ The stages of editing video are preparation, offline and online. New technology and non-linear editing systems using PCs are blurring the distinction between online and offline editing.

■ Options for compressing video so that it can easily be handled on the desktop include moving JPEG, MPEG and software codecs. The most common equivalent for the Web is RealVideo.

■ Codecs will usually have a range of data rates for which they are suited, so a Web codec may not work on CD and vice versa.

Recommended reading

Ozer J. (1995). *Video Compression for Multimedia*. London: AP Professional
Quantel Limited (1994). *The Digital Factbook*, 7th edn. Newbury: Quantel Limited
Watts H. (1984). *On Camera*. London: BBC Publications
Watkinson J. (1995). *Compression in Video and Audio*. London: Focal Press

Information on codecs for video compression can be found at Codec Central from Terran Interactive. The URL is www.codeccentral.com

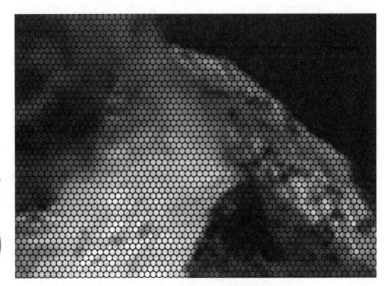

15

Graphics asset production

Project manager's responsibilities

- To assemble the necessary graphics team
- To ensure that the project definition is in a form that adequately briefs the graphics team
- To monitor the development of the graphics, and liaise between the client and the team over changes and misunderstandings
- To make sure that 'proofreading', the checking of any written material in the graphics, is carried out
- To make sure that the source graphics are archived at the highest reasonable resolution, no matter how they are displayed in the application
- To understand the processes involved in producing this kind of asset

A picture is worth a thousand words

No matter how innovative your interface design, how sophisticated your programming or use of HTML, the public face of your Web page or multimedia application and the major make-or-break factor is going to be your graphics. Your potential customer will feel able to make an instant judgement, for better or for worse, on the basis of that first impression on the screen.

Just as with software, the creation and manipulation of graphics is a complex business, and the purpose of this chapter is to provide some general background to the techniques and systems that you might wish to use, and to outline some of the problems that you might come across.

The two key parts of managing the production of graphics are the definition of the task and the selection of the personnel. There should be some definition of the approach to graphics in the project plan. In some cases a graphics artist or art director will have taken part in the definition of the application. On the basis of the graphic requirements a team will be chosen. It may be that you are working in an organization that has graphics artists on the staff or a pool of freelancers. This situation is more common for graphics and programming than for sound or video. In this case you might find that the project plan evolved to fit in some way with the abilities of a particular graphics person.

There are many kinds of process that go to make up artwork, and after a brief explanation of terminology for colour this chapter will look at the differences between them and how the way they are made may impact upon the management of a project. This will apply to two stages, because you should work with your images in the highest quality possible and then convert down if necessary to the standard required for delivery. Archiving should also be done so as to include the highest-quality versions.

Colour

A colour image on a computer screen is made up of red, green and blue dots or lines, which are close enough together to blend into each other when seen from a working distance. Red, green and blue (R, G and B) are what are called the **primary colours** for any colour displayed with light. You will find an example on the CD of how a colour image is built in this way. (For pigments, such as paint and printing ink, the primaries are red, yellow and blue. For practical reasons printers usually work with secondary colours – yellow, cyan and magenta – to which black ink is usually added to avoid the muddy effects of trying to make black from the secondaries.)

For this reason we refer to a colour image on the screen as an **RGB image**. Almost any colour can be produced by mixing the three primaries, and in a full-colour image on the screen each picture element or pixel is built up from varying amounts of red, green and blue light. Shades of grey are produced by making the amount of red, green and blue in the pixel equal. For black there is no light, and for white the light is 'full on'. In digital terms there are 256 shades to each of red, green and blue in a full-colour 24-bit image.

With fewer than 24 bits there will be fewer colours, but it is possible that each of the colours that can be shown can be predefined from the full range, or palette, of 24 bits.

Drawings

This word has a double meaning. To the person in the street, drawing is taking a pencil and creating a freehand work of art. Drawing, like painting, is the essence of fine art.

In computer terms a drawing is an image that consists of distinct segments or shapes, called **draw objects**. It is sometimes referred to as **line art** but this term could be ambiguous, sometimes also referring to an image on the screen that is made up of only black and white pixels.

The classic draw objects are lines, rectangles and arcs together with a range of wavy lines called **curves**, of which Bézier curves are perhaps the most familiar. Since the draw objects are based around lines they are sometimes called **vector graphics**. The important thing about a drawing is that the objects in it retain their separate identity, so that they can be manipulated independently of each other, even if, in the image as seen, the object is partially or completely hidden behind other objects.

Each object has characteristics, which can be changed. Drawing applications will allow you to rescale an object or a group of objects. The width of a line, and the pattern with which it is drawn, called the **pen**, can be changed. If the object has an 'inside', it can be filled with a colour or a pattern. A polygonal shape or a curve can be altered by moving the corners or changing the controls on the curve.

Changing one object has no substantial repercussions on the other objects. If the circle in the diagram is moved it would reveal the polygon behind it. The image becomes a pattern of dots on the monitor only when it is displayed or when you choose to 'fix' it. By definition the drawing does not have a scale, and can be expanded or shrunk or distorted as required with no ill effects, as seen above. An exception to this scale independence is the thickness of lines, since that tends to be fixed. As a result you might wish to increase line thickness as the size increases, and vice versa.

If changes are required, drawings are relatively easy to modify. Because it is based around these distinct and almost unconnected objects a drawing package is said to be object-oriented.

In some computing systems, particularly the Apple Macintosh, these draw objects are supported by the operating system at a low level, which makes it easy for different programs to work with them and even exchange them.

Although most graphics on the Web are bitmapped, there is a small but important use of draw objects in making small animation files. Flash is a particularly popular example of this, and by describing the objects that go to make up an animation, and describing how they move and change, Flash is able to produce sophisticated animations from a very small amount of data.

Bitmap or painting

In contrast a **bitmap**, sometimes referred to in computing as a **painting** (hence paint packages as opposed to drawing packages), exists only as the patterns of dots. To continue the example above, if the ellipse moves it leaves a hole. If the bitmap expands, the dots get bigger and the resolution of the image becomes cruder.

The bitmap may start out as a set of draw objects. It may be created in a drawing package and then turned into a bitmap, 'fixing' the pattern of lines and shapes. It could have been scanned in from a photograph. Scanners are devices that take a 'real' image such as a print, a slide, a transparency or even a photographic negative and scan across the image, from side to side and top to bottom, to produce a stream of dot information about the image, which can be stored in a computer file and so make its way onto the screen.

Making changes to a bitmap, such as changing text in the image, could have serious implications because of the holes left when parts of the image are removed. One way around this problem is to use a painting package, which allows control of layers of an image and the way they are combined, or composited, together.

JPEG and GIF are the two most common bitmap formats for graphics, and both are used extensively on the Web. On CD-ROMs JPEGs are also common, although GIFs are unusual. BMP (Windows) and PICT (Mac) are platform-specific bitmap formats used on CD-ROMs. The new Web graphics format PNG supports up to 48 bits (16 bits each for R, G and B), which allows the look of the graphic to be adjusted as it is displayed to compensate for differences between different computers' graphics displays.

Composites

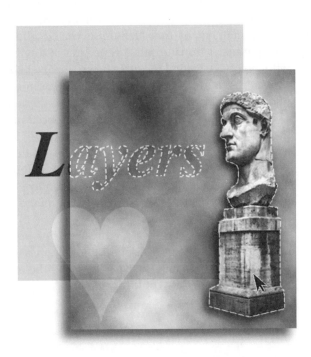

The addition of alpha channels and layers into paintings has helped to bring some of the advantages of draw objects to the world of the bitmap. Separate bitmap objects can be combined into a composite image. Even though changing a bitmap object itself is still difficult, the relationship between objects can easily be changed. Text (one object) over a photographic background (another object) can easily be changed. Each component of the final image is known as a **layer**, and the alpha channel determines how the layers blend with each other.

The simplest alpha channel is transparency or a simple mask. The GIF format allows for a colour to be transparent, which allows the background to show through, and helps the image to blend into the background of the Web page.

A true alpha channel is a graduated mask. It is essentially a fourth channel after red, green and blue, and it determines how much of the RGB image layer is shown at any point of the composite image and how much of whatever is underneath shows through. For most of the image the mask would be 'white', showing that all the RGB was visible and none of the underlying layers. Outside the image it would be 'black', showing that none of the RGB was visible there but the underlying layers were fully visible. At the edges of the image, where it would be designed to blend into its surroundings, the alpha channel would gradually change from white to black, and the depth of the 'grey' at any point would determine the visibility and mixing at that point.

In a montage, where there might be several small images grouped together over a background, each of the small images would have its own alpha channel and would exist in a separate layer. In this way changes can be made to each of these elements independently of the whole composite image. A further refinement of this technique would allow layers to be completely transparent or translucent. A reflection in a window would be transparent, with the image behind the glass being opaque behind it.

As a result of using layers in this way an image becomes easier to change under some circumstances. Let's use the example where a final image consists of a photograph with some text superimposed on it. If there is no layering to the image in your archive then to change the text you will have to find the original image of the background and build the image again from scratch. With layers you can change the text, which will be in the foreground layer by itself, without having to touch the background. A recent innovation is to use a version of layers to hold changes to an image, so that the changes can be modified or even reversed.

Paint packages can be biased towards creation, retouching or both. For many multimedia artists Adobe's PhotoShop defines the retouching package (although it is not alone), especially once it became available on the PC platform as well as on the Apple Macintosh.

3-D modelling and rendering

Quite often an application will have illustrations and montages that have a three-dimensional look. This may or may not include an animation such as a smooth movement of the viewpoint through a group of objects. 3-D packages are usually object oriented like a drawing package. You can build a solid object using techniques analogous to building with bricks, to using a lathe to turn, or to extrude (like squeezing toothpaste). Just as two-dimensional draw objects once became part of low-level operating system tools (sometimes called **primitives**), in time three-dimensional objects are joining them. This makes the creation of 3-D objects easier and cheaper because, again, programs will be able to make use of the operating system's objects rather than having to define their own.

Once the scene is designed and the objects in it are built and positioned you can choose the surfaces for the objects. This can include texture mapping, where a bitmap is spread over the surface of an object, bump mapping, where the object is given a bumpy surface, and setting the reflectivity or opacity of the object.

Then the lighting conditions can be set up with a balance of ambient (general) lighting and spot and floodlights, and the viewpoint chosen. All these parts of the process are part of the modelling.

Finally the scene is rendered to produce the final image or images. Unlike other graphical processes, which work more or less in real time, rendering can be very slow. A single image can take minutes or even hours to be rendered as the computer works out the view. The end result can be quite stunning, and can be genuinely referred to as photo-realistic. This is one reason why 3-D modelling is such a popular technique.

3-D images can take a long time to render, partly because of the time taken to work out the shadows and reflections in a scene. One very popular technique for determining reflections is **ray tracing**. In this case every ray of light in the view is traced as it 'bounces' from the light source, the objects in the scene and the viewer's eye. Ray tracing is very computationally intensive, and an alternative is environment mapping, where a view of 'the world as seen by the shiny object' is computed and wrapped around the object itself.

Three-dimensional modelling, like illustration and animation, is a special skill somewhat distinct from general graphics work, and you are likely to find artists who specialize in one or more of these areas.

A special case of 3-D modelling is VRML, Virtual Reality Modelling Language, which is used on the Web to make virtual worlds that the viewer can navigate at will. The VRML data defines the environment, and this is modelled in real time by a plug-in to the viewer's browser. The process needs a lot of computing and so is usually somewhat clunky compared with a sophisticated 3-D rendered image, but the real-time response to movement is very engaging, and it is possible to provide simple shading to enhance the experience. VRML is developing, and now includes animations and sound so that you can watch events unfold in front of you from whatever perspective you want.

A similar process to this kind of modelling is provided by QuickTime VR (QTVR), which is usually used to show the real world in a navigable way. The world is photographed as an interlinked series of 360° panoramas, allowing the user to look around and move from one panorama to another. QTVR can explore other worlds as well, since not only can the panoramas be computer-generated, but NASA published QTVR panoramas taken by a rover vehicle on Mars. QTVR is not the only such navigation software.

DPI and bit depths

In computing terms you define an image in a number of ways. For a bitmap the most obvious defining parameter is size. In printing, graphics artists are used to defining an image by its size in inches or centimetres, and then saying what the resolution is. This means that if you have a scanned image that is 2 inches across, with a resolution of 150 lines (or dots) per inch, there are 300 dots across the image. Print is defined in this way because print has a fixed size: the size of the final image on the printed page. Computer displays are not necessarily like that, and television screens are definitely not like that. In these cases the size in inches is not important, but the size in pixels is. So the computer person will give the image size as 300 pixels across and not really be worried about its physical size in inches. Note that to a printer a screen is part of the process by which an image made of continuous gradations of colour, such as a photograph, is turned into something that an ink-based printing press can actually reproduce. This book uses the word 'screen' to mean the image seen on the computer display.

Certainly a computer display has its equivalent of the printer's screen. Dots per inch is the usual way of defining a computer screen output as well. This is usually 72, 75 or 80 dots per inch (dpi), and each dot is a pixel. For a computer display of 75 dpi, the 300-pixel image will be 4 inches across. You need to be clear in your mind about the relationship between the size of an image in pixels, in inches, and the connection between the two, which is its dpi. If the image on the screen is to be 2 inches across again, instead of 4, then it can be shrunk by half in a paint or photo-retouching package.

There is a third dimension to computer screen images, which is the bit depth or colour depth. The number of bits in the screen display determines the number of colours or shades that can be shown. For a fixed size of image in pixels, the size of the file needed to store it doubles for most of the stages below.

- 1 bit gives you two colours (black and white).
- 2 bits give you four colours.
- 4 bits give you 16 colours.
- 8 bits give you 256 colours (GIFs are 8 bits or less).
- 16 bits give you 65 536 colours.
- 24 bits give you 16 777 216 colours (JPEGs are 24 bit).
- 48 bits give you 281 474 976 710 656 colours (PNG supports up to this depth).

Usually, when literature refers to 32-bit colour (as on the Apple Macintosh), this refers to 24 bits of colour information and 8 bits of alpha channel or mask, which is used for compositing. Also, a 16-bit system often gives five bits each to red, green and blue, and uses the sixteenth bit for a one-bit mask. Another technique is to give green more bits than red and blue because our eyes are more sensitive to green.

The CD includes examples of an image stored with different bit depths.

There are occasions when you will see a reference to colour of more than 24 bits, which is really just that. Colour scanners increasingly scan at 10 or even 12 bits per colour, making 30 or 36 bits. This is because the colour rendition of the object being scanned will not usually match that of the computer, and it is handy to be able to adjust the scanning to compensate for this. The difference usually shows in the darker and lighter parts of the image. This becomes especially true when working with photographic negatives, which have a particularly wide latitude (the film equivalent of dynamic range). The relationship between the colours at the input of a device and its output – for example, as how a monitor displays shades of grey – is called the **gamma** of the device. Every display device has a gamma, and PCs, television sets and Macs all have different gammas. This means that a 'correct' image made on a Mac will not necessarily look good on a PC or a TV. You can adjust the gamma of an image, but doing this to a 24-bit image results in some colours disappearing – a phenomenon familiar to anyone who uses PhotoShop's 'Levels' facility. Since PNG has 48 bits it will allow changes of gamma without sacrificing quality.

Of course you can substitute 'shade of grey' for colour. It is generally assumed that the eye can distinguish fewer than 256 shades of grey, which would suggest that you could represent a smooth gradation from black to white with 256 shades. Unfortunately this does not always work, because our vision is extremely sensitive to the transition between very similar shades. However, 256 grey levels is reckoned to be far and away good enough, and it certainly works for everyday images. For colour images the boundary lies between 16-bit and 24-bit.

Although 24 bits are best for a colour display, you can make do with fewer bits if the individual colours are chosen carefully from a 24-bit palette of colours, to match the colours in the image. Very few images run across the whole 16 million colours, and so using a **custom (or adaptive) palette**, as this is called, is a useful way of getting the bit depth, and also the size of the file, down. Often you can go down to 256 colours with a custom palette and the results will be virtually indistinguishable from a full 24-bit image. Unfortunately a custom palette is not always a practical idea, especially if several images with different custom palettes, and even the windows on the screen, are expected to share the same screen display and the screen is not a 24-bit one. The result will, at best, be an attempt by the operating system to reconcile the different palettes but, at worst, some of the images will turn psychedelic. There is a well-known palette for Web design that contains the 216 colours 'native' to Netscape Navigator under Windows.

The basic rule of reproduction, and this applies to print as well as to computer displays, is that you can trade spatial information for bit-depth information, which you could call **colour resolution**. This means that you can group pixels together and use the group, averaged between the individual pixels in the group, to show more colours than an individual pixel can. The group of pixels acts like a larger pixel that is capable of showing more colours. This technique has versions such as half-toning and dithering, which you can use as well as or instead of a custom palette. It is even possible to dither a one-bit image to make it look almost photographic, if the screen resolution is high enough and you do not look too closely.

Dithering.

As an extreme example, the illustration shows a grey-scale image of the Matterhorn that has been dithered from eight bits (256 shades of grey) to one bit (black and white). This is called a diffusion dither. You really have to squint and imagine really hard to see this as a grey-scale image, but the basic principle of dithering is there: groups of dots simulating greys.

Using what, when and why

For the designer of a computer-based application there are times when you will need to think very carefully about how your images are stored and reproduced.

In an ideal world, apart from special effects, you would always use 24-bit (or better) images in your Web pages and multimedia applications. However, you could run into problems in doing this, for reasons of display incompatibility and file size and/or download times. If the display of your target delivery system is not 24-bit then you need to know how it will react when fed a 24-bit image. If the display does not gracefully degrade it by, for example, dithering it, you might be better off dithering the images yourself. If there are palette problems, which are common in applications using windowing interfaces because of differing requirements of the windows on the screen, this can make your images look poor to the point of being psychedelic when their window is not active.

Custom palettes, especially when viewed on a display with less than 16-bit colour, present a potential difficulty in that, when switching from one picture to another in a sequence, the palette may not switch at the same time as the picture. This can lead to a brief flash of weird colours on the screen as the palette settles down. There is a brief moment while the beam scanning the image onto the monitor switches off as it moves from the bottom of the screen back to the top, called the **vertical blanking interval** or VBI. The VBI allows a short period during which both screen image and palette can be changed so that the palette flash is not seen – as long as the necessary changes can be made quickly enough.

File size is important for reasons of capacity and loading time. As well as taking up three times the space of an 8-bit image on your hard disk or CD-ROM, a 24-bit image takes three times as long to load. This could be crucial if you are expecting very fast response times and, of course, especially important on a Web site. As we have already discussed, you can reduce the size of an image by reducing the number of colours, and we discuss data reduction or compression of still images below.

You should also think carefully about whether you want to use 24-bit if it is available. It may be that some of your images will work very well in 8-bit, and so you should consider using them this way. This is particularly true of animations, where you might need to reap the benefit of smaller file sizes, or even use simple but fast compression methods (run-length encoding, for example) to avoid having to move too much data too quickly.

Even though your final delivery may not be a full 24-bit colour image, you should carry out all the retouching and compositing operations in 24-bit. Working on an 8-bit or a 16-bit version of an image will never give as good a result as working on the 24-bit original. This argument also extends to the archiving of graphics, and they should be kept at the highest reasonable quality as well as in their final form.

Anti-aliasing

Although text is essentially a one-bit image, there are circumstances when you would want to display text with more bits. It is all part of that trade-off between spatial and colour resolution. When converting from an object (such as text or a drawing) to a bitmap you have to fit the edges of the object to the pixels on the screen. If you do this and set the pixels black or white depending on whether the majority of the pixel is covered by the line or not, you get jagged lines on the screen, known as jaggies or staircasing.

The alternative is to colour the pixels along the edge in different shades according to how much of them is covered. This will disguise the jaggies, and usually renders them inconspicuous. The shades are blends of the foreground and background colours.

Because the effect of the mismatch between the real line and the 'quantizing' caused by trying to fit it onto the pixels in the image is known as aliasing, the kind of rendering that puts the grey pixels around the edge to smooth it out is known as **anti-aliasing**. Anti-aliased text, particularly, has become very popular with computer typographers and designers because it looks more like words on paper and less like a screen bitmap.

Some computer operating systems can render text to the screen in an anti-aliased fashion in real time, but in other cases the text needs to be built into the image as a graphic. However, even if the operating system is doing the anti-aliasing, it will be slower than simply printing non-anti-aliased text.

There are some occasions when you should think carefully about using anti-aliased text. This is especially the case when the text is small, because the grey wedges around the edge tend to make small text look fuzzy. This problem increases with the reducing of text size because the 'grey' pixels around the edge have a fixed size and so become a bigger proportion of the text size as the text shrinks. In some cases, more careful alignment of the text on the screen will optimize the appearance. The worst-case scenario is where the text is small enough, and misaligned enough, for some of the strokes of the characters to be almost completely grey. In this case they just look out of focus. Making the size of the characters such that their top and bottom edges lie exactly at pixel boundaries reduces this effect, but few characters have straight lines at their edges. Basically you have to check the images carefully.

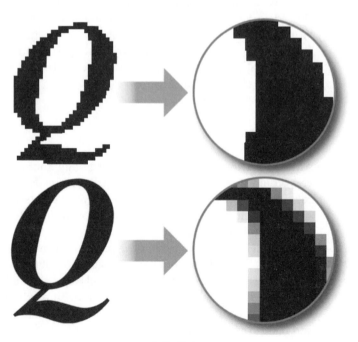

Anti-aliasing.

Look before you leap

Any graphic should be checked on the delivery system. Reducing the bit depth of an image can have all sorts of undesirable side effects, particularly **quantization**. This is sometimes also called **posterization** or **contouring**. It is the result of taking a smooth transition from one colour to another and replacing that with a series of discrete steps.

Posterization.

In this image, as an example, you see an extreme case of posterization. There is a risk that the 24-bit image on the left (subject to the vagaries of reproduction in print), which has 256 shades of grey in it, would come out looking like the one on the right if that computer screen could display only four levels of grey.

Unfortunately you can only be sure of this kind of compatibility if you have checked your image on every screen format, which is a bit problematic for a Web site because there are so many computers with so many browsers. Fortunately, there is a known group of colours, known as the **Netscape** or **Web palette**, which can be used for 8-bit images to minimize the risk of unforeseen changes. This palette also eases cross-platform compatibility between the PC and Mac. However, there is a final Mac/PC issue that often catches people out, and that is the difference in the display gamma between the two platforms. Gamma is the way in which brightness levels are shown on the display, and the result of Macs and PCs having different gamma curves is that images look darker on a PC than they do on a Mac. To overcome this you must either tailor the image to the platform – a CGI program or JavaScript can find out what platform a viewer's Web browser is using and call up appropriate image files – or accept dark or light images or attempt to compromise. In the future it should be possible to detect the characteristics of the computer display and adjust the gamma of an image accordingly.

Taking less space

You will usually need to reduce the size of graphics files. This can be for reasons of space, for example on a compact disc. It can also affect the time it takes to access the files, whether from the Web or from a CD.

One way of reducing the size of a graphic is by degrading it. The size of the file, in pixels, can be reduced. A 640 by 480 file could be shrunk to 320 by 240 and blown back up on display. This will lead to a dramatic reduction in quality. The colour depth of the picture can be reduced. One quite effective way is to change from a 24-bit image to an 8-bit one with only 256 colours. If the palette for the picture is carefully chosen a 256-colour version of a 24-bit picture can be a very effective substitute. This is known as an **adaptive palette**.

JPEG compresses photographic images substantially by losing the less visible elements of the picture using a process called a discrete cosine transform (DCT) to identify fine detail and remove it. JPEG at relatively low compression rates, such as 5 to 1, will usually be indistinguishable from the original. This means that JPEG is even more efficient than 8-bit with an adaptive palette.

Compare the two images below.

JPEG Matterhorn.

JPEG artefacts.

The first image was compressed using a high-quality JPEG compressor, but if we subtract this image from the original, and the range of brightness in the result is expanded so that the changes are easier to see, a mosaic pattern becomes visible.

In the second image, the finer the dots are, the more detail has been removed by the JPEG DCT algorithm. The reduction achieved by JPEG here is a factor of 3. If the image was colour the difference would be greater. You can find these images on the CD.

Reducing the size of a file reduces the time it takes to load that file. If the image needs to be decoded, as a JPEG image would, then you have to take account of the decoding time. Despite this, on a Web site you will find that the time taken to download and decode a JPEG image is still less than the time taken to download an uncompressed version – if your browser could display the uncompressed file type.

Computer graphics and video graphics

If your graphics artist has a background in video, he or she may suggest that you work with video graphics equipment. In general the facilities available on such equipment are similar to those on computer packages but more powerful (unless your computer is really high end). The main differences are that television is a 16-bit system (making use of our relatively poor colour resolution of vision), it is interlaced, and it has a set image size. On the plus side, this kind of television equipment (Quantel is a major manufacturer of such systems) has dedicated hardware and so can operate very quickly, often blindingly so. There is a large pool of experienced video graphics people. Also, if you are actually manipulating images from video, the facility will be able to handle this for you in an integrated manner.

Animated graphics on the Web

Animated graphics are somewhat different from movies, although an animation can be a movie. By animation what we mean is an animated line drawing, like a cartoon, rather than something that is, or looks, photographic. Some forms of animation can be efficiently compressed for use on the Web. We have already mentioned Flash, which takes draw object shapes and text and allows sophisticated animations to be made using them that require very little data. Animated titles or bullet point slides can be made this way with little data overhead over and above the Web page itself. The only disadvantage is that the viewer needs to have downloaded the relevant plug-in for the browser and to have installed it correctly.

Another form of animation that is web-friendly is **sprite animation**. A small animated object, called a **sprite**, can be moved around a larger stage. This sprite could be an animation of a walking figure, and the stage could be a line representing a road. Shockwave, which is based on Macromedia Director, allows animations of this kind to be made and distributed on a Web page. Director itself animates by using a sprite-based system, which translates well to the Web. Again, the plug-in is required.

Of course you could devise an animation that ran as a Java applet, and in this case it could be as sophisticated as your programming skill allowed. No plug-in is needed because many browsers support Java, but many users disable it and some companies restrict or ban its use for security reasons.

Asset management

It is possible that the number of graphics files you might have in your application is large. It could be the largest number of files, and if you take into account versions, sections of composite images, and animations then the number can easily run into thousands.

For this reason it is vital that from the beginning you adopt a known system of naming files. This was especially difficult with filing systems that did not allow long names, such as DOS, but is less of a problem now. It is tempting to use paths in your directory structure to identify files, but this has risks since files can become separated from their directories. Some kind of coding is probably going to be the only safe solution to this problem, with a short code identifying the image and its status. A suffix or extension should be reserved for the file type since some filing systems recognize files only by this extension. The resources in Apple files are potentially very useful, and very detailed information about a file can be put there as a special resource, but this does not help you if you are working on a PC. Also you will have to consider the problems of recognizing files from lists, including lists in archives.

In particularly complex cases a database may be required to handle the assets in an application, and several software companies have been addressing the problems of handling an image database of this kind. You may wish to write a system of your own, which can be used for different applications.

Image compatibility and quality

Since it is possible to display a photographic-quality image on a 24-bit display, you will need to take care that any compression does not noticeably degrade the image. In agreeing quality standards with a client you will need, as with audio and video, to align your quality with what the delivery system can display. However, there may be times, such as with a Web site, when the delivery system will encompass a range of displays, and under these circumstances you will need to check how the images look on all the platforms and try to make sure that they degrade gracefully as the display capabilities decline.

From a practical point of view the days of image standards for still pictures being incompatible are almost over, since there are a number of good conversion packages that can take an image in one format and convert it to another with no loss. You should be aware, however, of differences between uncompressed, compressed but lossless, and compressed with loss (or lossy).

An image that is compressed without loss, such as one compressed with run-length encoding, will be the same as an uncompressed one when it latter is expanded. Lossy systems are more unpredictable but the good ones, such as Photo-CD and JPEG, can be used as if they were uncompressed as far as delivery of the image is concerned.

There is a caveat. If you are going to manipulate an image you should start from an uncompressed or lossless-compressed image. Exceptionally, Photo-CD can be used for origination, as the compression system used for it is visually lossless, even though it does lose some information. This loss amounts only to information that we do not see since our eyes do not resolve colour as well as the brightness information.

Proofreeding!

In software they say that 'there is always one more bug', and the typo is the graphical equivalent. It will be important to check for any errors in the graphics, just as you will do with any voice-over script. Any text on screen should be checked for spelling and consistency of presentation before it is passed on to the graphics team for display on the screen. However, even the most experienced typographer can make a mistake, and if proper names or foreign languages are involved, extra care is needed.

Proofreading is a skill and, in any event, should not be carried out by the person who wrote the text because they will sometimes see what they expect to see rather than what is really there. You cannot rely on spell checkers because spell checking does not usually pick up misused words or typos that are valid words, such as 'if' for 'of' or 'reed' for 'read'.

Theory into practice 17

The CD-ROM contains examples of images with different resolutions and bit depths. You should familiarize yourself with the effects on different kinds of material and, using whatever image manipulation software you have, experiment with changes in the number of colours.

If you have access to a range of machines with different graphics capabilities, or if you can easily change the display on your computer, you can take a couple of graphic-oriented Web sites and see how they look under differing conditions.

Summary

■ There are two basic types of image, one that is object-oriented and known as a drawing, and can be changed relatively easily, and one that consists only of the exact dots displayed on the screen. This is a bitmap or painting, and is less easily manipulated.

■ Working with a composite image in a package that uses layers and alpha channels can give you the best of both worlds because you can separate the sections of the image and work on them independently.

■ Unless you are working with photographic images (usually 24-bit colour), you will have to select a range of colours carefully for representation of the image. This is known as the palette.

■ In transferring a 24-bit image to a smaller palette, say 8-bit, there are compromises that have to be made. However, the resulting file will also be smaller.

■ Reducing the number of colours in an image is not the only way of shrinking the file, since JPEG compression, which is an international standard, can achieve a shrinkage with less visible artefacts.

■ Whatever you do with images, it is vital always to check how the image will look when it reaches your end user. And don't forget to proofread any text.

Recommended reading

Siegel D. (1997). *Creating Killer Web Sites*, 2nd edn. Indianapolis IN: Hayden Books

Foley J.D., van Dam A., Feiner S.K. and Hughes J.F. (1996). *Computer Graphics, Principles and Practice*, 2nd edn in C. Reading, MA: Addison-Wesley

16

Integration

Project manager's responsibilities

- To assemble the necessary software engineering team to implement the application

- To ensure that the project definition is in a form that can be implemented in software

- To monitor the development of the programming, and liaise between the client and programming team over changes and misunderstandings

- To define the testing to be carried out, and oversee that process

- To understand the basics of programming logic so as to better understand the problems facing the programmers

Multimedia fusion or confusion?

Multimedia can be said to gather the best, and the worst, aspects of both computing and the audiovisual industry, and they have to be fused together in the core stage of multimedia development. This is the integration of the application. Here the underlying computer software is applied to the assets, and this is often the first time that anyone, including the designer, sees the jigsaw fitting together. The writing of HTML for a Web site is not often regarded as programming, especially because it is often carried out by another specialist, such as a graphics artist. Of course, any programming for CGI applications on the Web site is usually hard code, and can be just about as arcane as multimedia gets. In any event, since a program is a series of instructions written by a human so that a machine can carry them out in the intended manner, certain basic rules and principles apply, and the term 'programmer' is used here is this very broad way.

Managing a team in software development has much in common with the general principles covered in Chapter 12, *Team management principles*. The software team involved in an application can range from a single person upwards, although for multimedia your team is unlikely to be larger than four or five. If you have a single person working on your project it will be beneficial for that person to have contact with other programmers so that any sticky problems can be sorted out. Within a team you may wish to have one person who manages the team's work. Software is often written on a modular basis, with separate but self-contained parts of the application being written by different people. It can be necessary for someone with software knowledge to distribute the work and make sure the modules fit together.

The choice of people to program your project will depend on how it will be carried out. Different software engineers will have experience of using different languages and tools. Ideally you will have enough experience, or be able to get suitably impartial advice, to choose the environment and therefore know what kind of programmer to recruit.

A second part of managing software involves the specifying of what needs to be done and ensuring that it is carried out. Taking advice from a programmer during the early stages of the design can avoid problems later and can help you to describe the application in ways that a programmer can clearly understand. When specifying an application there will be input from every part of your team and from your client. For a consumer product your client could be replaced by information on what customers want, but the basic principle remains the same.

The purpose of this chapter is to give an overview of the software aspects of Web sites and multimedia, but it does not set out to show how to actually carry out the programming. Just as in the audio and video chapters, this chapter aims to help non-programming specialists to understand the processes and problems that arise in multimedia software development.

A computer program is a series of operations and decisions. Something happens as a result of the user carrying out an action, and the software will respond. It is the task of the designer to decide what that response will be, and of the software engineer, or programmer, to implement this as code. The software engineer will write the software that carries out this integration by using either an authoring tool or a programming language.

Authoring versus programming

There is no hard-and-fast rule about what constitutes authoring as distinct from programming. Packages with which you can write multimedia applications range from graphical packages such as Director and ToolBook, with which you can build basic interactive structures with a few clicks of the mouse button and a few pulled-down menus, through scripting languages such as HTML, which is not unlike English, to the hard stuff, such as Java and C++. In general the versatility and performance of your application will increase as you move towards a full-blown programming language such as C++, but it will be more difficult to implement.

An authoring package often lends its own look and feel to the application, and experienced authors can sometimes look at a program and say 'Oh, that was developed using Macromedia Director' or 'That's a typical ToolBook application'. This is partly the result of early users of such tools making good use of the facilities the tools provide – a package-led approach. Using authoring packages for Web pages has an extra aspect, in that often the HTML they produce is quirky in some way, even though it usually still does the job.

As time has gone by, the desired functionality has become more of a driving force than the obvious abilities of the tools. It must be said, however, that authoring tools do have their limits, especially when it comes to performance of offline applications.

So, how do you choose between the different options? In the end some kind of risk–benefit analysis needs to be done to compare your options, but there are a couple of underlying factors that you need to take into account.

As a general rule, the lower the level of coding you undertake, the longer it will take. This is partly because the code will take longer to write, but it will also be more prone to bugs that are difficult to track down. To counter this, if you have software engineers working in your team who have experience of lower-level coding then they may program very quickly. You, or your software team, should be building up a set of routines or libraries for your programming. This is particularly true if you are working in C or C++. You can incorporate these libraries in future projects as well. This is the main reason why it is a good idea for you to only license your code to your clients rather than grant them all rights; otherwise you will find it difficult to make use of your basic routines from earlier projects.

Besides the inherent abilities of the team at your disposal, you will also be judging the requirements of the particular application. In some cases it may demand low-level coding, for instance if there are any gaming elements, but for less responsive and more asset-led applications an authoring tool may be very appropriate.

The authoring tree

A good graphical authoring package or structure editor will have an underlying scripting language, and a good scripting language will allow you to build new commands with a lower-level language such as C. At the bottom of this pile, rather like the court of ultimate appeal, the low-level language could call routines in machine code for speed. Machine code written as part of an application is common in games but much less so in multimedia.

A graphical structure editor, or similar, lets you define the flow of an application's logic by drawing it on the screen in some way, often just like a flow chart in traditional logic. Examples of this kind of authoring package include Icon Author and Authorware.

Alternatively the flow could be predetermined, as in a card-based hyperlinked system, where you define hot-spots or buttons and then have a new card that is displayed as a result of activating the button. The buttons can also trigger other things besides jumps to other cards, and you can trigger events on opening or closing cards as well. Examples of this kind of system include ToolBook and Hypercard.

A third kind of authoring system uses a time line onto which you put events. The hyperlinks in this kind of system jump around on the time line. Macromedia Director is an authoring system of this kind.

Although these are in fact three different kinds of authoring system, what they have in common is that you can build a simple application or define the outline of a more complex one without typing in any commands. In almost every case, these authoring tools have scripting languages underneath, such as Lingo with Director and Hypertalk with Hypercard.

There is no hard-and-fast definition of an authoring or scripting language as opposed to a programming language. One definition is that a scripting language is a special type of computer language in that it usually appears to be in English. HTML is effectively a scripting language, although it actually sets out to mark up text to say how it should be displayed. As HTML has evolved to allow designers to control more of the look of a page it has become more of a program and less of a mark-up. (However, since HTML has no variables or structures to allow conditional looping and testing it falls outside any real definition of a computer program.) Scripting languages can also offer intuitive variables like 'it' so that when you 'get the time' the value of 'the time' is held in a variable automatically called 'it'. Then when the next command is 'show it' the value of the time will be displayed. Since the script says 'get the time, show it', it reads like English.

The definition falls down partly because well-written code in computer languages can sometimes be as relatively easy to read as English. Also C++, which is a very powerful programming language, has a variable 'this', which always refers to the current object. JavaScript and Perl are two languages used on the Web. JavaScript runs in the browser and appears embedded in the HTML, whereas Perl runs on the server. Both these languages are often referred to as producing scripts rather than code, but this just serves to illustrate how blurred the boundaries are since their syntax can be decidedly cryptic at times.

Another definition is that a scripting language will only be able to carry out a defined range of tasks, whereas a programming language is versatile. This one is closer to the truth but still not accurate. As long as a language can carry out basic arithmetic and logic it can, in theory, be applied to any task – even being used to write itself, just as C can be used to write a C compiler. But that may be the key. In practice, most scripting languages are good at some tasks but very inefficient in others.

To help with their core task, scripting languages for multimedia will have built-in support for sound and video, which would have to be specially programmed in a more general-purpose programming language.

Because of the hyperlinked nature of the HTML documents used on the World Wide Web, you could argue that HTML is a scripting language, and the kind of programs that read HTML (Web browsers) can handle pictures, sound and movies. It is possible to use HTML as a simple form of multimedia authoring on CD-ROM (as we have done on the CD with this book). HTML is designed to work in a distributed system – the Internet – and distributed multimedia is becoming increasingly important.

In an authoring environment you, as author, do not really have any control over the way your program interacts with the computer's memory, filing system and so on. This can result in problems if the authoring package you are using has any faults in the way it interacts with the computer. One example is where the program takes some memory to carry out a task but does not correctly free that memory after use. In this way it is possible for a program to very slowly eat into free memory until the computer runs out of memory and crashes. This kind of error, known as a **memory leak**, is extremely difficult to track down, and can be the cause of inexplicable crashes that also seem to be unrepeatable. In this case, using a utility program to monitor the computer can help. If you are working in a computer language that allows direct control of such things, such as C, then you have to take care of memory usage yourself.

A final analogy for programming versus authoring: you might be able to use a screwdriver (a low-level and versatile tool) to dig a hole in the street, but would you want to do so? The jackhammer or pneumatic drill (a rather blunt analogue of the authoring tool) is better suited to the job, but less versatile than the screwdriver. Conversely, think about trying to turn a screw with a jackhammer.

Stages

There is some confusion as to the stages of software development, since some of the terms mean different things to different people. In practice, because of the diverse backgrounds of people working in multimedia, a strict software-oriented development cycle might not be followed, or indeed be appropriate, as has been discussed earlier in Table 2.1. It is up to the development team as to how they manage their programming, but some clients will expect some of the more formal elements of software design. To help understand this, what follows is a brief outline of a more software-oriented offline procedure, and may not be at all appropriate for your multimedia application.

In addition, the quality standards (such as ISO 9000) that can be applied to any process lay down definite meanings. One common software approach is to write a user requirements document and a functional specification. The proposal to the client may well have covered some aspects of this, since the application structure might have been outlined. Ideally someone from the software team would have been involved in this process, or else the structure would have been based on previous work and therefore would be, to a large extent, tried and tested.

User requirements

'User requirements' is an ambiguous expression, and if it is mentioned, you will need to be sure of what is actually meant. There are two meanings, both of which are useful, and you might consider including both in the software process.

The first meaning is 'What are the needs of the user that the multimedia application can satisfy?' In this way the user requirement of a word processor is basically the ability to write and manipulate text, and this kind of information follows from the scoping of the project when the needs and objectives of the user are determined.

This is a very general interpretation, which allows the design team to lay down the functionality of the software in a general way. Sometimes this stage is called a **user specification**, and in order to help a potential client or sponsor understand what the application will do it could include short scenarios that describe (hypothetically) what it would be like to use the application.

The second meaning is 'What does the user require of the application?', which is a much more specific question. Here the answers are things such as 'a user-friendly interface', 'spell checking', 'automatic saving of work on a regular basis'. It may be that your client will have very specific requirements that the complete application must fulfil, and a strict user requirements list like this is a good way of expressing those. The software team use the list as input saying what needs to be done. It is their task to work out how to do it, which leads to the functional specification.

Functional specification

Whereas the user requirements outline what needs to be done, the functional specification gives much more detail about how a task will be carried out. At its fullest a functional specification will list the outcome of every action carried out by the user, and will say how that is to be achieved.

With a Web site some things are taken for granted: the way the links operate and the graphics are displayed are outside your control since the browser does that. So a functional specification is not appropriate for a Web site unless CGI programming is involved. However, the client and the developer need to agree on the structure of the site and the way it looks. So a specification for a Web site would concentrate on the look of the graphics – perhaps with template designs for page layouts – and the hierarchical structure of the site. Once a Web site moves on from HTML to CGI then a functional specification becomes a possibility. This can happen because the site is going to be very large and dynamic, perhaps something like a catalogue, with many pages that have a standardized layout. In such cases the Web site might be built dynamically by a database rather than being hard-coded in static HTML. The database will organize the site content, and the responses to queries will be output as HTML so that the browser receives what seem to be ordinary Web pages.

For a major software project (and this would include a big database-driven Web site, for example), the functional specification will be a very large document, and will be carefully researched and written. It can take many months to write the specification, and it is the document that defines the application. If clients have a software background, they may ask for such a document. Otherwise, the programmers will perform the same sort of task adapted to the constraints of multimedia, but clients will not necessarily be given it as part of the documentation because its use to them without a programming background would be minimal. If clients have requested a functional specification, then once this document is agreed and signed off, any changes have to be similarly discussed, agreed and signed off as change requests. A change request can then be evaluated in terms of its impact on time, quality and budget as discussed in Chapter 5.

There is a basic difficulty in applying a strict functional specification of this type to multimedia, which is why its use is intermittent in the industry. This results partly from the audiovisual nature of multimedia. A lot of the content of the application lies in the assets, and they can be very difficult to specify since, at the start, they will not have been researched. Also, time-based media are notoriously difficult to specify since the performance of the integrated application depends on so many factors, including the exact nature of the time-based asset itself. We are not yet at the stage in multimedia where our clients and viewers can take as read the quality thresholds that apply to assets in the way they can for radio or television. The concept of broadcast quality cannot yet automatically apply to multimedia simply because of the variety of display systems on people's desks.

A second problem with the functional specification lies in the difficulty of writing down what is a very dynamic process. For this reason many developers use prototypes, or demonstrator applications sometimes also called animatics, to define the task to be carried out. Even then there is an acceptance that not everything intended can be achieved. This would never be the case with a piece of accounting software. Sometimes for multimedia the only accurate definition of an application will be the application itself.

Finally, a recent trend in software design has been to forgo a functional specification altogether. With object-oriented programming, where distinct modules of the program are defined carefully so that they operate as independent objects and just communicate with each other, the important thing to define is the way the program will work. The exact detail of how the objects are coded is left to the software engineers.

For these reasons any kind of functional specification, and also the user requirements, are likely to be internal rather than external documents in a multimedia development. Their primary purpose is to help the software team to build the application rather than to define the application for the client. As a result the documents may even be called something completely different but would fulfil broadly the same purpose.

Alpha and omega

The actual development, as distinct from the talking about the development, also has names. Again, there is some variance as to what the terms really mean, but this is one set of meanings. Software people will sometimes refer to stages of a project in terms such as pre-alpha, alpha, beta, and golden master. A wider approach to testing than a pure software approach is discussed in Chapter 18. Using this as a reference, the point at which you would put your application out for external testing is what would be referred to as a beta version by software-oriented developers.

An alpha is more for testing internally in the team, and you might not even show it to the client. To extend the meaning of alpha into multimedia you might say that an alpha is structurally complete but does not have all its content in place, only enough to test functionality while you are waiting for the complete content. This is part of the type of testing referred to as **developmental testing** in Chapter 18.

In offline projects, the golden master is the one that is actually going to be sent for replication and distribution. The equivalent stage for a Web site is the point at which the complete site is ready to go online. It is fully tested and has survived all the testing you, and possibly your client, has thrown at it. The project is signed off or gets final acceptance.

As the software team gets bigger, the difficulties of keeping track of the development increase. In multimedia the problem of **version control** or **version tracking**, as this is called, increases as well because most of your assets will be going through changes too. As part of your version control you will need to devise a numbering scheme for everything you do, including the documentation. Here are some suggestions:

- Anything that is unfinished has a version number smaller than one, for example 0.3 or 0.99 (for 'almost there'). You can have more numbers after the decimal point to show very small changes but this is a rather subjective concept.
- A more complex numbering system, such as 1.2 B 24 would denote that this is the beta version of version 1.2 of the specification, and this is the 24th build of the application. The term 'build' implies a compiling process or some process that takes the software in one form and turns it into another.
- An odd or an even number beyond the decimal point could indicate whether the change from the last number was due to new functionality or a bug fix.

In a modular piece of software a version number should be given to every module, especially if different people are writing different modules. Use comments in code freely to explain what is going on, including the basics of what the module does. Images built as montages of other images will also require version numbers.

Bugs

Computers are, at best, very stupid but very logical. They never know what you mean, they only know what you say in your programs, and this can be extremely frustrating when something goes wrong with a program and it has to be investigated.

Legend has it that the use of the word 'bug', meaning a problem in a computer program, dates from Admiral Grace Hopper, who was one of the very early computer pioneers (and sometimes credited with inventing the software computer program). A big computer failed, and the cause was an insect (bug) which had crawled onto a logic module and died as a result of the heat or voltage. The logic module used a valve or vacuum tube. The legend is only partly true, since engineers have been finding technical bugs in things since the 19th century. Hopper's insect bug (a moth) did, however, die a legendary death.

There is a saying in programming, 'There is always one more bug', and unfortunately the reliability of complex systems decreases geometrically with the number of component parts. Since a computer program does not wear out like a car engine, its reliability is better defined as correct operation under all conditions. Things the user is not supposed to do – such as illegal keystrokes – should be catered for during software development; but reliability tends to decrease with the increasing complexity of the program. Even changing the delivery medium can show up a bug. As an example consider an application developed under Windows 95 or NT that is to be delivered on CD-ROM. Windows now allows very long file names, and it is a temptation to use them, but a Windows 95 or NT CD-ROM that uses what is called the Joliet extensions to allow long file names allows only up to 31 characters in the name, so the program that worked on a hard disk may not work on the CD-ROM. It now seems to be accepted that a complex computer program can never be tested for absolutely every eventuality.

This can be difficult for clients to understand. If they come from an area where it seems that absolute quality is achievable they might overreact to a bug. The onus is on the software team and the project manager to test as thoroughly as possible, bearing in mind cost and time constraints.

One option is to allow the client to use the software 'in anger' for some time and delay final acceptance until that period is finished. If you are going to do this then it is vital that the schedule and cost allow for it and that this has been agreed up front, not as an afterthought. See Chapter 18 for how to specify a full testing strategy.

If it is any consolation, even long-established software can have bugs, some known and some unknown. One very common microprocessor, which was for a long time a mainstay of 8-bit computing, had a low-level addressing bug that was never fixed. If a bug is known about, and software works around the bug, it is possible that the bug will never be fixed because this would affect the existing programs that are working around the bug.

With a Web page the difficulty in testing lies in the many different browsers and machine combinations that people will use. A recent survey of visitors to the Browser Watch Web site turned up so many differently identified browsers visiting the site (this information is sent to the server with the page request) that four different Web pages were needed to list them. Of course you can test the syntax of your Web page. Programs such as Weblint (which runs under Perl) will do this for you, and track down unbalanced tags (opened but not closed and vice versa) and the like. But sometimes a bug can appear as if from a clear blue sky. The author suffered from crashes of a Web site that suddenly started for no apparent reason, only when using Netscape, and could not be replicated on the local machine, only over the network. This was eventually traced to a background graphic that had somehow become corrupted and was only affecting Netscape under certain circumstances. Bugs like that are hard to find and, as usual, require a complex process of trial and error testing.

It can be difficult to test CGI programs because they need to run on the server and get data such as environment variables over the network. Environment variables can be passed to a CGI program so that the program can act on them. This makes it difficult to test them offline prior to installation. Often when a CGI has a bug and does not return the correct result you will not see anything on the browser because the server does not allow the CGI to return anything at all. For this reason some servers allow you to run your CGIs in a debugging mode, which allows you to see remote results clearly. This might be done by prefixing the program name with something that identifies it as a debugging run.

A further consideration is that the Web itself suffers from the equivalent of bugs. Some days it slows down and very occasionally it suffers from a major problem. The server could malfunction: it could have crashed because of some external event you could not control, or your CGI program may have seized up, perhaps waiting for an key-press acknowledgement that will never come. If you have an ongoing responsibility for a site it is a good idea to have someone check it every morning. That way, if the client telephones you can already be on the case.

The demo factor

In many organizations and projects there will be pressures to demonstrate Web sites or offline applications. This could be for the client, or other clients, or the board, or at a trade show. The demo factor brings two major implications to the development of the application.

First, and this is a negative factor, the timing is likely to be such that you will have to assemble a special version for demonstration. This is very likely to be the case if the demo is taking place early in the development cycle. If it is a networked application you may have to produce a stand-alone version, or you may have to put it on the server with password protection.

Second, and this is a positive factor, a demo can be a very good bug finder. There is something about letting a member of the company management demonstrate the software that brings the bugs out from the woodwork. Of course this means that the demo should be 'scripted' so that nothing untoward happens. Unfortunately people doing demonstrations do not always follow instructions. The author was involved in a project where the demonstrator was warned that under no circumstances should he do a certain thing because it was known to crash the program. He, of course, did just that – at the beginning of his demonstration to the chairman of the multinational company for which he worked.

However, this is a lesson that you learn very quickly the hard way, and it is a lot easier to lose a client than to gain one. The best approach is not to be pressganged into giving demos too early.

The only other solution is to make sure that even a demo is solid enough to continue working and not crash completely. Do not have buttons that call a routine that crashes; rather, make them 'blind' and not do anything. It takes minutes to restart most multimedia systems.

The jigsaw

Software engineering is becoming more and more like a mix-and-match jigsaw puzzle. Programs are made up of objects that interact with each other and can be reused in other applications. Multimedia applications will have three main sections that need to be fitted together:

- The **user interface** is the means by which the user controls the program. It may or may not include assets of its own.
- The **program logic** runs behind the user interface and carries out the tasks the user interface requests, and will possibly have an agenda of its own if, for example, the application includes any simulations.
- The **assets** are the audiovisual components of the program that the program logic will choose and activate, usually on the instructions of the user interface.

Even if the application does not easily break down into these three sections, there are reasons why you might wish to separate them from a logical point of view. The user interface may run remotely from the core program logic in a networked application. A Web page is essentially a user interface that runs on a Web browser. Assets will need to be proofread or otherwise checked, which is their equivalent of debugging, and replacing assets on a CD-ROM is easy if they are not inexorably entwined in the software, unless of course you have a CD-ROM that has just been shipped out to a thousand customers. Replacing assets on a Web page is fairly trivial at any time. Program logic is less platform dependent than the user interface and so is easier to port from one platform to another.

Risky business

There is a wish in most software teams for them to be exploring new territory and not continuously reworking the same old routines time and time again. It is considered a matter of pride to be asked to beta-test some new software tool or operating system extension. When surfing the Web you will often come across Web sites that require either a just-released browser or some plug-in or other. In many cases Web browser plug-ins – and this is also true of Java – provide tiny run-time environments in which the small programs can run, sometimes called **virtual machines** if they are particularly versatile. In fact these small programs have even been given a name: **applets**. Ironically, as you move further and further away from HTML, your online programming becomes more and more like programming for offline multimedia.

'Pushing the envelope' can be a dangerous business. The envelope is your current level of expertise, and when you push the envelope you try something newer and more challenging. To build an application you need to be able to plan and move forward through the development cycle, and if the sands shift beneath you because of bugs in the tools or changes in their functionality then you are in trouble. There are few things worse in computing than chasing a bug for months only to find eventually that the problem lies in the operating system, or the language, or some other third-party software such as a low-level driver.

Of course there always has to be a first time to use a new tool, so you can never be completely sure. The message is to think very carefully of the implications of using something new, and to allow for extra time for the learning curve in your planning. The time when you use a new version of a tried and trusted tool or of the operating system can also be problematic, and as a general rule upgrading should not be carried out in mid-project unless there is no alternative.

It is also possible that using a previously untried feature of familiar software can cause difficulties. Unfortunately it is not always possible to rely on documentation since a complex program, by definition, is very difficult to document fully. And as already mentioned, there can also be bugs in long-established software and even the operating system or processor.

The link between software and the client

The project manager's dilemma.

More than in any other area of multimedia development, the project manager or producer has to be able to act both as a buffer and as a translator between the client and the team. As project manager you have to trust your team to truly represent the status of the software. Sometimes they will give you what seems completely counter-intuitive advice as a result of some esoteric way the browser, compiler or authoring tool works or because of a known problem with the delivery system. The risk is that the client, if not familiar with software engineering and programming, will sometimes think that there is no substance to the real problems you will face. You are the liaison between the team and the client, and you need to be able to understand the problems the software hits in order to explain such things. There is a fine line between explaining a complicated problem to clients and blinding them with science, and the position of that line depends a great deal on your relationship with the client.

Theory into practice 18

Talk to people you know who have programmed multimedia applications and ask them what they liked and disliked about the process and about the tools and languages they used. You should take any opportunity you have to try new tools, and you will find demonstration examples of some on the CD-ROM and links to others on the Internet.

Summary

- Integration is the core stage of multimedia development, where assets and software are fused together to make the application.

- Choosing the software package, programming language or authoring system is key to this stage. Multimedia authoring systems will have built-in support for different kinds of asset.

- You will need to define names and numbering conventions for the different stages of your development and testing.

- Testing and fixing bugs in complex code will be time consuming and it is essential to avoid the possibility of bugs in tools and operating system routines as they will confuse the testing.

- Making use of browser plug-ins and Java results in a programming process more like offline multimedia than online Web page design.

- 'Pushing the envelope' is risky.

- The software development in multimedia is likely to be the least understood part of the process for a client.

Recommended reading

Apple Computer Inc. (1987). *The Apple Macintosh Human Interface Guidelines.* Reading, MA: Addison-Wesley

Vaughan T. (1994). *Multimedia: Making it Work.* Berkeley, CA: Osborne McGraw-Hill

The BrowserWatch Web site is at http://browserwatch.internet.com/ (Note: there is no www in the URL)

The Weblint home page is at http://www.cre.canon.co.uk/~neilb/weblint/

Rights, copyright and other intellectual property

Project manager's responsibilities

- To ensure that all assets used in the application are cleared for the correct use
- To avoid the rights status of the whole application being compromised by uncoordinated rights issues
- To consult expert opinion if there are any doubts

Rights and wrongs

Suppose I came round to your house for dinner one evening, and you showed me a beautiful model boat you had made. It had taken you several weeks to build it, and you had lovingly fashioned every plank on the deck and every line in the rigging yourself. It was well made and I liked it. To quote the Bible, I coveted it. So on the way out of your house I hid the boat under my coat and walked away with it. Is that theft?

Once I had reached my house I took your boat and put it into a machine that made copies of it: each copy indistinguishable from the original. I took those copies down to the market the next day and sold dozens of them and paid you nothing. Have I done anything illegal or immoral?

Suppose I came round to your house for dinner one evening, and you played me a beautiful song you had written. It had taken you several weeks to compose it, and you had lovingly fashioned every nuance in the melody and every line in the lyrics yourself. It was well written and I liked it. To quote the Bible, I coveted it. So on the way out of your house I remembered your song. Is that theft?

Once I had reached my house I took your song and sang it into a machine that recorded it and then made copies of it. I took those copies down to the market the next day and sold dozens of them and paid you nothing. Have I done anything illegal or immoral?

In law a copyright is as much an object as something you can touch. It can be traded and it can be passed on to your heirs. Unfortunately it is also intangible. You cannot actually touch it, and so it does not match our usual understanding of a property.

Copyright is one important aspect of what are called **intellectual property rights** (IPR). This chapter has two aims. First, it will provide some background to copyright itself, and why it is important, and second it will outline some of the rights models used in the media to see whether they can be applied in a particular multimedia application for the licensing of IPR and assets. There is a caveat. Intellectual property is a complex area of the law, and expert advice should always be sought if there is any doubt. It also differs from country to country, and even the basic philosophy behind rights differs between countries. The growth of the Internet has complicated the issues even more. This chapter is intended only as an introduction and not as a user guide.

In the beginning

Copyright as a concept in English law has its roots in new technology. In the second half of the fifteenth century the invention of printing made it possible for books to be mass produced, and as a result unauthorized copying of literature was a possibility. The book printers – the stationers – formed themselves into a guild, and were granted a royal charter in 1556. Under this charter lawfully printed books were registered with the guild, and the guild had powers to act against unauthorized copies.

The first copyright act in the UK dates from 1709, and gave the 'sole right and liberty' of printing books to authors and whoever they assigned rights to. Protection was for a period of 14 years from publication but could only really be enforced if, as before, the book was registered with the Stationers' Company.

Later revisions of the law widened the net to include other creative works such as engravings and music. Eventually the emphasis on copying had to be extended to embrace rights of usage for performances of music and drama, and eventually sound recordings, cinematograph films and broadcasting joined the fray, the concept of what is still called **copyright** extending to embrace new means of distributing intellectual property.

From this beginning has come international agreement on the protection of intellectual property. This covers inventions, copyrights and, to a lesser degree, designs and a recent addition, which is moral rights. To a great extent the introduction of moral rights into English law reduces some of the differences from, say, French law. The English approach has been that protection of copyright is protection of the material benefit of exploiting that right. This is why English law protected the rights of printers. The French and Belgian perspective is that copyright is in some way a recognition of the artistic achievement of the author. In fact in French law it is not copyright that is protected, but *droit d'auteur* – the right of the author.

Getting a copyright

In US, UK and European law a copyright is created at the same time as the copyright work. The situation used to be different in the USA, where you had to publish using a particular notice of copyright, or in some cases register a copyright for it to be in existence, but this situation was anomalous and recently changed. Timing is important, since the only infallible test of having a copyright lies in being able to prove creation of the copyright work before anyone else. In other words, you have the original. A common, and cheap, method of achieving this is to send yourself a copy by registered mail, which fixes a date to the copy in the envelope as long as it remains unopened.

You can have copyright in a work of art (painting, drawing, sculpture, and so on), literature (prose or poetry – even the source code of a computer program), music (more on this later), and in a photograph, movie, or television programme. There has to have been some effort exercised to create a copyright, so that by photocopying a drawing you do not create a new copyright – you only risk infringing the original one. US law requires that creative effort took place before a copyright is created. The condition, in English law, is sometimes called **sweat of the brow**, and is less demanding.

The advent of electronic reproduction and wide area public networking through the Internet has confused the copyright situation, and the law keeps changing to cope with it. Until the 20th century there was no need to recognize that there could be copyright in a photograph or sound recording, and as time has gone on whole new issues have been added to intellectual property, such as 'look and feel': can you protect the way your user interface works? – Apple and Microsoft have been battling over this issue for many years. Recently an important US court held the menu commands of a leading spreadsheet program to be uncopyrightable.

International agreement on copyright has been based on a series of conventions that are ratified by governments. Since the distribution of intellectual property is an international business it is only equitable that a country should expect the same kind of protection for its citizens' work in a foreign country as it gives to its citizens itself – or indeed gives to citizens of foreign countries. Needless to say, some countries have taken a more lax view of this kind of protection than others, as any visitor to certain parts of the Far East may have found.

Although copyright protection is automatic in the USA and UK, it is considered good practice to assert the copyright by printing a notice such as © 1998 Elaine England and Andy Finney. Other phrases such as 'all rights reserved' and 'if you copy this we will send the boys round and sort you out' or the prominent FBI shield that you see on American videos are arguably a bit over the top. The reason for them is to remove any possibility that a defendant in court could claim he or she didn't know the material was copyright. This is of course no defence to a primary infringement, but it could be considered to be mitigation since ignorance of copyright is widespread. Primary infringement is the initial production of an infringing copy. In cases of secondary infringement, ignorance can be a defence in the UK. This would happen if, for example, you imported an infringing work or licensed the work and were reasonably sure that the person who provided the material had cleared the rights. Even if an infringer acknowledges that 'copyright infringement is theft', as they say, there is also an attitude that copyright owners are rich and would not miss a few bucks. But we all have the potential to be copyright owners, and deserve not to be ripped off.

When you produce a copyright work as part of your employment, the copyright usually rests with your employer. However, when you commission a freelancer to produce it for you, the ownership of the copyright will usually rest in the first instance with the freelancer. For this reason, a commissioning company will often take copyright in a commissioned work under the terms of the contract, and this is probably the best way to avoid confusion. This situation is complex, especially when contributors are contracted via an agency, and a detailed discussion of this problem is beyond the scope of this chapter.

If you have to decide about copyright ownership you should think of it in terms of future use. If you as creator will have no further use for the work then you lose nothing by assigning copyright or granting an exclusive licence. Assigning your rights means that they are no longer yours: you have sold them, and an assignment is always exclusive.

As commissioner you have to be able to use the work for its intended purpose, which may or may not require you to own the copyright. (Computer program code is a special case, which is discussed later in this chapter.) Beyond these issues the copyright in something is as much a part of the deal as the money paid, and can be negotiated, since the copyright has a value in itself that is distinct from ownership or use of the work. It is also unrelated to the time it took to create the work, since a Picasso sketch remains a Picasso sketch whether it took him ten days or ten seconds to draw it. To be safe, all copyright assignments and licences should be in writing. In fact, under US and English law, an assignment of copyright can only be made in writing.

Moral rights

Moral rights are a relatively new addition to intellectual property in English law. This provides a method in law for you to be credited for your work (called **paternity** or **attribution**) and for your work to be used only in ways of which you approve and without unauthorized changes (**integrity**). Given the interactive nature of multimedia, moral rights are quite significant, especially integrity. It is worth noting that you can do anything with a work if the author consents. In the USA, moral rights are narrow and usually apply only to visual arts.

The composer of a piece of music has a moral right for the music not to be edited. You should not cut out the verses to leave just the chorus or change the order of the verses. If you design an interactive application that allows the user to do things like this then you risk infringing the moral rights of the composer. For this reason most music publishers will not allow you to include a song in your multimedia application under circumstances where the user can change the music because they do not have the permission of the composer to do so. Music will be discussed in more detail later.

When a graphics artist builds a montage of images from many sources there is a risk of infringing moral rights. A particular photographer might take exception to having something extracted from the image or to having the image cropped. Juxtaposition of one image with another might be problematic for reasons other than copyright because it is possible to libel someone by publishing an unwisely montaged or positioned picture, so great care should be taken with this. Is it real or is it PhotoShop? An extreme example would be to build a photograph of a notable teetotal politician drinking a glass of water into a montage so that he appears to be drinking in a vodka distillery. Because computer technology is now quite able to produce images of non-existent objects, such as the dinosaurs in *Jurassic Park*, in a way that is very difficult to distinguish from reality, this problem is only going to get more difficult.

Because moral rights are new to English law there is less guidance on what can and cannot be done than there is with more established areas of copyright. One possibly contentious area arises because the author or authors of a computer program have no rights of paternity or integrity. This is because computer programs are often written by large teams. But does this also apply to multimedia? As a creative person your future depends on people recognizing your past work, and it is important that credit is given where it is due. There will be instances where, as a multimedia developer, your client will attempt to deny you a credit. Your only straightforward way of achieving your just credit is to insist on it in your contract with the client, rather than by relying on the law. Conversely, many commissioning contracts will include a clause waiving moral rights.

Exceptions

One problem with copyright, if taken to extremes, is that while the owners have their rights, the rest of us should also have some leeway to enable life to go on; and the concepts known as **fair use** (**fair dealing** in the UK) and **insubstantial portions** come into play. In law, and in the right circumstances, these are two important exceptions to infringement. A critic reviewing a book has the right to quote from it without asking permission. A student studying the works of an artist has the right to photocopy illustrations to include them in a research paper. You can quote a small (insubstantial) extract from a literary work.

In the USA there are also exceptions for parody, news coverage and so on; even some commercial use may be fair if it does not injure the copyright owner.

Unfortunately we cannot always benefit from these exceptions in multimedia production. Recently, in English law, it has been ruled that some of the exceptions to infringement do not apply if you are making a commercial product, and a multimedia title for sale would be commercial. The term 'insubstantial portion' does not necessarily mean that anything short is OK, and two obvious exceptions to this are the denouement of a mystery novel and a line of poetry. The test is always one of degree, and there are no hard-and-fast rules about what constitutes an insubstantial portion. Importantly, this kind of exception applies only to literature, not a film or a piece of music for example, so you cannot argue that a four-second sample from a hit record is fair game because it is an insubstantial portion.

Alongside the exceptions included in copyright legislation there has to be an element of common sense. It is very difficult to judge whether a photograph will work in a montage or on a Web page without trying it out. Here, technology is actually making things more difficult for us. In the old days, to make a mock-up of a page of a magazine, you might cut out copies of photographs from the colour supplements and paste them onto a piece of paper. That does not infringe copyright in the photographs. Doing the same thing on a computer involves scanning the photographs, and so you infringe the copyright unless you already have permission to scan the image into the computer. In this case the intention is the same, but changing the means by which you carry out your intention has led to a possible infringement.

One very constructive idea to get over the mock-up infringement problem has been implemented by some stock photo libraries, who give you a blanket permission to reproduce their images for mock-ups.

Music

One area of copyright that causes confusion is music, and it is worth going into this rights situation in some detail. The confusion arises because there are several different rights in music, which have grown up in custom and practice over the years.

Music rights.

Once you write a tune it is copyrighted, and you have the exclusive right to exploit that tune, which you might do yourself, or by licensing the rights to a publisher, who then 'works' the tune on your behalf for a fee. (You can license the rights for either the full duration of copyright or for a limited time.) Once upon a time music was 'plugged' by a song 'plugger' going to the office of a band leader and playing the tune on a piano in the hope of the band's performing it. Today a 'plugger' is more likely to be taking a disc jockey out to lunch.

If you grant permission for someone to perform your tune in public, that is (logically enough) called the **performing right**. In the UK, performing rights in music are administered by a body called the Performing Rights Society (PRS), and they collect money from radio stations, concert venues and the like. In the USA the equivalents of PRS are ASCAP, BMI and SESAC. In offline multimedia you are unlikely to have to deal with the performing right although, because of the similarity of wide area network distribution (for which read Internet) to cable, you may find that a performance licence is needed for something on a Web site. If one of your multimedia productions is played at an exhibition, and it contains music, then permission is needed, otherwise the performing right is infringed. In the UK it is usually the responsibility of the venue to cover any fees due for public performance of music, and they probably have a blanket licence for this purpose, as do many bars and shops.

If your tune is recorded, another permission is required covering what is called the **mechanical right**. This right, administered in the UK by the Mechanical Copyright Protection Society (MCPS) and by the Harry Fox Agency in the USA, is quite distinct from the copyright in the recording. If you include a record or CD in your multimedia application you will need permission and a licence covering the music, which will come from a music publisher, and a separate licence for the use of the recording, which will come from a record company. This need for a dual licence has led to some publishers setting up special libraries for use in film and television – and now multimedia – where all the rights are controlled by the publisher, so they become a one-stop shop for music. Using these recordings is always cheaper, so **library** (sometime called **production**) **music** should be your first choice for music in multimedia.

With library music the licence is usually called a **synchronization licence** because the music is mostly used synchronized to images in films and television, and this generally does not attract a royalty payment, just a fee based on duration used. You and the library publisher can also negotiate for reductions, royalties or whatever you jointly agree.

Another significant benefit of library music is that it is provided specifically for you to tailor to your needs. The publisher will expect you to edit it to fit your requirements. This will not be the case with a commercial gramophone record where you would normally have to explain in some detail just what you want to do with the recording before permission is considered. The British Musicians Union also considers that interactive multimedia is a different usage compared with sale of a record or CD, and might require that you pay another session fee; this fee would be in addition to a licence from the record company and the publisher. The session fee is the fee paid to the musicians for playing the music at the recording unless they were members of a regular group, in which case they would probably receive royalties from sales.

When you license a music recording from a record company, the company may have to pay royalties to the principal performers from your usage, depending on the contract between the record company and the artistes. In many cases, use in multimedia, whether online or offline, would not be covered by their contract, and the record company would have to negotiate for the right with the artiste before being able to license it to you. This may be impractical, and so the record company would have to refuse you a licence.

Alternatively you could get the music specially composed and recorded, and a surprising number of multimedia projects do this. This ignores what a good library publisher can offer, but it does ensure that you have original music, which might be very important to your application. If you do commission music, you should make sure you take further exploitation rights. This would enable you to use the music in a sequel, or to release a record if (say) your games theme was a hit.

The World Wide Web

In general, countries want to make the effect of new technology on copyright fit into the existing legal framework. At its root a Web site should be viewed legally as any other publication. It has more similarity with a magazine or even a television programme than with a CD-ROM because it is (or should be) a living updated thing. Legally, Web sites can be considered to be cable programmes, and this is the basis on which music is currently licensed for them in the UK. This definition excludes videoconferencing, Internet telephony or chatrooms because these are two-way interactive things, but this is exceptional.

The technical way in which a Web site makes its way from the original server to the viewer's screen means that copies of the site can exist in caches and sometimes on mirror sites. All Web browsers use local caches to stop redownloading of data that has already been downloaded, and some Internet service providers have caches to reduce long-distance download times for pages frequently viewed by their customers. In an extreme case the original site, the cache or mirror and the viewer can be in three different legal jurisdictions.

Whereas a cache is a necessary and automatic part of the functioning of the Web, a mirror is not. (A mirror is a copy of a site on another machine, usually in another part of the world, to expedite access from a distance.) This means that it could be argued that anyone publishing material on the Web knows that transient copies will be stored in caches and so implicitly authorizes them. This is not so with mirrors, and explicit permission must be sought to mirror a site. An alternative point of view is that a cache is a necessary backup of software (the HTML being computer code) and so is legitimate, but since your browser will work if you turn off the cache this argument might not be so solid.

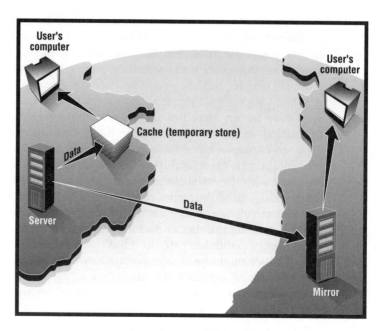

Caches, mirrors, and Web linking.

There are some programs that download a site quickly to allow you to read it offline at your leisure, and the otherwise transient caches of Netscape Navigator and Internet Explorer can themselves be accessed offline either using programs such as Netscape History or by the simple expedient of configuring the browser to never check pages for changes.

Caches and mirrors may also disrupt the usual logging of accesses of the site's pages, and if this is a crucial part of an agreement for advertising then we have a problem. In some cases a cache will check to see whether a page has been updated, and this shows on the site log in a distinctive way.

Linking from one page to another is a key part of the Web, and it is assumed that anyone can link to anyone else freely. When I find someone has linked to my pages I am delighted. However, not everyone would be so happy under all circumstances. A link can be seen as an endorsement or possibly as a claim of authorship. Consider the use of frames to show another Web site as if it were part of yours or using the image source HTML link to bring someone else's image into your page. In neither case is there any copying done since the final page is assembled only in the viewer's browser window. The much-publicized case between two newspapers in Shetland seemed to revolve around whether just linking to another page could infringe copyright. In fact the result does not appear to have revolved around this issue but rather around copying of headlines on the Web pages themselves. The Web community could breathe again.

There are so many interesting points arising from the way the World Wide Web works (in the meaning of 'interesting' used in the famous Chinese curse

'May you live in interesting times') that it may be that the only solution is to widen the scope of fair use and fair dealing to take account of it. This is a point made in Graham Smith's book *Internet Law and Regulation*, which is in any case a good place to start if you want to explore this field further.

Databases

A database consists of a collection of items that are stored in such a way that they can be found in a systematic way. If the database consists, for example, of photographs or articles from a newspaper then these, individually, are copyright. If there is creativity (or even just skill) applied in the selection or arrangement of the contents then the database is in itself copyright. Even if the contents are not copyright then a new European right called **sui generis** is applied, which protects the database for 15 years from publication. In the case of a living updated database this could continue for ever.

The sui generis protection of a database is a European concept and not an American one. The European protection is given only to 'owners' who are Europeans (as in the European Union), and this protection is not currently extended outside Europe unless similar protection is given to European databases in the other country. This means that an American database does not have this protection in Europe because the USA does not have the required legal concept.

The public domain and clip media

Copyright does not last for ever. As the concept of copyright in law developed, so the time for which a work was copyright grew. At the beginning of the 20th century copyright in the UK lasted only for the greater of 42 years from the date of publication or seven years after the death of the author. In the following 100 years the period has grown to allow the heirs of the author more time to benefit from the work, until the period in Europe reached 70 years after the year of death. This was 50 years in the UK until copyright was harmonized within the European Union.

In the USA the duration is much more complex than in Europe. Pre-1979 works are protected for an initial period of 28 years, renewable for a further 47 years. A work that first expired after 1963 was automatically renewed, but complex rules govern who actually receives the renewal rights. Currently the 50-year expiry term applies in the USA as it did in Europe, but a pending bill would raise this to life plus 70 years.

Any assumption that a work is out of copyright is fraught with danger, and you should seek professional advice, but in general a literary or artistic work is in copyright in Europe until 70 years after the end of the year in which the author died. This becomes more complicated for a translated work, where the translator has rights too, and similarly for illustrators and engravers.

In Europe, a sound recording expires 50 years after publication. So if you have an original 78 rpm gramophone record from before the late 1940s in your possession – an old Caruso recording, for example – then the recording is no longer in copyright. The tune, however, could well be in copyright since its copyright lasts for 70 years after the death of the composer. Similar arrangements apply to photographs, but for movies – known as cinematograph films – the situation is complicated since performance in public was not seen to be a publication. So some movies have surprisingly long copyright lives. The situation is not simple, and undoubtedly you can imagine the complexity of rights in a production containing multiple media forms, each of which has different copyright terms and needs world rights.

Incidentally, you should assume that a transcription onto CD of an old recording is copyright, especially if the sound was cleaned up in the process. It is possible to fingerprint digital files to identify the source, so if you wish to use an old record, you should clean it up yourself.

So now we come to the Mona Lisa. Since Leonardo da Vinci died over 70 years ago, the picture is out of copyright. It is so old that copyright did not even exist at the time. Therefore you might assume that you can include an image of the Mona Lisa in your application without permission. Unfortunately this is not the case, and the reason will become clear if you consider how you would acquire an image of the painting; stealing it from the Louvre is not an option.

If you owned the Mona Lisa you would have the right to control access to it and, as a result, to control reproductions. This is true of any collection of out-of-copyright works, usually in the hands of museums or art galleries. They will grant permission for reproduction, for a fee, as if the work was in copyright and they owned the copyright. The agreement you sign with the gallery allows you to use the image for a specific purpose. If you use it for another purpose you are not in breach of copyright but you are in breach of the contractual agreement. There will be a copyright in the photograph you receive from the library as well.

Going to the gallery or museum and photographing the picture yourself would not infringe copyright, but the museum would presumably allow you entry only on condition that you did not take photographs, or that if you were to do so, they would not be for publication. This is a contractual obligation on you, but it could be invalid if it was not brought to your attention before you bought your entry ticket. The Van Gogh museum in Amsterdam has a more straightforward approach. They do not allow anyone to take a camera inside. Incidentally, if you were able to take a photograph through an open window, you would not have infringed copyright or any contract. Whether the resulting image would be good enough to publish is another issue altogether.

In general the terms **out of copyright** and **in the public domain** are used to mean the same thing, but they are not exactly so. Copyrights expire after a time, but the owner has the right to give them away before this time if he, she or it (because an organization can own copyrights) so desires. The owner can also allow people to exploit the work without payment, with or without conditions attached. This is known as **placing it in the public domain**. However, just because an author places something, such as a piece of software, in the public domain does not mean that it is out of copyright. Often conditions are attached; so read the small print or the 'read me' file. The copyright on something placed in the public domain in this way will expire at the usual time.

NASA, like other US government agencies, places its material in the public domain. This means that you can use images from the space probes free of charge (apart from paying to get the picture itself). However, NASA does state that you cannot use the images in such a way as to suggest that NASA endorses your product. So there is a condition, albeit a relatively small one, attached. Since 1978 works of the US Government have not had copyright protection at all (Section 105 of the US Copyright Act), but this was not intended to extend outside the USA, which raises the question of European use and even of export outside the USA of finished works incorporating such material.

Some companies produce libraries of assets that are supplied **royalty free** for you to use on paper or in multimedia applications and Web pages. This is **clip art**, or **clip media**. This material is often still in copyright, and it is not really in the public domain either because you may have paid for a book or CD-ROM that contains it, and your use of the material is restricted. There is probably a restriction to make sure that you do not produce more clip media discs from their clip media discs, and you might be restricted to a certain number of images in a single production. But you do not have to pay anything else to use the material in as many productions as you like.

CD-ROMs of clip media range in price from tens to hundreds of pounds/dollars. You can even buy clip art in books, and the Dover Books series of clip art and design are a notable example of this. They often reproduce illustrations from Victorian books and magazines because they are, in themselves, out of copyright. If you own or have unrestricted access to hundred-year-old copies of the *Illustrated London News* or *Strand Magazine* (with its original Sherlock Holmes stories and illustrations) then you could exploit their contents because you have the actual out-of-copyright originals, assuming that the author and illustrator died long enough ago.

It is possible to obtain free material such as clip media by downloading it over the Internet. You should assume that something you can download is available for you to use only if you are explicitly told that this is the case. Usually there will be a page of contractual terms and conditions that you agree to by clicking on the link to start the download. Because Web pages can so easily be taken apart it is sensible to include a copyright notice on any image on a page as well as on the page itself, but bear in mind that the attitude to copyright on the Internet is loose, to say the least, and you should assume that someone somewhere will copy. On the Internet, infringement is considered to be the sincerest form of flattery.

As a multimedia developer you must think not only of the rights you take in assets you license but also of the rights you can take in any work you commission. You could be commissioning artwork from a graphic designer, photographs, music, or scripts. There is even the software written by your programmers.

As a rule of thumb you should explicitly acquire rights in any work done for you by your staff or freelancers. This would be included in the contract for the work but, for you to be sure, it has to be a contract with the person doing the work, not an agency or subcontracting company. If you are acquiring rights from a freelancer or subcontractor then he or she must be able to pass on those rights, and should indemnify you against any claims should that turn out not to be the case. You can acquire rights in future work if it is appropriate, and in Europe it is important to obtain all appropriate waivers of moral rights as well.

Some rights models

In order to make use of someone else's intellectual property in a project you have to get permission, and this will result in the granting of a licence for the use of the copyright material. It can be difficult to describe the rights involved, so one approach is simply to describe what the project is, how it will be used, and who will buy it. In some forms of media a number of specific rights have grown up that define the uses you can make of the material you have licensed. For illustration, here are a few examples:

■ **All rights**. As the name suggests, this type of agreement gives the developer all the rights for exploitation of the material. In practice this might be the kind of right taken in a small interview or script rather than a substantial contribution to an application. In the case of small contributions this kind of agreement might attract only a small fee, or maybe no fee at all. However, since an all-rights contract with no residuals (residuals being payments for further use of the material beyond the original purpose) is biased in favour of the producer or publisher rather than the contributor, it should be used with care. You should be careful when licensing material that was originally covered by all-rights agreements. Some publishers have been putting editions of journals into online databases on the assumption that this is covered by their original agreements with the freelance authors. Although this practice was endorsed by a US court there has been an appeal against the judgement, and it could be that this secondary use is an infringement of the authors' copyright. With older material it is also possible that an all-rights agreement might not include new media, on the basis that such things as Web sites were not known when the author signed the agreement. Similarly, a broadcaster's all-rights agreement might cover only broadcasting, and so on.

■ **Non-theatric**. In audiovisual publications, a non-theatric right is one that excludes broadcast, home video and theatric rights. This sounds a little back to front, but basically broadcasting is usage for radio or television transmission (and possibly cable), theatric is performance where the public pay to see the material (as in a cinema), and home video is performance where the public pay for the material. Non-theatric covers use in training, business, education, conferences and exhibitions. This is the case even if the public pay admission, because they are not paying specifically to see the material.

■ **Home video**. This right, applied to videos, allows you to sell or rent the material to the general public. The equivalent for audio is the gramophone right, whereby record companies pay musicians to include their contributions on records.

■ **Interactive right**. This is a term that has recently been applied to a permission to use material in any interactive form such as CD-ROM or, possibly, interactive services on demand (but this last example overlaps with cable). It is platform independent but has definite implications for moral rights if the viewer can modify the assets. A right to use something on a Web page would probably be defined as such, rather than being part of a general interactive right.

■ **Flash fees**. Still images, when used on television, are sometimes paid for on the basis of the time they are on screen. The common, but essentially impossible, question from picture libraries for multimedia is 'How long is it on screen?' Music will usually have a rate dependent on duration, but you do not 'still frame' a piece of audio. However, you could repeat a loop of music under a menu, for example. In this case you should negotiate a special rate for the use.

Split market.

The terms used above are some that you might come across, and they are not platform specific. There seem to be two schools of thought regarding the licensing of assets for multimedia. The first says that the licence should relate to the market for the product. Terms such as non-theatric apply to that method of licensing. The second school of thought says that the method of delivering the material is more important than the market, and will want to license differently for analogue and digital, for interactive and linear, and for on- or offline. It is unclear at the moment which way the licensing model will go, but the authors' preference as developers is for the market-led approach.

Unfortunately, in an immature market – and for immature read also 'small' – it could be considered restrictive for a developer to have to renegotiate if they want to port an application from one platform to another. If you make a single disc that will play on any computer platform, such as a Web site on a CD-ROM, this becomes totally impossible. To get around this you might ask for a licence for all platforms.

Similarly you have to consider whether a foreign language translation of an application that otherwise remains the same should require renegotiation of the licence for pictures or music.

One model, adopted by at least one major multimedia developer, is to acquire rights for all versions on all platforms for the life of the product. The 'life of the product' is a vague term, which has as yet remained untested; it probably allows revisions but does not allow the material to be used in a project on another subject.

In the offline world, licences are also granted for territories. These may be language specific (such the amusingly named GAS – Germany Austria Switzerland), or regional (North America or EU), or historic (British Commonwealth). World rights used to be considered to be all-encompassing, but the advent of satellites has led to a solar system or universe territory. Remember that anything you put on a Web page can be seen anywhere in the world, whether you intend it to or not, so a licence for the Internet is, by definition, a worldwide licence.

One usage issue that is exercising some multimedia developers is the question of contribution: 'Just what is the contribution of this asset to my project?' This is obviously a question that you should be asking when you assess a fee, but it can also become a negotiating point. Does an image that is seen only if the viewer navigates his or her way down through five levels to a particular screen of explanatory detail carry as much weight as an image in the main menu or home page?

The risk of following this path of argument is that, rather than lowering the fee for the less-seen image, it raises the fee for the one in the main menu. The question has to be judged on the basis of what is actually being bought. In practice it is the right of reproduction of the copyright image, related to the intended use, that is being bought. Trying to quantify how likely it is that a viewer will see the image is akin to differentiating between different pages in a book.

Because of possible ambiguity and misunderstanding, it is dangerous to rely on terms such as 'non-theatric' or 'interactive' instead of a clear specification in a licence of exactly what media, platform and so on is actually meant. A licence should also say who owns the rights not expressly granted in the licence.

The already confusing rights situation in multimedia is compounded by different asset owners' applying different models. Picture and music libraries work differently, and two picture sources may operate in different ways as well. Since there should be a known status of rights for the whole multimedia application it is important not to risk one asset's compromising the others in terms of such things as the duration of a licence, or territories in which the application can be sold. Failure to pay attention to this can result in the rights in the whole product being affected by the lowest common denominator of rights in its individual assets.

This is perhaps less crucial for an online project such as a Web site than it is for a CD-ROM, simply because a Web site can be changed at any time very easily whereas a CD-ROM would, in extreme circumstances, have to be withdrawn from distribution and destroyed.

Royalties versus buy-outs

Should you pay royalties or pay a one-off fee for use of material? And if you buy out rights, what multiple of the standard fee should be used?

Obviously, if the multimedia project is never sold then royalties based on sales are impossible. A Web page is never sold since it is usually freely viewable by anyone who accesses the URL. However, a Web page can attract income through advertising or other means, so it is possible for there to be an income stream without actual sales.

Although a creator has every right to share in the profits from his or her work there are compelling reasons why a buy-out can be a fair offer. In a small market it might be a very long time before a royalty stream amounts to much. A buy-out on the basis of an estimated number of sales may lessen the opportunity for making more money in the long term but it does give the asset owner 'money now', which may be much better than 'maybe more money much later'. Look upon it as repositioning the risk, and consider the interest earned by investing the extra money instead of waiting for a royalty trickle.

From a practical point of view it can be difficult for multimedia developers to administer royalties if they are small companies. Often the applications are made for clients who pay the developer a fixed fee for the development, and the developer may not get any royalties, which does not provide a basis for any downstream royalty payments to asset owners. Clients may not be willing to undertake to pay royalties because they had no control over the negotiations.

In more mature media, such as books, television and records, companies have whole departments that handle royalty tracking and payments, and in time multimedia publishing will probably follow this model.

Rights in code

The situation for rights in computer code is a little different from that for rights in assets because of the way code is written. It is often built up of fragments, libraries and routines that were written for other projects to carry out certain tasks such as drawing a picture to the screen or synchronizing sound and pictures.

It is custom and practice for software not to be sold but to be licensed. If you produce a multimedia application for a client you should not assign the copyright in the code to the client because that will make it difficult for you to reuse that work. Clients ought to accept this, but it does mean that you need to state it explicitly in the agreement with your client. You will, of course, have to grant a free licence to use the code, otherwise they cannot make use of what they have paid for, but they will not own it.

As a developer contracting software from a programmer you will have the opposite point of view, and will probably want to make continuing use of any code written for you. This means that you will have to explicitly take the rights you need from the programmer. If you have contracted a company rather than a person you need to be sure that they can assign you these rights because they have taken them. Should you ever want to license rights in code to your client then you have to have the rights yourself first. It's a basic rule – you cannot license rights you do not have.

A further point is that computer programs are specifically excluded from moral rights in Europe, although it is not clear how this exclusion would apply to multimedia applications given that they also contain literary, artistic, musical and other kinds of work. You might want to include a clause in any contract you make with your client to ensure that you get due credit for your work.

How to negotiate

There are no hard-and-fast rules, but a few guidelines will be helpful.

- Be fair and honest. Few rights holders are going to cheat you; they are just after an honest income. Similarly, you have a right to pay a fair price.
- Set yourself a target price, based on experience, but don't be unreasonable or inflexible. The more you do this the more you will have a feel for costs.

- Accept that some rates are just not negotiable, because the owner does not want to negotiate.
- Be prepared to say 'Sorry, I cannot afford your rates' – but make sure you have time to change your plans for the project.
- Remember that the asset owner who has only one asset to sell may want more money than a library.
- If you run into trouble with an asset after an offline application is 'finished', never admit that to the asset owner. Balance the cost against the cost of changing the application (plus a new asset) rather than your original target price, since paying an extra 100 for the picture will cost you less than paying 200 to go back and change the application. In general, because of the way Web sites are built, this is less of a problem on the Internet.
- Be consistent in your description of the usage to be agreed. This is much more important than worrying about one picture costing too much, since one asset that cannot be used in Japan means your whole application cannot be used in Japan.
- If the man with the big cigar says that the voice-over fee is $20 000, accept that he is really trying to say 'Go away!'.
- Build up working relationships with asset owners, partly because it will make the negotiations more convivial, but also because buying in bulk can be cheaper.
- Don't confuse the technical cost (such as dubbing the film or photographing the picture) with the licence fee, and make sure you know which you are paying and when.
- If you can, offer to return a picture to a photo library quickly. They might lower their fee as a result. For a bulk deal you could even scan the images on their premises with your equipment. Don't forget to ask for permission to digitize images as part of the process of deciding what to use.

The rights check-list

- Can we administer and pay royalties?
- What is our target fee for any particular kind of asset?
- What delivery platforms are we licensing for?
- Are we offline or online or both?
- Is excerpting for promotional editorial or advertising of the application included?
- What is the duration of the licence?
- What territories are covered?
- Are foreign language versions covered?
- How do the agreements relate to my expected pattern of sales in these territories and languages?
- Are further editions of the work covered?
- Are bug-fixes covered or would they be considered new editions?
- Are derivative versions covered?

■ Have the asset providers indemnified us against claims for infringement should they not have true title?

... and finally, jurisdiction, patents and data protection

One of the more significant things that the Internet has done to communications is to internationalize it. Anything you put on your Web site can be seen by people in most of the countries in the world. Before the Internet, worldwide publishing involved making licensing or distribution deals with different people in different countries, and arranging for shipping of items of software between continents. Now all that it takes is to tell someone that your URL exists and say 'Please come and look'. Unfortunately this raises the issue of legal jurisdiction. Jurisdiction is basically the law you come under.

This could be important in multimedia publishing on the Internet, partly because everything you publish that way is available internationally. Just because your Web site is situated in Denver, Colorado doesn't mean that you have to clear rights only for the USA. People in the UK or Egypt or Russia or New Zealand can see what you have published. But rights are not the only issue. A libel committed on the Internet, such as in a Usenet news group, could be read anywhere, so a legal action could in theory be taken anywhere. Recently, the state of Minnesota declared that its consumer protection legislation was applicable to any online purchases – even if the purchase did not involve a buyer, seller or recipient in that state. Basically the internationalization caused by the Internet lays any Web publisher or supplier – including you with your home Web page – open to action anywhere in the world. So be careful.

The territorial restrictions placed on DVD (in its movie form) by the film companies are a similar issue to that of jurisdiction. Here, DVD discs have a territory flag in the data that says which part of the world the disc is licensed for. A disc licensed for the USA will not, for example, play in a European or Japanese machine. It is likely that any equipment or technique that might be employed to circumvent such a restriction would be, in itself, illegal. This might become a multimedia issue if you were to produce a movie-playing application that played a DVD movie disc on a computer but ignored the territory flag.

You cannot copyright an idea, only the form in which the idea is expressed. The idea that a television transmitter and receiver could be put in an orbit so high above the earth that it appeared to be stationary, and could then be used to relay television signals, cannot be copyrighted. It could be patented – or could have been in 1944, when Arthur C. Clarke wrote his famous *Wireless World* article on the subject. The article itself, being the expression of the idea in literary form, was copyright, and indeed will be for at least the next 50–70 years since, at the time of writing, Mr Clarke is still very much alive.

A **patent** is a document given to you by the government granting you the exclusive right to exploit and control exploitation of a process for doing something. You have to be able to describe the process in such a way that any reasonably capable person could carry out the work from your description; so you cannot be vague and, say, patent time travel without describing how to do it. The process must not be obvious (patently obvious?) since there has to have been an inventive step in the process that you have seen but others have missed. Finally you have to have done it first. If you were beaten to the idea by someone who can prove it then your patent will not be granted, or could be declared invalid, even if you genuinely knew nothing about the other idea. This is called **prior art**.

Prior art can come from the craziest places. One, possibly apocryphal, instance tells of a patent examiner who was trawling through literature to see if a particular new idea had been described before. He finally found a reference, but it was not in a scientific journal or a PhD thesis: it was in a comic book.

In most countries you have to keep quiet about your invention, since disclosure can invalidate the patent as well. So do not be tempted to give a learned paper on the subject too soon. Timing is critical, and swear everyone you discuss it with to secrecy – that is, **non-disclosure**.

If you have been granted a patent, you have the right to control use of your idea for (in most countries) up to 20 years from the date of filing. A patent does not actually have to be taken out by the inventor. Often employers will take out patents based on work done by their employees. The employee will be the inventor but the employing company will have the patent rights if the work is done during the course of the inventor's employment.

The process of getting a patent is both time consuming and costly. It is important that a patent is carefully worded so that it can stand up to scrutiny for inventiveness. A particular kind of lawyer called a **patent agent** should be involved in this process. Currently there is no such thing as an international patent. The patent will have to be applied for in every country for which protection is required. This should be the countries in which your product would be used or manufactured. You have the right to stop both sales and manufacture of an infringing item – or to negotiate a royalty payment.

In Europe a computer program cannot, as such, be patented. However, a technical process can still be patented even if a program is key to how it is done. It is the technical process that is patented, not the software behind it. But this distinction is more easily seen in an industrial context than in the kind of work done in multimedia.

However, since software patents are granted in the USA that would not be granted in Europe, it is important that possible patent infringement is considered when learning from other people's techniques on the Internet. The risk is probably slight, especially given how much code is freely available under such things as the GNU Copyleft (sic), but should not be ignored. Fortunately, the possibility of multimedia *per se* being covered by a patent has gone away.

A final point is that in the process of granting you the 'letters patent' the government will also publish your invention. This will happen even if you decide not to pursue the patent.

As the inventor you have the choice of patenting your invention. If you decide not to patent it you should consider finding a way of establishing your prior art by publicizing your idea. If you do this, someone else trying to patent the same process later on will not be able to gain a patent and so stop you making use of your 'own' invention. Altruistically, publishing your idea allows other people to make use of it. It is the equivalent of shareware.

Although you cannot copyright an idea, and many ideas cannot be patented or would not be because of the cost and time involved, you can protect your idea by contract. If you need to discuss your idea with anyone you should get them to sign a **non-disclosure agreement** (NDA) in which they agree not to disclose your idea. That will afford you a measure of protection, and, along with terms and conditions of trade, every company should have a stock NDA.

Data protection is a broadly European concept in law, and it is only occasionally going to be an issue with a Web site or CD-ROM. Basically, under English law, anybody who uses data relating to living people may have to be registered under the Data Protection Act. The definitions of a data user and a data subject are carefully set out in the UK Act and in the guidelines for registration. People who operate data bureaux also need to be registered.

If you produce a database that contains personal information about living people you are a data user and must be registered. Your customers, if they are not able to change the data on the site or CD-ROM, are not data users and so do not have to be registered. If you give them the power to change the data then they may become data users as a result. Any company or person who uses a computer may have to register. Although simple use of mailing lists and word processing are excepted from registration it is worth noting that use of email is not.

Data protection is not dealt with in the same way by every country, but within the European Union there are further steps being taken to harmonize legislation. There is no such thing in the USA.

Theory into practice 19

On the CD-ROM you will find some licence agreements used by asset providers. These are worth studying, and will give you a basis on which to consider your own negotiations.

Summary

- Copyright is a property like any other and, as such, should be respected. A copyright is automatically granted when certain kinds of work are produced, including artistic and literary ones. In some countries, besides the copyright by which the owner controls reproduction, there are moral rights that protect integrity and paternity.

- Any asset you wish to use in multimedia is going to have copyright implications but music is perhaps the most complex of these with composer, publisher and sometimes recording company having a stake in the exploitation.

- There are exceptions which allow some limited use of copyright material without the need for clearance, but usually free use is possible only when the work is out of copyright.

- Ideas cannot be copyrighted, only the expression of them. If you have an idea for a process for doing something then a patent may be the appropriate course of action.

Recommended reading

You should always take careful legal advice on rights issues, but it is useful to have some basic background. Most of these books are based on English law. When reading books on copyright, make sure that they are up to date. The last major revision in UK legislation was in 1988.

Henry M. (1994). *Publishing and Multimedia Law*. London: Butterworths.
This book covers more law than IP. It is fairly expensive but includes 52 sample contractual documents on paper and PC disk.

Holyoak J. and Torremans P. (1995). *Intellectual Property Law*. London: Butterworths
This book is aimed at students, and gives substantial background on all aspects of intellectual property including patents and copyright. Some international issues are covered as well.

Philips J.J., Durie R. and Karet I. (1993). *Whale on Copyright*, 4th edn. London: Sweet & Maxwell

Smith G.J.H. (ed.) (1997). *Internet Law and Regulation*, 2nd edn. London: FT Tax and Law.

Strong W.A. (1993). *The Copyright Book: A Practical Guide*, 4th edn. Cambridge, MA: MIT Press
This is a guide to US law for non-specialists.

Wall R.A. (1993). *Copyright Made Easier*. London: ASLIB

The American Information Superhighway initiative has produced some useful documents with a background to American rights law. They are available as of mid-1998 on the Internet at http://www.uspto.gov/web/offices/com/doc/ipnii. The report can be found under 'Speeches, Testimony and Documents' in the 'Documents' directory.

The Chartered Institute of Patent Agents (Staple Inn Buildings, High Holborn, London WC1V 7PZ) publishes information leaflets that explain the functions of a UK patent agent.

The Office of the Data Protection Registrar publishes guidelines to data protection as it is implemented in the UK. Copies are available from the Information Services Division, Data Protection Registrar, Wycliffe House, Water Lane, Wilmslow, Cheshire SK9 5AF.

18

Testing

Project manager's responsibilities

- To match testing methods to the project
- To devise a testing strategy in conjunction with the team and the client
- To create enough time and budget for the testing to be carried out effectively
- To manage the acceptance testing process in order to get final sign-off for the project

Multimedia and testing

There is a good deal of confusion about testing and multimedia. Is testing really necessary? Does it have to be done by people outside the team? Should software testing techniques be applied to multimedia applications? How much does it cost? What's the value? ... and this list can continue ad infinitum.

There is also fear of testing, probably linked to the dread of examinations from everyone's school years. It is a subject that is generally avoided in multimedia circles, but hopefully this chapter will show that it is essential to have a testing strategy for each project, and to make clients fully aware of the extent of the testing outlined in the strategy.

The confusion of terminology doesn't help either. **Testing** and **evaluation** are the main culprits. They are both to do with making improvements, which is why they are difficult to separate. However, the main difference appears to be that testing implies matching a prescribed set of quantifiable criteria against performance to find errors; evaluation is wider in that it is looking not for specific errors but for improvements to the design during development or when the program is finished. **Validation** is another term that causes confusion. The problem here is that the interpretation of the term changes depending on the context in which it is used. In evaluation, validation means checking that the methods used are ones that will provide the type of data that is wanted. If one of the needs specified is detailed user reaction to the concepts, it will be invalid to select internal testing alone as a test method, for example.

Testing data categories.

The subject of testing is complicated because there are so many types that can be applied at every stage of a project. Also, the mix of disciplines in multimedia means that different approaches to testing might be employed. Concept testing with focus groups, prototypes, peer review either within the project or with external review of the design documents, usability tests, field trials and acceptance tests are some of the varieties that could be employed.

The type of data collected with any of the processes veers between quantitative and qualitative, objective and subjective, formative and summative. There are arguments for and against all the different methods, and you will have to decide which approach serves the project's requirements, time, cost and quality constraints.

You need to become acquainted with the varieties so that you can devise a testing strategy that will serve your projects. You'll need to understand how to cost the different ways and also consider subcontracting the specialist forms of testing. This whole area can be a specialism in itself.

As a brief introduction the varieties mentioned above will be summarized, but it is worth your taking time to explore this area in greater depth with further reading.

Concept testing

This approach comes from marketing. It means trying out the main project ideas on selected groups of people representative of the intended user group. The ideas may be presented in a paper walkthrough or through discussion. This is conducted very early on so it would be prior to any prototype stage of development. The project may not have had complete agreement to proceed, and the findings may influence further agreement. A facilitator opens up discussion around the concepts, perhaps relating them to competitive products. The aim is to check whether the predicted reactions to the new product match the wishes of the users. This is done early in development so that the design can be adjusted in line with the findings, and so that there is more confidence that the intended direction will be successful. Concept testing is also known as **focus groups**. This is a commercial approach to checking out predictions about a product with prospective customers against competing products in the market.

Prototyping

This is derived from software development, and is a mock-up of several of the key features from the program. It is designed to get feedback on the general look and operation of the design as early as possible during development. The practice grew because of the mismatch between the expectations that the clients had from reading the formal specification documents and the reality of the way programs actually worked. This was often explained as the gap between written and visual understanding. The gap caused problems of redesign at a late stage in development, and was costly.

Prototypes can also be used with users to gather their reactions to the main operations at a stage where changes in the design can be made efficiently.

Online projects can actually be easier to prototype than offline ones. If you set up a password-protected area of the Web site and put the new design ideas there, then it is easy for any authorized person to have a look and comment, and for you to gather and process the feedback. The ability of a Web page to accept updates at any time can be both an advantage and a disadvantage. If you have an ongoing responsibility for the site then it is quite reasonable for certain decisions to be taken on the understanding that user feedback may modify them later, but if you are providing the client with something based on a template that they can maintain then this argument no longer applies. It is important to separate the two key elements of a Web site: the structure and design from the actual content. Some people will find it very easy to imagine a template with changing content but others will not. You could explain it to the client as being like the design of a newspaper or magazine, and so early proto-types of the Web site will have dummy content in them.

If the Web site is dynamic, and the Web pages are built on demand by a CGI program from a database, for example, then it is likely that the CGI pro-gram will be complex enough to need prototyping and testing in the same way as a CD-ROM application. An extra stage here could be offline prototyp-ing followed by online prototyping. Of course, a static Web site can be protoyped offline from a hard disk or CD-ROM, but there is nothing really different in running a site off disk than running it on the server. Adding CGIs to the site changes this because you have to have the site on a server for the CGIs to work, even if you have tested and debugged the CGI program on your computer.

Peer review

A faster approach to testing the concepts of design is to get colleagues to bring their experience to bear on them. As indicated, this is important because of the mix of skills needed in the multistrand design. However, this relies on prediction according to factors that have been identified, and prediction is not a science. Experience gives insight but multimedia is relatively young. External peer review can extend the range of experience and insights, particu-larly if the reviewers are selected for their experience in the respective multimedia application areas. The aim is to refine the design at an early stage to help faster development.

Usability tests

These are rigorous tests, usually applied when the project has been integrated and is ready for release. They originated in software development as a method of proving that the program met the needs of the users. Often the tests are carried out in specially adapted usability laboratories that simulate the workplace. The users are monitored electronically with cameras, microphones and records of key-presses. They are observed through two-way mirrors. The very large amount of data is analyzed to determine where and why the users experienced difficulty so that redesign can take place. Multimedia projects do not usually employ usability tests to the extent of computing application testing, but research projects where data on user reactions is needed, or market-led projects such as applications that are meant to sell products, may have some requirement to apply these rigorous methods for market research.

Field trials

Here the application is tested *in situ* with the users. They are observed and interviewed. There are a number of different methods of observation and interview that can be employed. The users may also be required to fill in questionnaires. The data is collated and analyzed, and the recommendations for redesign are given. Again, this is not as common with multimedia as with software applications, but in some cases, such as accredited multimedia training programs, the accreditation body might need to see that the application conveyed the correct level of information with a certain number of trial users. Some retail applications might also require proof of use in the field.

Acceptance testing

If there is a clear specification of what is required, then testing can be carried out to prove that the application conforms to the requirements. This relates more to the operation and functional performance of the code, and is derived from software development.

We are going to concentrate on **developmental** and **acceptance testing** as they indicate categories of test related to the stage of the project rather than specific methods that will have to be agreed with your clients. Developmental testing means the numerous checks that are carried out during the course of development to ensure that each part of the project meets its specifications. Many developers have come to use the terms 'alpha test' and 'beta test' in the same sense as developmental and acceptance tests are defined here. These are referred to in the integration chapter (Chapter 16), since that is concerned with the influences from software development. This chapter tries to provide an umbrella for the whole issues of testing that can be met during projects by amalgamating insights and methods from different disciplines.

What is testing?

Testing means examining the project performance according to the specifications that have been agreed. This will include the robustness of the code or compatability of the Web site across different browsers, the structure and content of the programme or Web site, the interface, the interactivity, the

Testing = examining aspects of performance.

performance of the programme or site, the look and feel. It is obvious once this is stated that unless you have the specifications agreed, you cannot prove that your application passes the final test. You will not be able to draw a line to show that you have completed the contractual agreements. The lack of understanding of what constitutes completion of the application is a risk that you need to control to ensure that final sign-off runs smoothly.

Developmental testing

Another point that is self-evident once stated is that testing the programme against specifications is a continuous process during development. Each of the sign-offs that have been suggested is part of the process: the overall structure, text, audio and video scripts, the audio and video edits, the look of the graphics, the look and feel of the navigation. This is not always recognized as being part of the testing process, but it is. A lot of testing occurs during project development. Each of the people on the team is concerned to produce a professional product, so they care about their own performance. If it is a good team, they'll monitor each other's performance in a constructive way. But however much they pool their expertise to predict how the users will react and how the code should operate, there will always be weaknesses.

Many of the weaknesses will be spotted and corrected. Some will be noticed and left alone. This might appear to be a strange admission, and you will not find it stated in much of the literature, but it will be true of the majority of projects. Some design errors will be impossible to change because of the repercussions on the whole of the rest of the project. They need to be spotted very early in the project to be implemented without adverse effects on other parts of the application. Sometimes clients insist on certain features that you know will be detrimental in release; remember the drastic changes to the video sequence caused by an executive in Chapter 12, *Team management principles*.

Acceptance testing

Sometimes design defects become apparent only in use. One or two factors might show up where what appeared logical from past experience does not apply well in new circumstances. The main problem in trying to get final sign-off is to find what is acceptable for both parties. This can be any point on a scale between 'impossible to use' and 'perfection'. Even the most frequently used and maintained programs, such as word processing software, undergo evolution from the first release to maturity and beyond. Sometimes they are released with a statement as to 'known bugs'. Complex multimedia applications will naturally be able to sustain improvement if there is a proper allocation for an improvement cycle. Now, this is not granting the right for developers to abdicate their responsibility for the quality of the delivered product. It is just trying to establish what is fair and equitable in an unsettled set of circumstances.

The program has to operate without failing. That is the first standard that will not be disputed by both parties. This will drive the acceptance test. But even this becomes problematic. We know of at least three projects where a bug in third-party code in the development software had a severe knock-on effect on the operation of an application. This is actually more likely to occur with offline multimedia because the limited level of use of code may not have found all the bugs. This means that the more obscure problems in code occur even when software has been around for some time and appears stable. Use in a new set of circumstances will tease them out.

HTML is a fairly simple form of code, but different Web browsers will interpret the code differently, and it is practically impossible to test Web pages on every combination. We tested the Web pages on the CD-ROM with the first edition of this book with the browsers available at the time. Unfortunately there was a bug in the code, something as seemingly trivial as a missed quotation mark, and our browsers were tolerant of this and so we did not catch the bug. Later browsers changed the way they decoded (or parsed) the HTML and the bug showed up.

It is highly unlikely that a bit of poor HTML will crash a machine, but it can make the Web page unreadable. Unfortunately it is possible for a legal Web page to crash a browser, and the authors had a problem whereby a client's Web site was crashing Netscape online. The problem did not show up when the site was viewed off a disc, and Internet Explorer was unaffected. The problem hit PCs and Macs. To add to this curious situation the problem appeared after the site had been running happily for several months. The bug was finally traced to an innocent-looking background GIF graphic file, and it was replaced.

Perhaps the most common 'bug' on a Web page is the broken link. This could be a link to a graphic, and is most likely to happen if the graphic is not in the site being built. It could be an advertisement, for example. Similarly, any links to other sites can change, and although this is a maintenance issue rather than a developmental one, the client needs to be aware that it can happen and needs policing by someone.

With a Web site any CGI programs will, again, need testing just as in an offline project. An added problem is that the risk of incorrect input from a user is greater on the Web. The chance of a hacker trying to break your code or get into your site is small, but it exists, and you should make sure that your code traps erroneous inputs coming in through the environment variables that pass parameters to CGI programs.

What happens when a bug is found in a finished and delivered application? Is it your responsibility? Is it the client's? Is it the original developer's? Here, your own developers fall foul of the problems that others face in trying to reach perfection in software. Remember to include a limited liability clause in your contract to cover this risk. See Chapter 10, *Contract issues 2*.

Defects in the program will range in severity, knock-on effects and frequency. You need to identify the problems, the severity and the effects on the robustness of the program. This will include correcting any data that is wrong, whether it is a typing error, words in the wrong place, text layout and so on, as well as code defects – wrong sequence, failure to operate a navigation path, or corrupted screens, for example. Your aim is to present an application that will work efficiently and perform correctly within a span of correct use. If the specification did not mention it needed to be 'hacker' proof, you do not have a responsibility to test it under the most extreme circumstances. However, users do have a knack of using programs in ways that are not logical. So a span of unexpected use should be tried out as well as expected normal use.

All these points should indicate that acceptance levels should be specified in advance, and that testing has to be systematic and thorough to prove robustness across a span of use.

The test phase is cyclical. Developmental refinement occurs to ensure each sign-off stage. The assembly of all the parts according to agreement leads up to integration of the pieces and acceptance testing. This sounds as though there should not be too much to do at the end, if all the pieces have been approved. That is rarely so with multimedia because the integration can have repercussions on previously agreed pieces.

The size of text approved in isolation may be illegible because of encoding deterioration, overpowering graphics near it and so on. The colours may shift and in turn affect the legibility of text or clarity of the graphics. A module that

The test cycle.

worked perfectly on its own may fall over when you try to activate it from a subroutine. The development platform might be different from the delivery platform specification, and someone might have overlooked some of the issues of transfer from one to the other.

A Web site can be fully tested only when it is up and running on its own server under the anticipated load of accesses. This assumes that you have already tested the interaction between static HTML and dynamic CGI programs, together with such extras as how a submission form might send emails. Don't forget that some parts of the picture – the server itself and the mailing program – may not be under your control at all if the site is being hosted by an ISP.

Systematic testing has to be done once all the parts are assembled and integrated. A testing plan should be drawn up to ensure that all paths will be explored and all data checked for accuracy, that all interactivity operates as expected, that the right data appears in the right sequence, and that any records that the user builds up during use are faithful and accurate. Each application will have its own features, so these are examples of the more generic aspects that might need systematic testing.

If an application is complex, and extensive use will be made of it by a range of users, then it becomes more important to use one or more testers from outside the team at acceptance testing. During production, the team will have developed patterns of use for themselves based on their experience of the project. It becomes increasingly difficult for them to predict use from a naive perspective. An external, experienced tester will help to draft a test specification to simulate a variety of experience while checking the accuracy of all the data. It will be necessary to use formal test sheets to keep records of the errors and the sequence of actions that caused them, and to have some code of severity to help decide where correction time will be best deployed. Then, because the error needs to be retested to prove that it has been corrected successfully, the person who corrects it should initial and date the correction and the retest should be initialled and dated. See the sample acceptance test report sheet.

The sheet may seem over-bureaucratic, and it should be adapted or discarded depending on the type of project at the discretion of the project manager and depending on the level of testing required by the client. For more complex projects the sheets can help because there is a tendency for revisions to the code to cause knock-on effects. Retest after retest can take place, gradually whittling away the errors. Because there are retests, it is easy to work on the wrong version, so dating and version numbering become more important. See Chapter 16, *Integration*, for a further explanation of versioning.

What is a testing strategy?

A testing strategy sounds complicated but it isn't. It means stating in writing what measures will be taken to ensure that the final program meets the client's requirements. This will include noting the number and type of sign-off stages, the responsibilities of the team members to meet the technical and functional requirements at each stage, the analysis of the users if applicable, a peer review process if applicable, the building and trialling of a prototype if necessary, and whatever other methods you decide to employ during the development stages.

The developmental testing is part of the testing strategy. You can indicate that prior to and around sign-off points for the project the team will be testing to ensure that each part of the application meets the specification that has been agreed for sign-off.

If you have agreed to carry out any of the specific tests that occur early in the project, such as focus groups and prototyping, these will form part of the development testing strategy.

The acceptance test description should be as detailed as you can make it so that it is clear when your team have discharged their responsibilities. If you have had to build a multimedia presentation for an executive, it is straightforward for the individual concerned to try it out and approve it. But if you have a Web site application with items for sale to the general public, then it can be

Table 18.1 Sample acceptance test report sheet.

Project name: **Version number:**   **Programmer's name**
Tester's name: **Date:**
Retester's name: **Date:**
Machine no./spec.   **Platform description**

No.	Error description	Priority code	Programmer's comments	Status: Fixed/Left	Initials	Date	Retest status	Initials	Date

time consuming to collect the data to prove its usability prior to release. It is relatively easy to collect the data once the site is live but the feedback will drive adjustments. If you haven't agreed that the adjustments arising from use are post project and subject to extra costs, you'll find that the client refuses to give final sign-off and effectively gets free updating in the name of the original project.

You may decide that one internal round of testing, record error, resolve error and recheck until satisfied will be enough. Alternatively you may decide on this and then an external round of testing, perhaps done by nominee(s) from the client company and/or by external testers. Your decision will be based on the complexity of the project, the time and cost of the testing agreed, and the wishes of the client.

Any of the specific tests such as usability and the use of an external tester that occur in the latest stages of the project will form part of the acceptance testing strategy.

A word of warning here about nominees from the client company: often they will ask several others to try the program out and even set up a small sample of use with the target audience. This is laudable only if that is exactly what you understood was going to happen. If the client expands the testing specification spontaneously then the odds increase against their signing off.

The wider the acceptance testing, the more likely it is that insights about the users will emerge and point towards design rather than code changes. This is normal in emerging fields where user reaction and use are guessed at. Clients need to recognize this and accept that their application may not be perfect in every detail but that you have faithfully tried to achieve the best given the constraints. Both you and the client will learn from the process, and will be able to assess the user needs better for future applications based on the reactions. Until multimedia markets have matured, and sound analysis of user likes and dislikes has been carried out, this will be the situation. It is unfair of the client to expect more, so you need to state and re-state their responsibilities and the risks that they are taking, and spell out the possible consequences.

You can agree that all text will be spelt correctly and that the screen layouts will conform to the agreed specification. You can agree that the program will function as specified, save for code errors in third-party software and hardware. You can agree that the final product will be tested for robustness according to a testing plan that will ensure that all functional paths are tried and that a normal span of use, accounting for differences in the users, will be tried out. All these would constitute an acceptance test strategy that both your team and the client would find acceptable.

So, it is prudent to explain in the strategy plan that design defects are picked up during development, and operational errors are the main focus of the acceptance phase of testing. If the client is concerned to refine the design you can offer several alternatives during the development stage, such as a prototype trial, but it must be the client's decision to bear any time and cost implications or sacrifice adjustments to the design. If this is clearly stated and agreed you will have done your duty both to your client and to the team so

Stages of testing.

that the level of expectations is set. For example, if there was no agreement for a user trial with end-users, and then modifications to the application are made on the results, any request for this would clearly form an extension of the original project in terms of time and cost.

Prediction of use can be based on experience, but actual use will differ. Unless user testing and redesign have been part of the project specification, your part of the contract is to use your knowledge and experience to guess use. The client acts on the users' behalf to vet your specification. If there is no needs analysis as such built into the project plan, the client's responsibility is to act on their users' behalf in good faith, to allow a proper user trial, or to accept tests designed to test the robustness of the application.

Your testing strategy should be written up as part of your detailed contract documents, and should be alluded to in the scoping document.

Very often the cost of extensive testing and redesign is left out of a multimedia project specification because to do them properly adds so much to the nominal cost of development that a developer fights shy of them. At the very least the testing time risks being eaten into by overruns. This is more true of offline than of online developments. Multimedia is still a difficult market, so any means of pruning project costs is used to arrive at a proposal cost that will make it competitive. But to ignore this completely by pretending that the development stages of multimedia run smoothly is, in the great majority of cases, unrealistic. The final sign-off will then stand more risk of getting into a never-ending loop.

This can cause dreadful problems for a project manager just at the time that everything seemed to be sewn up. Some projects spin out of control right at the final stage, mainly because of readjustments. The client refuses to sign off until these are completed; the developer is certain the adjustments are extras that should be paid for. Small adjustments can be absorbed, but often there will be one or two seemingly small changes that have large repercussions. It is also likely that your team will be in the process of being disbanded or reallocated onto other projects at this stage, so it becomes far more problematic to implement even small changes.

It is at this point that decisions taken early in the project acquire significance. Did you suggest a structured testing plan as part of the project plan?

Did you suggest user trials with prototypes? Did the client reject it? Did they understand the significance of saving money on these items at this time? Did you explain?

If you take the time to plan the testing strategy at the beginning of the project and, if necessary, refine it with your client during development, mindful of time and cost factors, it will pay dividends at final sign-off.

Insights into software testing

Acceptance testing in multimedia is the closest to pure software testing because it addresses the code underlying integration. Some of the problems, such as third-party software bugs and corruption of data that was stable, have been mentioned, but some of the insights from pure software testing should be noted.

Testing is a black hole, and the project manager cannot accurately predict how much time and effort it will take to make the program robust. Usually, the deadline for how much time can be devoted to it will be forced on the team by the amount left prior to the release date or handover date to the client. This is why it becomes important to define the priority of defects so that best use can be made of whatever time is left.

There are problems inherent in the nature of changing code, and effectively this is what happens when the programmer addresses the errors found in tests. There is a 20–50% chance of introducing another error. So it is possible for retested code to end up displaying more errors than on first testing. This is not automatically a reflection on the programmer. Testing is like diagnosis; it spots defects that can be symptoms. The programmer may ease the irritation but may not cure the main infection. Other symptoms can then occur that, when studied, show a coding problem that may warrant extensive rework.

Experienced programmers recognize that the more original code is changed, the more likely it is that the integrity of the overall logic will suffer and break down. Another lesson from their experience shows that there are different ways of treating errors. You might be asked if you will take the risk on a 'patch' or 'quick fix', or negotiate an extension from the client, because to address the error in depth might jeopardize the delivery date. You will have to take the decision.

It will help if you recognize that despite the acceptance test being the final test phase for the project, it is the first full test for the integration. So, in effect, the integration stage has a development stage of its own where it needs time to shape up. Depending on the complexity of the application, you should create enough time and space in your project plan for a few test cycles. You might decide to call the first cycle 'integration testing' to allow the recognition that this is the first chance to address the robustness of the integrated code, and then call the retest 'acceptance testing'.

Testing and error correction have traditionally been handed over to more junior programmers. There are dangers in doing this, and you need to make sure that your original programmers are involved to the end of the project. It has been found that other programmers don't have the overview of the project, and therefore address the errors in isolation. They cannot link the symptoms to a main cause as effectively as the original code writers. Fixing errors can therefore take longer for them. Also, there is more likelihood of the introduction of new errors from inconsistencies between the original programmer's code and the new code.

It should be evident that the end of the project is a vulnerable time for the project manager. There are pressures from the team, the client, and the management. These are over and above the pressures from the diminishing time and budget factors.

Final sign-off

If the acceptance test is prespecified and understood by all parties, then final sign-off will follow smoothly. It is important to have this agreement in writing just as with other sign-offs. This will act as the end of your team's and your responsibilities to the client so that final payment can be claimed.

Your specification for the acceptance test can form the basis for the components listed for sign-off but you should add a sentence or two stating that this sign-off concludes the project and that your company has carried out all its obligations according to the agreements.

Theory into practice 20

Which of the symptoms of a poorly defined testing strategy have you known? Tick all that apply.

1. Clients asking for extras before final sign-off.
2. Clients refusing to sign off the project.
3. Poor version control re-introducing errors which had been corrected.
4. Never-ending testing and error correction cycles.
5. Little testing done because the project ran out of time.
6. No original programmers left to correct errors.

Are you clear now on how to avoid these problems in your next projects?

Summary

■ Multimedia does not have a strong tradition of testing. It has not developed a clear relationship with the methods of testing from other disciplines, and has not devised its own.

■ There are many forms of testing. Each has its strengths and weaknesses in relation to the needs of an application.

■ The project manager has to balance the needs of the application with time and cost factors to devise a testing strategy.

■ The client has to agree to the strategy in the full knowledge of what it includes and what it excludes so there are no last-minute recriminations.

■ Developmental testing is the combination of sign-offs of the completed parts of the project as well as the natural refinement of the individual assets during the development process.

■ Acceptance testing takes place at the final stage of the project to predefined criteria specified in the testing strategy. The integrated code is tested, and the robustness of the project is scrutinized.

■ Final sign-off agrees that the team has met its responsibilities and that the application performs as specified.

Recommended reading

Brooks F.P. Jr (1982). *The Mythical Man-Month. Essays on Software Engineering.* Reading, MA: Addison-Wesley

Dumas J.S. and Redish J.C. (1994). *A Practical Guide to Usability Testing.* Norwood, NJ: Ablex Publishing Corporation

Humphrey W.S. (1990). *Managing the Software Process.* Reading, MA: Addison-Wesley

Roper M. (1994). *Software Testing.* London: McGraw-Hill International (UK) Ltd

19

Archiving

Project manager's responsibilities

- To build into the schedule enough time to archive effectively
- To carry out any company policies for archiving projects
- To rationalize all documentation, assets and budget information

Archiving: the rationale

Chaotic archiving.

If the project has been a large-scale production then there are lots of ends that need to be tidied up. This can seem like bureaucracy running amok, but once you have been caught out by clients requesting individual graphics from their application for marketing purposes, clients returning after several months to do an update that had never been mentioned, your colleague wanting to see the budget breakdown to help in costing another similar project, another colleague wanting the name of the voice-over artiste and agent, your management dealing with an enquiry from the corporate client company's inspectorate about exactly who had signed off the content in the project a year earlier, an enquiry from the musicians' union about the 15 seconds of a record used, a museum insisting that they are one slide short and claiming four months' penalty fees, and so on, then the value of the time put into archiving in a structured way pays for itself.

What needs to be archived?

Companies may have their own policies for archiving their projects. Many have different systems and locations for storing text, audio tapes, videotapes, code and graphics. There will be different versions of the assets from

Successful archiving.

different stages of the project, and during production you will have held on to them all because quite frequently you revert to parts of an earlier version as the project progresses. Keeping the different versions also allows you to keep a check on how much is changing and whether you could absorb the time and cost or need to renegotiate.

Once the project has received final sign-off, all the assets need to be sorted to ensure cover in all aspects for any further requests. This is an onerous task, which usually falls on the project manager and/or admin. assistant as the only ones left working on the project. If no archive check-list is provided by the company it will be in your interest to draft one, because it is easy to forget one or two major items – such as getting the master tape back from the encoding company, if you used one. They often hold on to them in case of any rework needed.

You need to make sure that you have scheduled enough time for yourself to archive the project after final sign-off. It will take three to four days of initial administration for a commercial, large-scale project. The amount of text material that will have been generated might fill most of one filing cabinet. You may have electronic folders of text files representing the final Web page scripts, drawers full of content documents that helped in constructing the final text scripts, several versions of graphics that led to the final graphics files, a few boxes full of videotapes, copies of the master tapes, voice-over tapes, music tapes, photos, slides, or a stack of CD-ROMs from testing! You will be pressured to get the graphics and code off the development system to free space for other projects.

So it will help to have a systematic approach to archiving. The paper from the project can be split into formal documents, scripts, and budget information. There may be a set way of boxing the files or a separate store room with filing cabinets devoted to archiving. You may already be using a coding system according to the project number or project name you have worked on, so that any assets stored in any location will need to be cross-referenced with them. If there is no system, it will be wise to cross-reference by name anyway.

As electronic archiving becomes increasingly popular, and the need for automated multimedia documentation increases, the archiving of projects will become an accepted way of working. (See the references at the end of the chapter to articles on Bulldog's Web site about companies migrating to complete multimedia archiving systems, and the increasing need for businesses to do so.)

Formal documents

These will include all contractual documents, such as the final proposal document, any terms and conditions agreed as per the firm's policy, any agreement to ways of working, all sign-off documents for the intermediate stages, and the final sign-off. They should also include all confidentiality agreements from the team members if this was a condition accepted from the client. Copies of all contracts drafted for subcontractors or freelancers should be held with the formal documents. All rights agreements for the text, video, audio and graphics assets should be sorted and filed accordingly. You'll need an index of what the files contain for quick access later. Finally, a list showing where assets such as video master tapes, audio tapes, and code backups are being held is necessary for a full formal record to be complete.

Scripts and assets

Text copies of the final scripts for all the components should be held with their electronic files. This will mean sorting out the versions and updating any of the scripts with the inevitable last-second changes that were probably written in on copies. All assets that belonged to the client should be returned. Make a list for the archive files and date it showing exactly what was returned and when.

If you had to use external assets from picture libraries or museums then a similar list should have been compiled for those. Many of them should have been returned and recorded during the course of the project but there are often quite a few of the more important ones left over in case they were needed again. Whoever was managing the rights and clearances for the project should have made good records showing what has been returned and what is outstanding and why.

The company may have a policy to recycle video and audio tapes for other projects, or may choose to archive them as well. The masters may well be held off site for security purposes so these will need to be clearly marked in an appropriate way for easy identification later if necessary. There may be packaging guidelines for off-site storage that you need to conform to. Wherever audio, video, graphics and code are held, you need to make sure that their location and date of transfer are recorded for the formal set of documents.

Budget information

During the project you will have been monitoring the actual time and cost against the predicted time and cost as stipulated in the final proposal agreement. These are important records, so detailed files are essential. If your finance department has been collating the team's time sheets against tasks or sign-off points, and costing according to the internal and external rates you gave them, then you should already have a file with their printouts. They should be able to provide you with a detailed printout for the complete project soon after final sign-off. However, for many reasons this rarely seems to happen, so often you have the best understanding of exactly where the project stands in relation to the actual expenditure. Record your understanding.

You need to rationalize the details that you hold with those that the finance section holds. For example, you will have the detailed breakdown of numbers of assets cleared from each source, so it will probably be easier for you to arrive at a final cost for asset rights clearances than the accounts section. You will then be able to match the figure against the predicted figure to see where the project stands on this. You should have been on top of this type of equation all through the project, so that refining the information should be relatively easy.

It is a good idea to write a budget report to put with all this information comparing the predicted and actual spend and the predicted and actual time spent. It will help you for future projects, as well as colleagues and the management, if you indicate the reasons for any overspend in any section or any extra time incurred.

It is easy to forget the causes of problems on a project, but they will help you to become better at predicting time and costs on other projects and to make sharper decisions about risk factors. Some of the factors may point towards organizational issues that should be resolved by management to help all projects to run more smoothly, as well as some showing where you yourself might improve.

The time record systems and therefore staff project spend information are becoming integrated into improvements to standard software packages. Electronic time sheet systems are more common now, and the tasks for each staff member can be pulled into the project plan to update on certain aspects of the project's progress. It is as well to keep track of these developments as there is a point when the saving on admin against the cost of a system will make sense even for a small company.

Closing the project

Once all the archiving is in place, all assets have been returned if required, and your work area is probably the tidiest it has been since you started the project, then the project is properly finished. If you don't take the responsibility to do all this at the end, you will find that the project can haunt you as the small requests from all quarters become harder to implement. You will have lost interest in the project, and your own understanding of the files will fade quickly.

Many organizations do not pay enough attention to archiving. You may need to fight for the time as legitimate time to build into the schedule at the beginning, but it is in your interest. You need to bear in mind that by the end of the project you'll probably hate it, and just want to finish at all costs. It takes mental stamina to persevere with archiving, particularly when your other team members have moved on to more interesting things.

Summary

- Spending a few days archiving at the end of a project has good payback even in the short term. Fight for time in the schedule if necessary.

- Archiving is a neglected area. Employ the company's policy if one exists or define and use one yourself.

- A systematic approach to archiving projects will benefit both you and the company.

- File and index all formal documents together.

- Sort out the final versions of all scripts. Return all assets; list and date the returns.

- Trace, list and store all internal assets – video masters, audio tapes, and so on.

- Gather all relevant budget data together. Write a report on the project management aspects of the project and learn from it for future projects.

Recommended reading

http://www.bulldog.ca
Technology Bullpen section: Articles by Peter De Vries
What is media management?
Media asset management: managing complex data as a re-engineering exercise

20
Marketing and marketing research

Project manager's responsibilities

- To understand marketing and distribution concepts
- To keep up to date with marketing information
- To recognize the implications for interactive products
- To focus the project team on marketing issues when appropriate
- To influence the design of a product according to market information
- To liaise with marketing staff, if part of the company

The relevance of this chapter

Project managers can be forgiven for wondering why we have included this chapter. Most of them have to combine several roles already without facing the fear of also having to do their own marketing and distribution. However, some of the biggest criticisms of interactive media companies are: that their projects overrun, that they produce products that are too expensive, and that they are media and technology led rather than market led.

As part of management, and perhaps as part of your own development plan, you should consider wider perspectives recognizing their place in your work context. It is with this in mind that we introduce the concepts here and provide references for further study.

What is marketing?

The marketing perspective.

For many, the concept of marketing is linked only with advertising and selling. However, it concerns a wider two-way process of exchange in which the supplier identifies, anticipates and satisfies customers' wants, and the customers choose to buy because the goods or services meet their criteria. This is a continuous process since the customer's criteria change according to many influences – economic, cultural, legal, technological, social, informational, and political. The supplier needs to recognize any shifts in requirements and even anticipate these to satisfy the consumer before the competition does, or risk losing business.

The path that the interactive products will utilize to reach their target market is referred to as the **marketing** or **distribution channel**. Effectively this means that you might have produced a good product at a winning price for a certain target market, but if the customers don't know it exists and where to buy it, then it can't make a return for you.

Why are these concepts important?

If your company is producing commercial products these concepts are essential or the company is at risk of failing not from lack of good products but from lack of exposure and opportunity for the customers to buy. For example, a lot of the publishers who tried producing interactive products have pulled out of the consumer market. The production process was difficult, the size of the market that wished to buy products was uncertain, the type of product they wanted was indeterminate, the price they were willing to pay was unknown, and the distribution was flawed. For years, if you wanted to see interactive products, even games, where did you go – a bookshop, a consumer electronic goods outlet, or a video outlet?

In many countries this lack of a proper distribution channel has been addressed. Now there are high street retail outlets for software, but the size of the market and the understanding of sales is still difficult. Unfortunately, even if there is a channel, getting your product taken on and distributed is not straightforward. You may have to go through a series of middlemen who all take a percentage of the final sales. This is as true for the Internet as it is for offline products. If someone else guarantees you more visibility and potential sales because their site, shopping mall or whatever gets a good hit rate, they will ask for a fee or percentage of your sales.

If a product takes too long to produce, the market opportunity may have moved from the point that the product was originally meant to serve. With technology, the market is difficult to understand in the first place, and it can shift dramatically in a short time. The speed with which the World Wide Web took off, for example, was not predicted, and even the largest players in the software market had to run to keep up.

If the product is too expensive, it may price itself out of what the market wishes to pay. The pricing policy for new products in software changes quickly in line with the expectations of the market. You may sell more and get a good return at a low or middle price than selling few with no return at a high price.

The message that a project manager should be picking up from this information is that when producing a commercial product, even if it is on behalf of a client, there are more factors to consider about slippage and its impact on the saleability and the cost for development, because the market might not support the end price that the development cost forces.

If we return to the time, cost, quality equation that we started the book with, for commercially viable products you may now be prepared for a further layer of consideration. The cost of development may be driven by the price that the market will support for a particular type of product according to the expected number of sales. You can work this backwards to find a relevant price for production that can influence the time for production. Alternatively, if the main drive for a product is to get it out by a particular time – interactive products based around successful toys for Christmas, for example – the time as well as the cost of the final product can influence the development time and cost. Whatever the driving factor among time, cost and quality, we can now recognize that it will have an effect on the other two.

Understanding the impact that market factors and distribution factors can have on the product development cycle and costs should broaden your own perspective. If it has, your team need to become as aware. It will help them to recognize that their personal drive of how the product should be shaped might need to be tempered by the wider vision.

The same can be true of the client. They may forget the overriding need to produce the product for a window in the market. You may need to remind them by asking whether their new requests for modifications to the specification should be implemented despite this meaning two months' extra development time, or whether the agreement to add to the time and costs for development may mean that the end-product price will not be supported by the market. Larger companies can spread the return on investment (ROI) of a product over several years knowing that there will be a loss for some years then an increase to a beneficial return within five years, for example. Smaller companies can rarely afford to wait for the return for this length of time. You need to understand the risks and take decisions accordingly.

Marketing and new media

The concept of marketing has gradually been recognized as a determining factor that can affect the philosophy of companies. If all sections of the company coordinate their efforts towards putting the customer first, this is a sign of a company's applying the marketing concept. There is also an emphasis on profitability rather on the volume of sales. This concept will be alien to many interactive media companies because most of them are small and do not have marketing departments.

Generally, within the industry, the emphasis has been on the innovative use of technology rather than on who the customers are and what they want. There is some justification for this approach in an emerging market or in a speculative market where customers are few. But times are changing, and there are now some parts of the market that are more mature than others, and where feedback from the customers is essential.

The key principles of marketing and distribution have been difficult to apply to interactive media until recently. These principles are: know your customers, know your competition, know your strengths, know your market, and know how to reach your customers with information and products.

Even when these principles are applied in a mature market marketing is not an exact science, and many predictions are wrong. But all decisions have to be made on available data, so market and competitor intelligence and the interpretation of this information are important aids to targeting the market or a particular part of it. This is why the larger corporations invest in technology trials and use their marketing departments to process the data. Even a little information on an emerging market might allow the development of a strong product line ahead of the competition and establish the company's credibility with the customer base. This can lead to loyalty and further sales.

Who are the customers?

From a marketing perspective it is essential to know who your customers are and what they want from a product so that you can meet their needs and increase sales ahead of the competition. It may seem an easy question but it isn't as straightforward as it seems. Are your customers those who commission a project or are they the end-users? Are your customers internal and part of your company? Are they the retailers that stock your titles? Are they the buyers or the recipients of the title?

Because interactive media is an emerging market, it has been difficult to gauge what has made an impact from a consumer point of view. This means that developers have produced applications according to their experience, the technical limitations and current trends from the respective disciplines of programming, computer graphics, video production and so on. Very often the expense of prototyping with users and redesigning according to the feedback has been considered too expensive and time consuming. Often, as well, the developers have been divorced from feedback from the end-users after the release of the application. They consider their job finished when the product is released.

But with the emergence of a market certain customer traits can be identified. The market can be divided into certain types of consumer behaviour and wants. This leads to products' being developed specifically for particular segments that are identified as being sufficiently large and lucrative. Offline interactive media have begun to segment, and so can be equated with a maturing market. Developers are beginning to target specific sectors, such as point of sale, point of information, commercial training, corporate training, education and games. Online products are now showing signs of being an emerging, unstable market. Many people are trying to understand where the commercial value lies, because there is at least the confidence that there are significant numbers of potential customers involved. But the 'free' culture of exchange of information and goods that underpinned the Internet has meant that traditional ways of identifying trends are confused. Marketing companies are trying to establish new business models for the new ways of doing business. The potential for making money is known to exist, but very few are actually doing so.

For applications that are developed for a market segment other than the consumer – the corporate market, for example – the premise of 'know your customer' still applies. We have seen that poor specification by people commissioning projects can cause problems. By working with the commissioners as suggested, you will move nearer to an understanding of what they want and what you can produce for them. The commissioners/clients are your customers because they are buying your services. But, since the users are the clients' customers, the premise applies equally to the clients. They will serve their companies' needs better if they focus on the needs of the users.

Interactive media companies that ignore the first principle – know your customers – will find that their successful competitors will be spending time and effort analyzing their clients' and users' wants. They will get to know more about their likes, dislikes, aspirations, beliefs, attitudes, lifestyles, sense of humour, and so on, to tailor applications to suit the trends.

Know the competition

The companies that are successful in terms of repeat custom and sales are offering goods and services that meet the needs of their particular market. By studying what they are offering and comparing it with what you offer, you'll begin to understand their competitive edge.

Once you try defining your competition, you will find that it is even more difficult than knowing your customer. Your competition can originate from several sources – direct, close, similar products, substitute products and indirect competition.

Identify your competitors.

Your direct competitors are usually the easiest to identify. In interactive media terms they will be other companies who compete for the same group of clients/customers and offer the same type of applications. Let's say that your company specializes in developing multimedia CD education titles for schools. Your direct competitors would be similar firms with a similar orientation.

Close competition offers products that have similar benefits for similar customers. If you specialize in CD education titles for sale to schools, and another firm is producing edutainment titles that can be suitable for schools and home use, they would be close competitors.

If we continue the education scenario, similar products could be information or reference CDs. A museum might have a point-of-information kiosk application developed for a special dinosaur exhibition. They might then offer CDs based on this for sale in their shop. Schools often visit museums, and teachers and children might buy the title. Would you have considered the museum a competitor?

Substitute products are ones that might be bought instead of the multimedia offering. In the case of this museum exhibition, the museum shop may be selling general books and videos on dinosaurs as well as their own CD. The substitute products – the books and videos – might prove more popular than the CD in the shop sales. Looking at this in a wider context, educational video titles and, of course, books offer information in ways and at prices that could influence buyers away from CDs. Perhaps the museum featured here should have considered producing their own video and book as 'substitutes' for the CD. Then more of the sales would be of their own titles, and so make a return on the investment in the original kiosk application. Of course, online products for schools would also be substitute products that would be seriously competitive.

It is wrong to become complacent about the competition, because the worst threat might come from an indirect competitor. Broadcasters, for example, are experimenting with interactive TV. In the future, TV or cable companies might offer schools a package. The schools would receive many more materials for a year's subscription than they might get from the total supply of educational online packages or educational CDs from several suppliers. Both you, as a multimedia CD educational company, and your direct competitors might suffer in this case. Your indirect competitor, the TV or cable company, offers a different form of product, which can appeal to and win away your customers. Alternatively, you might have watched and planned for this change in the market and have built bridges with the emerging competitors. Then, instead of selling to the schools yourself, you might be looking to produce for the TV or cable company instead. The Internet's success came quickly and was a surprise to many businesses. It was an indirect competitor but suddenly, because of its popularity and the computer literacy of its users, it offered a realistic market platform and possible distribution channel for interactive products.

Know your strengths

It is probably easier to define your own company's strengths once you have defined those of your direct and close competitors. Interactive media companies tend to have historical bias as described in Chapter 2. A company might have computer graphics strengths or a publishing orientation. The resources and way of working will reflect the strengths but may also help in pinpointing weaknesses when deciding why a competitor is succeeding better than you in a particular market. A well-known method to help with this type of analysis is known as **SWOT**. This method asks you to consider your company's strengths, weaknesses, opportunities and threats.

Your strengths are your competitive edge, and you need to consider whether you are using their entire potential in relation to the market opportunities. You can also consider whether the strengths can be enhanced or focused to give better results. At the same time, once you recognize your weaknesses, you are in a position to start counteracting them. The same is true of the threats.

By matching the analysis of your strengths to the market, you should be able to assess whether you are working on the best business for you. You may also be able to target business opportunities that will fit your strengths better. The state of the market will be important here. In an emerging market, companies take business from wherever it is offered rather than target specific areas, because opportunities are diverse and few. As a market matures and segments, then companies within the market begin to specialize and line up with particular needs.

Know the market

Larger companies pay for market research, and use the information for competitive advantage. They are the only ones who have the capability to do such large-scale research in new and emerging markets. But as a market becomes bigger, market research companies start to do their own research because they know there will be enough people interested in buying the reports. Gradually, as segments mature, the research companies follow the trends and write more targeted reports to sell.

There are many ways of gathering information and equally many ways of interpreting what is found. Research companies will employ their own techniques, and these will be addressed later in this section, but less formal sources can also be invaluable. Articles in journals or the trade press can indicate where a competitor is putting effort into a new initiative. Attending exhibitions and monitoring competitor trends/products/pricing is also fruitful. Talking to distributors can gain their perspective on the various strengths of each product and company as seen by customers, and so on. These form part of a micro picture about the market. More rigorous and formal methods need to be applied to gain a macro picture of what is happening and where key players are heading.

Companies themselves can gather information continuously about total sales in relation to products and geographic variance, for example. This will allow them to see whether their marketing strategies are working, and to help identify trends. This type of data is called **continuous market research**. Research companies also employ this method of continuous research to build up macro marketing trends. They may decide to gather data on an emerging market every year. They will cover the same ground to monitor shifts and so identify emerging trends, scale of operation, increased investment and so on. With established market segments, they may produce more regular reports – monthly breakdown of interactive sales by sector and country, for example. The opposite of continuous research is ad hoc research that is carried out for a specific reason. This might be to help a company make a particular decision – to find out why a popular series has dropped sales, or why hits on a highly popular Web site have declined and are therefore putting the advertising revenue it gets at risk, for example; and what to do about it.

There are two categories that describe the type of data that is gathered – quantitative and qualitative. Most market research data is **quantitative**. This means that the information can be conveyed in a numerical way. The number and total of sales are obvious examples but percentage sales to age groups and success rates on repeat sales are also quantitative. Many questionnaires are devised to be analyzed numerically. The continuous research reports will have processed the data collected from their questionnaires into graphs, charts, percentages and so on to help people compare one set of figures against previous results.

Qualitative data is reflected in descriptions and unstructured reactions. This type of research is used to predict customer behaviour/attitudes and so tailor a new product to suit as yet unrecognized needs. Inductive methods such as asking the interviewee to project into a situation and comment freely on their reactions are used. The qualitative research methods are found most helpful in establishing the categories of market segment. The concept of lifestyle – leisure activities, interests, social habits and so on – for example, has largely replaced that of social class as being a key determinant of customer behaviour.

The sources of marketing information are either primary or secondary. **Primary** data is that collected by direct involvement in such methods as observation, surveys, interviews, inductive techniques, and experimentation. **Secondary** sources are those where the data has already been analyzed and collated in some way. This can come from internal company records such as sales records and royalty returns – if the products are marketed to the public, for example. Alternatively, the data might be compiled from records of use of an application, a Web site or a kiosk, for example. The external sources of data will come from market research reports, trade reports and so on.

It is important to check the reliability and accuracy of the information. Reliable information means that the same results can be repeated or reproduced. The information also needs to be valid. This often depends on the size of the sample used to collect the data and whether the sample was representative. You need to consider: if the information were extended, would it be true of the market as a whole? Relevance is another principle to apply. If product groups are lumped together and you need information on a specific type of product, can you use the information? Finally, you need enough data to make the decisions you want, and the information must be current.

Know how to reach your customers with information and products

... or face the consequences.

It seems common sense that if you are in business to produce products for the consumer then they will buy more of your applications if they are easily available, the price is right, and they compare favourably with competing products. But how will they know where to find your interactive products? It is still difficult to decide where to advertise your company and products to reach the people who will be receptive to buying them. If you work for a large media company that has moved into interactive media and has a marketing department, then their usual forms of advertising and distribution will not cover the emerging interactive market adequately.

If the marketing department does not fully understand the scope of interactive media, they may not recognize that a new strategy might have to be devised. In smaller companies many of the applications they develop will be for clients directly and not for the general public. Their clients might have commissioned the product to sell on the open market and so they will have to take the decisions of how and where to introduce the product to the potential buyers.

If we take the UK as an example, one of the first attempts at establishing a distribution channel was to sell the applications side by side with the hardware in major media hardware chains. This included audiovisual and computer chains. In the next phase, the applications were more readily available in the larger shops of the stationers' chains. These shops were the type that sold audio CDs, videos, and limited computer accessories. Finally, dedicated software stores for a range of computer-related software and multimedia applications have been established in the major high streets. Distributors have emerged and have refined into ones for particular sectors.

Education, for example, relies more on mail order channels with established suppliers of educational materials. (If you need to find a distributor, you'll find them listed in the multimedia directories – see the references.)

When it comes to the Internet, many falsely believe that the distribution problems are over because all potential customers need do is search for the sites and the browsers are there to help them. However, how and why sites are accessed, either directly or via searches, is not straightforward. There are tricks of the trade to help get your site recognized over and above competitors. You have to know how searches are carried out and what triggers the browsers are looking for. New consultancy practices are emerging that specialize in Web marketing and distribution because they are different from other practices (see the references at the end of this chapter).

Companies have found that using traditional advertising and including the Web address gives increased traffic on the site. Only some direct advertising on the Web is successful, but again, why and what works is still being identified. Predicting consumer interactive behaviour on the Web cannot be directly based on their non-interactive behaviour off the Web.

An introduction to market analysis

Although we touched on broad methods such as quantitative and qualitative research in the section above, it will be useful to explore some techniques further.

A market research company will gather different types of data according to the needs defined in the brief. The information will be processed and presented in a variety of ways. One of the common techniques used is a **perceptual map** or **matrix** as demonstrated below.

Perceptual map of multimedia competitors.

If you had commissioned a market research company to evaluate the perception of your company (Number 1) against your competitors in your market segment, they might collate the results in this way. This demonstrates your position in relation to price of development and perception of quality of the multimedia titles/products produced. You would be able to discuss strategies for changing their perception of your company for the better while trying to increase pricing in line with what they said they value. Other variables can be used for the axes, but the variables should be ones determined by the customers as important to them during the research.

Another form of analysis that is used in marketing research is the **Pareto method**. This is valuable in defining which segment of the business is making the best contribution and what type of customer group might be the most valuable to target. The sales/contribution analysis is arrived at by finding the current sales or turnover by customer or segment accounts. This is plotted against sales revenue minus all variable costs. The company might like to be producing high sales volumes on valuable products but may be producing variable sales on lower-value products. The analysis again helps to decide which type of product/customer group offers the best return and where the effort for winning a particular type of business might make a big difference. It can also point out productions that have not made an impact for the business and might need to be discontinued. The example chart below demonstrates this in a figurative way. Each dot represents a type of product that a hypothetical interactive media company produces and shows the value on the return for the company. Each dot might represent the product type, such as kiosk, presentations, Web sites, educational titles and so on.

These few examples provide a basis for understanding where and how marketing analysis can begin to serve a company. Although marketing is a relatively new discipline it has made a significant contribution to business

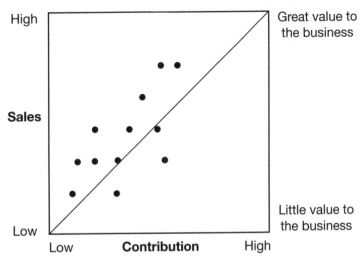

Sales contribution chart.

studies, and is refining its techniques to help business decision making all the time. It needs professionals well versed and trained in its discipline to perform the collection, analysis and interpretation of data. The intelligence that they can give a company needs to be considered carefully but cannot be ignored. We hope that this short introduction will encourage professionals to be receptive to marketing information and better informed as to the value of the decisions taken in relation to the business objectives.

What of the smaller companies that cannot afford to have marketing personnel or to commission research? These need to rely on surveys and reports produced for the industry. A listing of relevant companies and the types of report they offer is given at the end of the chapter. However, a lot can be gained informally through the grapevine as long as everyone in the company knows who wants the information and sees that it is appreciated.

Theory into practice

There is no task set for this chapter since it is outside the project cycle and used for background development of knowledge rather than skills.

Summary

- This chapter defines the concepts of marketing and marketing channels and explains the relevance of them for a multimedia project manager.

- The possible implications for product development – how the time, cost and quality can be affected – are raised.

- The key concepts of know your customer, know your competition, know your strengths, know your market and know how to reach your market are covered.

- Some insights into marketing analysis practices are outlined.

Recommended reading

Adcock D., Bradfield R., Halborg A. and Ross C. (1995). *Marketing Principles and Practice*, 2nd edn. London: Pitman.

Brinson J.D. and Radcliffe M.F. (1997). *Multimedia Law and Business Handbook: A Practical Guide for Developers and Publishers*. Menlo Park, CA: Ladera Press. Contains a chapter on negotiations with publishers and distributors.

Dibb S. and Simkin L. (1996). *The Market Segmentation Workbook: Target Marketing for Marketing Managers*. London: Routledge.

Hagel J. and Armstrong A.G. (1997). *Net Gain: Expanding Markets Through Virtual Communities*, Cambridge, MA: Harvard Business School Press

Hammond R. (1996). *Digital Business*. London: HarperCollins

Judson B. (1996). *Netmarketing*. New York: Wolff New Media

Henning K. (1998). *The Digital Enterprise: How Digitisation Is Redefining Business*. London: Random House

Schuyler N. and Ocampo R. (1995). *The Business of Multimedia*. New York: Allworth Press. Contains a chapter on how to get products on the shelves.

Technology/media market research

Directories

The Directory of New Media Market Research (1998). Peterborough: Multimedia Ventures

The Multimedia and CD-ROM Directory (1998). London: Macmillan Reference

Who's who in UK Multimedia (1998) London: The Simpkins Partnership

Agencies

Pull together various reports from sectors
Global Information Inc
http://www.gii.o.jp/english/plms.htm

Companies

These produce reports on various aspects of the markets. Some reports are continuously updated and revised; some are specially commissioned as trends appear.

OVUM Ltd.
http://www.ovum.com
INTECO
http://www.inteco.com
CIT Publications
http://www.telecoms-data.com
SIMBA
http:// www.simbanet.com
TFPL Multimedia
http://www.tfpl.com/TFPLhome.htm
FT Media
http://www.ftmedia.com
Cyberatlas
http://www.cyberatlas.com

Companies specializing in Internet research

Zona Research
http://wwwzonaresearch.com
NOP Research Group
http://www.nopres.co.uk

General recommended reading for developers

Burger J. (1995). *Multimedia for Decision Makers. A Business Primer*. Reading, MA: Addison-Wesley

Vaughan T. (1997). *Multimedia: Making It Work*, 3rd edn. Berkeley, CA: Osborne McGraw-Hill

The Multimedia and CD-ROM Directory (1998). Vol.1 Marketplace. Vol.2 Titles. London: Macmillan Reference

..... and what's next?

This final part of the book will probably turn out to be full of errors. Predicting future trends is a dangerous business but here, briefly, we shall look ahead to see what may affect multimedia in the future.

If we look back to the mid-1980s, when interactive video was a promising new medium, we can see four key things that have changed: entertainment technology, telephony, networks, and computing power.

At the time of writing in 1998 we see that computing power has increased as predicted, and there is no reason to suppose it will not continue to do so. This is the underlying cause of the technological change that new media industries will exploit. The kind of computing power that was found in a 1970s mainframe now sits happily in the palm of your hand. But what of the other three?

Fifteen years ago the idea that millions of homes around the world would sport satellite dishes seemed unreal. Admittedly, the North American experience with cable was beginning to show that hundreds of channels of television could be provided for consumers, but we equated dishes with telephone companies and NASA.

Mobile telecommunications was the preserve of the rich and the emergency services, and the idea of using thousands of low-power transmitters rather than a few powerful ones was unheard of. This simple approach to telecommunications – cellular radio – has freed up the airwaves to allow millions of people to carry a 'phone in their pocket.

The Internet existed, but it took a long time for someone to devise a way to make it easy to use. But when the World Wide Web appeared the Internet became a mass medium, and the term 'wide area network' took on a whole new meaning.

So what are the likely major changes coming in the near future that will have an impact on multimedia? There are key changes coming in broadcasting (television in particular) and mobile communications.

Broadcasting is going digital. By the time you read this, digital terrestrial television and digital audio broadcasting will be a reality in some parts of the world. The first model digital television will use MPEG-2 as its video standard, and will also have a configurable data channel (shared with the pictures). Electronic programme guides (EPG) will be produced to help viewers find their way around the increased number of channels, especially from the satellite broadcasters. Early interactive ideas only scratch the surface of a new potential market for multimedia. There has to be more to interactive TV than choosing camera angles and joining in quiz shows.

But as television viewers join the multimedia fold, will they play by our existing rules or will they force us to rethink? After all, there may be a lot of computer users but there are many more TV viewers out there. They are used to changing channel and, in Europe, to interacting with Teletext. A windowed environment is not part of their grammar. They are used to smoothly streamed audio and video of high quality.

The next generation of mobile communications, called UMTS (universal mobile telecommunications services), will come on stream in the middle of the first decade of the new century. Plans are already in place for mobile video telephony and conferencing, and for travellers in trains and planes to be able to hook up to the Internet during their journey. There are already signs of the boundary between a computer and a mobile telephone becoming blurred, and this will continue.

Alongside these changes are extensions to standards. The multimedia world traditionally has followed de facto standards set by major manufacturers, and because of the fluid nature of the computing platform we are able to adapt to cope with these. In the bigger world of broadcasting and telecommunications, the manufacture of millions of television sets (or whatever consumer appliance) requires internationally organized standards. We already make use of some parts of the MPEG work: MPEG-1 is Video-CD, and now available in software on faster PCs; MPEG audio levels are widely used; MPEG-2 is used in DVB and DVD.

MPEG-4 and MHEG-5 are two more recent developments. MPEG-4 started out as a lower bit-rate progression from MPEGs 1 and 2 but it has become much more than that. Now MPEG-4 allows the definition of arbitrary objects to make up a scene or a soundtrack. The future viewer of an MPEG-4-compliant television picture will be able to choose viewpoints and, perhaps, even modify the components to suit personal taste. You want a female newscaster? You got it!

MHEG-5 (Multimedia and Hypermedia Experts Group) defines a coded representation of a scene including text, icons, buttons, menus and graphics as well as audio and video. A user can interact with an MHEG scene within constraints set by the program author. MHEG is not new: it has been around for over five years. But fitting MHEG into the MPEG hierarchy (hence the 5) suggests that it will become part of the wider audiovisual picture.

What these things mean for multimedia is unclear. However, it seems certain that both broadcasting and telecommunications will embrace multimedia as their technology develops. And that, we hope, will increase the market for our skills.

Glossary

3-D Three-dimensional, appearing to have depth.

3-DO Consumer multimedia player

8-, 16- or 24-bit image The more bits a colour image has, the more colours can be shown in it. An 8-bit image can have 256 colours because eight bits can be used for numbers from zero (00000000 in binary arithmetic) to 255 (11111111 in binary arithmetic). However, these colours can usually be chosen from a larger palette of perhaps millions of colours. If the 256 colours are all shades of grey then a photographic-quality monochrome image can be reproduced. A 16-bit image will have thousands of colours, and can look photographic in many circumstances. For a truly photographic colour image the millions of colours available in 24 bits is necessary (or even more). Note that on the Apple Macintosh an 8-bit matte or alpha channel can be added to the 24 bits, and the image can be referred to as being 32-bit.

above-the-line cost A cost that you would not be paying as part of the overhead of running the company. Your in-house resources and/or staff are a below-the-line cost whereas a freelancer hired for a particular job is an above-the-line cost. These two kinds of cost are both real, since somebody has to pay them, but your attitude to them is likely to be different.

ADPCM Adaptive delta (or difference) pulse code modulation. Delta PCM is a sound-encoding method that reduces the data rate by storing only changes in the size of samples rather than the absolute value of the sample. The adaptive part is where the encoding of the difference values adapts so as to more accurately follow large changes between samples.

aliasing Occurs when the way something is recorded produces errors that look or sound as if they should be parts of the real thing. The wheels of racing covered wagons in a Western movie, which often seem to be going backwards, do so because of aliasing. In this case the 24 frames per second of the film is not fast enough to accurately record the motion of the wheel. In digital audio it is possible to produce false sounds if the rate at which the sound is sampled is not fast enough to accurately represent the waveform. See **anti-aliasing**.

alpha channel Besides the red, green and blue channels of an image that determine the colour of each pixel, there can be another channel that sets how transparent the pixel is. This is known as the alpha channel. The effect is similar to a matte except that a matte is usually only 1 bit deep so that the transparency is either full (so the background shows through) or opaque. In television this is known as *keying*.

alpha disc The disc on which an alpha version of an application is distributed.

alpha test The first, internal, test of a complete or near-complete application. The term originates from computing, and is not always used by multimedia companies originating from other disciplines.

analogue Strictly speaking an analogue is any kind of representation or similarity. However, analogue is used in multimedia (and in audio and video and electronics in general) to differentiate from digital. In digital, a signal is turned into a series of numbers, and the numbers are stored or transmitted. In analogue the signal itself is either stored or transmitted directly, or is converted into another medium that can follow its variations and itself be stored or transmitted. Whereas analogue systems are prone to distortion and noise, digital systems are much less susceptible.

animatic An application that demonstrates and prototypes the final application.

animation Simulated movement of objects using computer or video effects. A simulation of a building rising from its outline foundations to completion is an example of an animation.

anti-aliasing In graphics it is possible for edges of objects to look jagged because the resolution screen display is unable to accurately represent the object itself. To alleviate this problem the colours of the pixels around the edge of the object are mixed gradually between the object and its background. In this way the colour resolution compensates for the lack of spatial resolution that causes the jagged edges. By definition, this technique cannot be used where only pure black-and-white pixels are available. Some computer displays will now automatically anti-alias text to make it look cleaner on the screen.

applet A very small computer application (usually in the Java language) downloaded from a Web site to run on the user's computer as part of a Web page.

application A general term for a multimedia title or project.

application-based program A program that is either self-contained or which runs entirely within one environment, such as an authoring package.

artefacts Disturbances and defects to an image or sound that are not supposed to be there, but which are the results of errors in digitization or display.

assets The media components of an application – audio, video, graphics, animations, text – that combine to form the content.

authoring tool A computer program designed to be simple to use when building an application. Supposedly no programming knowledge is needed, but usually common sense and an understanding of basic logic are necessary.

bandwidth The amount of data passed along a cable or communications channel of any kind. Sometimes the data channel, or pipe, is described as *fat* if it has a high bandwidth and can carry a lot of data quickly, or *thin* if it cannot. Bandwidth is usually expressed in bits per second or bytes per second. Because of this confusion you should be clear whether bandwidth is being expressed in bits or bytes to understand how fast the data can be transmitted.

BCPL A computer language, one of the ancestors of C and C++.

beta If your application has 'gone beta' then it should be finished but needs testing. This testing may be carried out by people outside the production team and even outside the production company.

bit depth The more bits a colour image has, the more colours can be used in it. An 8-bit image can have 256 colours, but you can usually choose those colours from a larger palette of perhaps millions of colours. If your 256 colours are all shades of grey then a photographic-quality monochrome image can be reproduced. A 16-bit image will have thousands of colours, and can look photographic in many circumstances. However, for a truly photographic colour image the millions of colours available in 24 bits is necessary (or even more). Note that on the Apple Macintosh an 8-bit matte or alpha channel can be associated with the 24 bits, making 32 bits.

bitmap A graphic image that represents the image by a matrix of every pixel, usually going from top to bottom, left to right. Bitmap images usually have a resolution in pixels per inch and a size in pixels.

bit rate reduction Audio and video engineers often use this term to mean compression of data, as the term compression has another use, especially in audio. See **compression**.

bookmark A function of an application whereby users can store their place so that they can quickly go back there later, even saving the bookmark for retrieval many days later. The electronic equivalent of a piece of paper between pages of a book.

browser A piece of software that allows the user to look through a number of resources, usually held in a variety of formats. A Web browser is designed for viewing World Wide Web pages on the Internet. Netscape Navigator, Internet Explorer and Mosaic are examples of Web browsers.

buffer A place for temporary storage of data, often to smooth out differences in speed between a data input and output.

build The process of taking all the component parts of a multimedia application (or indeed any piece of software) and making the finished version.

bump mapping In computer graphics, a technique for giving a surface texture to objects by slightly distorting the shape.

buy-out Paying for all the necessary rights in one go rather than paying royalties.

C, C++ Powerful computer languages, often used to write sophisticated code to carry out specialized or difficult tasks in multimedia applications. C++ is more recent and is designed for object-oriented programming. Java is based on C.

cache Computer memory or disk space used for temporary storage of data in order to speed up a task. A Web browser has a cache on disk to hold recently downloaded pages and graphics so that if a page is revisited and has not changed the information can be quickly loaded from the local disk rather than downloaded again over the network.

cartogram A style of illustration in which a map shows statistical information in a diagrammatic way.

CD burner A machine that can write compact discs, including CD-ROMs. The discs were originally called WORMs (write once read many) and so sometimes the machines are called WORM burners. The term CD-R is more common now, and there is a re-recordable version called CD-RW, which has limited compatibility with standard CD-ROM drives.

CD-i Compact Disc-Interactive is an interactive multimedia platform that uses a television monitor with a CD-i player as the delivery system. Primarily developed by Philips for the consumer market, it allows use of all media on the system. It has its own set of authoring tools, and conforms to the Green Book technical specification standards. With the decline of consumer CD-ROM CD-i remains in a niche market for training and other professional applications primarily because of its inexpensive player cost and use of a television set rather than a computer monitor.

CD-ROM Compact disc read-only memory has progressed from allowing only text and data onto the disc to now include audio, graphics, animations and video. It conforms to the Yellow Book and ISO 9660 technical specifications. CD-ROM drives vary in the speed for transferring data. Quad-speed drives are usually regarded as the target for multimedia delivery.

CD-TV A short-lived consumer multimedia system based on the Commodore Amiga.

cellular radio A system for radio communication that uses a large number of low-powered transmitters, each operating in a small area called a cell. Mobile telephones use this system.

CGI Common gateway interface: Internet standards for the passing of information between applications such as Web browsers and pages and the server. Programs that make use of this, called CGI programs, allow sophisticated generation of Web pages based on dynamic data, and mean that such things as forms and databases can be used on the Web.

change management A system set up by developers to monitor and control the number and type of changes made during development, whether the changes originate in house or from the client. Also known as *change control*.

channel See **distribution channel**.

character generator A piece of software or hardware designed to make captions for video and superimpose them on the picture.

clearances The portmanteau term for copyright permissions.

coincident needles A stereo meter for showing volume of sound where the two needles of the meter, representing left and right signals, revolve around the same point.

competences The definition of skills evident from practices carried out in the workplace. This term has become prominent in training circles through the link to NVQs (National Vocational Qualifications). These are new-style qualifications that are concerned with accrediting people for the skills they employ naturally as they carry out their work.

compile To take the source code of a computer program and turn it into machine code using a compiler. The source code is written by the programmer. Extra code from programming libraries is incorporated at this time.

component A video image in which the colour information is kept separate from the luminance or brightness information. Usually two signals are used to represent the colour information. This is similar to RGB, and the RGB signals can be extracted from the three components. The components are also specified to take into account the eye's response to different colours.

composite A video image in which colour and brightness are encoded together in the same signal. PAL and NTSC are composite television systems.

composite image In video, an image in which colour and brightness are encoded together in the same signal; in graphics, an image made up of several other images, blended together.

compressed but lossless A compressed signal from which the original signal can be retrieved without any changes or errors.

compressed with loss A compressed signal from which it is impossible to retrieve the original signal, in which a version of the original is retrieved that is satisfactory for its intended purpose.

compression In computing, reducing the amount of data needed to carry something; also known as bit rate reduction. When the term video compression is used it will almost certainly have this meaning, and will refer to such systems as MPEG and Cinepak. In audio, reducing the dynamic range (range of loudness) of a sound recording.

computer-based training Often referred to as CBT, computer-based training is a method in which some or all of the training content of a course is turned into an interactive computer program.

concept testing Testing of ideas on an audience chosen from a sample market. The aim is to check the feasibility of the ideas for the market before incurring expense implementing them. The method for implementation can but may not involve interactive methods. Concept testing originated with marketing, and may be called *focus groups*.

contingency In project management, predicting the need and reserving funds, time and/or resources to cope with unforeseen circumstances that affect the project schedule. Multimedia project management needs more contingency than many other forms of project because it is a volatile environment.

contouring An artefact in graphics reproduction whereby smooth changes of brightness or colour become changed so that discrete steps are seen. Sometimes also called *posterization*.

copyright The right of a creator of a work of art, literature, music, and so on to have control over the use of the work.

credit The linking of people to the tasks they performed. This is normally done by listing the name and function performed, as in credits at the end of a television programme.

critical path The identification of the optimum sequence to carry out tasks to achieve a project on time and within budget. See also **task analysis** and **network analysis**.

cross platform Describes the development of applications that will run on more than one delivery platform.

custom palette A palette of colours chosen specifically to represent an image.

DAT Digital audio tape, a format using 4 mm tape in cassettes originally designed for digital audio (48 kHz sampling 16 bit) but also used to store data when it operates as a streamer tape format.

debug To study an application to remove errors.

decompile To take the machine code version of a program and change it back into something a human can understand.

decryption To remove the encryption from something so that the original is produced.

delivery medium The system used to distribute an application. The World Wide Web can be considered to be a delivery medium.

delivery platform The multimedia system or systems that people will use to interact with the application. The total specification of the platform is important so that the application is developed within the capabilities. A Web browser can be considered to be a delivery platform.

development platform The multimedia system that is used to develop the application. This may not be the same as the delivery platform. It is important that the final application is tested on the delivery system to check that it will perform on the specified platform.

diaphragm In a microphone, the membrane that is vibrated by sound and so causes the production of an electrical signal that represents the sound.

digital In a digital system, the signal (including such things as sounds and pictures) is turned into a series of numbers, and it is these numbers that are stored or transmitted. In an analogue system the signal itself is either stored or transmitted directly, or is converted into another medium that can follow its variations and itself be stored or transmitted. Whereas analogue systems are prone to distortion and noise, digital systems are much less susceptible.

direct competitors Companies that are in the same line of business, competing for sales from the same people.

discovery learning A learning situation that is structured to allow the learner to explore and find answers rather than be told the information.

distance learning A learning situation in which the student studies a course away from the institution using any medium that is provided. This may include interactive programs. See also **open learning centres**.

distribution channel A well-defined and sustained system for moving goods from production out to the people who will buy the products.

dither Small, seemingly random perturbations to a signal or image designed to fool the eye or ear into thinking that it has greater quality than it really does. In graphics a dither is a seemingly random pattern of dots of a limited range of colours that, when viewed from a distance, appear to have a greater range of colours. When digitizing a signal a dither is used to reduce the effect of digitizing errors because our eyes and ears are less distressed by noise (which dither looks like) than by the sharp changes in a signal that the dither disguises.

document-based programming Programming in which the format of the document is standardized and one or more applications can be used in concert to read or display it. The World Wide Web is an example of this.

Dolby The company (and inventor) famous for a system for reducing noise in an audio recording and for systems providing multichannel (surround) sound in cinemas and the home. The name is often used ambiguously for either.

domain name The Internet equivalent of a street address, showing the route to a particular computer. The name will end with the high-level domain name, which designates a user sector, primarily in the USA, such as .com for commercial, .gov for government or .edu for education. There are also internationally agreed country names such as .us, .uk, .fr and .dk, and a machine will usually be situated in that country. The US sector high-level domains are often used by organizations wishing to show an international presence even if they are based outside the USA. In an email address the domain name appears after the @ symbol.

dot pitch The distance between dots of phosphor on a colour television or monitor tube. Figures of .23 to .28 millimetres are common.

dpi The density of dots in an image or on a computer screen. Most computer screen displays are 72 or 75 dpi (dots per inch).

draw object In graphics, an image that is defined in terms of simple graphics 'primitives' such as lines, arcs and fills.

dub To copy something, usually an audio or videotape recording. A dub is the copy itself. In digital terminology a direct digital copy is often called a *clone* since it will be indistinguishable from the original.

dumb terminal A computer terminal with a keyboard and screen that does nothing other than show a display generated at a distant computer and send back your typed input.

DVB Digital video broadcasting.

DVD Digital versatile disc. Originally called digital video disc, this is the successor to CD-ROM and has many incarnations that are starting to appear. The capacity of a DVD disc is much greater than that of a CD-ROM because the system packs the information more tightly on the disc, has the possibility of two information layers per side, and can have information on both sides of the disc. As with CD, recordable, re-writeable, audio and ROM versions are possible.

DVD-ROM Use of DVD to hold a large amount of data (up to almost 18 gigabytes), which can then be accessed by a computer. Basically a big equivalent of CD-ROM.

educational technology The study of the ways in which the use of media and structured approaches to organizing material can aid teaching and learning.

edutainment A term derived from the words *education* and *entertainment* coined to describe a category of interactive titles. These are designed to be used in the home to inform and motivate through the use of media.

electrostatic Describes a system for microphones, and less commonly, loudspeakers and headphones, whereby electrostatic charge is used to detect or cause the movement of the diaphragm.

emulator A system that pretends to be something it is not, such as a software system that pretends to be a piece of hardware.

encryption Changing a data file so that it is unrecognizable but can be turned back into its original form on receipt, if the receiver has the key to decode it.

environment map In computer graphics, a method of reproducing reflections on the surface of an object by determining what the object 'sees' from its position.

environment variable Information passed to a Web server when a distant browser requests a 'page'. It includes information on the computer making the request and what Web page included the link being followed (if any).

evaluation Often confused with the term 'testing' and used interchangeably, but when used in a strict technical sense, there are differences. Evaluation of an application is the broad appraisal of any factors that influence the development, delivery and reaction to it. See also **testing**.

Exabyte A type of computer streamer tape using 8 mm cassette tape in the same format as Video-8. This is a brand name of Exabyte Corporation, who are the only company making such drives. Streamer tapes are usually used for backup and archiving but sometimes for software and assets (such as MPEG-compressed movies).

exclusive assigned rights Copyright passed on to someone else so that the original copyright owner no longer has rights in the material.

external clients People who are not part of your organization who commission you to do a piece of work. They define the brief and specifications. Budgets are agreed and negotiated between you.

Extranet A private network whereby the main company allows some other companies to share some or all data on their **intranet** with strict controls on access.

fair dealing or fair use In copyright law, an exception to infringement under certain limited circumstances because your usage of the material is very slight and/or under circumstances where free usage is seen as reasonable. Examples of this include use of extracts from books in a review.

field trials The use of the product *in situ* with the intended users prior to release to identify problems for correction.

fixed-term contract A contract that cannot be extended beyond its original duration.

focus groups See **concept testing**.

force majeure A condition in a contract where neither party has control over the circumstances. This might include war, loss of electrical power and acts of God.

formative A term used to describe evaluation processes carried out during the development cycle. These are contrasted with summative evaluation processes, which occur at the end of development. In this context, team review meetings that occur during the project could be called a formative evaluation process. See **summative**.

frames In video a complete single image, which forms part of a moving sequence of images. On the Web, a technique that allows several distinct parts of a Web page to be defined, and which can be operated separately by the viewer. Usually used to allow an index to be shown alongside the different things referred to in the index.

functional specification The document that says how an application works. The application will be written by reference to this document.

gallows arm A kind of microphone stand with a vertical part to which is connected a horizontal extension. This is like the arm of a gallows, and it is used to extend across a table (for example). The mic is fixed to the end of the arm.

gamma The relationship between the brightness of an original (such as a digital image) and the way that signal is displayed by a monitor or on a printed page.

GIF Graphics Interchange Format: a standard for 8-bit graphics, widely used on the Web. One version of the standard allows part of the image to be defined as transparent.

gigabyte 1024 megabytes.

golden master The final version of an application; the one that will be distributed.

grabber board A piece of hardware that takes in an analogue signal, usually audio or video, and digitizes it for storage in the computer.

graduated mask In graphics, a mask that determines how much of a second image shows through the first. It is graduated because it has values such that a mix of the two images is seen.

graphical structure editor In programming, a programming environment whereby the author can lay out the relationship between sections of the application in a graphical way, like a flow chart.

hacker A person who uses considerable computing skill in deviant ways, including introducing computer viruses into a computing community. The term is also used less often, and informally, to denote a skilled computer programmer with no malicious intent.

half-toning In graphics, a method for reproducing shades of grey by using black dots of varying sizes.

hardware A piece of equipment; as distinct from software.

high-level design The first attempt to define the interactive structure and content of a program. The term comes from software engineering. See also **outline design**.

hits, hit rate Either the number of individual requests for data that a Web page receives or the number of different visitors who have called that page up.

host machine The computer on which a program runs.

hot-spot A section of an image on the screen that instigates an action when the pointer enters or clicks in it.

HTML Hypertext mark-up language: the definition system used in Web pages to say how a page should be displayed by a browser. Originally HTML was intended to describe the attributes contents of a page, but it is being increasingly extended to allow tight description of layout as well.

HTTP Hypertext transfer protocol: the Internet communications protocol used in the World Wide Web. Basically, a browser calls up a Web page by sending an HTTP request to the server.

hybrid Web/CD A multimedia application that needs both a Web connection and a CD to work to the full. This could be a CD-ROM that updates itself from a Web site or a Web site that uses a CD-ROM to hold large multimedia assets such as movies.

hypertext Non-linear text that is read by following jumps and links in the text itself.

icon A pictorial symbol or representation used on the screen to denote an active area. It will allow access to further data or trigger an interactive reaction of some type. It has become common for a text explanation to appear when the user positions the cursor over the icon to help the user understand its significance. See also **picon** and **micon**.

indemnity A guarantee that if any cost is incurred as a result of your action, you will cover it.

indirect competitors Companies that are in related lines of business to you who may win sales from your potential customers with their products.

instructional design The study of methods of teaching and learning with particular reference to the section and use of media to aid instruction. The term is widely used in the USA. Europe tends to use the term **educational technology**.

instructional designer A person who applies the principles of instructional design to convey information using a variety of media and methods.

insubstantial portion In copyright, a qualitatively small proportion of a literary work that can be reproduced without infringing copyright.

integrity (of moral rights) The author's right for the work not to be changed.

intellectual property A general term for rights such as copyright and patents.

interactive design The definition of how to structure the content and interactive paths through the material for an interactive application.

interactive television Interactivity applied to broadcast television. As yet this is ill defined, but certainly includes multimedia electronic programme guides, information systems, and adjuncts to the transmitted programmes allowing viewers more involvement.

interactive video An interactive system that uses an interactive videodisk to deliver sound and pictures and combines them with text, sound and graphics from a computer source. More a system of the 1980s, used by large corporations for training, its use is in decline, and DVD will probably seal its fate completely. Also denoted by IV.

interface The way an application is designed for people to use. This includes the screen designs, the use of icons or menus, the way interactivity is set up, and the overall structure of the application.

interlaced Describes a television picture that is made of two halves, which interlace with each other like the lines of a comb and the spaces between.

internal clients People – part of your own organization – who define a piece of work for you to do. Budgeting for the work might be affected by company practices.

Internet A worldwide interconnection of computer networks, originally set up between the American military and its suppliers to make a network that; by virtue of its multiple interconnections, would be safe from destruction. Up to the 1990s the Internet was largely the preserve of the academic and research communities, but the invention of HTTP, HTML and the World Wide Web has made the Internet the latest mass communications medium.

intranet A local area network, such as in a company, which operates using Internet protocols and systems. This will now usually include a local implementation of the World Wide Web with Web pages read by browsers. Intranets have changed the way most large companies communicate with their staff.

ionizing The process of electrically charging something by removing or adding electrons.

ISP Internet service provider: the organization that connects you to the Internet, usually by means of a dial-up telephone connection with a modem. Some ISPs operate nationally and internationally (such as AOL, MSN and Demon), while others operate locally.

jaggies See **staircasing**.

Java A computer language based on C and devised by engineers at Sun originally for the control of household appliances. It allows efficient sending of small applications (applets) across the Internet, which are then executed on the user's computer.

JavaScript A scripting language that runs in recent browsers and allows more sophisticated control of pages and interaction than HTML.

JPEG A standardized method for compressing still photographic images so that little is lost from the image with high rates of compression. The acronym JPEG stands for Joint Photographic Experts Group.

layer (of graphics) Several layers of images can be combined together in graphics to make a new single image. The relationship between the layers is controlled by their alpha channels.

leadership The employment of appropriate management styles to ensure and maintain progress of a team towards common goals.

learning styles Part of the theory of learning, which indicates that people develop preferred ways of learning. This has implications for designing learning materials so that people can process the information in ways appropriate for their preferred style.

letters patent The document that defines a patent.

limiter In audio, an electronic circuit that automatically controls volume to stop short peaks of volume exceeding a certain amount.

link On the Web a word, phrase or graphic on a Web page that, when clicked by the user, sends an HTTP request to the server, usually calling up another Web page. Sometimes referred to as a **hot link**.

look and feel Common name for the interface of an application. See **interface**.

luminance The black-and-white or monochrome part of a colour television signal or picture.

machine code Zeros and ones in a program that a computer can execute directly.

magneto-optical disk A type of disk used for data storage for which both a laser and a magnetic field are required to write data.

mainframe A very large computer.

market research Information about the changing behaviour of people and their habits, gathered by a variety of methods and organized into statistical or analytical representations.

master tape The definitive and original recording of something.

mechanical right The right to record a piece of music.

megabyte 1024 kilobytes of data.

menu A set of options listed or otherwise available on screen for the user to select. A main decision point in an application might be called a *menu screen* even if it does not contain a conventional menu list.

MHEG-5 Part of the MPEG family; MHEG is an ISO standard for the definition of multimedia objects.

micon An icon that has moving images. Few make the distinction between icon and micon and generally icon is used to cover all selection images. See also **icon**.

milestone Defined key points of the project's development. Milestones are often linked to the end of a phase of development, and can be linked to phased payment stages of the project as well.

mirror site A Web site that contains the same content as another Web site. This is usually done so that access speeds can be optimized depending on where in the world the user is. Mirroring a Web site requires permission, otherwise it is infringement of copyright.

modelling In 3-D graphics, building a scene by defining objects in the scene and arranging them and their environment.

montage A single graphic made from several sources.

moral rights Rights, related to copyright, which protect a work from unauthorized changes or misattribution without the author's permission. This is currently mainly a European concept.

morph To change one shape into another in a smooth transitional movement.

MPEG audio The MPEG standard includes three levels of audio, of which level 2 is the most common. Level 1 is used for DCC (digital compact cassette), and level 3 gives better compression but is more complex.

MPEG Motion Picture Experts Group; a group of ISO standards for compression of video and definitions of multimedia objects.

MPEG-1 The version of MPEG that compresses video to a data rate of around one megabit per second. The quality is similar to that of S-VHS.

MPEG-2 The version of MPEG for broadcast quality video at bit rates of the order of 8 megabits per second. The European standard for digital television; digital video discs (DVD) and Sony's Betacam-SX use MPEG-2.

MPEG-4 An extension to MPEG introducing object-oriented structures to audio and video.

multiscan Referring to a computer monitor that can work with a range of displays.

multi-session disc A CD-ROM that can be/is written to more than once.

multitasking Able to do more than one task at once.

needs analysis The primary stage of a training project where the definition of the criteria for success takes place. The competence level of the target audience and the gap between this and the proficiency needed is analyzed.

network analysis Also referred to as *critical path analysis*; this is the definition of the core tasks and the dependent tasks needed to complete the project. These are mapped out in a network diagram to show their relationship to each other. See **critical path**.

non-exclusive rights A licensing of rights that still allows licensing to other people.

NTSC The television system used in North America and Japan, with 525 lines in a frame and 30 frames per second.

object-oriented programming Programming as interaction between self-contained mini-programs or objects.

objective A precise definition of a result that is wanted, in terms that will allow the result to be measured. Objectives are used particularly in education and training applications where the results of learning need to be stated, and ultimately measured, to demonstrate the effectiveness of the materials. Objectives are often confused with aims. Aims are more general statements of direction rather than measurable statements.

objective evaluation Evaluation carried out with preset criteria that give a measurable indication of the results. See **subjective evaluation**, **qualitative evaluation** and **quantitative evaluation**.

offline A multimedia application that works in isolation on a computer and does not need a network connection. A CD-ROM application is an example of offline.

offline editing Video editing with working copies of the 'real' tapes and low-quality equipment in order to prepare for online editing.

on-demand services A method of providing entertainment and other audio-visual material to consumers (and others) whereby they can demand a particular item, such as a film, and it will be sent to them immediately down a communications link. Some early video-on-demand systems even sent MPEG-1 video to consumers down their telephone lines.

online applications that operate over a network, such as the World Wide Web.

online editing Video editing with the 'real' tapes on high-quality equipment.

Open learning centres Centres usually set up in the workplace where a variety of learning and training materials are gathered for people to use. They can have access to the materials as and when they want. Many use interactive materials as well as videos and books. This approach to learning reflects the need for quick access to training in organizations that are changing faster than ever before.

open plan An office arrangement that assigns space according to changing need. There are no or few permanent partitions between desks, so that the space can be reorganized efficiently when needed. An extension of this principle allocates desks and even computers to workers as they are needed, and is known as *hot desking*.

operating system The lowest level of computer software in a computer. It manages the operation of the hardware and provides the programmer with ways of controlling the machine. Often the term *operating system* is taken to include the graphical user interface as well.

option bars Part of a graphic on the screen that provides hot-spots, buttons or icons grouped together for the user to make a choice.

OS Operating system.

outline design The first attempt to define the interactive structure and content of a program. The term comes from interactive training design. The later stage from this discipline is called the *detailed design*. See also **high-level design**.

palette The colours available for use in a graphic.

pan Moving the viewpoint of a camera from side to side by swivelling it and not actually moving the camera.

Pareto method An analytical representation of data in graphical form; used to help identify the products that can make the best contribution to the company.

patent agent A lawyer who drafts letters patent.

patent The right to exclusive implementation of a process as defined in the patent document.

paternity The moral right whereby you have a right to be identified as author: also known as *attribution*.

peer review Appraisal by colleagues or people performing similar jobs, where the sharing of experience and insights is used to adjust, in this case, the design and functionality of the application.

perceptual map Analytical representation of the results of a survey; used to understand the relative positions of two variables plotted in a matrix.

perceptual matrix See **perceptual map**.

performance monitoring A management process in which people agree criteria of acceptable achievements for a period and review performance according to the criteria at the end of the time. The performance agreement might be linked to bonus payments. Any shortfall of performance accredited to lack of skill might prompt training initiatives.

performing right The right to perform a piece of music to an audience.

Perl A computer language widely used on Web servers to produce dynamic Web pages based on data received from users. It has powerful string manipulation capabilities, which make it well suited to generating HTML on the fly.

picon An icon that shows a realistic image or picture rather than a representation or symbolic image. Few make the distinction between picon and icon, and generally icon is used to denote all selection images. See also **icon** and **micon**.

pilot projects Experimental projects designed as a run-up to a full-blown development.

pixels Picture elements, the basic building blocks of a picture: sometimes used to be called *pels*.

placeholders A temporary use of images, audio and/or text that are representational of the navigational feel of the final version but not part of the real content.

plug-ins Small extensions to the functionality of a piece of software such as a Web browser. The use of the term *plug-in* refers to the ease with which they can be added, usually involving simply copying the plug-in into a particular computer directory.

port (to and a) Move a computer program from one machine/platform to another.

posterization Reduction of the smooth variation in colours in an image to a series of discrete steps. Also known as *quantization*. Although this is usually seen as an error, posterization is sometimes used for artistic effect.

pre-alpha A very incomplete version of a program.

pricing policy The decisions made on the price of goods based on the understanding of the market, competitors' prices and what people are prepared to pay.

primitives Basic building blocks of a computer system.

prior art In patents, a patent can be invalidated or refused if the idea has been publicized before (the prior art).

programming language Since computers can work only with zeros and ones it is rather difficult for mere mortals to program them. To alleviate this problem, programming languages have been developed that understand almost real English.

project management The specification, planning and control of time, cost, quality and resource issues to complete a project on time and within budget.

project manager A person who carries out project management. Used here to describe the leader of a multimedia team.

proposal The document in which the developers outline the application content, development schedule and cost for the commissioners of a project.

prototype A limited working version of the application; used early in the project to get reaction to the general design and interface so that adjustments can be made.

psycho-acoustics The science of hearing, taking into account the psychological aspects of the way the brain interprets sounds as well as the pure acoustics and physics.

psychometric tests Psychological tests that use measurable factors to attribute a score for the person being tested. The tests are used in recruitment and career management decisions, particularly in large organizations.

pushing the envelope Trying something new, usually without sufficient experience.

qualitative evaluation Evaluation that takes into account a wide variety of factors that might influence the results being analyzed. The attitudes of the users, the culture of the institution or country and the general environment would be examples of qualitative factors. See also **quantitative evaluation**.

quantitative evaluation Evaluation that is concerned with measuring the results against predetermined criteria to assess whether they have been achieved. The number of times that help is used might be used as an indicator of how effective the interface of an application is, and the percentage of correct responses after taking help might be used to indicate the effectiveness of the help messages. These would be examples of quantitative measures of evaluation for multimedia packages. See also **qualitative evaluation**.

quantizing Inaccuracies in the digitizing of a signal caused by the integer distance between levels of sampling.

RAM Random access memory; basically the memory in a computer.

ray tracing A technique used in computer graphics to produce realistic images.

refractive index The amount by which light changes velocity when it passes between media, usually between air and glass or water. The refractive index is different at different frequencies and therefore colours; hence a prism is able to break white light into its constituent colours.

relational database A database with a complex structure allowing the data items to relate to each other in many ways. If the relationship is simple the database is often called a **flat-file** since its structure resembles that of a card index.

render In computer graphics, to build an image.

residuals Extra rights in a licence that are not involved in the primary use but which may be applied later. Also called **secondary rights**.

return on investment (ROI) A measure of the effectiveness of capital invested in a project, calculated by expressing average profits from the project as a percentage of average capital invested in it.

RGB Red, green, blue: the three primary colours from which virtually all colours can be built. Also refers to an image that stores the three primary colour components separately.

rights Permission to reproduce and/or sell something.

RISC Reduced instruction set computer: a microprocessor with relatively few built-in operations but which can execute what it has extremely quickly.

ROI See **return on investment**.

role play A technique used in teaching and psychology, in which a person acts out a situation, perhaps from different perspectives, to get insight into decision making and reactions.

royalties Payments based on the number of copies sold or distributed.

run-length encoding A form of compression that stores the colour of a pixel followed by how many subsequent pixels are of the same colour. This works best with images made up of large areas of flat colour, such as a cartoon.

run-time The execution, or running, of a program.

sample rate The frequency with which an analogue signal is sampled on digitization. For accurate representation the sample rate must be at least twice the highest frequency in the signal.

scan To convert a flat image such as a photographic print into a digital form by measuring the relevant parameters of sections of the image in an ordered fashion, usually left to right, top to bottom.

scanner A device that converts a flat image such as a photographic print into a digital form by scanning across it.

screen resolution The number of pixels on a screen. The most common in multimedia is 640 pixels by 480.

scripting languages Computer languages that are designed to be used without detailed knowledge of programming. They are specialized to particular tasks.

segment An identifiable part of a market that has enough common needs to influence products being designed for it.

server In a local area network, a server is basically the hard disk that is not on your own computer but elsewhere. You can use it to store your files or you can look to it to supply material available to the whole network. In a wide area network or video-on-demand system the server is the centralized repository for data. On the Web a server is the distant computer that holds the Web pages and carries out your requests for them.

session fee A payment for performing in a music recording as a session musician. A principal performer would probably take royalties on sales, not a session fee.

set-top box A computer-based system that is designed to be like a piece of home entertainment hardware (for example, a VCR or CD player), and may actually sit on top of the television set. Satellite receivers and decoders for video on demand and digital TV are usually referred to in this way.

severance In employment, the terms under which the employment is ended.

sibilance Exaggeration of 's' sounds in a voice, sometimes natural but sometimes caused by poor acoustics or microphone placing.

sign-off The signature of a person given the authority to agree that a phase of work has been completed satisfactorily. Sign-offs are often linked to milestones in the project, which can coincide with staged payments.

simulation A technique used to reproduce a situation as realistically as possible to allow people to develop the skills needed to handle the situation. This is often used in management training. The easiest computer-based example to quote is that of a flight simulator used to train pilots, and in many ways this kind of simulation is better known as *virtual reality*.

site log Record kept by a Web servers of every HTTP request it receives, with details including the time and date, who asked for the page, and how much data was transferred.

slippage The amount of time that has been lost according to the agreed schedule and the present project position.

software A computer program or computer programs in general. Usually used to differentiate from the equipment or hardware.

source code The human-readable version of a computer program before it is compiled into machine or object code.

staircasing Appearance of lines on a screen that are almost, but not quite horizontal, and under some circumstances will appear jaggy. Also referred to as *jaggies*.

standards conversion In television, conversion of a video signal between the PAL and NTSC standards.

standing waves In sound, self-reinforcement of a sound wave when it is reflected back on itself by a wall or the end of a tube. Between two walls this will reinforce certain frequencies and so colour the sound.

storyboards A scripting convention that includes mock-up visuals; used in video production originally, and now sometimes used in multimedia projects.

streamer tape Magnetic tape, usually in cartridges or cassettes, onto which computer data is recorded or streamed for archiving and backup purposes. The most common formats are DAT; Exabyte and DLT.

streaming On the Web, playing of an audio or video file over the network so that it is heard or seen instantly as it arrives. The audio or video file does not usually remain on the user's computer, and it is possible to stream a live event, rather like a radio or TV broadcast.

stylus In computer graphics, a special pen without ink that is moved across a special tablet in order to draw a line or shape on the computer screen. In audio, the tip, usually diamond, on a gramophone pick-up that actually makes contact with the disc groove.

subcarrier A secondary frequency added to a signal in order to carry extra information, such as colour in a TV signal.

subjective evaluation Evaluation that is based on observation and analysis of non-quantifiable factors, and is affected by the experience and bias of the evaluator. See also **objective evaluation**.

summative Term used to describe evaluation processes used at the end of development. This can include testing but could also include such practices as the end of project review, or debriefing procedures. See also **formative** and **evaluation**.

SWOT A method of analyzing a company's position against competitors by defining its strengths, weaknesses, opportunities and threats.

synchronization licence A licence to take music and juxtapose it with pictures in a film or video.

synchronization pulse Part of a video or digital signal that identifies a position in the signal, such as where a frame of video starts.

take In a take, or a recording: an attempt to record something. If you have to try again, then you do another take.

task analysis Identification of all the processes and subprocesses needed to complete a project.

technical specification Document describing a task to be undertaken in terms of the equipment and techniques required.

telephony Ordinary telephone traffic, in which people talk to each other.

teletype A teleprinter or telex machine, used to communicate with computers before monitors, or VDUs, were available.

testing The use of methods and procedures to check the performance of an application according to predefined criteria. Testing is often confused with evaluation. It can form part of evaluation, which has a wider remit. See also **evaluation**.

texture mapping In computer graphics, adding a texture to the 'surface' of an object drawn in 3-D.

time and materials contract A contract for work in which the cost is directly related to the time spent and the materials used. It is the opposite of a fixed-price contract.

time code Information added to video and to audio for video, to uniquely identify the individual frames. This is a great help when editing.

time-lapse photography Photographic technique in which a camera remains in position and records events in detail over a period of time. The film is then speeded up when shown, to allow people to see the changes take place in seconds rather than days. An example would be the change of a flower from bud to bloom to death.

time-based media Media that change over time, such as audio and video.

uncompressed Describes the original form of an image, sound or other data.

Universal Disc Format (UDF) A newly defined standard for the directory structure (etc.) defining the dataspace on a DVD-ROM disc.

Universal Mobile Telecommunications Services (UMTS) A future standard for mobile telephony that includes high data rates and the use of multimedia.

UNIX A computer operating system used extensively in tertiary education, industry and for Web servers.

usability laboratories Specially constructed rooms where people are observed using applications and their actions are recorded on video, through the computer and on paper by the observers. The information is analyzed to indicate the efficiency of the program and to make recommendations for improvements.

usability testing The recording and subsequent interpretation of people's usage of a computer-based system through a combination of methods that can include observation, electronic records, and video taping. See **usability laboratories**.

user requirements The needs of the users; studied to determine how the application should be structured and how it should operate.

validation An appraisal of the methods that have been used to check that they are consistent with the results. It is sometimes used with the sense of evaluation but strictly it is part of an evaluation process. Also sometimes used with the meaning of field trial as validation exercise. See also **field trials**.

version tracking In software development, keeping track of changes to the software so that development is coordinated. This is especially important where more than one person is writing code.

vertical blanking interval (VBI) The part of a television signal between the bottom of one picture and the top of the next. Used for teletext, time code and test signals. In computing the VBI is useful because it provides time to change a displayed image.

video CD A compact disc, actually a Mode 2 CD-ROM, which contains MPEG-l video and audio, and can be played on a television or PC screen like a videocassette. Although this early digital videodisk has not been widely accepted by consumers in the West, it is very widespread in the Far East.

video compression Reduction of the amount of data needed to carry something; also known as bit rate reduction. The term is used to refer to such systems as MPEG and Cinepak.

video on demand A system whereby a home subscriber can access television material stored remotely on a server. Some systems use high-bandwidth cable and others use ordinary telephone wires for the link between the server and the consumer's television. See also **set-top box**.

video conferencing Basically the combination of a telephone conference call and television or a video telephone. Recent video-conferencing systems operate using personal computers, allowing both ends of the conference to work together on documents that each can see.

videodisk See **interactive video**.

virtual machine A layer of software between a computer program and the computer such that the interface between the program and this software is standard no matter what actual machine is used. The new software exists in different versions for different machines.

voice-over An audio commentary that accompanies video or graphics. Hence *voice-over artiste*, a person who reads the commentary.

waveform A visual representation of a signal, usually electronic in nature, that changes over time, such as recorded sound.

Web browser A piece of software that takes as its input a Web page – with all its text, images, links and even sounds and moving images – and formats and displays it on the user's computer.

Web pages The individual documents, based around HTML, that make up a Web site. Analogous to the pages of a magazine.

Web site A group of Web pages and possibly other networked resources that are designed to be viewed as a distinct entity in the same way a magazine is made up of pages and separate articles.

Web surfer Person who accesses the World Wide Web and looks at Web sites.

Web-television Display of Web pages on a television set rather than a computer screen.

wide area network Computer network that extends beyond the home or office building or complex. Often consisting of linked local area networks, as in the Internet.

wide latitude Of film, able to record a wide range of brightness levels in a scene, or cope with under- and/or over-exposure.

World Wide Web (WWW) The multiplicity of HTML documents on Web sites spread around the Internet. On a technical level the Web uses Hypertext Transfer Protocol (HTTP) for communication between Web browsers and Web servers, although other Internet protocols such as FTP (File Transfer Protocol) are also used in tandem.

WORM In data storage, Write Once Read Many, a type of computer disk that can be written to but not changed. Often used to denote a CD-ROM that has been written rather than pressed or replicated. The process is known as burning a WORM.

WYSIWYG Describes an application that shows you the end result of your work exactly as it will be seen by the end-users: What You See Is What You Get.

zoom To increase the focal length of a lens in video or photography. It magnifies the scene and looks similar to, but not exactly the same as, moving closer to the subject.

Index

Note: When page numbers are highlighted in bold, the reference appears in the glossary.